Empire
AND THE LITERATURE OF SENSATION

mela

multi-ethnic literatures of the americas

AMRITJIT SINGH, CARLA L. PETERSON, C. LOK CHUA, SERIES EDITORS

The MELA series aims to expand and deepen our sense of American literatures as multi-cultural and multi-lingual and works to establish a broader understanding of "America" as a complex site for the creation of national, transnational, and global narratives. Volumes in the series focus on the recovery, consolidation, and reevaluation of literary expression in the United States, Canada, and the Caribbean as shaped by the experience of race, ethnicity, national origin, region, class, gender, and language.

Lin Yutang
CHINATOWN FAMILY
EDITED AND WITH AN INTRODUCTION BY C. Lok Chua

Pauline E. Hopkins
DAUGHTER OF THE REVOLUTION:
THE MAJOR NONFICTION WORKS OF PAULINE E. HOPKINS
EDITED AND WITH AN INTRODUCTION BY Ira Dworkin

EMPIRE AND THE LITERATURE OF SENSATION:
AN ANTHOLOGY OF NINETEENTH-CENTURY POPULAR FICTION
EDITED AND WITH AN INTRODUCTION BY Jesse Alemán and Shelley Streeby

Claude McKay
A LONG WAY FROM HOME
EDITED AND WITH AN INTRODUCTION BY Gene Andrew Jarrett

SHADOWED DREAMS: WOMEN'S POETRY OF THE HARLEM
RENAISSANCE, 2ND EDITION, REVISED AND EXPANDED
EDITED AND WITH AN INTRODUCTION BY Maureen Honey

Empire AND THE *Literature* OF *Sensation*

AN ANTHOLOGY OF
NINETEENTH-CENTURY
Popular Fiction

EDITED AND WITH AN INTRODUCTION BY
Jesse Alemán and Shelley Streeby

RUTGERS UNIVERSITY PRESS
NEW BRUNSWICK, NEW JERSEY, AND LONDON

Library of Congress Cataloging-in-Publication Data

Empire and the literature of sensation : an anthology of nineteenth-century popular fiction / edited and with an
introduction by Jesse Alemán and Shelley Streeby.

     p. cm. — (Multi-ethnic literatures of the Americas)

  Includes bibliographical references.

  ISBN 978-0-8135-4075-7 (hardcover : alk. paper) — ISBN 978-0-8135-4076-4 (pbk. : alk. paper)

  1. American fiction—19th century.   2. Popular literature—United States.   3. Imperialism—Fiction.

  4. Indigenous peoples—America—Fiction.   I. Alemán, Jesse, 1968–   II. Streeby, Shelley, 1963–

   PS653.E67 2007

   813 .309358—dc22

                                             2006039168

A British Cataloging-in-Publication record for this book is available from the British Library.

This collection copyright © 2007 by Rutgers, The State University

Introduction and scholarly apparatus copyright © 2007 by Jesse Alemán and Shelley Streeby

Text design by Adam B. Bohannon

Visit our Web site: http://rutgerspress.rutgers.edu

Manufactured in the United States of America

To Danizete Martínez,
because your help with this book
was not thankless.

CONTENTS

CHRONOLOGY

1803	The Louisiana Purchase between the United States and France creates a boundary dispute with Spain regarding ownership of Florida and the Spanish colony of Texas, near the Rio Grande River.
1810	The Mexican War for Independence from Spain begins.
1812	The War of 1812 between the United States and Britain begins.
1815	Treaty of Ghent ends the War of 1812.
1817–1818	First Seminole War in Florida between the United States and the Seminole Indians.
1819	The Adams-Onís Treaty settles the boundary dispute between the United States and Spain created by the Louisiana Purchase. The United States gains Florida and a boundary along the Sabine River in Texas, extending over the Rocky Mountains and to the Pacific Ocean. The treaty ends the First Seminole War.
1821	Mexico gains its independence from Spain, and the new government agrees to allow settlers to colonize the Texas region. Abolitionist and independence movements begin to appear in Cuba. Edward Zane Carroll Judson (a.k.a. Ned Buntline) is born.
1822	George Lippard is born.
1823	James Monroe delivers the State of the Union address known as the Monroe Doctrine, announcing U.S. neutrality in European affairs and Western Hemispheric sovereignty that bars further European colonization in the Americas.
1826	Mary A. Denison is born (dies in 1911).
1830	Mexico closes Texas to colonization and outlaws slavery in the area because Anglo settlers outnumber Mexican citizens in the region and refuse to recognize the authority of the Mexican government.
1832	Black Hawk War between the U.S. Army and the Sauk and Fox Indians.
1833	Antonio López de Santa Anna elected as Mexico's president. His attempt to centralize government power incites federalist revolts across Mexico, including in Texas.
1835	Texas revolution begins. Second Seminole War begins in Florida.
1836	Texas declares independence, and Santa Anna marches to San Antonio, Texas, to quell the rebellion. He lays siege to the Alamo for thirteen days, killing nearly all of the trapped Texans; he then defeats the Texan army at the battle of Goliad and executes 445 prisoners. In April, he meets General Sam Houston's army at the battle of San Jacinto and is taken prisoner. He is forced to sign the Treaties of Velasco and concede Texas's independence.
1837	President Andrew Jackson recognizes the independent Republic of Texas, Santa Anna is exiled to Cuba, and the closure of Philadelphia's Second Bank of the United States creates a financial panic.

1842	Second Seminole War ends in Florida. The Mexican army returns to San Antonio, Texas, and recaptures and occupies it twice during the year. In December, a volunteer Texan army retaliates with an expedition to Mier, Nuevo Leon, Mexico, where they are captured.
1843	The Mier Expedition prisoners face a lottery-style execution: seventeen are shot and the rest continue to Perote Castle prison. E. E. Barclay publishes *The Female Warrior: An Interesting Narrative of the Sufferings, and Singular and Surprising Adventures of Miss Leonora Siddons*.
1844	James K. Polk, a Democrat supportive of Texas annexation, is elected U.S. president. Remaining Mier prisoners released from Perote Castle.
1845	Texas annexed into the Union. Santa Anna exiled to Havana, Cuba.
1846	United States declares war on Mexico on May 13, 1846. General Taylor wins the battle of Palo Alto on May 8; the battle of Resaca de la Palma on May 9; and the battle of Monterrey on September 20–24. Acting on a pact with President Polk, Santa Anna is smuggled through the Veracruz blockade in August, but rather than end hostilities, he takes charge of the Mexican army.
1847	Taylor wins the battle of Buena Vista on February 22–23. General Scott's forces land at Collado Beach, south of Veracruz, on March 9; Scott's forces bombard Veracruz on March 22, and the city surrenders on March 27; Scott wins the battle of Cerro Gordo on April 17–18 and begins the march to Mexico City in July. He wins the battles of Contreras and Churubusco on July 20, the battle of Molino del Rey on September 8, and the battle at Chapultepec on September 13, and occupies Mexico City on September 14. Narciso López arrives in New York to escape punishment for his plot to overthrow the Spanish government's rule of Cuba. Ned Buntline's *Magdalena, The Beautiful Mexican Maid* is published [?].
1848	The Treaty of Guadalupe Hidalgo ends the U.S.-Mexico War and cedes much of Mexico's far northern frontier. George Lippard's *'Bel of Prairie Eden* is published.
1849	Zachary Taylor becomes president. Narciso López's first expedition to invade Cuba stopped by the U.S. Navy.
1850	Zachary Taylor dies. López invades Cárdenas, Cuba, but retreats to Key West when Spanish reinforcements arrive. The Compromise of 1850 attempts to balance the interests of free and slave states and establishes the Fugitive Slave Law.
1851	López invades El Morro, Cuba, and battles the Spanish army. López and his volunteer army are captured: most of the filibusterers are imprisoned, and López is executed. Santa Anna is exiled from Mexico. E. E. Barclay publishes *A Thrilling and Exciting Account of the Sufferings and Horrible Tortures Inflicted on Mortimer Bowers and Miss Sophia Delaplain*.
1853	Santa Anna returns to power in Mexico. William Walker and a small army invade Baja California and Sonora on a short-lived filibustering expedition.

	The issue of slavery continues to provoke turmoil in Cuba. José Martí is born in Havana, Cuba.
1854	The Ostend Manifesto discloses the U.S. plan to buy Cuba from Spain, an idea Spain rejects. George Lippard dies.
1855	William Walker escapes to Nicaragua as a mercenary. Santa Anna exiled from Mexico. Third Seminole War begins.
1856	William Walker declares himself president of Nicaragua; his presidency lasts until the following year.
1858	Third Seminole War ends.
1860	Beadle and Adams publish the first dime novel, Ann S. Stephens's *Malaeska, The Indian Wife of the White Hunter*, which was originally written and published in 1839. Beadle also publishes Mary A. Denison's *The Prisoner of La Vintresse*.
1861	The U.S. Civil War begins. Benito Juárez becomes Mexico's president.
1862	Sioux uprising. Indian wars will rage across the Plains and the West until 1890.
1863	Sam Houston dies.
1864	Maximilian I becomes emperor of Mexico.
1865	The U.S. Civil War ends.
1867	Maximilian I executed and Juárez returns to the Mexican presidency.
1868	Cuba's Ten Years' War of Independence from Spain begins.
1876	Antonio López de Santa Anna dies.
1878	Cuba's Ten Years' War ends without Cuban independence but with freedom for the slaves who fought in the war.
1879–1880	Cuba's *La Guerra Chiquita* (The Small War) continues hostilities between the island and Spain.
1886	Ned Buntline dies. Slavery abolished in Cuba.
1890	Wounded Knee massacre brings an end to the Indian wars.
1893	Frederick Jackson Turner delivers his "Frontier Thesis."
1895	Cuban War of Independence begins. Martí dies.
1898	Cuban War of Independence ends. USS *Maine* explodes. The Spanish-American War begins and ends by December with the Treaty of Paris, which grants Cuba its independence and gives the United States Spain's colonies: the Philippines, Guam, and Puerto Rico.

INTRODUCTION

"Oh, there is to the guilty something more terrible in *memory*, than in all other things. It gives a double terror, for it links the past with the present and the future."

—Ned Buntline, *Magdalena*.

The narrator of Ned Buntline's novelette, *Magdalena, The Beautiful Mexican Maid*, captures the impulse of *Empire and the Literature of Sensation*: it is a collection of nineteenth-century popular fiction that reminds us of the early history of U.S. empire-building in the Americas before 1898. Although conventional wisdom often locates the beginning of imperialism in the Spanish-Cuban-American War at the end of the nineteenth century, the pieces collected here—most republished for the first time—document the intimate, ambivalent relationships between popular literature and the cultures of imperialism from the 1830s through the early 1860s.[1] This was a culture vested in the acquisition of previously held Spanish territories in the Americas, especially Mexico and Cuba, and it is also a legacy that is foundational to the nation's emergence as a global power. The memory these popular texts invoke, in other words, is of mid-nineteenth-century imperialism, the Manifest Destiny, that, in Buntline's time, was a repetition of the past and proved to be a harbinger of the future.

Often designated as the antebellum period, the years before the Civil War were marked by violent conflicts over Indian removal, territorial expansion, and slavery. The War of 1812 established the nation's independence from England, but by the 1830s, a second war with the Seminole Indians in Florida had begun, and U.S. settlers in the Mexican province of Texas rebelled against Mexico and fought the battles of the Alamo, Goliad, and San Jacinto before Texas established itself as an independent republic that the United States annexed in 1845. A few years later, the 1846–1848 U.S.-Mexico War ended with the Treaty of Guadalupe Hidalgo, which doubled the size of the United States by seizing Mexico's far northern frontier. The war also reignited the filibustering spirit that reached its zenith during the 1850s. Although the word *filibuster* would take on different meanings in the twentieth century, during the nineteenth century, it referred to efforts by independent agents and groups to take over foreign lands without the official sanction of the state. Many of these adventurers were veterans who joined armed incursions into Cuba and Latin America, most notably the Narciso López campaigns against Cuba and William Walker's invasion of Nicaragua. By the time the South seceded in 1861, most of the Civil War's major combatants—Jefferson Davis, Robert E. Lee, Robert Jackson, Pierre Beauregard, George McAllen, Ulysses S. Grant, and William T. Sherman, to name a few—had already seen action in the

Florida campaigns against the Seminole Indians, the U.S.-Mexico War, or filibustering schemes across the Americas.

The designation of the period between the 1820s to the 1860s as antebellum thus begs the question: before which war? The U.S.-Mexico War? The first or second war against the Seminole Indians? The Texas rebellion? López's assaults on Cuba? Walker's war in Nicaragua? Or the various armed conflicts waged against Native America, including the 1832 Black Hawk War, the 1835 Trail of Tears, and the war of extermination that California's governor declared against the newly annexed state's indigenous Indian population? These conflicts are buried deep within the nation's cultural memory partly because the antebellum periodization's focus on the Civil War obscures the other wars that took place before 1861.

If this standard periodization of nineteenth-century literature is fraught with amnesia, so is the usual understanding of the history of empire, for according to many scholars, the war of 1898 marks the watershed moment of U.S. imperialism. Indeed, in earlier scholarship, 1898 was often isolated as an aberrant episode of imperialism when the United States accidentally and innocently acquired an empire. Amy Kaplan, Philip Foner, Angel Smith, Emma Dávila-Cox, and Pedro Cabán, to name only a few, have criticized the idea that the nation became an "empire by default" in 1898.[2] Nonetheless, many historians continue to view 1898 as the definitive moment in U.S. imperialism, especially in relation to the global market, but identifying 1898 with the emergence of empire elides a long history of U.S. interests in global markets, the Asia Pacific, the Caribbean, and other overseas parts of the Americas, as well as overland paths of commerce. Although it is important to remember the differences between continental and overseas empire-building, it is equally important not to misconstrue continental imperialism as a natural or inevitable process of expansion into adjacent lands that was radically discontinuous with later forms of overseas imperialism. In this sense, the history of U.S. empire spans the nineteenth century rather than starts at the end of it.

The point here is not to establish a definitive origin story for empire but to understand how national memory recollects 1898 as the beginning of U.S. imperialism while forgetting the mid-nineteenth century as an era that set the stage for the nation's fin de siècle encounter with Spain, Cuba, and the Philippines. John O'Sullivan penned his famous Manifest Destiny editorial during this era, although long before the *Democratic Review* proclaimed it, many politicians, capitalists, slaveholders, and others were scheming for hemispheric dominance.[3] Most notably, the 1823 Monroe Doctrine pronounced the Western Hemisphere off-limits to European powers, but the gesture also opened the Americas to inter-American encroachment that might explain why, despite the 1818 Neutrality Law, filibustering broke out throughout the 1830s and 1840s for Mexico's northern frontier, Canada, and Yucatán, Mexico's embattled southern state.[4] While the filibustering spirit culminated with the López expeditions into Cuba, the war with Mexico brought expansionism to a head and made the Union seem more like an Old World empire than a New World republic. The 1848 Treaty of Guadalupe Hidalgo also intensified the sectional divisions that would lead to the Civil War and incorporated a Mexican American population that troubled nativist definitions of national identity as essentially Protestant and Anglo-Saxon.[5]

The U.S.-Mexico War was also, as Rick Stewart explains, "the first event of its kind to be photographed, the first to be reported by war correspondents for mass circulation newspapers, and the first to be extensively recorded in lithographs intended for a broad audience."[6] In fact, because of emerging technologies in the mid-nineteenth century, imperialism was already an entrenched ideology in the United States by the beginning of the Spanish-Cuban-American War. The idea that the nation was destined and even entitled to expand westward toward the Pacific in the name of democracy rather than empire thus links 1848 to 1898 through cultures of imperialism that, while often forgotten, are preserved in the cheap, popular literature of empire, penned during the heady times of the so-called antebellum period. The sensational fiction of the era, then, is one of the many forms of collective cultural memory that embodies and enacts the desire for and the excitement, confusion, and trepidation about empire, despite the ideological impulses to justify, deny, and forget the nation's history of conquest.

The Other American Renaissance

As David J. Reynolds demonstrates, sensational literature and popular writings contributed to the literary formation known as the American Renaissance. Beneath the writings of Melville, Hawthorne, Whitman, Thoreau, and Emerson, Reynolds suggests, is a bedrock of travel narratives, seduction tales, reform writings, urban gothic stories, and women's rights fiction that the Renaissance writers transformed into highbrow art.[7] Yet the American Renaissance era also witnessed a general renaissance in U.S. print culture following the print revolution of the late 1830s and 1840s, when the development of stereotyping and electrotyping, the invention of Napier's and Hoe's presses, and improvements in paper-making made it possible to produce printed texts more quickly than ever before. These technological changes, along with the emergence of railroads and new inventions such as the telegraph, supported the production of a popular literature that included mass-circulation newspapers, pamphlets, story papers, and dime novels that appealed to multiple classes and audiences.[8] The Renaissance writers competed in the literary marketplace with writers and publishers of this popular sentimental and sensational literature, but although they adapted and transformed sentimental and sensational conventions, their literature did not satisfy the tastes of an increasingly diverse national readership and they were never popular during this era.

Hawthorne's envious reference to that "d—d mob of scribbling women" has often been cited as evidence that female authors of sentimental novels dominated the literary marketplace, but an emerging body of scholarship has suggested that many sentimental writers were men and that sensationalism was at least as popular as sentimentalism. Much of the 1970s and 1980s recovery work on sentimentalism focused on it as a specifically female genre, written by and for women, and singled out for critical analysis novels such as Harriet Beecher Stowe's *Uncle Tom's Cabin*, Fanny Fern's *Ruth Hall*, and Susan Warner's *The Wide, Wide World*. While Ann Douglas argued that sentimentalism, with its emphasis on feelings, tears, and sympathy, represented a declension from a tough-minded, rigorous Calvinism, Jane Tompkins contended that sentimental novels had the power to engage deeply held cultural beliefs and thereby change the world.[9] In the 1990s, Shirley Samuels and the contributors to *The Culture of Sentiment* reconfigured the Douglas-Tompkins debate by examining sentimentalism as a cultural matrix that extended beyond the literary into other realms and as a "set of cultural practices designed to evoke a certain form of emotional response, usually empathy, in the reader or viewer," but this culture was still largely identified with women.[10] More recently, however, the editors of *Sentimental Men* have challenged the idea that sentimentalism was an exclusively female genre by emphasizing that both men and women read sentimental novels and by showing how male authors such as T. S. Arthur, Frederick Douglass, Henry Wadsworth Longfellow, and even Herman Melville participated in the culture of sentiment.[11] In Melville's case, the incorporation of sentimental conventions and tropes into *Pierre; or the Ambiguities*, for instance, was partly a desperate, failed effort to win the attention of readers, who had refused to respond to complicated, experimental novels such as *Mardi* and *Moby Dick*. By setting out to write a sentimental novel, Melville hoped to appeal to the huge audience that eagerly responded to the narratives written by more popular authors such as Stowe and Arthur.

Melville and other canonical authors of this era also engaged the tropes and conventions of the sensational literature that was incredibly popular during this period. This literature was one of the products of the print revolution and was initially linked to the penny press. It included trial reports, criminal biographies, mysteries-of-the-city novels, and narratives of war and imperial adventure. Most of this literature was published in New York, Philadelphia, and Boston, but improvements in communications and transportation, such as the completion of national railroad networks in the 1840s and 1850s, helped it to reach a much wider audience, especially in the later part of this era, when it was also produced in places such as Cincinnati, New Orleans, and California.

During the 1830s and early 1840s, broadsides, pamphlets, and newspapers were especially important and prominent forms of sensational literature. In these early texts, authorship is often difficult or impossible to verify, since this was a period when it was still hard to make a living as a writer, and the intentions of individual authors are not as significant as the conventions of genre when analyzing this ephemeral and often anonymous or pseudonymous literature. But starting in the late 1840s, as Michael Denning has shown, authors such as George Lippard and Ned Buntline were able to support themselves and become famous by editing and contributing to newspapers and story papers and by writing best-selling mysteries-of-the-city novels such as *The Quaker City; or the Monks of Monk Hall*; *New York: Its Upper Ten and Lower Million*; and *The Mysteries and Miseries of New York*.[12] City and empire were closely connected in this literature, for most of these authors also wrote sensational novels about the U.S.-Mexico War and other scenes of empire-building, and their mysteries-of-the-city novels often connect urban plots to foreign locales. By the early 1860s, after Beadle and Adams introduced the dime novel as a standardized package of around a hundred pages, distinguished by its small size and by the striking illustrations and dime trademark on the cover, prominent authors such as Ann Stephens, Edward Ellis, Metta Victor, and Prentiss Ingraham were able to reach a national, mass audience with their stories of urban crime and imperial adventure. Throughout this period, writers we now think of as major, such as Hawthorne, Melville, and Poe, both borrowed and sought to distinguish their writings from this flourishing literature.

Sensationalism and sentimentalism are related literary modes, but sensationalism's lowly place within emerging literary hierarchies, its characteristic structure of feeling, and its ways of connecting bodies and the body politic distinguish it from sentimentalism. During the print revolution, emerging distinctions among a largely non-popular highbrow literature, middlebrow sentimentalism, and a lowbrow sphere of story paper fiction and dime novels began to stratify the literary field. While these spheres overlapped, sensational literature, which was connected to a larger culture of sensation that included journalism, blackface minstrelsy, and Barnum's American Museum, occupied the bottom tier within emerging literary hierarchies. Although both sentimental and sensational literature reached a broad audience that cut across classes, Richard Brodhead suggests that sentimental fiction especially appealed to people "already possessing, or newly aspiring to, or at least mentally identifying with, the leisured, child-centered home of middle-class life," while sensational narratives were read by "farmboys, soldiers, German and Irish immigrants, and men and women of a newly solidifying working class."[13]

Like sentimental fiction, sensational literature is a form of melodrama that aims to move its audiences to experience intense feelings, but it emphasizes thrills, shock, and horror more than virtuous and socially redemptive feelings. While sentimentalism elicits emotions in order to regulate them and emphasizes the refinement and transcendence of the body, sensationalism swerves away from sentimental didacticism to linger on bodies and explore intense emotions rather than regulating, refining, or transcending them. Harriet Beecher Stowe's *Uncle Tom's Cabin* (1851), for instance, channels the intense emotions of little Eva's death-bed scene toward the novel's Christian, abolitionist cause, but the primary aim of the representations of tortures and bodily suffering endured by Sophia Delaplain and Mortimer Bowers, two of the characters in one of the sensational pamphlets that we have included in this collection, seems to be provoking squeamish thrills.[14] Both modes translate political, social, and economic questions into affect-drenched narratives about relations among individual and collective bodies and both make women's bodies allegories for races, classes, and nations, but sensational literature is more outrageous and less respectable, more connected to a lowly world of popular entertainment than the middle-class home, and more concerned with exotic and foreign spaces than the domestic sphere, making it an excellent archive of popular fantasies and fears about U.S. imperialism.

This anthology offers three important forms of nineteenth-century sensational literature: the pamphlet narrative, story paper novelettes, and the dime novel. The earliest narrative, *The Female Warrior*, was issued in 1843 as a pamphlet in New York by E. E. Barclay, who published 163 titles in the course of the nineteenth century, including *A Thrilling and Exciting Account of the Sufferings and Horrible Tortures Inflicted on Mortimer Bowers and Miss Sophia Delaplain* (1851), a story of female adventure, cross-class romance, and a Cuban filibustering expedition gone awry, which also appears below.[15] Both pamphlets claim to be first-person accounts, although in both cases authorship cannot be verified and it is quite likely that both Siddons and Delaplain were made-up characters. Both are also part of a larger female picaresque genre that can be traced to songs and ballads, seduction novels, and other popular narratives of crime, war, and empire. During the early 1840s traveling agents working mostly in the North sold Barclay's imperial adventure and crime pamphlets door to door, but by the early 1850s the pamphlets reached markets in other parts of the nation. The original title page of the Delaplain narrative, for instance, lists Charleston, South Carolina, as the place of publication, although Barclay is known to have indicated "Richmond, Charleston, or St. Louis when it served his purpose."[16] As Dawn Keetley has shown, the shorter pamphlets (around thirty pages) sold for about seven cents each while the longer ones (forty to sixty pages) sold for nineteen cents, making the prices of both "significantly lower than the 25-cent editions that Ronald Zboray has identified as the most inexpensively-priced paperbacks available (of American authors) in the antebellum period."[17] These pamphlets are difficult to align with particular political positions in this era, for they emphasize action rather than ideas and avoid taking a clear stand on the divisive issues of the day as they attempt to appeal to a mass audience.

Story paper novelettes, which usually sold for twelve-and-a-half or twenty cents, reached many more readers and were more closely connected to regional and national transportation and distribution networks. Sensational novels took on different meanings when they were produced for and serialized in story papers, where chapters ran alongside news stories, editorials, and letters to the editor about slavery, immigration, empire, and war. Our anthology includes two U.S.-Mexico War novelettes by two of the most popular authors of the nineteenth century, Ned Buntline and George Lippard. Lippard penned several best-selling urban gothic and imperial adventure novels and even edited his own story paper, *The Quaker City* (1848–1850), where he serialized one of his two U.S.-Mexico War novels, *Legends of Mexico*. Buntline, who wrote influential plays and novels about New York bowery boys and Buffalo Bill, also briefly edited his own story paper, *Buntline's Own*, but his two U.S.-Mexico War narratives, *Magdalena, The Beautiful Mexican Maid* and *The Volunteer; or, the Heroine of Monterey*, were initially issued by two of the most successful publishers of cheap literature during this period: the Williams Brothers and Frederick Gleason. The Williams Brothers, who also published the New York story papers *Uncle Sam* and the *Flag of the Free*, issued *Magdalena*, while the most popular story paper of the era, Boston's *Flag of Our Union*, serialized *The Volunteer* before publisher Frederick Gleason reissued it as a cheap book. These story papers, along with others, flourished during the war years, as readers hungry for news about Mexico contributed to their rapidly increasing circulations.[18] Although all of the story papers supported the war with Mexico, their politics varied significantly. While the Williams Brothers' publications often expressed Whiggish views, Gleason's *Flag of Our Union* tended to support the views of the Democrats, and although Lippard's radical democratic and antislavery perspective shaped the *Quaker City*, Buntline's story paper and much of his fiction promoted nativism and supported slavery.

The 1860s heralds the era of the dime novel, but this new cultural form had roots in the sensational literature of the earlier decades, for some of the first dime novels had been published earlier in story papers and publishers initially enlisted authors who had already established a readership. Although men wrote most of the U.S.-Mexico War novelettes, and although dime novels are often (mis)remembered as books for boys, women wrote many of Beadle's early novels, including the first one, Ann Stephens's *Malaeska; or, The Indian Wife of the White Hunter*.[19] The present anthology includes selections from another early dime novel, Mary Andrews Denison's *The Prisoner of La Vintresse; or, The Fortunes of a Cuban Heiress*, a narrative of international intrigue and romance that Beadle published in 1860. Before she became one of Beadle's authors, Denison already enjoyed a significant literary reputation as a contributor to story papers and as the author of *Gracie Amber* (1857), a seduction narrative about a working-class girl, and *Old Hepsy* (1858), an antislavery race melodrama. Denison's fiction, like most of the novels issued by Beadle and Adams, can be aligned with a Northern Republican party politics that was opposed to slavery but still strongly invested in racial, ethnic, class, and religious hierarchies. Since dime novel publishers, as Alexander Saxton notes, "maintained a linkage to the Republican party comparable to that of the impresarios of blackface minstrelsy to the Jacksonian party," it is not surprising that Denison's *La Vintresse*, which raises concerns about intimate relations between the United States and Cuba, also voices white egalitarian ideals that consolidate the interests of whites across class lines at the expense of nonwhites.[20] These early dime novels were published just before and during the Civil War, so they reflect more of a partisan, sectional perspective rather than muting the differences between North and South to appeal to a mass audience.

But writers of English-language narratives, sensational or otherwise, were not the only ones flourishing in mid-nineteenth-century America, for Spanish-language narratives also enjoyed a "renaissance." Spanish-language political pamphlets, historical literature, and newspaper production thrived in urban centers and in the former Mexican territories that, after 1848, comprised the Southwest. Philadelphia and New York rivaled Louisiana's crescent city in the proliferation of Spanish-language newspapers edited and published by Cuban political exiles. These papers were not ideologically homogeneous venues. The Manhattan-based *El Filibustero*, which ran from 1853 to 1854, hawked filibustering as an avenue for Cuban independence, although the paper was dubious about U.S. annexation; New York's *La Verdad* likewise decried Spanish rule in Cuba, but during its 1848–1860 run, the paper also advocated the island's annexation into the Union; and *El Mulato*, another New York paper that ran during 1854, called for Cuban independence and the abolition of slavery, a link between white and black Cubans under the Spanish crown that most elite Cubans were unwilling to accept.[21] If discussions of filibustering dominated the Cuban exile press, however, cultural conflict and colonial displacement were the central concerns of the Spanish-language press in the Southwest, especially in gold-rush California.[22] Thus, the Los Angeles–based *El Clamor Público*, which spanned from 1855 to 1859, informed Spanish-speaking citizens of their new legal rights and criticized the social injustices of the region. Certainly this alternative, Spanish-language archive conveys a history of anti-imperialism directed against the United States and Spain, but at times it also betrays complicated expansionist sentiments, especially regarding the annexation of Cuba, and equally complex attitudes toward slavery in the Americas. It is an archive of empire, in other words, that is not simply a counter-discourse to imperialism but is sometimes, especially during the 1850s, a contribution to it.[23]

The exiled Cuban writers nonetheless understood the threat historical amnesia posed to national memory, so in 1856, *El laúd del desterrado* (*The Exile's Lute*) was published in New York. It is the "first anthology of exile literature ever published in the United States" and is a compilation of exile and filibustering poetry that mostly appeared in the Spanish-language press.[24] In many ways, *Empire and the Literature of Sensation* is a similar project since it recovers from historical obscurity the popular images, representations, and discourses that Spanish-language writers of the same era were contributing to or contesting. Very few international romances and imperial adventure novels of the mid-nineteenth century remain in circulation because this literature was ephemeral and because of changing literary values and canons. The selections shed considerable light on gaps in the nation's literary history; the development of its print culture; and how readers across classes and ethnicities consolidated or complicated white identities during this era by reading sensational novels about racial, ethnic, and national "others." Sensational fiction is not good literature in an aesthetic sense, but it is a good way to begin to understand the significance of empire-building in nineteenth-century popular and mass culture. The stereotypes, stock characters, and stunning jingoism; the debates about imperial manhood and womanhood and the nation's gender troubles; the class and race conflicts and gothic frontiers are all traces of a longer history of imperialism that may be read in a body of literature erased from national memory perhaps because, unlike the exile's lute, it does not carry a melodious tune about home.

Slavery and Empire in the Americas

Although we began by arguing that an emphasis on the Civil War as the defining moment in antebellum literary history has enabled a forgetting of U.S. wars of empire in the Americas before 1898, we want to insist on the connections between empire and slavery in sensational literature and on the importance of putting together these two histories rather than substituting one for the other. We are not calling for the replacement of a literary history focused on domestic divisions, the Civil War, and slavery with one that emphasizes international conflicts, transnational movements, and empire-building, for the story of U.S. empire is inseparable from the story of struggles over slavery and changing hierarchies of free and unfree labor. After all, the cheap literature of the U.S.-Mexico War era often compares Mexican labor arrangements and race relations to slavery and likens the hacienda to the plantation, as free (white) labor advocates worried about slavery's extension and the incorporation into the nation of other forms of unfree labor associated with nonwhites. Questions about Mexican debt peonage and about relations between Creoles and Indians haunt U.S.-Mexico War narratives, then, even as borderland spaces are represented as vulnerable to slavery's incursions or as alternative sites where U.S. laws, including those supporting slavery, may be turned topsy-turvy.

The filibustering ventures to Cuba were likewise embroiled in a complex history of slavery that created a confluence between the South's peculiar institution and the Spanish empire's legacy of the slave trade in the Americas. Cuban exiles who belonged to the island's elite, landed class were not unaware of the connection between the Spanish empire and slavery, but the freedom that elite *criollos* imagined was strictly one of white independence from the shackles of monarchy.[25] To be sure, there were some Cuban exiles and print organs, such as *El Mulato*, that imagined freedom in more expansive terms, but throughout the 1850s and through Cuba's Ten Years' War (1868–1878), an ambivalence about slavery and Cuba's mixed-race population hovered over debates about the island's independence and possible annexation into the United States or, during the Civil War, the Confederacy.

Debates about annexation and empire, then, were intimately and immediately tied to debates about slavery in transamerican contexts but not always very clearly. *The Female Warrior* and Delapain's *Thrilling and Exciting Account*, for instance, do not strongly mark regional differences or directly comment on the issue of slavery, though slavery is important in both texts. This strategy probably derives from an interest in muting sectional and political differences to appeal to a broad audience, and it also corresponds to the political strategy of compromising over slavery to preserve the Union in the decades before the Civil War. Although the protagonist of *The Female Warrior* is a Southerner who leaves Alabama for Texas, she does not clarify her beliefs about slavery, though she casually remarks that her family includes "a black servant," Mary, who "insisted on accompanying us" (5). While Siddons frees Mary just before she herself dresses as a man and launches "forth into the world . . . another being" (6), Mary is represented, in ways that echo proslavery literature, as a loyal and dependent slave who must be forced by a white person to assume her freedom. Thus even though the Texas borderlands are imagined as a space of revolutionary transformation, where women take on masculine duties and privileges and where slaves may be freed, the narrative remains ambiguous on the issue of slavery, despite its real historical presence in Texas.

Delaplain's narrative is also muted on this issue. Although the captain of the ship characterizes filibustering as "an enterprise intended to strike off the chains of slavery from the inhabitants of the island" (219), López and his comrades focused on liberating Creoles from the Spanish empire rather than freeing slaves. And though the pamphlet suggests that filibustering is a dangerous project, it does not naysay the filibusters' goal of ending Spanish tyranny; indeed, it may support that goal by lingering on torture scenes to help the reader "form an idea of the nature of the Cuban Spaniard" (225). But the narrative also avoids commenting on the issues of annexation and slavery, exploring instead the vaguer notion that foreign entanglements may be dangerous. In fact, Barclay seems to have understood that the Narciso López campaigns would interest Northerners and Southerners, which might explain why the story is set in New York but ostensibly published in Charleston. Both texts, then, provoke questions about slavery in a transamerican frame, but the pamphlets avoid answering such questions as they aim to appeal to a broad national audience that was divided over slavery.

The U.S.-Mexico War narratives often contained more substantial discussions of race, slavery, and other forms of unfree labor, perhaps because the war brought these issues to the forefront in ways that were more difficult to sidestep. Buntline's *Magdalena*, for instance, addresses Mexican debt peonage and slavery as well as the relations between Mexican *criollos* and Indians, which are depicted as eerily similar to those between white masters and mistresses and their happy slaves in Southern plantation fiction. Questions about Mexican debt peonage and its relationship to chattel slavery emerge when the Mexican officer, Alfrede, threatens to turn Magdalena and her family into peons if she refuses to marry him. Such comparisons among debt peonage, chattel slavery, and free labor were common during the U.S.-Mexico War era and even into the Civil War period in dime novels such as A. J. H. Duganne's *The Peon Prince* (1861).[26] This comparison could either undermine or support the annexation of Mexico and the extension of slavery, but Buntline uses it to mobilize readers' sympathies not in opposition to slavery as such, but in response to what is represented as the horrifying possibility that the white woman Magdalena may be reduced to the status of a slave. Debt peonage in Mexico is worse than chattel slavery in the United States, Buntline suggests, because whites as well as nonwhites may be subjected to it. On the other hand, Buntline naturalizes and romanticizes the labor of nonwhites on behalf of whites in scenes where an Indian, Zalupah, faithfully serves Magdalena and even sacrifices himself for his "mistress" and his "new master," Charles Brackett (75). Buntline makes a point of insisting on the "vast difference" between the *criolla* Magdalena and Zalupah even after she "stains" her hands and face "dark" and dresses like him to rescue her lover (76). In effect, Buntline includes Mexican Creoles within the circle of whiteness by distinguishing them from nonwhites who, like slaves in paternalist plantation novels, cheerfully serve their master.

While Buntline was a prominent author and advocate of the white working class who also supported slavery, George Lippard opposed slavery but was still invested in a version of white egalitarianism that represented nonwhite characters in racist ways. Lippard's '*Bel* implies that slavery is partly to blame for the tragedies that it records, for the colonist Jacob Grywin, a "broken bank director" from Philadelphia, brought slaves with him when he moved to Texas to start over. Slave labor helped to build Prairie Eden, and so slavery extension is fully implicated in the novel's bleak conclusion. But even so, at the end of the novel Lippard depicts a Philadelphia slum as an especially degraded environment because blacks and whites share the same spaces, and in his writings he prioritized the struggles of white workers over those of nonwhites. Such a contradictory response to race, slavery, and empire can also be traced in Lippard's story paper, *The Quaker City*. In his story paper, Lippard spoke out against slavery but singled out white slavery as the most pressing issue facing the nation, and he yoked utopian hopes for land reform to the Democrats' project of national expansion through empire-building even as he worried that the war would unleash dangerous passions and that slaveholders and other corrupt capitalists would chiefly benefit from it. Indeed, his white egalitarianism resembled that of the Wilmot Proviso, the amendment that would have protected the interests of white labor by banning slavery and other forms of involuntary servitude from any territories acquired from Mexico after the war.

This worldview helped to shape the Northern Republican position that emerged in the Civil War era and that defined white egalitarian ideals of free soil and free labor in opposition to Southern chattel slavery and the plantation economy. In *The Prisoner of La Vintresse*, Mary Denison combines antislavery sentiments with white egalitarianism by making the villains decadent Spanish slaveholders and by defining the whiteness of the heroine through contrasts with nonwhite servants and slaves, who are represented either as unthinkingly loyal or as sadistic accomplices of their masters. The novel idealizes the rural, republican independence of Herman's father, who is "king on his own soil," by contrasting his manly self-reliance to the Cuban aristocrats' dependence on slaves (275). In these ways, Denison connects empire to slavery by suggesting that annexing Cuba might mean extending slavery's sway and incorporating more nonwhite people into the nation, even as she includes Cuban Creoles within the boundaries of a hierarchically structured whiteness that privileges English over Spanish "blood."

Transnational Transvestism and Racial Masquerade

The narratives collected in this anthology thus remind us that Thomas Jefferson's "empire for liberty" was also an embattled empire of slavery well before the Civil War, making it difficult to forget that legacies of empire, slavery, and revolution across the Americas linked together the United States and Spain despite their differences.[27] Indeed, U.S. cultures of imperialism are part of a greater hemispheric history of conquest and struggle that brought the United States and Spain to war in 1898 perhaps because the United States followed in Spain's footsteps as an empire-builder in the Americas in 1848. The transamerican contexts of empire and slavery also illuminate how gender, sexuality, and race were unsettled and redefined in the United States in this period. In "Manifest Domesticity," Amy Kaplan suggests that "narratives of domesticity" were "inseparable from narratives of empire and nation-building" and that ideas about gender, sexuality, and race "at home" were entangled with and transformed by "foreign" affairs, war, and imperialism in the borderlands and other parts of the Americas.[28] This insight about how international conflicts and imperial encounters reshaped gender, sexuality, and race can help us to understand the ubiquitous scenes of gender and racial masquerade in the sensational literature of empire, which registers anxieties about slavery, the incorporation of nonwhites into the nation, the changing boundaries of home, and challenges to traditional gender roles in times of war.

Leonora Siddons's *The Female Warrior* is part of a well-established subgenre in nineteenth-century fiction: the first-person account of a female heroine who cross-dresses during national conflict. The narrative of Lucy Brewer, *The Female Marine*, sold widely in the early part of the century as it recounted Brewer's transvestite participation in the War of 1812, while Eliza Allen's 1851 *The Female Volunteer*, another first-person account, narrates her participation in the U.S.-Mexico War as George Meade. Sophia Delaplain's cross-dressed filibustering in Cuba picks up on the same theme, and the subgenre finds its culmination in the 1876 *The Woman in Battle*, a narrative that recounts Loreta Janeta Velazquez's cross-dressed support of the Confederacy during the Civil War. The authenticity of these autobiographical adventure narratives is suspect, yet the volume and consistency of such accounts in literary history, plus the appearance of other female cross-dressed characters in the popular literature of the time, indicate that transvestism embodies the cultural conflicts and boundary-crossings that emerge during times of expansion.[29] The Civil War, for instance, challenged Victorian sensibilities as women participated as nurses, spies, and, in the South, as the overseers of slaves and plantation work. So it is not surprising that the cross-dressed figure appears in fiction as a symbol of women's transgression from the seclusion of the home front to the dangers of the frontlines. In this sense, the transvestite figure in fiction indicates a "category crisis elsewhere," and in the sensational literature reprinted here, the cross-dressed figure expresses the domestic instability of national expansion into the other Americas.[30]

These cross-dressing texts might be considered critiques of normative gender codes, but they are also reactionary re-entrenchments of female roles and the nation's borders. That is, while transvestism demonstrates that gender is performative rather than natural (as Judith Butler teaches us), transnationalism threatens to undermine the sanctity of the nation's domestic borders and the woman's place in the home.[31] Both accounts warn against the threat imperialism and filibustering pose to the home, nation, and their related gender roles as female domestic angels enter the public sphere as masculine subjects but return to the safety of the home following their harrowing encounters in imperial locales. In the Siddons text, the Texas rebellion leads to the demise of patriarchy (Siddons's father); signals the collapse of slavery as Leonora frees Mary; and, with Santa Anna's courtship, even imagines a seamy alliance between Anglo Texas and Mexico. Similarly, expansion and filibustering in the Delaplain narrative threaten New York's class and gender codes; highlight the potential for civil war (figured by the mutiny aboard the *Henry Clay*); and most important, Cuban filibustering raises the specter of Catholicism and the so-called Black Legend in the Americas. Cross-dressed female adventurers thus buck class, gender, and even racial norms, yet their narratives also reinforce social order as each heroine returns to the domestic front and pens a transvestite tale that warns readers about the threats imperialism poses to womanhood and the domestic sphere.

Still, these texts trouble the international romance genre that was a staple of the cultures of imperialism. Many U.S.-Mexico War novelettes feature a romance between a U.S. soldier (usually an officer) and a Mexican woman (usually landed and light-skinned) that concludes with their marriage or the prospect of their postwar nuptials. As with other "foundational fictions," the war's popular fiction often imagines Mexico as a feminine body (sometimes in drag) waiting to be liberated and loved by the masculine and chivalric army officers from the north.[32] But although the usual erotics of empire identify heterosexual conquest and desire with political intervention and social transformation, the Siddons and Delaplain pamphlets disrupt the international romance genre by enacting gender reversals that question the masculinity and heterosexuality of U.S. imperialism. In the

Siddons narrative, Texas history becomes a drag show of female adventure as young Leonora's heroics displace the leading men of Texas's independence—Stephen Austin, William Travis, Davy Crockett, Jim Bowie, and even Sam Houston—and thus question the hyper-masculinity often associated with Texas's famed rebellion. The Delaplain narrative invokes its own crisis in masculinity as the text offers two ostensibly male adventurers: Mortimer Bowers and Delaplain in drag. Delaplain's male garb does not keep her from playing a stereotypical feminine role next to Bower's heroics during the *Henry Clay*'s mutiny, but once they are captured and Delaplain's disguise has been revealed, their roles reverse: Delaplain becomes the adventurer proper, effecting her escape disguised as a Cuban servant and making her way back to Baltimore, while Bowers meets his demise when he is forced to hug a statue of the Virgin in what must be read as a gothic reversal of the heterosexual erotics of U.S. empire.

As Delaplain's escape suggests, transvestism also appears as racial cross-dressing, a trope that signals confusion in national identity exactly when expansionism raised the problem of racial integration and the fear of miscegenation. As Senator Lewis Cass proclaimed in 1847: "It would be a deplorable amalgamation [uniting the United States and Mexico]. No such evil will happen to us in our day. We do not want the people of Mexico, either as citizens or subjects. All we want is a portion of territory, which they nominally hold, generally uninhabited, or, where inhabited at all, sparsely so, and with a population which would soon recede, or identify itself with ours."[33] The U.S.-Mexico War novelettes in this collection highlight how racial transvestism registers an anxiety in U.S. culture that annexation of Mexico would lead to amalgamation between its peoples.

In Buntline's *Magdalena*, Charles Brackett's mixed identity (Castilian and Anglo-American native of Texas) makes him a perfect candidate to dress as a Mexican to spy across enemy lines, where he meets, falls in love, and marries the eponymous heroine. Brackett's mixed blood raises questions about the racial purity of Anglo-Saxon America, and the text exacerbates the racial confusion by mirroring Brackett and his Mexican foil, Colonel Alfrede. They vie for Magdalena's affection through a romance structure that pits progress and liberation (Brackett) against exploitation and oppression (Alfrede). Yet, in the final scene, it is Alfrede who dies by Brackett's dagger (the usual weapon of choice among Mexicans, according to most narratives) and Brackett who dies by Alfrede's pistols (the usual Anglo-American weapon). The reversal is slight but significant because it is the culmination of the racial and national confusion first signaled by Brackett's racial cross-dressing and border-crossing.

In a much more gruesome ending, Lippard's *'Bel* narrates the haunting transformation of John Grywin, the story's hero who, after a series of gothic experiences in Mexico, returns to Philadelphia as Juan, and brings with him his Mexican corpse bride. The uncanny transformation from John to Juan is all the more haunting because it collapses rather than maintains the difference between the United States and Mexico in the same way that Charles Brackett's Mexican disguise highlights the fact that the U.S.-born soldier is already a Mexican American. Racial transvestism, in other words, registers the shifting, constructed nature of racial and national identities and responds to how these identities were transformed during the war and after the signing of the Treaty of Guadalupe Hidalgo, but it also enacts an anti-imperial amalgamation anxiety that sees contact with Mexico as a threat to the purity of Anglo-Saxon American identity.

Anxieties about imperial manhood and womanhood and the boundaries of racial and national identities are also evident in Denison's *La Vintresse*, where entanglement in Cuban filibustering provokes radical transformations in the heroine and threatens white U.S. manhood. The novel focuses on Minerva, an heiress who disobeys her uncle and tries to elope to the United States with the "Americano," Herman Goreham. Initially, Goreham seems to be an exemplary figure of national manhood, but after he is waylaid by authorities as he tries to leave Cuba and is imprisoned in the slave quarters of an abandoned plantation, he is transformed from a "self-reliant, dignified man" into a "pale, bowed down captive," who longs for freedom (254). Since Minerva leads the expedition to free him, the narrative inverts the rules of sensational melodrama, whereby heroic men save endangered women: here the woman rescues the man. The narrative's inversions and transformations of gender and sex roles link concerns about filibustering and the amalgamation of Cuba to Northern Republican ideologies of free labor and white egalitarianism as well as to fears of the extension of slavery and Southern power. Filibustering and U.S. involvement with Cuba, the novel warns, threaten to enervate white American manhood by subjecting young men to the passions of slaveholders and the cruelties of slavery. The idea that involvement with Cuba and Cubans could reduce a man like Goreham to the condition of a white slave held captive by a malevolent black slave also illustrates the dime novel's anxieties about Cuba's black people, despite Denison's antislavery beliefs.

In Denison's novel as well as in the other popular narratives that we have included in this anthology, race and gender are not what they seem to be, and neither is the nation, for as this collection documents, U.S. imperialism in the Americas predates 1898. While the standard view of the 1898 Spanish-Cuban-American War as the origin of U.S. empire may lead to the forgetting of earlier imperial encounters and conflicts within the United States and across the Americas, the antebellum literary periodization practically erases from national memory the significance of other nineteenth-century wars before the great one between the states. At the same time, the emphasis on the literary formation of the American Renaissance obscures an alternative renaissance: the popular and sensational literature produced during the era, much of which responds more directly to the excitement and anxiety of this era of empire-building. *Empire and the Literature of Sensation* thus seeks to remember the literary, historical, and cultural ties that connect 1848 to 1898 in order to place U.S. imperialism within its transamerican contexts of empire, slavery, freedom, and print culture throughout the long nineteenth century.

Notes

1. During the 1970s, imperialism was an important topic in work on the Vietnam War and in studies of internal colonialism in ethnic studies (especially Native American Studies and Chicano Studies). Beginning in the 1980s, the impact of postcolonial theory on the U.S. academy made scholars more attentive to issues of empire. Amy Kaplan and Donald Pease's anthology *Cultures of U.S. Imperialism* (Durham: Duke University Press, 1993) was an especially significant contribution that inspired the study of empire in U.S. literary studies. Some key texts include Kaplan, *The Anarchy of Empire* (Cambridge, Mass.: Harvard University Press, 2004); John Carlos Rowe, *Literary Culture and U.S. Imperialism: From the Revolution to World War II* (New York: Oxford University Press, 2000); and José David Saldívar, *Border Matters: Remapping American Cultural Studies* (Berkeley: University of California Press, 1997).

2. See Kaplan, *The Anarchy of Empire*; Ivan Musicant, *Empire by Default: The Spanish American War and the Dawn of the American Century* (New York: Holt, 1998); Philip S. Foner, *The Spanish-Cuban-American War and the Birth of US Imperialism, 1895–1902*, vol. 1 (New York: Monthly Review Press, 1972); Angel Smith and Emma Dávila-Cox, eds., *The Crisis of 1898: Colonial Redistribution and Nationalist Mobilization* (New York: St. Martin's Press, 1999); Pedro A. Cabán, *Constructing a Colonial People: Puerto Rico and the United States, 1898–1932* (Boulder, Colo.: Westview Press, 1999).

3. John O'Sullivan, "Annexation," *Democratic Review* 17 (July 1845): 7.

4. Robert E. May, *Manifest Destiny's Underworld: Filibustering in Antebellum America* (Chapel Hill: University of North Carolina Press, 2002), 7–14.

5. See Reginald Horsman, *Race and Manifest Destiny: The Origins of American Racial Anglo-Saxonism* (Cambridge, Mass.: Harvard University Press, 1981).

6. Rick Stewart, "Artists and Printmakers of the Mexican War," in *Eyewitness to War: Prints and Daguerreotypes of the Mexican War, 1846–1848*, ed. Martha A. Sandweiss et al. (Fort Worth: Amon Carter Museum, 1989), 4.

7. David S. Reynolds, *Beneath the American Renaissance: The Subversive Imagination in the Age of Emerson and Melville* (Cambridge, Mass.: Harvard University Press, 1988), 170–171.

8. Shelley Streeby, *American Sensations: Class, Empire, and the Production of Popular Culture* (Berkeley: University of California Press, 2002), 11–13. See also Michael Denning, *Mechanic Accents: Dime Novels and Working Class Culture in America* (London and New York: Verso, 1987); and Ronald Zboray, *A Fictive People: Antebellum Economic Development and the American Reading Public* (New York: Oxford University Press, 1993).

9. Ann Douglas, *The Feminization of American Culture* (New York: Anchor-Doubleday, 1988); Jane Tompkins, *Sensational Designs: The Cultural Work of American Fiction* (New York: Oxford University Press, 1985).

10. Shirley Samuels, "Introduction," in *The Culture of Sentiment: Race, Gender, and Sentimentality in Nineteenth-Century America* (New York: Oxford University Press, 1992), 3.

11. Mary Chapman and Glenn Hendler, eds., *Sentimental Men: Masculinity and the Politics of Affect in American Culture* (Berkeley: University of California Press, 1999).

12. Denning, *Mechanic Accents*.

13. Richard Brodhead, *Cultures of Letters: Scenes of Reading and Writing in Nineteenth-Century America* (Chicago: University of Chicago Press, 1993), 79.

14. Jonathan Elmer, *Reading at the Social Limit: Affect, Mass Culture, and Edgar Allan Poe* (Stanford, Calif.: Stanford University Press, 1995), 102, 207. Elmer uses the example of little Eva's death scene to explain the distinction between sentimentalism and Poe's sensationalism. He suggests that sensationalism repudiates "the openly recuperative didacticism of sentimentalism" (103).

15. Dawn Keetley, "Victim and Victimizer: Female Fiends and Unease over Marriage in Antebellum Sensation Fiction," *American Quarterly* 51, no. 2 (1999): 344–384. See also Thomas M. McDade, "Lurid Literature of the Last Century: The Publications of E. E. Barclay," *Pennsylvania Magazine of History and Biography* 80 (October 1956): 452–464.

16. McDade, "Lurid Literature of the Last Century," 457.

17. Keetley, "Victim and Victimizer," 345.

18. On U.S.-Mexico War novelettes, see David Kazanjian, *The Colonizing Trick: National Culture and Imperial Citizenship in Early America* (Minneapolis: University of Minnesota Press, 2004); Richard Slotkin, *The Fatal Environment: The Myth of the Frontier in the Age of Industrialization, 1800–1890* (Middletown, Conn.: Wesleyan University Press, 1985); and Streeby, *American Sensations*, 81–149.

19. *Malaeska* is included in Bill Brown, *Reading the West: An Anthology of Dime Westerns* (Boston: Bedford Books, 1997).

20. Alexander Saxton, *The Rise and Fall of the White Republic: Class Politics and Mass Culture in Nineteenth-Century America* (London and New York: Verso, 1990), 322.

21. Rodrigo Lazo, *Writing to Cuba: Filibustering and Cuban Exiles in the United States* (Chapel Hill: University of North Carolina Press, 2005), 65.

22. See Nicolás Kanellos, *Hispanic Periodicals in the United States, Origins to 1960: A Brief History and Comprehensive Bibliography* (Houston: Arte Público Press, 2000), 76.

23. Kirsten Silva Gruesz, *Ambassadors of Culture: The Transamerican Origins of Latino Writing* (Princeton: Princeton University Press, 2002), 11.

24. Kanellos, *Hispanic Periodicals in the United States*, 11.

25. Rodrigo Lazo, *Writing to Cuba*, 83.

26. Streeby, *American Sensations*, 189–213.

27. Thomas Jefferson, letter to James Madison (April 27, 1809), in *The Writings of Thomas Jefferson* (Washington, D.C.: Thomas Jefferson Memorial Association, 1904), 11–12.

28. Amy Kaplan, "Manifest Domesticity," *American Literature* 70, no. 3 (September 1998): 583, 584.

29. Jesse Alemán, "Authenticity, Autobiography, and Identity: *The Woman in Battle* as a Civil War Narrative," introduction to *The Woman in Battle: The Civil War Narrative of Loreta Janeta Velazquez, Cuban Woman and Confederate Soldier*, by Loreta Janeta Velazquez (Madison: University of Wisconsin Press, 2003), xxvi–xxxi. See also Daniel A. Cohen, ed., *The Female Marine and Related Works: Narratives of Cross-Dressing and Urban Vice in America's Early Republic* (Amherst: University of Massachusetts Press, 1997).

30. Marjorie Garber, *Vested Interests: Cross-Dressing and Cultural Anxiety* (New York: HarperPerennial, 1993), 17.

31. Judith Butler, *Gender Trouble: Feminism and the Subversion of Identity* (New York: Routledge, 1999), 173–180.

32. Doris Sommer, *Foundational Fictions: The National Romances of Latin America* (Berkeley: University of California Press, 1991), 6; Streeby, *American Sensations*, 102–138.

33. Lewis Cass, "The Mexican War," Senate of the United States (February 10, 1847), 5–6.

A NOTE ON THE TEXTS

Extant copies of the titles included here are housed in libraries across the country either as bound pamphlets or in serial newspapers. The most readily available copies of the texts, however, are found in the Wright American Fiction microfilm collection. All of the texts reprinted here derive from the Wright collection housed in the University of New Mexico's Zimmerman Library because it is the most accessible venue for each text but also because the microfilm copies allowed the editors to handle the texts in ways we could not handle originals. Considering the nature of popular fiction, there are certainly variations across publications, especially the ones that first appeared serially and then in pamphlet form, but we have made no effort to establish authoritative texts. Instead, the texts were transcribed from their microfilm form to an electronic document. They have been edited for this collection. All of the original copyright pages and illustrations were expunged, as were the original chapter synopses in Buntline's *Magdalena*. Some of the chapters of Denison's *La Vintresse* have been redacted for the sake of space. We did not correct content related to characterization, vernacular, or foreign words or names, but we did standardize the texts to American spelling and punctuation. We silently corrected anomalous misspellings and typographical errors, and we modernized punctuation marks such as quotation marks and dashes. Invariably the transcription process generated textual slips, and while we have made every effort to catch these mistakes, we nonetheless regret any egregious corruptions in our edited reprints.

Empire
AND THE LITERATURE OF SENSATION

The Female Warrior

Published in New York in 1843 by E. E. & G. Barclay, *The Female Warrior* is an example of a popular literary genre—the first-person account of a cross-dressed female soldier—that circulated in the United States as early as the Revolutionary War and continued through the Civil War. These accounts often balanced patriotism with sensationalism. Transgressive women were standard fare for the Barclay publishing house, which circulated pamphlet novels of similar length, style, and form that recounted the criminal adventures of female murderers, prostitutes, or insane housewives. Although it purports to be autobiographical, then, the Siddons narrative is not a true, first-person account but a form of fictional autobiography that dominated the early sensational market. The author remains unknown. The story derives its sensationalism by combining the popularity of events in Texas with the titillating focus on a cross-dressed female soldier on the brink of exposure. The link between Texas and transvestism seems to offer a cautionary tale about the young republic's annexation into the Union, viewing it as a threat to the domestic stability of the United States.

As with Leonora's gender identity, the text's historical background is not clear. The story is set in Texas, where the Siddons family arrives in 1837, a year after Texas gained its independence at the battle of San Jacinto. Contrary to the narrative, though, Texas and Mexico were not at war in San Antonio between 1837 and 1838. Instead, Mexico invaded and occupied San Antonio in March and September 1842, a year before the Siddons text was published. The narrative thus recounts the 1842 skirmishes but places them in 1837 and 1838, perhaps as a way of capitalizing on the current events in Texas and making Leonora's story seem more historical than fictional. Either way, Leonora comes of age during the Texas-Mexico conflicts that preceded the U.S.-Mexico War, so her adventures depict the border tensions the nation inherited when it annexed Texas in 1845. The war with Mexico would start a year later, and with it, as the Siddons narrative warns, would come the domestic instability that led the nation to civil war.

THE FEMALE WARRIOR.
AN INTERESTING NARRATIVE OF THE SUFFERINGS
AND SINGULAR AND SURPRISING ADVENTURES
OF MISS LEONORA SIDDONS.

Narrative of Leonora Siddons

*T*he following lines may appear strange, and perhaps incredible to you at first; still they are not the less true. To use the language of Byron, "Truth is strange, stranger than fiction."[1] And I think upon the attentive perusal of the following pages you will find it, at least for this time, verified.

What I have suffered, pen can but faintly portray. But I have set myself down to the task; and, as far as I am able, will endeavor to give you a clear, and at least a correct account, of my privations and sufferings.

I shall not trouble you with a long detailed account of my birth and education, which are matters of but little importance compared to what I am about to relate, and which would weary me in writing, as well as you in reading.

Suffice it, therefore, to say, that I was born in the city Mobile, Ala., in the year 1822; making me at the present time 21 years of age.

My father was once a wealthy merchant, and did an extensive business there for several years. But owing to some speculative scheme which he engaged in, and the great money pressure of '37, which all will recollect, he, like thousands of others, was completely ruined.[2] My mother dying about the same time, overwhelmed him with grief, and he determined on removing from a place which had been so unfortunate to him, and was connected with so many associations, recalling to his mind and contrasting the present with the past.

Accordingly we removed to the village of Galveston, in Texas.[3] Our family consisted of but three persons, my father, myself (who, by the way, was an only child,) and a black servant, who had lived in our family in more prosperous days, and who insisted on accompanying us. Here my father engaged in a retail business, which yielded him a fair compensation, and our prospects became again somewhat cheering.

But on the breaking out of the war between Texas and Mexico, he deemed it his duty to enlist, and assist in protecting his adopted country from tyrannic oppression.[4] To this I made no objection, for I held it, and do still hold it, to be a duty both binding by the laws of God and man, for every citizen to aid his country, by every means in his power, to drive back her tyrannical invaders, and erect the noble standard of liberty, from which the banner of freedom triumphantly may wave o'er all the land.

I took an affectionate, alas! a final leave of my father. Poor man! He now fills a soldier's grave.

News was brought me of his death by one who saw him fall; to whom he told my place of residence, and requested him to bear the sad intelligence. His lasts words were, "Sir, you will find my daughter as I have described; say to her, her father died defending the glorious cause of liberty. Tell her, also, to serve her country by whatever means fortune may place in her power. I can say no more: farewell."

When this news reached me, I was for a short time completely overpowered; and I felt that I was truly alone in the world, without a friend or protector. For several days my mind was wandering and unsettled; I knew not what or how to dispose of myself. Then came my father's words ringing in my ears, "Serve your country!" I felt that I ought to do something, but what, I knew not.

Thoughts like these perplexed me for some time, until at length I resolved to join the army, then rallying under General Houston.[5] This to you, reader, will undoubtedly seem a strange and novel idea, and truly it was: but in the spirit I then felt, it mattered but little with me what came of it. The very novelty gave it an additional charm.

I longed for excitement,—something to drive away the gloomy cloud that was hovering over my mind. This I thought would gain my end, and, what would be still far better, at the same time, be assisting my country.

My mind once made up, and with me there was no hesitation. I believed in a maxim which was strictly adhered to by my father, "When you would choose, consider well. When chosen, never halt between two opinions." I mention this, merely to show with what firmness I undertook my purpose; for had my mind been wavering, I should never have completed such an arduous undertaking. I told the black, who still lived with me, that my mind had become so depressed since my father's death, that I intended travelling to regain my health, both of body and mind.

She tried by every means in her power to have me give consent for her to accompany me, but I steadfastly refused, nor did I dare to let her know of my real intentions, for she would have exposed the whole scheme—for the sake of saving me from ruin. When she found she could not prevail on me to consent, she cried like a child. I felt sorry for her, but my mind was made up, and we must part.

For some time I was troubled to know how I could procure a male dress, and not be suspected. At last I hit on a plan which worked to my satisfaction.

I told Mary (the black) that I should first go back to Mobile, and that I had a cousin there who was to accompany me in my travels, and that he had requested me to get him a dress made in Texan style, and bring with me.

This, however implausible story, Mary readily believed; and accordingly procured the garments, which I told her were about my size. I then sold what little furniture I possessed, gave Mary a part, and told her that henceforth she was her own mistress. Our parting was in tears.

As soon as we had separated, I arranged myself in my new habiliments, which I found to fit well, and launched forth into the world as it were another being.

How strange our fortunes! how little do we know, who pretend to know so much! Had any one, a few years ago, told me I should have to pass through even half what I have, I would have laughed him to scorn.

I proceeded immediately to Houston, where I found a number of volunteers, whom I joined, and we together joined the main army. I do not think my sex was suspected, although I attracted considerable attention, and frequently overheard some very flattering compliments relative to my beauty, &c.

We were not ordered out under about two months after my joining, and I began to feel very uneasy, and was on the point of deserting, when an order came for us to take up a line of march to St. Antonio.[6] This was glorious news to me; I fairly leaped for joy. I longed for excitement—for battle—something to rouse up my dormant energies.

It had been a constant theme in my mind, wondering how I should feel when standing where death rode upon the sword and steel. I longed to satisfy my curiosity. And when word came to march, as I said before, I fairly leaped for joy.

We were not long in reaching this place, considering the distance. At St. Antonio we found a good deal of bustle and preparation, for a rumor was afloat that the enemy was marching directly for this place.

This, to me, good news, was again contradicted by a statement that the Mexicans had taken another route, and it was considered very uncertain whether they would show fight or not. This caused much uneasiness among many of the soldiers, who I found were as anxious for the affray as myself. But we did not have long to wait; this last, it seems, was a false rumor. In a few days news was brought by some who had been sent out as scouts, that the enemy were fast approaching, having found it impossible by a feint to throw us off our guard.

We were again ordered to be in a readiness for a moment's notice. The next news we received was in the evening, by which we learned the enemy had en-camped within a few miles, and that a battle was to be fought the next day which would decide, perhaps, the fate of Texas.

This intelligence created considerable confusion in our corps, and I saw many with pale cheeks, who the day before had boasted how much they could do, should the cowardly Mexicans, as they termed them, dare to give us battle.

There are ever many brave hearts when there is no danger. But I have found, by observation, that those who boast the most and talk the loudest are the first to run away when danger is near; while they who say the least, as a gen-eral thing, turn out to the contrary. But, heaven be praised, there were but few cowards among us; most of them were brave staunch fellows, who feared not death, so that they died in a good cause.

Early in the morning I was awakened by the roll of the drum, calling each to his post. Alas! thought I, as I ran my eye down the lines, how many of these brave fellows this day must sleep the sleep of death!

And I, ay I, perchance, may be one of the number. Am I prepared, am I ready? As I asked myself these questions, my blood coursed coldly through my veins. It was not fear. For had fear formed a part of my nature, I should never have undertaken what I did. But there is an undefinable something, which forms a part and being of the boldest hearts when death is apparently near, and, given, time for reflection, will make them pause, and think of the uncertain future. It was this which affected me, as I thought what might be my fate ere the sun was lost in night.

But conscience did not prick me with her darts; I felt that I was doing my duty, and if I died it was in a noble cause.

My reverie was disturbed by an order to march. The enemy, we soon learned, were already on their way, and but a few hours could elapse ere a tale must be told of weal or woe.

We marched to a plain not far distant from St. Antonio, where we did not arrive until about ten o'clock, owing to some unavoidable delay. Here we were ordered to halt and prepare for action, for the enemy were already in sight— at the farther end of the plain their bright armor glittering in the sun, as on they came, with martial tread, to the sound of the rolling drum.

As they neared, we could perceive their numbers to ours to be about ten to one. What a sight! was not this enough to try the courage of the bravest? Still we stood undaunted, waiting in dread suspense for the moment to arrive when we should be called upon to strike for Texas and freedom!

At length that moment came. It was about noon; the sun shone with such intense heat that it seemed as if we must melt. The air was thick and sultry, and it was with difficulty that we could breathe. We were again ordered to march, and when within about pistol-shot of the enemy, both armies halted, as it were by common consent. For a moment and all was still; it was a sickening, death-like stillness, for well each knew, when that stillness again was broken, it would be the death-knell of many brave hearts. It was but a moment.

Still I believe I suffered more fear, more agony of mind, in that short space of time than all before or since.

Now came the word—fire! and ere the sound had died away the roar of musketry took its place, mingled with the cries of the wounded and dying soldiers.

It was truly a heart-rending scene! Shriek upon shriek arose from the unfortunate—some crying for help, for mercy, and some for death, to relieve them from their pains. The next instant all was confusion and uproar, and ere five minutes had elapsed from the first order to fire, I, who shuddered at the first groan, could look on death with perfect indifference. It seems to me that I was borne along by excitement, for I felt doubly strong, and I thought, while charging upon the enemy, "Though they can muster ten to one, they cannot boast of an easy conquest."

How the battle was going, I could not tell. I at times caught sight of General Houston, fighting hand to hand with the Mexicans. He was attired in a very poor dress, used, I suppose, to disguise him from the enemy.

We fought for two hours with a bravery worthy of a better fate, and it was plainly perceptible to all that we must finally be conquered by overpowering numbers. Still our little band fought on, nothing daunted, until even hope itself had become extinct.

Many now yielded themselves to the Mexicans as prisoners of war. But I determined to fight to the last, as became a true soldier, and if I must die, thought I, let it be on the battle-field in preference to a Mexican dungeon. I found a few others who were of the same mind, and as our ranks were broken, we thought it best to bear round and attack from the other side. In attempting to do this we were surrounded by a party of about five times our number, who, it seems, were coming around on our side for the same purpose. We had nothing left us now but to fight.

We formed into a solid square, and with cutlasses and swords, with which most of us were armed, (having picked them up on our way,) we made a noble resistance.

But what could we do against such odds? One by one our numbers became less, until by some, as it were, miraculous providence, I stood alone. "You are my prisoner!" said one, a large, stout-built man, slapping me on the shoulder.

(He spoke in Spanish, but being acquainted with the language, I readily understood him.)

"Never!" cried I, as I thought of my sex. "Liberty or death!" and as I spoke I made a pass at him with my cutlass, which I still held in my hand.

This he was prepared for: catching it on his with a quick dexterous turn, he wrenched it completely from my grasp.

"Lost, lost, all is lost!" exclaimed I, in agony; then perceiving a brace of pistols in his belt, I sprang with the desperation of a madman, and, ere he was aware of my intentions, drew one, and shot him through the heart.

At that instant I saw the flash of another, and all was dark—I fell.

When I recovered my senses it was night. At first I could not recall to my mind how I came, or even where I was. But by degrees it broke upon my mind. Then it was with sickening horror, as, partly raising myself, I gazed around, and by the light of the moon discovered the ghastly countenances of my companions in battle. Feeling a dizziness and a curious sensation in my head, I reached up my hand and drew it back wet with clotted blood.

So then, thought I, I am wounded—perhaps mortally—and am left here to perish, without even one on whom I can call for assistance. Better by far had the bullet pierced my brain and ended life at once.

I tried to get on my feet, but it was in vain; and after several unsuccessful efforts, I fell back upon the bloody soil, completely exhausted.

At length I felt a heart-sickening feeling. Every thing began to grow dim and more indistinct. This, thought I, is death, and inwardly did I rejoice to think that soon I should be past all suffering. All again was lost.

When I recovered from this fainting-fit, it was broad daylight. As I again raised myself to look around, I perceived a foraging party of Mexicans but a few paces from me, apparently examining the body of one of the soldiers. On discovering, they immediately turned their attention to me; and perceiving by my dress that I was a Texan, part of them were for dispatching me on the spot; the others objected to this, and said I "ought to be taken as a prisoner, and confined in some dungeon, to eke out a miserable existence," rightly judging it was by far the worse punishment of the two.

After holding a short consultation, it was decided that, as they were on their return, I should be taken with them to the city of Mexico, and thrown into a dungeon. Any thing was preferable to this, and I begged of them to shoot me on the spot.

But they paid no attention to my cries and entreaties, no more than if I were a beast. One of them seized me very roughly by the arm, and jerked me upon my feet. But I could not stand; faint with the loss of blood, fatigued by over exercise and excitement, and being without food for twenty-four hours, with a wound in my head, it will naturally be imagined that I was in a truly deplorable condition. As the ruffian let go after jerking me up, I sank to the ground. As there was a surgeon among them, he was ordered to examine my head, and, if he thought the wound any way dangerous, I was to be shot, and save all further trouble.

After examining it carefully for a few minutes, he pronounced it not dangerous. The ball, he stated, had come in a slanting direction, and striking my skull, had again glanced off without doing any material injury other than stunning me, and confusing my brain. He then took a strip of cloth and bound it around my head, while two stout fellows seized me, one under each arm, and bore me away. I suppose I must have again fainted, or lost my reason, for I have no recollection of any thing that passed after this until I heard the rippling waters dash against the prow of the vessel.

When I awoke from this second trance, as it were, I saw that I was on the deck of a ship, and some of the party who had captured me were standing near, evidently disputing some point. Among these was the surgeon, who seemed to argue his case almost alone. A part of the conversation I overheard, which I will here mention.

"I tell thee, Rialto, to grant me but twenty-four hours, and if in that time he does not recover, I will agree to your proposal."

"But see here, surgeon," replied the other, "you have put us off this way for several days, and the lad is as crazy now as ever; for my part, I am for heaving him overboard directly. What see you in him so peculiar, that you wish to save his life?"

"Have I not told thee, Rialto, that he would be worth a thousand dollars for me to experiment upon, if he recovers his reason before reaching Mexico?"

Oh, horror of horrors! Reader, you can better imagine my feelings than I can describe them, when I perfectly understood this conversation to relate to me. This, then, thought I, is the *disinterested* kindness of the surgeon. I am to be spared merely for doctors to practice upon.

As these thoughts passed through my mind, I was wrought up to such agony that I uttered a groan.

Hearing this, they immediately turned their attention to me. "Ha, did I not tell ye so?" said the surgeon, clapping his hands for joy, as he saw by my look that I understood what was going on. "I knew he would come to his senses."

"Where am I?" said I, appearing not to notice his remark.

"Where are you, young fellow? why, you are where you will be safely taken care of. You are on board the noble vessel St. Juan, and by good luck will soon be in Vera Cruz.[7] From there, sir, you will be conducted to the Capital by an escort of the great Santa Anna, where you will find a place that you can call your home, built expressly for you and a few other villains, where you can sojourn while you deign to stop in the city."

As he spoke this in an apparently sneering tone, it drew forth several coarse hearty laughs and a burst of applause from his companions. But I thought I detected something in his manner and look, when the others were not observing, that told of far different feelings at heart.

It may be possible, thought I, that I have wronged him with conjectures. And perhaps what I overheard was only some plausible tale to pacify the crew, until he can find an opportunity to set me at liberty.

This last I found to be correct: for passing me soon after, he said, in a low hurried tone, "Be of good cheer, all will yet be well." These kind words came like balm to a wounded heart. They were the first I heard in kindness since I had been taken prisoner; and though I could think of no chance of escaping, still they gave me much relief. I had the consolation of thinking there was one who cared for me.

In the evening he brought me some light food, (for I was still very weak,) and pretending to examine my wound, he bent over his head, and in a low voice said, that if I would obey his directions he thought I might regain my liberty.

"Who are you," said I, "who speak to me in this manner, at the risk of your own life?"

"Hist," said he, "or we may be overheard; I am a Texan."

"A Texan," said I, "and fighting against your own country? if so, I will hear none of your proposals!"

"Nay," said he, "you do me wrong. It is a policy which I have adopted to save my countrymen; and many a Texan has owed his escape from the Mexicans to me."

"This is indeed joyful news," said I, "but how can you mange my escape?"

"By the appearance of the western horizon," he replied, "I judge we shall have a storm ere tomorrow morning. My plan is briefly this: should all work to my expectations, I will arouse you when the gale blows the hardest, (for if we escape it must be then,) and I have a boat in readiness, fastened on the larboard side, which we must enter as carefully as possible, then cut the ropes, trusting ourselves to the mercy of the wind and waves."

"And do you intend going also?" said I.

"I do. Will you be in readiness?" said he.

"Never fear me," was my reply.

"Enough; I hear some one coming this way. Tonight. Remember."

And with these words, he turned upon his heel and walked away. Soon after I heard him in conversation with some of the crew, relative to my wound, &c. I heard him say, he thought by the time I reached Vera Cruz I would do for his purpose.

But this gave me no uneasiness, as I rightly judged it was said to blind them as to his real intentions.

That night came on a heavy storm, as the surgeon had predicted. According to agreement, he came to my berth about twelve o'clock, and in a whisper said, "All's right."

This was the signal; and creeping from my berth with as little noise and delay as possible, I followed him upon deck. It was a terrible night. The wind blew tremendously, accompanied with rain. While far in the west the forked lightnings played incessantly; and every now and then came the booming roll of thunder, each clap growing louder and louder, telling us a shower was rapidly approaching.

As yet the lightning was too far distant to show objects distinctly, where we were. But as every moment's delay was likely to expose us, we felt impatient to be in our boat.

When we came on deck we secreted ourselves behind the forecastle, in order to ascertain that all was safe for us to proceed. As ill luck would have it, the watch was between us and the boat, and how to overcome this difficulty was a matter of no small importance.

"There is but one way," said the surgeon to me sternly, (whom I shall hereafter call Allen,) "but one way, and it must be done, or we are lost. The shower is rapidly nearing; every flash gleams brighter, so that what we do must be done quickly. We will try to pass him quietly, but should he discover us, and attempt to raise alarm, I have a dagger; come, not a word." And taking me by the arm he led the way as still as possible.

Every thing seemed to work to our desire. We had already passed the guard or watch by great precaution, and were about to enter the boat, when, striking my foot against something, I stumbled, and fell against the side of the vessel. This the watch overheard, and demanded "Who goes there?" no answer. Again, "Who goes—" A bright flash of lightning at this instant seemed to light the whole universe, as it were, in one grand blaze. Oh, what a sight! never, while breath animates this body, shall I forget that scene! But a few feet from me, with his dagger in his hand, dripping with blood, stood Allen. Just in front of him, and in the act of falling, was the sentinel, his features horribly distorted, the blood gushing from his heart, while around the two the lightning danced, as if in mockery of this awful deed.

The next instant all was dark. I felt an arm around my waist, and in a moment more Allen and myself, in an open boat, were tossing on the angry deep.

"I would have spared him, Henry," (for such I previously told him was my name,) "but had I done so, all would have been lost. It was indeed horrid; how the lightning did play over his features!"

"Come, come," said I, wishing to turn the conversation, "do not grieve about it; you know it could not be helped, without the risk of our own lives; and as we are not safe yet, let us take our paddles and row from them as fast as possible."

"Good heavens!" said he, feeling in the bottom of the boat, "I have forgotten them. We are lost. Yes, Henry, we are lost!" And, true enough, owing to the hurry and confusion of our escape, they had been forgotten.

What was to be done? We were twenty miles from the nearest land, in an open boat, the storm raging with fury around us, without even a thing wherewith to propel our boat; and, to add to our dismay, we could perceive, by the flashes of lightning, a bustle on board of the ship, and active preparations for manning a boat to go in pursuit of us, for we were equally visible to them. As we saw this at a glance, it seemed to both that our fate was inevitable.

"Well," said Allen, "we must do our best. I feel that my time has come. However, they shall find it no easy conquest; I have with me two loaded pistols and two cutlasses; take one of each, Henry, and let us defend ourselves to the last; for my part, I will never be captured alive. See, they have already shoved off. Possibly something may turn up to save us, although I do not expect it. Let us fight to the last, and when all hope is lost, rather than be taken, we will leap overboard and end life at once. Are you agreed to this?"

"I am."

"Then let them come; we are ready." We sat down in the bottom of the boat with the pistols in our hands. By the continual flashing of the lightning we were able to mark their progress—now on the top of some mighty billow, now plunged out of sight, on they came, as fast as their own oars would propel them. They were six in number. In a few minutes they were alongside. "Now is our time!" shouted Allen, and quick as thought we simultaneously discharged our pistols, each of which took effect, and two of our pursuers rolled into the deep, and sank to rise no more. With a desperate leap, cutlass in hand, Allen sprang aboard their boat, and lunged another through the body. The next instant—a flash—a crack—and the waves rolled over him. I saw all was lost, and was about to leap overboard, when a blow on the head laid me senseless.

When I recovered my senses, I found I was in the hold of the St. Juan, my hands manacled, and my feet in stocks, so that I could scarcely move. I now truly felt the horror of my situation. My life, thought I, is spared for some horrible punishment—perhaps my sex discovered—and I tried to invent some way to put an end to my existence. My head was very painful from the blow, which I suppose was struck by a paddle.

In about three days we arrived at Vera Cruz. During this time I could learn nothing in regard to my fate. A rough-looking Spaniard brought me my food, (which was coarse bread and water,) but to my interrogations he merely shook his head, making no reply.

At Vera Cruz, I was taken from the St. Juan (my hands still manacled) and placed behind a cart, which was to convey part of the soldiers to the city of Mexico. My hands were tied to the cart, to prevent the possibility of escape. In this disgraceful manner I found I would have to walk the whole distance.

As the cart, which was drawn by horses no faster than a walk, passed through the streets of Vera Cruz, hisses and groans saluted me on either side. Some were not even content with this, but hurled missiles at me, many of which took effect and wounded me severely.

I travelled about twenty miles each day, sometimes over burning sand and uncouth roads, with the tropical sun pouring down, as it were, melted lava upon me; my skin blistered, my feet so swelled and sore I could scarcely walk, with scarce food enough to keep me alive, for thirteen days, making a distance of over two hundred and fifty miles.

At night only I was allowed to enter the cart to rest myself, first being securely bound, with the plank under me for a bed, and the canopy of heaven above for the covering—a sentinel stationed near who was armed with a musket, with orders, if I stirred, to shoot me at once. But this last was unnecessary, for I was so bound that I could not move, had I been so disposed.

In this manner I reached the Capital, so worn out and exhausted, that I do not think I could have lived through another day of such fatigue.

I arrived at the Capital, as near as I can recollect, in August, 1838. I was immediately conveyed to prison and placed in a dungeon, where daylight never reached; and, as on the St. Juan, my hands were manacled and my feet were put in the stocks, there to await my trial, or rather sentence, when Santa Anna should arrive.[8]

For several days following my imprisonment, I partook of scarce any food. My jailer, a rough, uncouth-looking figure, visited my gloomy apartments but twice a day, bringing me a small chunk of stale bread, not infrequently alive with vermin, and a cup of water.

A sickly taper, which burned a part of the time, was the only relief from total darkness. My cell, I should judge, was about ten feet square, and some fifteen under ground. It was truly a gloomy looking place. The walls were covered with a thick slime, formed, I suppose, by the vapors arising from the dampness of the ground. For the first week or two I was so stupefied that I took no notice of anything, and it has oftentimes been a wonder to me how I lived through what I did. But it is impossible for us to tell what we can undergo and yet live, and, at the same time, how little it takes to end our existence. I know not why my feet were kept in stocks, unless it was to prevent me from committing suicide, for there was not the least chance of escape.

I remained in this way about six months, until I had despaired of ever seeing daylight again, thinking it was probably my punishment to be forever buried alive, when one day the jailer, who had spoken but once or twice to me, informed me that Santa Anna had arrived, and he had orders to bring me before him. This was joyful news to me, for I felt that any change, any punishment, however hard, could not be worse than solitary confinement in that gloomy dungeon. A faint spark of hope, too, was alive in my breast, for I had determined, upon receiving my sentence, to throw myself on his mercy, and reveal my sex. I say a faint ray of hope, for I hardly expected this would save me.

When brought into the presence of this great general, (as he is termed,) my heart sank within me—hope fled. I saw an inferior, squalid-looking man, with such a stern, deceitful, bloodthirsty (if I may so use the expression) look about his countenance, that for the first time my eye quailed before a human being.

In a dry, husky voice, he inquired, "What are the charges preferred against this young man?" (meaning me.)

An officer in waiting replied there were three. First, I had been taken as a prisoner of war. Secondly, for mutiny committed on the high seas. Thirdly, for murder of officers when performing their duty.

"Can these be proved?" inquired Santa Anna.

"They can," was the reply.

Santa Anna then turned to me and said, "Young man, for each of these offenses you shall receive one hundred and fifty lashes on your bare back, for three days in succession, one for each offense; and if you survive this, you are then to be shot. One hundred and fifty now. The sentence is passed; officers, do your duty."

In an instant I was seized by two stout fellows, who instantly commenced stripping off my clothes to perform their barbarous operations. The first tore off my coat and vest, and then one of them commenced tearing open the bosom of my shirt, when he started back with a look of surprise, and exclaimed, "A woman, by heavens!"

"A woman!" exclaimed Santa Anna, also rising in amazement, "a woman did you say? this must be seen to; remand her to the cell until I have more leisure to inquire into it. I forgo the sentence." Scarce had he ceased speaking ere I was hurried away, (so readily are his orders obeyed,) and again confined to my gloomy dungeon. The next day the keeper said he had orders to remove me to another part of the prison.

I was now taken to the second floor from the ground, where there was plenty of light, and, compared to what I had left, the place was as a palace to a hovel. My shackles were all taken off, and I was told they would not be put on while I remained above. I was also told, if I attempted to escape I should again be shackled and remanded to the dungeon.

With this sort of admonitory information, which I received from the jailer, the door was bolted on me, and I was left alone in my new apartments.

From this cell there were two windows, or gratings, which overlooked the yard, admitting both light and air. The room was very large, I thought, for one person to occupy, being, I should judge, about 15 by 20 feet. In the center of the room stood a chair and also a table, on which were several books, pen, ink, paper, half a loaf of bread, and a cup of pure fresh water. As I gazed at each article in turn, as a miser at each piece of gold, I scarce knew how to act or what to think. Hope sprang up anew in my breast, and I could not think but that something would yet turn up to give me my liberty. I took the pen and paper, and thought I would amuse myself by writing a sketch of my adventures. And there it was that most of these pages were written.

I had been there about a week, when one day, as I was sitting at the table looking over the books, the door opened, and to my astonishment Santa Anna entered. His manner was much more pleasing than when I last saw him; still there was a wild voluptuous look about his eyes which pained and startled me.

"Fair lady," said he, "I trust you will not consider this an intrusion, when I tell you that I have been drawn hither by your beauty." This was said in a soft, bland manner, accompanied with a slight bow.

"What is the meaning of this?" said I, somewhat alarmed.

"Meaning?" said he, "it means simply this: that you are young and handsome, and moreover my prisoner. You have been tried and found guilty of mutiny and murder, and by my order can in a moment be led to execution. I now come here to offer you life—on one condition."

"On one condition!" said I, almost breathless; "name it."

"That you become—my mistress."

"Never!" said I, with a burst of indignation I could not control. "Lead me to the scaffold, to the rack, or, worse than death, to the dungeon; but never Santa Anna, ask me to be your victim! No! while I live, while I have strength to move, my virtue shall be untainted!"

"But consider," said he, "I have money, you shall not want; I have power, you need not fear."

"I have considered," I replied, "and you have my answer! What! Shall I, an American, be a mistress to the cruel, bloodthirsty Santa Anna and thus disgrace my country? Never! You have your answer. Go! I would that you leave me."

"You shall repent this!" said he, and turning on his heel he left me. This, then, is why I am thus favored, and my life spared, thought I. O that I were dead! Then came the thought that perhaps I might escape; this was the first time that it had entered my head, and I immediately commenced examining my room, grating, &c., to see if there was any chance of my succeeding.

My windows were double grated, so that to attempt to escape that way seemed like madness. But still I might succeed if I only had the implements to work with; without them there was no chance; and save through the window there was no means of escape. I had looked at every place, and was on the point of despairing, when my attention was attracted to a small spot on the wall which I thought appeared somewhat different from the rest. To satisfy my curiosity, I went to it and commenced scratching it with my finger nail, when, to my astonishment, I found it was soft. Encouraged by this, I worked away diligently, until I had made a hole about half the length of my finger, when I picked out a dirty piece of paper written on with pencil. I hurried to the light and read what follows: "My time has come for execution—I cannot escape. But should this paper fall into the hands of any here confined, they may reap the benefits of my industry. By running your finger into the hole from whence this is taken, you can remove a stone where you will find a saw and a file. The grates of the south window are almost off.

(Signed)   A Criminal."

Mad, as it were, with joy, I rushed to the stone, and in a few minutes succeeded in removing it, where I found the implements as described. The saw was made from the mainspring of a watch. I then went to the window, and found it, by careful examination, just as the paper had stated.

Now, thought I, Santa Anna will find his bird has flown when he least expects it. Then came the fear of my being removed before I should be able to accomplish my purpose. But I determined to manage this by policy.

The next day Santa Anna came again to see me. He said perhaps I had thought better of my treatment to him, and wished to know if it was so. I told him in a measure it was: but I could hardly bring my mind to agree to his proposal as yet; I wanted time to think of it. I told him if he would give me one month to consider, at the end of that time I would give him a decisive answer. At first he objected to the length of time, but finding me inexorable, he finally consented. Then, waving his hand, he bade me adieu, thank heaven, for the last time.

After this arrangement had been completed, I felt much elated. I now looked upon liberty as almost certain. The jailer, as usual, came only twice a day, morning and evening, so that all the rest of the time I was left to myself. I now proceeded to my work in earnest. As I had to file or saw carefully, for fear of being overheard, my progress was naturally very slow.

In about ten days I had succeeded in cutting off all the bars, so that I could remove them whenever I chose.

I now determined leaving the first dark stormy night. From my window I could see there were pickets on the top of the yard, which I thought would assist me rather than otherwise, as I could prepare a sort of rope from my bedding, and after landing in the yard, throw it up until caught by the pickets, then drawing myself up, could thus escape.

After getting every thing in readiness, I had to wait a couple of days before I found a night that would answer my purpose. At last such a night came. It was very dark, the wind blowing from the east, but for the first part of the night unaccompanied by any rain.

About ten o'clock I removed the bars, and with a rope which I had made, by tearing my blanket in strips, I let myself down into the yard; then managing as I had before mentioned, with the other rope I drew myself to the top of the wall; drawing my rope up again, I let it down on the outside; then sliding down myself, I was once more at liberty.

I could hardly restrain myself from shouting for joy, so happy did I feel to think I had escaped from prison and the clutches of a tyrant.

But I had not overcome all my difficulties. Not being aware that there were sentinels outside the prison, in my heedlessness I came near ruining all, and it was only by a desperate move that I escaped.

I was gliding away very rapidly from the prison, paying no regard to any thing, when a heavy hand was laid on my shoulder, and a rough voice said "Stand!"

I was completely paralyzed with fear, for I thought I had been missed, and this was one of my pursuers.

"Wherefore go you, young lad, in such haste at this time of night?"

I knew by this I was only apprehended for the untimely hour in which I was out.

I stammered forth some excuse, for I was taken so aback that I knew not what to say.

"'Twill not do, sir," replied the sentinel, (for such I supposed he was,) "you must with me to the guard-house; perhaps you have been assisting the escape of some prisoner; if so, it will cost you your life."

What was to be done? If I attempted to escape from him, he would raise an alarm. If I remained peaceable, I should be discovered the following day, and again be sent to the dungeon.

And must I be captured with liberty in my grasp? These thoughts almost drove me mad. Meanwhile we were proceeding to the guard-house, and I knew if I did not make an effort ere I reached there, all was lost. We were but a few paces distant from it, when, by a sudden gleam of light from one of the windows, I discovered a dagger in the sentinel's belt. Tempted by the devil, and the love of liberty, with a maniacal desperation I drew it, and, quick as lightning, stabbed him to the heart.

He fell without a groan!

I now ran with all speed, I knew not whither, and as little cared, so that I escaped. After leaving the city, in about two hours time I found myself in a dense forest. Here I wandered on until daylight, when, finding an old tree with a hollow in it, about ten feet from the ground, I ascended and entered it, where I remained during the day. As I knew that I should be pursued, I dared not travel but little, save in the night. On making some observations, I found I had taken the direction to Vera Cruz. This was the nearest seaport city, therefore I determined on going there. As I had travelled the main road when a prisoner, I was rarely at a loss how to proceed. Keeping as near to it as I deemed safe, I thus retraced my steps, subsisting a part of the time on fruit I found in the woods, occasionally obtaining something from the outhouses of the settlers; travelling nearly the whole distance by night, in about a month I arrived in sight of Vera Cruz, early in the morning.

Not caring to be seen in the daytime, for fear I might be recollected by some, I waited until night, and proceeding direct to the wharves, I found a vessel just on the point of sailing.

Not caring whither I went, so that I escaped from the Mexicans, I walked leisurely aboard, (for I deemed it safest to work by policy,) and inquired of the captain whither he was bound. He replied, "For the East Indies."

This took me all aback; I knew not what to do. I did not want to go so long a voyage, and I feared I could find no other ship which was to sail soon. Besides, while waiting for another, I might be retaken. The fear of this determined me to venture. Better take a two or three year cruise, thought I, than to be taken and sent to the dungeon, perhaps for life. So I told the captain, that not enjoying the best of health, I should like to sail with him, and that, as I had not the means to pay I was willing to assist all that I could. He at first objected; but to my urgent entreaties, he finally consented. This was in the spring of 1839. Owing to bad weather, and some unexpected delay in business, we did not return as soon as expected. But as there is nothing to interest you, reader, in this voyage, and thinking your patience is perhaps already wearied, I shall now draw to a close. Let these few particulars, therefore, suffice.

On our return we touched at Havana, where, after returning my thanks to Captain Dedham for his kind treatment, I left the noble vessel Alhambra, which had been a home to me for three and a half long years. This was in the fall of 1842.

From here I sailed to Galveston, Texas, where I had some affairs to settle, and arrived there in January following.

From there I took passage to Mobile, (where I am now residing,) arriving here in March, 1843. My friends looked upon me as one arisen from the dead. As I have previously stated, I commenced this "Narrative" while in prison; by the urgent solicitations of my friends, I have been induced to finish and give it to the public. And now, reader, farewell; you that have followed me attentively through these pages, while I have been recounting my adventures, trials, and sufferings, that you may never undergo the like calamities, is the prayer of your humble servant,

LEONORA SIDDONS.

Magdalena, The Beautiful Mexican Maid

N ed Buntline is one of Edward Zane Carroll Judson's (1821–1886) pseudonyms. Judson was one of the most prolific writers of popular literature in the nineteenth century, and his life reflects those turbulent times. Judson served in the navy as a midshipman, fought in the Second Seminole War and for the Union in the Civil War, and, following his trek west in 1869, he made Buffalo Bill Cody a popular literary figure. He also penned over a hundred novels, countless tales, sketches, and articles, and several plays. He is most remembered for his dime novels, but even before Beadle went into the business of publishing sensational fiction, Buntline was publishing novelettes about sea adventures, urban intrigues, and colonial encounters in Mexico, Cuba, and the Caribbean. He also ran his own newspaper, *Buntline's Own*, which voiced an urban, working-class nativism that could turn violent. In fact, Buntline served one year of hard labor for his role in New York's 1849 Astor Place Riots, and he was connected to an election day riot in St. Louis in 1852.

Buntline wrote two U.S.-Mexico War novels. Boston's *Flag of Our Union* story paper serialized *The Volunteer; Or, The Maid of Monterey* before Gleason published it as a novelette in 1847, and New York's Williams Brothers published *Magdalena, The Beautiful Mexican Maid*. The original copyright page lists 1846 as the publication date, but it was probably published in 1847, since the titular battle of Buena Vista was not waged until February 1847, and the John Greenleaf Whittier poem included at the novel's end was not published until May 20, 1847. As its many historical references indicate, the narrative demonstrates how news from the warfront made it into the popular press as the excitement of fresh battle scenes and the melodrama of romance create a sensational story that turns individual characters such as Magdalena and Charles Brackett into social and sexual symbols of the U.S.-Mexico War. Their romance ends badly, which could be understood either as an antiwar sentiment that challenges the novel's otherwise pro-U.S. stance, or as a statement against the interracialism Brackett and Magdalena embody.

MAGDALENA, THE BEAUTIFUL MEXICAN MAID.
A STORY OF BUENA VISTA.

BY NED BUNTLINE;
LATE OF THE UNITED STATES NAVY

CHAPTER I

A work like this needs no preface,—it carries its own history along with it. If it is not written with all the beauty and force which a subject so interesting and eventful deserves, an apology, certainly, will not make it anymore acceptable to the reader, therefore he may e'en take it as it is, and make as much of it as he chooses.

It was on the sunny morning of March 11, 1847, that the "Army of Occupation" broke up camp at Corpus Christi, preparatory to crossing the Rio Colorado, and taking position on the Rio Grande, the stop which hastened the present war with Mexico.[2] Our story commences with the sunrise of this day. All of the tents save that of the commander in chief had already been struck and stowed away in the baggage wagon preparatory for a march.

Within his tent and seated upon a rude camp stool, with a map of Mexico spread out upon his knees, was an officer, whose person seen lithographed at every shop window in the country, scarce needs a description. It was that great general, who within a single year, has won a world-wide fame, one who, whether spoken of as General Taylor, or "Old Rough and Ready," is known to all who hear the name.[3]

Beside the general stood several of his staff, all watching the lines which he drew upon the map, for already the prospect of war was before them, and as soldiers, they looked forward to a broad and ripe field in which to gather a soldier's laurels. The general was tracing along the map a line of march which he knew would be necessary should hostilities ensue upon his crossing the Rio Colorado, as had been already threatened by the Mexicans. With that intuitive perception of the future which has rendered Napoleon and others so remarkable, he was already planning a campaign which he knew was inevitable, and was already glancing over the ground which was soon to become the garden of his glory.

The general paused in his examination, and looking up addressed a young officer near him:

"I wish you would have Captain Walker sent for, Major Bliss—I want him!"[4]

In a few moments, a small, finely formed man, possessing a keen and flashing eye, and a face much resembling the description which we have of South Carolina's gallant Marion, dressed in a hunting dress of the Texas Rangers, stood before the general, with his broad rimmed hat in his hand, awaiting orders.[5]

The eye of the old general on seeing him, brightened.

"Ah, Captain Walker, I'm glad to see you. I sent for you to inquire if you have not such a man in your company as I now require for a perilous and delicate service; a duty which requires courage, tact, keen observation, retentive memory, and all the qualities which are valuable in a spy."

"I have good men in my company, general," responded the young ranger, "but I had rather go on a duty of this kind myself, than to trust others with it, sir!"

"You will not do, sir," responded the general, and then he saw the face of the young ranger, redden, he hastened to add—"Not that I doubt either your bravery or your tact, but you are not dark enough, nor look sufficiently like a Mexican. I must have a man whose looks and knowledge of the language will enable him to pass for a native of Mexico."

"Then, sir, Charley Brackett is your man. I've not a braver man in my company, he was born and educated a gentleman, speaks Spanish perfectly, and as his mother was a Castillian, is full as dark, but not quite so yellow as a real native. If he was stained with a shade of butternut color and rigged up a la ranchero, he'll make as good looking a Mexican as I ever drew lead on."

"Is he faithful, will not his Spanish blood, cause him to lean toward the other side a little?"

"If to hate the Mexicans as few can hate; if to thirst for their blood, as the desert thirst for the dews of night; if to live under the weight of a fearful oath to revenge an outraged mother and sister, whose corpses are now mouldering in a bloody grave near San Jacinto, will ensure his faith to us, then feel secure that Charles Brackett will never prove a traitor."

"Has he seen service?"

"He fought like a demon on the field of San Jacinto. He was with me on the Mier expedition, and had there been twenty more like him in our band, we never would have suffered as we did.[6]—He is now with me waiting for the outbreak which is threatened, ready when it does come, to take a man's place, and do a man's duty."

"He will not have long to wait," said the general with a smile, and then added, "you may send the young man here, sir!"

In a short time the ranger was announced. As he entered the tent, General Taylor arose and took a calm and steady survey of the person who stood before him.

He was about five feet eight or nine inches high, with a slight but well knit figure, in which muscles seemed to make up for a deficiency in size: erect, and in form he looked every inch a soldier. His age was probably about twenty-five years. His hair and eyes were of a jetty blackness, his skin was rich brunette, his features betokened plainly his Spanish descent. There was that in his looks which showed that courage and resolution were his by nature: and there was a certain quickness in the flash of his large eye; and the restlessness of his motions, which told that like the curbed but impetuous war steed, he wished for action,—action, the very soul and life of a true man. His weapons: the rifle, bowie knife, and a brace of revolving pistols, were in keeping with his looks.

Standing in a respectful attitude, he awaited the orders of the general, and underwent the severe and searching scrutiny without a change of look or color.

The latter after a few moments addressed him,

"Your name is Brackett, young man, is it not?"

"Charles Brackett, general," responded the ranger.

"Your captain speaks well of you as a soldier, and recommends you as the best man in his company, and as likely to suit me for a piece of service which I have on hand."

"Captain Walker always says more for his friends than himself. I hope I may deserve his praise, but I am sure I have had no chance to do so yet."

"Young man, you shall have your chance," said the general, then turning to his officers with a kind smile he added, "gentlemen, excuse me in requesting to be left with Major Bliss and this young man for a short time. I will join you on the march—it is time for the columns to advance."

All of the officers, except Major Bliss, left the tent.

General Taylor seated himself, and calling the ranger to his side, spread the map out before him and again opened the conversation.

"You have already been in Mexico, and seen service," said he.

"I have, but I hope that the day of my service is but just dawning, for what I have done, like the smell of blood to the famishing tiger, only excites my thirst for more."

"Look upon this map, Mr. Brackett. Follow that pencil mark to the mouth of the Rio Grande, then up its banks to Matamoras. Let your eye mark each point. Very well, sir, now follow up the river—how high can it be navigated with steam boats?"

"To Camargo—I crossed it not far from that point when we were on our route to Mier."

"Very well, sir,—now which think you is the most direct route from Camargo to Mexico?"

"I have never been beyond Camargo on the lower route, but I think that from there, about south-west, or a few degrees more westerly, to Monterey, then south-west a little westerly to Saltillo, thence south to San Luis Potosi, would be the nearest and most passible way."[7]

"You are right, young man, quite right—I've marked out this very route, and now, sir, you shall know the service I require. It is probable that we shall have to travel this path before long. I wish the route examined, the state of the country carefully noted. I wish to know the condition of the fortifications: the prospects for obtaining water and supplies of provisions on the road; in short, sir, I wish to know everything which would be useful to me in case of a war of invasion becomes necessary."

"I am ready to perform this duty, sir!" responded the ranger, readily, "but disguise will be necessary. I am well known to many Mexicans, yes, they have known me as I have known them—to their sorrow."

"You must, of course, disguise yourself as a Mexican—you will receive funds and all other things that you require by applying to Major Bliss."

"How far do you wish me to penetrate into the country?"

"At present no farther than Saltillo and the passes of the mountains near there on the road to San Luis Potosi. Do this and return with all speed, for we may be at work before you come back, and your arm may be needed here!"

"I will go and return in twenty-five days, general, if you give me funds to freshen my supply of horse flesh now and then, for I am a hard rider."

"Major Bliss will furnish all you require," responded the general, smiling at the last remark of the young ranger, and then he added: "the sooner you are fixed and in the saddle, the better, for time is precious!"

"I will be on my route in an hour, general," responded the ranger, and as he spoke he hastily left the tent.

"I like that youngster, Major Bliss, promptness is a great virtue in a soldier's character," said the general, when he and his adjutant were left alone.

"It made Napoleon; and the want of it has lost many a noble opportunity to other generals!" was the brief reply of one who says but little, but thinks a great deal, Major W.W.S. Bliss.

The general responded not to this remark, but looking at his watch, changed the tenor of the conversation by remarking that it was time he was in the saddle. Then hastily folding up his pocket map, he deposited it in a breast pocket of his old blue surtout and left the tent.

One hour afterward the head of the advance column was passed by a man at full speed, well mounted on a fleet and heavily built black horse. The rider was dressed completely a la ranchero.[8] At his saddle hung the ever useful *laseo*; a short, rifled carbine was slung over his back; holsters were in their places, and though closely covered with oil-cloth to protect their contents from the weather, no one would doubt after a single glance at the rider, that the weapons were within and ready for use. A short saber or *machete* was suspended from his belt, in which was also placed a brace of revolvers, which, however, were hidden from sight by the neat poncho, or Mexican blanket which he wore carelessly over his shoulder. His legs were cased in the wide trousers of the country; upon his boots, made of untanned hide, he wore a pair of spurs heavy enough to tire a common leg to carry them, the rowels being at least an inch in length, the chains and braces in proportion. From beneath a broad rimmed Panama hat, peered a pair of flashing black eyes, and these were set in a face complexioned much like a bright chocolate color, though nearly two-thirds of it were hidden in a mustache and beard, so long, black, curling, and glossy that even Charley May would have envied a beard so perfectly *magnifique*. As the rider passed by the column and rode along the flank of the rangers, who as scouts led the way, he cast a fierce looking glance at them, and as he twisted the end of his jetty mustache, he spoke in no gentle tones.

"Malditos Americanos! A done vas, hijos de infierno?" Cursed Americans! Where are you going, you sons of hell? and as some who understood the language answered in language full as coarse and scornful, he burst out with a wild and contemptuous laugh, and dashed on, as he turned for the last time to look upon them, "froco—froco!" an expression equivalent to saying "wait a little time!"

Little did those hearty rangers dream that in that fierce and vindictive looking Mexican was their especial favorite Charley Brackett, he who in the field was reckoned the bravest and most expert of them all in their guerilla mode of warfare.

As Brackett rode on out of their hearing, he checked his horse down into a speed which, though rapid, would not over tax his power, and, as he kept on in a laughing soliloquy, he expressed his pleasure at the completeness of a disguise which had blinded the eagle eyes of his most intimate comrades.

It was indeed necessary that he should be well disguised, for many a Mexican had heard his battle-shout, many a fugitive from the strife of blood had as he turned rein from the battle-field, seen the flash of his jet black eye, and heard the crash of his saber as it dealt out death to those who were more tardy than he in flight.

Yes, there was one, who now held rank in the Mexican army, who had twice almost miraculously escaped from the revengeful hand of the son and brother, whose home he had made desolate, and Colonel Gustave Alfrede would have given half his weight in gold to know of the death of young Brackett, for he had heard of the "oath of revenge" and he knew but too well that while Charles Brackett lived his own life was in as much danger as if he walked through a prairie stocked with deadly serpents.

On through the warm, sunny day, over the broad and bright Savannas and through the occasional chapparal, pressed the coal black steed and his rider, on swiftly to fulfill his dangerous, but important mission.

CHAPTER II

A beautiful place is that which has lately become so noted as "the bloody field of Buena Vista"; a spot which took its name from the grand and romantic view which it presented. Reader, see a valley which hangs in evergreen beauty between a range of dark and lofty mountains; not a level monotonous plain, but a beautiful "rolling" country, interspersed here and there with little hills, pretty groves, rushing rivulets which supply the channel of the little river San Juan, which flows along the western side of the valley. Springs like blue spots in a white-cloud-mottled-sky, are seen here and there; in some parts of it fields of green and broad leafed corn are waving in the breeze; in others herds of cattle are grazing, or lolling in the shade of luxuriant trees; while here and there may be seen some lazy laborer attending to his duties on the hacienda.

You see that stone house on the Saltillo road; it is built like a castle, has its watchtower and its battlements, and is built of the dark, reddish stone which the hills on either side display.

That building is the residence of Don Ignatio Valdez, the owner of the hacienda or estate of Buena Vista. We enter it, reader, and pay Don Ignatio and his family a visit.

Don Ignatio is a Castillian noble, he left his country when ten years since in consequence of the failure of the attempts which Don Carlos made to gain the throne of Spain. Ignatio was in heart, aye in very soul a Carlist. He was a contemporary with Zumelacarraguei, the greatest guerilla chieftain who ever led men forth at dead of night to form the quiet ambuscade, or defend the narrow mountain pass; but Zumelacarraguei fell, and with him the hopes of Don Carlos.[9]

Then Don Ignatio sought domestic happiness and quiet in this beautiful valley, and here he buried Seberina, his beautiful wife; the better angel of his early days; the living memory of his ripened life.

But when she left the cares of life for the joys of heaven, he was not alone. Two fair daughters, Magdalena and Ximena, were left unto him to soften down the grief which might have overwhelmed even his stern soul.

The first—and, reader, she will soon be better known to you—was at the time when our visit is made, a girl of sweet seventeen, but one who seemed several years in advance of her age;—not that she *looked* old, but her manners, grace, and accomplishments, were beyond her years. Let me describe her.

She is above the medium height; yet her form is so full, so perfectly proportioned, that she does not look *too* tall; her low-necked dress reveals shoulders that are graceful as a sculptor's ideal, and a neck which Canova would have copied; her bare arms are round, full, and taper beautifully down to a dear little hand, which looks as if it was only made to hold the most delicate flowers of nature. Her face bespeaks a warm and enthusiastic heart, for she has a large, beaming eye of jetty blackness; lips full and rosy; cheeks which, though quite brunette, are transparent as the rind of the pomegranate. Her eye-brows are arched as the moon on its birth-night; her features are as classic as Salvator Rosa's beautiful Madonna; her hair is like waves of curled silk:—and this, reader, is the heroine of our story. Oh! Well was she known to all the noble cavaliers of Saltillo—and even as far as the golden city of the Montezumas—as the beautiful "Maiden of Buena Vista"! In disposition she was gay and dashing—much like the "Die Vernon" of Walter Scott.[10]

Her sister Ximena was a different being, both in person and in character. The latter was a delicate, fragile flower of humanity, a kind of fairy in appearance. Though one year older than her sister, she was small, delicately formed, more pale than the other, and so quiet and dreamy in her ways, that she had gained among those who knew her the name of "La Pensarosa," or The Sentimental.

Her features were fully indicative of her Castillian origin; her eye, however, was not as flashing and bright, like her sister's, but soft, dewy, and soulful.

So much for the daughters—now for their father. The hair of Don Ignatio, or what little he had left, for he was nearly bald, was white as the snows which cap Orizaba's mighty peak; his features were of a Roman cast, and his face wore that look of habitual dignity which seems so natural to a Castillian.[11] His form, though it bore the weight of nearly sixty winters, was firm and erect; his step had all the elasticity of youth, and his voice, when he spoke to his well-loved children, was soft as the tones of a troubadour. He ever wore his sword, and had a hand not only ready, but able to use the weapon, which had been the plaything of his boyhood, the companion of his whole life. If he had a fault, it was that he too much adored his two children. He was open-hearted, liberal to an extreme, and though once blessed with a considerable fortune, so careless of it had he been, that he was now involved in embarrassments; and even Buena Vista, his beautiful estate, was only held under a mortgage, the interest of which he scarce could meet.

These pecuniary troubles were excessively mortifying to his pride; yet Don Ignatio managed to keep his place in society, and to keep an "open-house" for his friends.

Among these the military were predominant, in consequence of the tastes which he had imbibed with his early life; and it of course will seem quite natural that soldiers, who, like sailors, are ever warm admirers of beauty, would flock to the house of Don Ignatio, as bees gather unto a flower-garden.

Of course the young ladies found plenty of admirers. Of these none were more attentive than was one Colonel Alfrede, to Magdalena. The colonel was a man of rather prepossessing appearance, whose age might be thirty, but not more. He was rich, commanded a regiment of lancers, and had a reputation for gallantry both in the battle-field and ladies' boudoirs, which rendered him quite an object of envy to his brother officers, and a subject of much fear to such Mexican husbands in his vicinity as had young, gay, and pretty wives.

Strange to say, this good-looking and very redoubtable officer could produce no impression on the heart of Donna Magdalena. She scarce knew why, yet she felt an unconquerable repugnance to him. Her father favored the suit of Alfrede, for the latter had always seemed to him to be very noble and generous. Repeatedly he had unasked proffered loans to him, when those loans were very acceptable; and he had never had the impertinence to assume the character of a *dun*. Don Ignatio had, almost unawares to himself, become indebted to Alfrede for several thousand dollars; and this perchance added to his willingness to have him for a son-in-law. But Donna Magdalena used every effort to avoid even meeting the colonel, and when in his company, took but little trouble to conceal her distaste for it.

At the time when our history commences, this officer was so busily engaged in preparing his regiment for service, according to the orders of his government, that she was in a measure relieved from his odious attention.

His quarters were in Saltillo, about seven miles north of her father's place. He used, as often as he could withdraw himself from his duties, to ride out of Buena Vista, generally accompanied by an escort of his lancers, more for show than use, for as yet Buena Vista was a valley of peace and quiet.

We have now introduced the reader to Don Ignatio and his family, and made him partially acquainted with the situation of its members.

Without following the course of Charles Brackett from the American camp, we will slide quietly over the space of a few days, which were to him barren of adventure, and meet him at the "Pasado del Estrangeros," or hotel of the strangers, which stands fronting the Plaza in the city of Saltillo. He had come thus far without discovery, had carefully reconnoitered Monterey and all of the points which were embraced in his orders, and had now nearly reached the farthest point of his travels. This was a source of pleasure to him, for already had the news overtaken him of General Taylor's arrival at the Rio Grande, and from the "curses loud and deep," which he heard around him, and took good care to echo, he knew that war was inevitable, and he sighed to return in time to take a leading hand in the first game.

It was night when he arrived in Saltillo—a clear and beautiful evening.— He had his horse carefully groomed immediately on his arrival at the hotel, and then partook in a hasty supper, after which he intended to take a walk round the town and reconnoiter its position and defenses. But on coming out into the open air, and finding it to be a clear, moonlight evening, he determined to hire a fresh horse and ride a few miles further on, as he had been directed, so that he might be able to retrace his route on the next day. He easily procured a steed, and rode on toward the mountain gorges, which he had been directed to examine.

His path led directly past the house of Don Ignatio, which he was passing carelessly, when a voice so rich and full fell upon his ear, that he involuntary reined in his steed, and stopped to listen.

He caught but one verse of the song, which seemed to be a simple, but exceedingly sweet Spanish air.

The verse which he had heard was peculiar. Here it is. Reader, get "Bareth's dictionary," "Josses Grammar," "Mordentes exercises," and translate it.

The Song of Magdalena

"Es Cierto que en casa yo viva saltera
No tengo disgusto, ni nada me altera,
Pero un buen marido, major me sera,
Si, un buen Esposico, mi amor pide lla!"

For fear the reader cannot get the books we have mentioned above, we will furnish a translation of the verse:—

"'Tis true that I'm living in maidenly leisure
With nothing to vex or cross me in pleasure;
But a dear little husband far better would be,
Oh a dear little husband were a treasure to me."

When Brackett heard this song in tones rich and lively, as if the singer cared very little about having the boon which in her happy ignorance, she pronounced "a treasure," he remembered it as one he had heard years before from the lips of his loved sister, and prompted by he knew not what, he followed the song by adding the next verse, but simply altering the masculine terminations into the feminine, so as to make the song apply to a wish for a dear little wife—thus—

"Es Cierto que en su casa yo soi la senor
Papa me quiere, mama me adora,
Pero un buen marida mejor me sera,
Si, un buen espocica un amor pide lla!"[12]

As his clear voice arose in this pretty cadenza, he looked up to the window casement whence he had heard the voice of the female, and caught one quick glance at a beautiful face, which seemed full of fun and mischief, as it glanced out in the moonlight to catch a glimpse of him. The eyes of both the singers met, but hers was in an instant withdrawn, and the next moment the swinging lattice of the window was closed.

Brackett looked for another view of her face in vain, and after waiting for a moment, he rode on, murmuring as he passed—"beautiful as an angel." Perhaps she heard his words, at any rate, a sweet musical laugh fell upon his ear from behind that lattice immediately after.

Putting spurs to his horse, he dashed rapidly along the road; but that voice seemed to follow him wherever he went, he could not banish it from his mind. Ere midnight was past, he had completed his reconnoiter, and returned to the city. In passing the mansion at Buena Vista on his return, he paused and tried to get another glimpse of the fair singer, but he paused in vain. All was still. She was probably reveling amid the joys of dream-land.

"She was beautiful!" he exclaimed, as he rode on toward the city. Little dreamed he that he had met Magdalena Valdez, one who was reputed the fairest maiden in all Mexico, yet much he pondered as he rode back to his hotel, whether he should ever meet her again. Perhaps he thought how horrible would be the scenes of war to such as she, and almost shuddered while he thought to what dangers a war exposed beautiful maidens and helpless women.

CHAPTER III

*I*t was but a little after sun rise. Donna Magdalena and her sister Ximena stood at the corner window which she had been seated at when Charles Brackett had passed on the previous evening, and heard her song.

And he was the subject of their conversation.

"Who could he be? I thought that I knew, by sight at least, all the noble cavaliers within leagues of Buena Vista—and he was *so* handsome, so manly in his bearing. Oh, sister, you know not what you have lost by retiring to your bed so early. You should have seen him and heard him!"

This was the effect which the single glance that she had caught of the ranger, produced upon Donna Magdalena. Her sister laughed as she listened to her earnest tone, and cried:

"I think you must have given your heart to that unknown stranger, sister; I never before heard you say so much for a man!"

"I never before saw a man who appeared to be worth saying so much for!" replied the other.

"What did he look like—did he resemble Colonel Alfrede?"

"Oh, why do you mention that hated name, Ximena? The stranger looked much more noble than he, as looks the proud war-steed nobler than a crop-eared, shaggy pack-mule!"

"Well, that is a comparison, indeed."

"Yet, methinks it suits very well;—*truth* will often make similar comparisons—I am sure there are as many asses with two legs, in the world, as there are four-legged ones!"

"Perhaps more—but look, sister—look toward the city! See that cloud of dust. Surely, Alfrede is not coming with his lancers to breakfast with us!"

"Heaven forefend the infliction of *his* presence," cried the other, quickly glancing in the direction pointed by her sister, and then she exclaimed, "What may it mean? I can see horsemen riding at full speed this way. Get the little field glass that father used to carry in Spain, Ximena, it will enable us to discern the objects plainer!"

The older sister hastened to get the glass, and in a moment Magdalena was looking at Saltillo through it.

"What see you, sister?" asked Ximena, as she saw the face of her sister flush with excitement.

"I see a large company of Alfrede's lancers! They ride this way—they seem to be in pursuit of one who rides upon a coal-black horse. They are close upon him, but he rides with the speed of the wind. Ha—he turns his steed in the road, and pauses. He fires a shot from his gun, and the foremost lancer falls from his horse. Oh! What may it mean?"

"Perhaps it is some robber escaping.—Look again, sister, and tell me what you see."

"He again speeds swiftly down the road—they seem to close upon him—his horse looks worn—ha! He fires a pistol—another lancer falls—another, and yet another—*four* are down! They fire at him, yet he still rides on, as if unharmed! He must be a demon to stand that volley. Ah! He stoops in his saddle—he must be wounded—but no! he comes on—on, swifter than before. The lancers follow close in his rear."

"Is Alfrede there?"

"Yes; I see him; but he is not in the front of his company—but the pursued.—Oh, how rash! He pauses again—he has loaded his gun, it was for that he stooped in his saddle. He raises his piece—he fires—Oh, Ximena! I am free from persecution; Alfrede falls—thank God, for that shot!"

"Oh no, sister, it cannot be—give me the glass?" cried the other; and she now became the watcher of the scene.

"Is it not so—has he not fallen?" asked Magdalena.

"No—he is up again; it was only his horse that was shot; he dismounts one of his lancers, and takes his horse and pursues. The pursued is coming near very fast. His black horse is becoming white with foam. That rather looks like a noble cavalier, may be it is your stranger of last night, and Alfrede is jealous of him, and wishes to destroy him!"

Ximena spoke in jest; but little dreamed she how near the truth she came.

The sister started, as she heard this remark, and again taking the glass, looked forth. Her cheek paled as she looked—her whole form quivered, and her voice trembled, as in a husky whisper she said,

"It is—it is! Oh, God grant he may escape. See, he fires his pistol again, and another lancer falls. Alfrede is encouraging the rest to follow, and leads them now with his drawn sword flashing in his hand. The stranger's horse reels; he is bleeding. The rider, too, is wounded. Oh God, save him!—but why do I feel this strange interest?"

The scene was now rapidly approaching Buena Vista. The ranger, for it was Brackett who was pursued, was urging on his steed toward the house, and already was he near it. Donna Magdalena, wild with terror and excitement, rushed from her chamber, down into the open court she sped, and out to the gate of the dwelling. Ximena, of a frailer nature, fainted in the chamber. Don Ignatio was not in the house, he was absent somewhere on the plantation. At the moment Donna Magdalena reached the gate, she saw the horse of the stranger, who was within an hundred yards of the house, fall dead upon the ground. The rider pressed on—but his steps showed that he was weak and wounded. The lancers were close upon him—and Alfrede was at their head. The beautiful girl rushed forward—but ere she could reach the side of Brackett, Alfrede had struck a sweeping blow with his saber, aimed full at the head of the ranger. The latter had received the blow upon his sword; but the blade of the weapon snapped near the hilt, and he was defenseless. At this instant, as he fell fainting to the ground, Magdalena sprang before him, and, while she *looked* upon Alfrede a scorn which she could not *speak*, she cried:

"Cowards! Would you strike a fallen foe? Back if you are men! What has this stranger done, that ye seek his life?"

"He is a traitor—a Texan!" shouted some of the band; but their colonel, respectfully dropping the point of his sword, in a gentler tone, said:

"Donna Magdalena, this is no place for you—this man must be my prisoner!" Then turning to his men he added, "Harm him not at present, but secure him—he shall be properly *tried* before a court-martial, though to do so but renders his fate quite as certain."

"What fate—surely he must not die simply because he is an enemy and has fallen in your power? And besides, he cannot be a Texan, he is of your own nation. Look at him, his face, garb, and all tell it!"

The colonel smiled as he bent down over the fallen man, and removed the false beard and mustache which covered his face, and then the maiden gasped with wonderment and increased anguish as she saw that he was young and more handsome without, than with his beard.

"Is he badly wounded?" she asked as she saw the officer examine the wounds.

"No, very slightly—nothing but flesh wounds which have wasted his blood as much as to weaken him—nothing more. I shall have to use your father's home for a prison, however, until tomorrow, when I can remove him to the city for trial."

The maiden seemed pleased at this idea, and made no objection to having him borne into the house.

The reader is, doubtless, anxious to know how the ranger's disguise became penetrated, and his discovery made. We will gratify him.

On rising in the morning, at the Posado, and ordering his horse, he saw that the Plaza was occupied by a regiment of lancers at drill, and he stood for some time at the door, watching their evolutions. He did not observe an officer who stood near him, whose eye was not upon the lancers, but upon himself. That eye was scanning him with a dangerous scrutiny—that officer was Gustave Alfrede, the murderer of his mother and sister—the perpetrator of the nameless crime upon them, which sinks all other crimes into nothingness. He had recognized the ranger, and was now thinking how he could get him into his power, with the least danger to himself, for he knew that he was ever in danger while his foe lived;—he knew of the "oath of revenge"—an oath sworn over the bodies of those whom he had violated and slain.

After a few moments of delay, carelessly spent in watching the drill of the lancers, Brackett mounted his horse, and started to ride around and examine the city, turning his horse's head toward the south gate. He had scarcely got into his saddle, when he saw an officer pass out from the inn, mount a horse, which was held by a soldier near the door, and dash at full speed across the Plaza, to the head of the body of lancers.

The ranger, at a single glance, recognized his enemy—he saw him speak to the lancers and point toward him; and then he knew that he was recognized. His first thought was to turn, and single-handed meet the foe: his next told him how important his mission was to his country—and he put spurs to his horse, followed at full speed by the shouting lancers. His horse was tired with a weary route of travel, but the noble animal bounded off, at first, with a speed which threatened soon to leave pursuit behind; but ere five miles were passed, he began to flag, and soon the foe came within shot of the ranger. The reader knows the rest of the adventure, up to the moment of capture.

CHAPTER IV

It was midnight, and Don Ignatio Valdez was closeted with Colonel Alfrede in his private chamber. The prisoner was confined in a lower room of the casa, with a guard of two soldiers over him, while all the rest of the lancers had been sent to their quarters in the city.

It was midnight, the end of the day which had commenced with his capture. The reader is permitted to listen to the conversation of Don Ignatio and his companion, in order that he may have a full comprehension of the situation and intention of all parties.

"Don Ignatio, it seems to me that a little more of your parental authority, a little more severity of manner, might at least induce her to treat me with common respect!"

"Don Gustave, she is wild and willful, I know; but Magdalena has never heard a harsh word from my lips, and it is hard for me to begin now, when each day renders her, if possible, more and more dear to me!"

"I ask you not to speak harshly to her, Don Ignatio; I only ask you to advise her to treat me with more respect—more kindness—not as if I were a slave, unworthy of a kind word, or a smile!"

"I will talk to her, Don Gustave. You know how desirous I am that she should be pleased with you—how desirous I am to have her accept your proffered suit—if you will only be patient, her repugnance to yourself will wear away, and all will be as you desire."

"Patience, senor! Patience itself can be worn out. I have wooed your daughter for three years—aye, sought with all the devotion of my heart to please and win her affections. By her daily conduct, you can see how I have prospered—and still, sir, you say *have patience!*"

This was spoken in a tone so impatient, that it somewhat touched the pride of the Castillian noble, and he haughtily answered:

"You need not expect to use force, sir, to win either her love or her hand. The daughter of a Valdez has a heart which can never be chained save by its own consent!"

The colonel saw that he had been rather hasty and in a milder tone said:

"Pardon me, Don Ignatio; I meant not that force was required—yet methinks a kind father's words of persuasion would be influential with a daughter ever dutiful, as is Donna Magdalena. Pardon me, if I have urged too strongly my suit. A passion so deep and fervent as mine, is like the swollen torrents which run down yon mountain's side; check or dam its course, and it will swell beyond the banks which should confine it."

"You are pardonable, certainly, Don Gustave; the more so that your present nature is so much like mine at your age. I will speak to the girl; I will urge your claims!" said Don Ignatio, who with his generous disposition was quite as easily pacified as angered, and as he said this, he bowed and left the apartment.

"Yes—for your *own* sake you had better urge my claims upon the proud girl; aye, and for hers! Little dreams she, or little thinks he that I own the roof which shelters them—the domain which surrounds them. The mortgage is mine, and one act of mine would drive them forth, or even make *peons* of them all."

This was the soliloquy of Alfrede, uttered as Don Ignatio left the room, and the last threat was a fearful one; for it is a common custom to *sell* a debtor in Mexico, until by his labor for a term of years he pays his debt, and there are authentic instances where such a slavery has been contracted for *life*.

It was the same hour. In a small room near the opening of the court of Don Ignatio's house lay Charles Brackett sleeping upon a rough settee, which had been before time used as a resting place for the porter, whose apartment this was.

He slept soundly, as if fatigue had overcome him. Though his face was a little pale, still his breathings were sufficiently heavy to show that his wounds had not left him in a dangerous situation. The bandages and dressings which were applied looked clumsy and awkward, as if applied by some hand unused to attending the wounds. The regular step of the sentinel in front of the door did not serve to disturb him—like those who have become used to danger and peril, he cared little apparently for the situation in which he was placed, even though he knew himself to be at the mercy of an inveterate foe. Besides, he had been worn down with the toil he had undergone, having been constantly in the saddle for many days, and all of this left him but little disposed for wakefulness.

The sentinel was almost as drowsy, and as he leaned against the door-post at the intervals when he paused in his walk, he would yawn and exhibit other somnambulic symptoms.

It was twelve, and he had yet another hour to watch, before the time when he could wake his relief, who lay upon his poncho asleep, in the entrance of the court. We know not whether the sentinel believed in ghosts or not, but he started very much and trembled violently as he saw the door of an apartment which led from the center of the building opened, and a figure dressed in white silently advance toward him. He did not tremble quite so much as the figure came nearer, and he recognized in it the form of Donna Magdalena, and he bowed respectfully as she approached. On her arm she bore a basket, which, as it was uncovered, exhibited a tempting display to one who belonged to a proverbially ill-fed army. There was wine, bread, meat, and fruit.

While he placed himself in front of the door, the soldier looked wistfully down into the basket, and though by his position he showed that the lady could pass no farther, still his manner betokened a respect, which possibly might have been heightened by the contents of her basket.

"The prisoner has not had any food or wine yet: I have brought him some," said the lady as she approached.

"My orders, senorita, are not to admit—"

"You have no orders not to admit refreshments to him, surely," said the lady, interrupting him, and then as she saw the direction in which his eyes involuntarily wandered, she added—"I knew that you too must be fatigued with your long watching. I have brought a bottle of wine for you, and also some food!"

The soldier's eyes sparkled as he heard this welcome piece of information, but he moved not from before the door which he guarded.

The lady stopped, and taking the bottle of wine and other articles which she had brought for him, set them upon the end of a rude bench which was placed at one side of the door, and then, with a beautiful smile said:

"Surely you will not refuse to let a helpless foe share in the necessary refreshment to sustain life—that would be unlike a cavalier, very unlike a true-hearted soldier!"

"Lady, I wish that I dared to please you in this, but my orders are to admit no one, not even to unbar the door myself."

"I will unbar it for you—you need not see me enter, you surely need not fear that he will escape. He is too weak."

"Lady, I fear not that—but my orders—"

"Your orders, you say, are not to unbar that door to anyone—now, do you sit down on that bench and partake of the refreshments which I know you need. Sit with your back to the door, then I can give the poor prisoner some food, and you will neither unbar the door, nor *see* it done. You know that he cannot escape—you see that you will not transgress your orders. All are sleeping in the house—this is an act of Christian mercy, and such acts are seldom *seen*—you need not fear."

The soldier tried to look sternly—but the lady smiled very sweetly—and then she put out her small white hand, and laying it upon his rude shoulder, pushed him very gently toward the bench where lay the food and wine. Her touch was so light that it would not have crushed a flower, yet, strange to say, it moved the stalwart guard from the door. She led him to the bench, and when she seated him, smiled sweetly and said—"Now don't look around—I will give him the refreshments and soon return!"

"Matilda! But she is a queen—and this wine is very good!" muttered the soldier as he took a breath after a hearty draught of the latter. He then proceeded to "lay in" the more substantial articles, taking particular care not to turn his eyes toward the door.

We will again enter the prison, if such we may term the room wherein Brackett was sleeping. When Magdalena went in she saw that he was asleep, and setting her basket upon the floor she cautiously approached his side.

Long and ardently she gazed down into his manly face, and then murmured:—

"So young—so handsome—and yet Alfrede says he must die! No! it must not—shall not be so. What if he is a Texan? He was taken in arms, and he shall not be murdered!"

Again she bent her head down to his brow, and impressed a warm, pure kiss upon it. He moved slightly as she did this, and in his sleep murmured: "Mother—sister!" Oh, where were then his dreams? Had the dream spirit borne him back to his boyish days of happiness? Oh, what a blessed power has a good Providence placed within our minds; that of permitting it in sleep to return to scenes of joy that are past and gone forever; that of dreaming that we still hold communion with loved departed ones. There is an angel up in heaven who often comes down to me in dreams and when my spirit almost faints with the toils of this world, she whispers cheering words, and tells me that the hour of rest is approaching. Oh bless God, for the power of dreaming!

But to return from our involuntary digression:—When Magdalena heard these words, she seemed to feel that none save a mother or sister held sway in his heart, for one ever whispers his dearest secrets in dreams; and again she pressed her lips to his brow, perhaps more fervently than before, for the touch awoke him. For an instant he seemed unable to recognize her or comprehend her presence, but the confusion of awakening passed, and he was about to speak.

Quick as thought, Magdalena laid her finger upon his lips and whispered:

"Be silent, senor! Your life is in danger—yes, *he* has said that you must die! But I will save you. Are you strong enough to ride?"

"I know not," he answered in the same low tone; "I am very weak, but if once in the saddle, I think it would still take trouble to unhorse me!"

"Another day would strengthen you much, would it not?"

"Not if as today, I am left without care or nourishment."

"Ah, I had forgotten! I have brought you wine and food!"

She hastened to administer these, and after a cup of wine he seemed much strengthened. His color heightened, and without much effort he raised himself to a sitting posture.

"I am better, lady—and I now remember that to you I owe my life. It is not worth much to me, yet I truly feel grateful to you, who are a stranger!"

"Senor, I did but my duty to a fellow creature. I would do more—I would save you from your present peril!"

"What is that peril?"

"Colonel Alfrede says that you are a traitor—that you must die!"

"*He*? he knows that if I live *he* must die! He, the murderer, the worse than murderer of my mother and sister!"

"Your mother and sister!—those of whom you but now whispered in your dreams. Did *he* murder them?"

"Yes, lady—after committing that nameless wrong which would render life itself a curse to a virtuous woman! He slew them, and their bones lie beneath the plains of Texas. I have sworn to revenge the fearful wrong—if I live, that oath shall be accomplished!"

The maiden shuddered as she heard these low-toned, thrilling words—and turned pale as she gazed upon his flushed face, and saw how flashed his jet-black eye, but she answered:

"You shall live, senor! Gustave Alfrede is my persecutor—my enemy too!"

"Then, lady, we are friends, even by the hate we hold!"

The lady's blush was deeper still, as she answered:

"We will be friends—but you must fly from here!"

"How can I?—My horse was ruined in this morning's skirmish."

"My father has fleet horses in his stable—but another thought strikes me. Alfrede has the fleetest horse in the country. You shot his usual road horse this morning, and he sent for his favorite war horse. It is now in the stable—but I fear you are too weak to ride at once!"

"I am used to the saddle, let me be once seated in it, and I can long sustain myself there!"

"I think another day can be gained, and that will revive you. It will give you strength to make a forced march, which will take you beyond his reach!"

"How can this delay be caused?"

"Feign excessive weakness. I will be more complaisant to him than usual—and thus easily prevail on him to delay for another day your removal to the city, where you are to be court-martialed. Tomorrow night all shall be ready for your flight!"

"But my guards!"

"I have conquered one of them with a bottle of wine—tomorrow night he shall have another, but it shall be drugged! All shall be prepared, fear not!"

"Lady, how can I repay you for all this kindness?"

"By not forgetting Magdalena Valdez when you return to your own country, and if as I fear, there should come war with all its horrors upon my country, and you should be among our foes, if you are kind to the helpless, then will I be repaid!"

"Lady, I never will forget you—and I will spare all who fall within my power save *him*—but when I meet Gustave Alfrede, he must *die*!"

She smiled sadly, and simply said:

"He is my *foe* too!"

"He shall not live long to persecute you, lady, but beware of him, and be ever on your guard!"

"I surely should not fear him!" said she, as she showed the pearl hilt of a dagger, which she carried in her bosom, and then she added: "remember to feign entire exhaustion on the morrow. You shall have more wine and food sent you in the mean time, and be ready tomorrow night. Your weapons, or others, shall be ready for you, and I will make your escape sure!"

Ere he could answer her, she had left the room.

"Beautiful as an angel, and kind as—as a woman!" said the prisoner when he looked around, and then he added in a tone which was anything but lover-like, "yet after all she is a Mexican—one of the cursed nation whom I have sworn to hate!"

When Donna Magdalena came out from the prisoner's room, she found the guard still engaged at the employment in which she had left him. Barring the door as she had found it, she approached him, and handing him a piece of gold, said:

"The prisoner's very low and weak—he seems hardly to have life in him!"

"I should think he wouldn't have much, after all the blood that was let out of his veins; I'm sure I wouldn't," said the soldier, and then looking round, he asked: "Is the door barred, lady?"

"Yes," she replied, "it is just as I found it. Be careful not to have this visit known to your colonel—you will be no loser by your discretion!"

"I shall be careful, for my own sake, if for no other," said the soldier, and the next moment the lady was gone, bearing with her the basket and bottles, to prevent discovery.

CHAPTER V

*I*t was a hot and sultry day that of the eighth of May, 1846. Our troops were on the march with a train of provisions and artillery, from Point Isabel to Fort Brown; General Taylor commanding in person.

The troops were much excited. They had heard by the signal guns from the Fort, that it was surrounded, on the previous day, and now that not a gun was heard from that direction, they were left to fear that the gallant Brown and his brave companions, had fought in vain against overpowering numbers. Under these feelings they pressed rapidly on, but ere noon their advanced scouts reported that the enemy were in large force, and that though the day was then hot, it was like to be hotter ere it closed. At two o'clock, they found themselves beside a small stream, in front of a grove, which from its tall timbers was called Palo Alto, a name which is written in letters of blood in our history. Here they saw the enemy before them, and here they paused to fill their canteens with water, and to prepare for the fearful struggle which was soon to commence. While the line of battle was forming immediately under the supervision of "Old Rough and Ready," Lieutenant Blake made a most gallant reconnaissance of the enemy's line, and as soon as his report was made to General Taylor, the action commenced. First, the fire of the Mexican batteries opened, then ours returned the salute, while steadily and firmly our whole line pressed on to meet them. But we need not give a history of this battle. Enough has already been written of it to sicken the reader. Oh, it was a glorious and yet a fearful sight. Calvary wheeling here and there; cannon pouring out their iron hail upon masses of infantry, which melted before the tremendous fire, as snowflakes falling into the sea; lances and sabers meeting and clashing; bayonet to bayonet, and breast to breast; on the open prairie and in the dense chaparral, thus met the foes, gallantly fighting and all too thickly falling. Here fell Ringgold and Page, and many of those gallant souls who are nameless on the page of history, because they were *privates*![13]

Oh, it was a sad and harrowing sight to see so many human beings lay mangled upon the bosom of their mother earth, yet the sun went down upon it. The armies had ceased through fatigue, and the approach of darkness. Under cover of this cloak the enemy retired to a more defensible spot, whereon to renew the fight once more.

Few slept that night of all our little army, though they were permitted to lay down upon the tentless ground, with their arms beneath them ready for instant use.

Their general neither lay down or closed his eyes. Beside a small campfire, beneath a clump of trees, upon a fallen tree-trunk, receiving the reports of the different officers, and giving orders preparatory to resuming his march in the morning, he sat, calm as if the fatigues of the day, and the peril of the fight, had made no impression on him. True, his face flushed and his breast heaved when he heard that Ringgold and Page must die, but he grew calm again when he thought that the battle was but half won, and must be resumed with the morning's light.

It was after midnight, when he arose from his seat, and wrapping himself in an old gray surtout, walked around his camp. He paused by a camp fire which was near the outer edge of his advanced lines. Around the dim embers were stretched several men, and at a little distance at the root of an old tree, lay one by himself. As the general approached the fire, he asked a soldiery sentinel, who hailed him, if Captain Walker was near.

The figure which was reclining near the tree, at once arose and advanced. It was Walker.

"I am here, general, not asleep, though resting, after today's ride!"

"It is well for you to rest, sir, you will need all your strength tomorrow—but I have sought you to ask about our spy. He should have been here before now—I fear some casualty has befallen him! You are sure of his faith?"

"Yes, sir, as sure of him as I am of myself. If he is not killed, he will be here soon, but you gave him a long and hard route!"

"True, but he has been gone nearly two months—he must have heard of the death of Cross, and Thorton's capture ere this, and such news would hasten his return!"[14]

"If he is still alive he will be with us before another blow is struck, perhaps by morning!" replied Walker.

"I hope he will, for now that the war is commenced, I am determined to push it, aye, to *force* a peace. The only way to make a victory valuable is to improve upon it—to push ahead. If a woodsman in clearing up a piece of ground simply cuts down the trees, they are more in his way than ever. He must burn them up, as well as cut them down. So with us; we must not only whip the enemy, but we must disperse or destroy him!"

"I don't know much about the theory of rules of war, general," answered Walker, "but I'm willing to learn. I'm like the tailor's good apprentice—you cut down the clothes and I'll sew 'em up! No offense to your name, sir!"

The general laughed, and said: "It would be hard to make me offended with so good an apprentice as you have proved yourself, within the past ten days—in fact, I think it were no more than justice to dub you a *journeyman*!"

"I thank you, general—I'll try and do honor to the profession tomorrow, for you can hear by the drums and bugles on the road ahead, that the bloody yellow-skins are getting ready for another scrimmage!"

"Yes—and if they have stopped at the dry ravine a few miles up the road, they will bother us some!"

"Not much, general. A little of the bayonet and broadsword, will start them as it did today, and then we'll have more use for the spur than anything else."

"You must not think too lightly of them. Some of their corps fought well today, and their batteries were well served!"

"We mustn't let them use their batteries, sir. Leave them to Charley May's dragoons and my mounted rangers, and see how long they'll hold their guns!"

"You shall have a chance at them, if they stand!" said the general, smiling, and then he turned away.

His next steps were to the temporary tent where rested poor Ringgold. By his side knelt Ridgely, his gallant friend and subaltern, who had so long been assisting him in drilling and forming his artillery corps. Tears were coursing down his sun-bronzed cheeks—he knew that his commander and friend must die. May was there—the Murat of our army, with his jetty beard and flowing hair; and others as brave and true, were also near, but all fell back as their beloved general approached.[15]

The eye of the wounded man brightened, as he saw who it was that knelt down on the ground where he lay and took his cold hand. The general could not speak—his heart was full—he saw that he must lose his most valuable officer. Let it be said as no disparagement to the rest of the brave band; but beside the general himself, that army could better have spared any two of its officers, than one Ringgold.

"General, I have done my duty—have lived a soldier's life—I must have a soldier's fate!" said the wounded man, faintly.

The general's eyes filled, his lips trembled as if he would speak, but he could not. Pressing warmly the cold hand of the wounded officer, he arose and hastily passed from a scene which was far more terrible to him than the mad havoc of battle,—the death-bed of a friend.

It was morning once more. The troops were up at the first tap of the reveille drum, and everything was ready for the renewal of their march. The spies had given the position of the enemy, and it was known that another scene of carnage was at hand, and though they knew that the foe was far more numerous than they, still the Spartan band formed calmly into column and line, and advanced as steadily as if they were on parade. They were not long in finding the enemy. The general's order of battle on that day was simple; his directions few but strong. Keeping his artillery in the wood where it could be used, and flanking it with his infantry, he advanced upon the foe, his few mounted men under May and Walker, kept in reserve near himself, ready to act when their time came. "The Ball" opened, and then not long had May and Walker to wait. When the enemy's battery came into full play—then Taylor rose in his stirrups, and pointing toward it with his field glass—cried to Captain May:

"Your time has come, sir, there is the enemy's battery, take it, *nolens volens*!"[16]

Then did the gallant dragoons shout in their mad glee as their dark browed leader rose in his stirrups, and pointing with his bright saber toward the foe, shouted,

"Forward, men! Follow!" And they did follow—on, on with bloody spurs, bright steel flashing in their hands, and brighter eyes flashing in their heads, they rode; soon they were beside the gallant Ridgely's battery, and as he cried:

"Stop one moment, Charley, till I draw the fire off the battery!"

They reined in to his right, then after he fired and received in return the fire of the enemy, again they dashed on to their leader's shout of—"forward! Boys, forward!" and the next moment they were upon the foe, though met by a deadly fire which strewed near one-half of the plain. On, on like the tempest through the grain-field they swept, and the enemy reeled before the shock. Back once more they wheeled upon the same gory path, and the battery was taken. The noble La Vega was a prisoner to us, but our Inge—"Fred Inge," the beloved of his corps and all the army, was dead; and many a bold dragoon lay cold in that bloody trench. Walker and his rangers, though they shared not in this charge, were in as perilous a fray in another part of the field, and at this moment came up to join May, who had already delivered his distinguished prisoner to Colonel Twiggs, his immediate commander.[17]

The enemy were not yet conquered, and were fighting desperately in dispatched parties through the chaparral. May and Walker were observing a body of lancers in their front at this time, who seemed preparing for a charge upon them, when suddenly they noticed a confusion in the enemy's ranks, and in a moment more they saw a soldier mounted on a magnificent white horse, dashing right through the ranks of the lancers, cutting right and left with a sword which was red with blood. Though he was dressed like a Mexican, his actions served to show that he was not of them but rather of their foes, and a fearful one at that; for as a mower lays a swath with his scythe, so did the strong horseman sweep a path before him. In a moment more he was free from them, and with a loud shout of joy, he dashed down toward May and his little squadron. His horse was spotted over with blood—his appearance seemed like a demon of the battle-field.

"By heavens, 'tis Brackett, my own Brackett!" cried Walker, as he struck spurs to his horse, and rode out to meet the spy.

"For God's sake, off with that sombrero and green jacket, Charley, or you'll be shot for a yellow skin!" he added, as he neared the horseman, who was, indeed, the spy, safely returned.

In a few moments they had returned to the ranks, and a hasty, and at that crisis, very necessary, change was made in Brackett's dress.

"Now you look more like yourself, Charley!" cried Walker; "but how you must have astonished the yellow skins when you dashed through them single-handed!"

"They did seem a little scared!" answered the spy; "but I saw that I was late to dinner, and thought I'd try and make a meal off the first grub that came my way. Where's the general?"

"God knows—I don't; he's somewhere about where fighting is going on, sitting cross-legged on his old white horse, laughing in his sleeve to see how our boys use up the yellow skins."

"I must find him—I've important news for him!"

"Which way did you come?"

"By the stockade—and its gallant commander, Major Brown, is killed—but Hawkins is of the right breed, he'll hold it till all's blue again."[18]

"What has detained you so long—the general was asking for you last night."

"It would take me all day to tell you; but I must find him, and report my arrival!" The spy now galloped off across the battle-field in search of Taylor. He soon found him, for he was very conspicuous, as he sat carelessly upon his large white charger.

The eye of the general gleamed with pleasure, as he saw the ranger approach, and he hastily asked:

"Have you succeeded, sir?"

"Perfectly, general!"

"Well, sir, I'm glad to hear it. The day is now our own, and this spree will soon be over. Come to me when all is quiet, and I will receive your report."

The ranger bowed low in his saddle, and was about turning to join in that which now was a pursuit and massacre, rather than a battle, when the general added:

"Take care of yourself, sir—I don't want to lose you anytime, but especially not till I have a report of your reconnaissance. Keep near my side."

This order Brackett, of course, obeyed; but he chafed to hear the shouts of the distant pursuers, and not be permitted to join the melee.

CHAPTER VI

It was night, and the victorious American army was encamped upon the ensanguined field of Resaca de la Palma, a name which, though spoken in a foreign tongue, thrills through every American heart, as warmly, too, as that of Saratoga, Yorktown, and Brandywine.[19]

The surgeons were employed in alleviating, to the extent of their power, the sufferings of the wounded. All were treated alike—both friend and foe, officer and private. Though it was late, yet the noble patriot, Taylor, was passing another sleepless night. Though he knew that the foe was thoroughly vanquished, yet he knew that his own force was small, poorly provided for, and far from succor, and it required all of his stern energy to meet the emergencies which surrounded him. This night again he passed without a tent between him and the blue sky—his solitary camp-fire glimmered up from beneath a clump of trees, and by its light he was examining a map of the country, taken on that day, from the baggage of General Arista.[20] By his side was Brackett, pointing out the different fortified parts of the road toward Mexico, and explaining, as he went along, the state of the parts of the country.

"Can Monterey be taken easily?" asked the general.

"Not easily, sir. It is a strong place. Three thousand good American artilleries and riflemen could hold it till doomsday; but it can be taken by Americans!"

"You are right—perfectly right, sir. I could take the world, if all America turns out such men as have fought these two battles for me—but this Monterey is an important point. I must have it!"

"You will, sir, if you try!" was the enthusiastic reply of the young ranger.

"How is the road from there on to Saltillo?" asked the general.

"Good, to the city, but narrow and rough beyond—it was there I met with the mishap that caused my delay, and an adventure which would be worth something in the hands of some poor devil of a novel writer!"

"Well, sir, let us hear it. I see that Captain Walker is in nettles to know what it is."

"I was taken prisoner by a man who is my sworn and deadly foe—a colonel in the lancers."

"By what plea did he dare to take you?—the war had not commenced then!"

"He recognized me as one of the Texans who helped to whip him and his comrades at San Antonio, some few years since, and knew that I had *sworn* to kill him![21] He murdered—worse than murdered—my mother and sister."

"*Did* you kill him?" asked Walker, who had listened with breathless anxiety.

"No; my horse stumbled as I fired, and I shot too low, killing his horse instead of him; but I laid out a few of his men before they got me down!"

"You were wounded, then?" asked the general.

"Certainly, sir, or they never would have taken me. That alone has delayed me!"

"But how did you escape?"

"That is the romance, sir! I was assisted by a young woman who was near as pretty as an angel, and quite as good as one. I'm sure that in this case she was my 'better angel,' for she certainly saved my life in two instances. In the first, she prevented them from killing me outright when I was taken. In the second, she effected my escape—supplied me with a fresh horse, arms, and all that I needed!"

"How did you escape, Charley, tell us that!" asked Walker, whose attention had been marked.

"Why, the lady got my sentinel drunk or asleep, I hardly know which, then unbarred my prison door, led me out through her father's garden, mounted me on the lancer colonel's own favorite horse, said 'God bless you!' and sent me off."

"Who was she?"

"The daughter of an old planter, who has a very pretty romantic place, called Buena Vista, just beyond Saltillo, where the mountain gorges commence. It is a magnificent spot for a fight—hills on both sides—lots of ravines and tree-clumps!"

"You fell in love with the lady, did you not?" asked Walker again.

"Why, no—not exactly. I do feel a little grateful for her kindness in getting me out of a bad scrape, and I'd like very much to see her again, but I'm not in love!"

General Taylor, who had been steadily gazing down upon the map, raised his head at this remark, and said, with a singular smile:

"You shall soon see her, sir, if she does not remove from the position. It lays directly in the road which I shall take to Mexico!"

This was a singular prophecy, but the reader knows how well it has been fulfilled.[22]

We will now pass back to a scene which occurred in the house of Don Ignatio Valdez on the morning when the escape of the ranger was discovered.

Colonel Alfrede had risen early and passed the room of the prisoner to order him to hold himself in readiness to be taken to Saltillo for trial. The sentinel was pacing to and fro before the door; the door was barred as usual. The colonel ordered the sentinel to open it. The order was obeyed, but neither the astonished sentinel, nor the enraged colonel could discover the prisoner. The nest seemed alright, yet the bird had flown.

"What means this, sir? What treachery is this? Where is your prisoner?" demanded the colonel, in tones of thunder, of the trembling sentinel.

"I know not, senor. Antonio said that all was right when I relieved him, about an hour after midnight, and I will swear by all the saints in heaven, that he could not have escaped in my watch!"

"Where is Antonio—bring him here?" thundered the officer again.

In a moment the other guard was awakened from that which seemed a very deep slumber, and stood before his colonel.

"What has become of the prisoner?" asked the latter.

"Is he not in the prison, senor?"

"No, dog! Where is he? Who aided in his escape!"

"As I love the Holy Cross, senor, I do not know! He did not escape in my watch!"

"There is a lie between you two!" thundered Alfrede; "and if I won't find out the truth, I'll have you both shot!"

"I have not moved one step from before this door, since Antonio called me," said the first sentinel.

"And has no one approached the spot?" asked the colonel.

"No one, as I live!" answered the sentinel; but while he spoke the keen eye of Alfrede was watching the countenance of the other, he saw it flush up as he asked this question, and at once mistrusted him.

"And you, Antonio—can you say the same? Beware, villain, how you deceive me, for I can read something in that blushing face of yours, which must and shall be told!"

"No one, senor, but the lady Magdalena, and she only brought the prisoner some wine and food."

"Did she not give you some, too?"

"Yes, senor," said the trembling soldier, for he knew now that a lie would be worth his life.

"And did you sleep afterward?"

"I could not help it, senor; I never felt so sleepy before in my life!"

"I believe you, you cursed fool. I see through all this now—she has played the traitress, and released him. By heaven, but she shall rue it. Quickly saddle my horse and your own. One of you ride at full speed to the city, and let patrols take every road in pursuit. He must be taken. I will give five hundred pesos to the man who takes him, dead or alive, I care not which!"

The soldiers hastened to obey these orders, while the colonel returned in a fierce and angry mood to the sitting room of Don Ignatio.

The latter marked his flashing eye and darkened brow as he entered, and asked what was the matter.

"Matter enough, senor; matter enough, when my prisoner must not only be better loved than myself, but must be set free from my hands by your daughter!"

"What! The prisoner loved—set free by Magdalena!"

"Yes, Don Ignatio. Now, methinks, it is time to exert a little of the parental authority, of which you have been all too sparing, when she leagues with the enemies of her countrymen."

"By my honor, I cannot believe this—I must hear it from her own lips!"

The old Castillian arose, and stepping to a window which overlooked the court, bade a female servant to call her young mistress and send her to him.

Meantime, with long and hasty strides, the enraged colonel was striding to and fro across the room, but he paused as he heard a step approaching through the passage way. It was one of the soldiers.

"Well, sir, what want you now? Why are you not mounted?"

"We have nothing to mount, senor," answered the man. "Your horse and saddle is gone—our saddles are where we left them; but there is not a horse left in the stall."

"There, sir, see more of your daughter's honor and *patriotism*! She has leagued herself with a horse thief, as well as—"

Alfrede paused in his bitter and sneering speech, as the maiden herself, dressed purely in white, stepped forth from an inner apartment.

"Well, sir," cried she, in tones quite as contemptuous as his own had been, "why did you not finish your tirade of abuse. It well becomes one who could deliberately determine to murder a brave and defenseless foe, who had become his prisoner; it well becomes such a one to abuse the fair fame of a woman!"

"Donna Magdalena, did you not aid and connive at the prisoner's escape?" asked he, in tones more mild and respectful than one would have thought he could assume. The father spoke not, but when he heard this question, he bent forward, expressing in look and attitude, his deep anxiety.

With a firm, but clear tone, while she gazed steadily in the eye of her questioner, she answered:

"I assisted a wounded and helpless man, whom, to your cost, you knew to be brave, to escape from the hands of a man devoid of honor, truth, or any of the qualities which make a man a soldier and a cavalier!"

As she thus spoke, he ground his teeth together through his lips, till the blood streamed down upon his jetty beard; his eyes seemed like burning coals of rage; at first he laid his hand upon his sword, as if he mediated to attack her there upon her father's floor, then he turned to the father, who stood with his head upon his hand, and his face expressing the agony of his mind and cried:

"Now, Don Ignatio, you have heard—judge for yourself."

"Magdalena, what have you done?" asked the father of his child, in tones so sad and subdued, that they called the tears to his eyes in one instant.

"My duty to a helpless fellow creature, who was in imminent peril!" said she, calmly, but in a tone far different from that which had marked her address to Alfrede.

"Rather say, lady, that you preferred a *new* lover to the duty you owe your country!" said Alfrede, with a cold sneer; but the lady paid not attention to the remark or its tone, but again spoke to her father:

"I could not bear that he, so young and so brave, should be deliberately taken to the city to be shot! You heard Don Gustave plan his doom; you know that dastardly as it would have been to execute a foe taken in arms, gallantly fighting, nothing but the step I have taken would have saved him from that fate!"

"Do you not love him, daughter? Is the reason of your conduct not that which is given by Colonel Alfrede?"

"It is not, my father. I do not love him. My heart would have prompted the same for any other in his situation!" said the beautiful girl, and her tone was so steady and confident, that her father could not, did not doubt the truth of her declaration.

Not so with the officer. With a frown upon his brow, and a curse upon his lips, he turned away, ordering his soldiers to find horses somewhere, and speedily bring them; then, while his clenched hands and frowning brow alone told how deep and wild his anger was, he stepped closer to her side, and in a tone low, but deep, said:

"He has not escaped, lady! No, by the bright heavens above,—by the love I have borne for you, I will retake the miscreant, *and you shall see him die*!"

"He will not die till his *mother* and *sister's* fearful wrongs have been avenged!" answered she, in a tone as low and deep as his, a tone which did not reach the ear of her father.

Don Ignatio wondered as he saw Colonel Alfrede turn so suddenly pale, and utter with a curse:

"Has *he* told you *all*? Then indeed he must die. There is now no time to tamper!" But he knew not the cause of the paleness or remark. As he said this, without even the courtesy of a parting salute, the officer strode from the room.

The daughter kissed her father's care-worn brow, and retired to her own and her sister's apartment. The lovely twain shared the same room and the same bed. The room was that whose latticed window opened out toward the road, the window through which she first had seen him. She had denied that she loved Charles Brackett, but she knew not her own heart. Let the future tell.

CHAPTER VII

*W*e do not intend to make our story a history of the Mexican war, and will only touch upon such scenes and incidents as are actually connected with the tale. Therefore the reader must not be surprised when we pass entirely over the capture of Matamoras, and the onward progress of our victorious army to Monterey; nor must he expect from us a description of the glorious battle, which placed "the flag of the free" upon the hoary battlements of that ancient city.[23]

The thread of our story recommences after the capture of the latter place, at the time when our scouts were already dogging the footsteps of the retreating foe, who were hastening to join Santa Anna, at San Luis Potosi. Alfrede with his regiment of lancers, had participated in the shame and defeat of the Mexican army at Monterey, and had retreated with his corps to Saltillo, which was already threatened by the intended advance of General Worth.[24]

The spies of the Americans, and the Texan rangers, were already hovering above the latter place. Don Ignatio Valdez, still remained at Buena Vista, for he had learned that the Americans never harmed the peaceably disposed inhabitants of the soil, who did not join in the war, and he was rather too old to take the field against them, especially when he knew that in doing so he left his daughters without a protector.

After his return from Monterey, Colonel Alfrede had been more than usually attentive in his visit to Buena Vista, and so far as remarks or actions were to be judged, appeared to have forgotten or forgiven the agency of Donna Magdalena, in the escape of the young ranger. But she knew full well that in this he was concealing the true feelings of his heart; that his was the most consummate hypocrisy. Her father, however, placed a far different construction on this conduct, and gave Don Gustave credit for a nobleness and generosity, to which he surely had no right. He even urged the suit of Don Gustave upon his daughter, and began to assume a tone of authority, which was as new to him as was strange to her.

Colonel Alfrede supported this effort with a gentleness of manner, which won much upon the father's regard, and even the gentle Ximena, began to chide her sister for not being more kind to one who appeared to love her so devotedly.

It was on a sweet moonlight evening shortly after the capture of Monterey, that the two sisters sat at their window enjoying the pleasant air which came down from the mountains, for though it was in the winter time, the atmosphere was soft and balmy. The hour was late, or rather we should say early, for it was past midnight.

Months had passed since Charles Brackett had left Buena Vista, yet Donna Magdalena had not heard a word from or of him. Alfrede had studiously concealed the fact, that he had again narrowly escaped from his inveterate foe, in the siege of Monterey; had carefully kept from her that he had even see the ranger. Still that her thoughts were upon him, let the following conversation testify.

Magdalena while seated by the side of Ximena, frequently looked out upon the Saltillo road, as if she expected some one to come from thitherward, and even as she looked in that direction, a gentle, half-suppressed sigh, would rise from her heaving bosom.

"Why do you sigh, sister?" asked Ximena. "Are you thinking of the young American?"

"I was thinking of him then, Ximena.—I often wonder whether he succeeded in regaining his countrymen in safety, and wonder if he be amongst those who are invading our country. I hope he is safe!"

"Sister, I fear much that you *love* that young stranger!" said Ximena, gravely.

"No," responded the other—"I do not love him, yet I often feel as if it would please me to see him once more—at least to know that he is in safety!"

"Ah, my sister, such interest is very near akin to love. It is too strong a feeling for a virtuous and patriotic Mexican maiden, to hold for one who belongs to the cruel nation which has invaded her plains, and drenched them with blood, who are even now revelling in the halls of our most beautiful city, and perchance may soon come to drive us from our happy home."

"Ah, sister, do not call my feeling *love*, or chide me now. I am sad enough already. My father is pressing the odious suit of Alfrede upon me. Indeed he has given me no choice, and says that within two short weeks I *must* wed—*must*, Ximena, must! 'Tis the first time he has ever spoke so to me!"

"He acts for our welfare, my sister!" responded the gentle Ximena, "but let us change the theme. Take your guitar, love, and sing for me. Sing my favorite, 'La Ausencia.'"

The fair girl, with another sigh, raised her guitar to accede to her sister's request, and in a voice sad and sweet, sung:

"Se fué el hechizo
Del alma mia,
Y mi alegnia
Se fué tambien."

She was about to continue with the second stanza of the song, when a rich manly voice beneath the window, took up the strain, and she heard the very words she was about to sing.

"Y en un instante
Todo he perdido
Donde te has ido
Querida bien!"[25]

"Oh, Cielo! 'tis he—'tis the stranger!" cried the astonished Magdalena, as she let fall her guitar, and bent far out of the window, to look down in the shadow of the wall beneath. She saw a horse fastened beneath a tree at a short distance; she recognized the magnificent charger which the stranger had rode away, the same which had belonged to Don Gustave. While yet she peered down into the dense shadow beneath her window, the singer stepped out into the moonlight, and she at once recognized the young ranger, dressed in a handsome uniform, and armed to the teeth. He had recovered his health, and the astonished girl fancied that she never had seen a more noble looking cavalier than he.

"Look, Ximena, 'tis he!" she cried, and the other sister, as she gazed out upon him, replied—

"He indeed is the same, and he is handsome—but, beware my sister of love, remember that he is our *foe!*"

"Oh, fear me not, Ximena, but see he recognizes us—oh, I must see him and talk with him a moment. He is surrounded with dangers here. I must advise him to return to his friends!"

"No—oh, no!" cried the timid Ximena, "you surely will not seek an interview with him?"

"I surely shall, sister!" replied the beautiful girl, and as she spoke she waved a 'kerchief from the window. The ranger approached nearer, and she spoke in a low tone:

"Hist, senor! Oh, you are very imprudent. Quickly, remove your horse from sight; meet me in the garden in the rear; the gate shall be open."

The ranger turned to obey, and Magdalena hastily prepared to descend to the garden. Her sister in tears now besought her to remain.

"Oh, do not go, sister; you know not the peril you encounter, both of reputation and discovery."

"The innocent have their own safeguard, sister; fear not for me. Await my return in quiet and peace; I shall be gone but a moment. I only go to warn him of his danger."

"I shall await you in prayer," replied Ximena, as she saw Magdalena with flushed cheek, and trembling form, pass forth to meet the stranger.

When she arrived at the small gate which opened into the rear of her father's garden, Donna Magdalena found the ranger already there. As she opened it, he stepped within, and taking her fair hand within his own, raised it to his lips.

"Oh, senor!" she cried—"Why—why have you come here, when the whole country is in arms. It is scoured daily by Alfrede's lancers. A price is set upon your head. If you are taken, nothing could again save you!"

"Is my life an object of interest to you, lady?" he asked.

She answered but with one word, yet the look which accompanied, and tone which uttered it, expressed more than a thousand words could have done. "*Senor!*" was all she said, but her look asked if she had not already proved that his life was dear to her.

"I beg your pardon, dear lady," he continued, "I was near here on duty, and I could not refrain from coming to try and see you once more!"

"But the danger, senor!"

"I am used to danger, lady—I have long been inured to it. I wished once more to see you, and express my thanks to you for saving my life, and to assure you that your last requests have been fulfilled!"

"The requests, senor?"

"Yes, lady, those made when last we stood near this spot, when you bade me not to forget you, and if war occurred, to be kind to your countrymen. Those words, lady, and the remembrance of you, have saved more than one life in the mad rush of battle. The foe who cries to me for quarter, speaks in the name of Magdalena, and speaks not in vain!"

"Oh, I thank you noble cavalier: I can almost forget that you are a foe!"

"Oh, *quite* forget, beautiful lady, for Americans are never foes to such as you. We oppose men like men; we meet the helpless with kindness!"

"Oh, will it ever be so; will not our beautiful valleys be laid waste, will not the helpless yet fly in terror before your conquering arms?"

"When my countrymen forget mercy, and make war upon women and children, then will I desert them; but that time will never come!"

"I pray God it may not!" said the fair girl, and then she added, "but you must fly from here—it will soon be day, and you will be fearfully exposed. Alfrede and his lancers are out early and late!"

"Aye, and they will always be too late for me!" responded the ranger with a stern smile; "they were early in leaving Monterey, though!"

"Did you see *him* there?" asked the maiden.

"Ask him! Nothing but the flag of capitulation saved him from my arm; but we will meet again. He has had his warning."

"The consummate hypocrite told me that he had never seen you or heard of you since your escape," said Magdalena; "but now I see through his drift—he attempts to conceal all his feelings, and is using every means to urge on his odious suit!"

"Does he still persecute you?"

"Oh, senor, if to inflict his presence upon me daily; if to ever be pouring his fulsome compliments upon my loathing ear, then I am persecuted!"

"This shall not last long. Within a month our troops will occupy Saltillo. If he dare to resist, we will soon silence his persecution; if he flies, he will leave you far behind, for you and yours shall have safety and protection guaranteed to you here. Your father surely will remain?"

"Alas, senor, he this day swore upon his honor that I should wed the hated Alfrede, and gave me but two weeks to prepare for the sacrifice. Two short weeks only!"

"Ha! Force to be employed, and that so soon?"

"Alas! Senor, I speak that which is but true!"

"Then force shall be met with force, lady. You never shall wed *him*—never!"

"How can I be saved?"

"I shall be ever near you and ever on the watch. Fear not but that I will foil all plans that are attempted against your peace. Have you a servant in whom you can place all confidence?"

"I have one, senor; a faithful Indian boy, who would die for me!"

"Then if anything should occur which should cause you to require sudden assistance, send him with a single lock of your hair to a ranger camp which is in a wood near the forks of the road which turns from the Monterey road to Capellana. Bid him turn into the forest where it is most dense on the left, and sound this whistle. It will be answered speedily."

As the ranger said this, he took from his pocket a small silver whistle, which he presented to her, and she replied:

"I will accept it, senor, but never use it without my peril is imminent. I cannot forget that you are a foe to my country!"

"Oh, lady, do not say so: I would fain forget all things save that to you I owe my life—to you I have given my love!"

"Your *love*, senor, Oh! Say not so!"

"Is my love so displeasing to you—am I so unfortunate as to love without hope?"

"Oh, senor, I know not what to say. You are the foe of my country!"

"But not *yours*! Oh, lady, forget that I am anything but your lover!"

"Senor, it is impossible—Oh, what would my joy not be if this war had not occurred!" cried the maiden, and then as she felt that her unguarded expression had exposed more of her own feelings than she wished, she blushed and added, "Oh, leave me, senor, present at least. We may meet again when this hateful war is past!"

"Oh, lady, one word with you have dropped, gives me hope. Say, at least, though we may not meet soon, that my love is returned!"

"Senor, I dare not say all that I feel. You shall not be forgotten. I will never yield heart or hand to another!"

"I can ask no more than this, lady; you shall see me again; and, now, farewell."

"Oh, be guarded, senor; dangers will ever attend you in this vicinity!"

"I will be careful, lady. For your sake!" responded the ranger. He bent his lips once more to her beautiful hand: the next moment he was gone.

For a moment the lady listened to his footsteps as he passed away, then she heard the rattling sound of his horse's hoofs as he galloped along the mountain base which ranged back of Saltillo. When all was still again, she burst into tears, and wept as if her very heart was running over.

Was it grief? No, she loved for the first time, and knew that she was beloved. The fountain of true grief is one where from few tears spring; it is the spring of joy, which, in a woman's heart, overruns its margin.

CHAPTER VIII

When Donna Magdalena returned to her chamber, she found her gentle sister still bending on her knees by the window casement, a golden crucifix in her hand.

Oh, how beautiful that young girl looked, with her hands holding the sacred symbol of her religion, and folded meekly across her heaving bosom! Her dark eyes were looking calmly up toward the blue sky, as if already she saw that there was a place of rest prepared for her; and her pure young lips were silently moving, as if she communed with unseen spirits.

When she heard the step of her sister, she arose, and hastening to her side, impressed upon her cheek a pure warm kiss of love and truth. When she saw the trace of tears, she asked:

"What ails thee, my sister?" in tones soft as the cooing of the wood dove.

"Oh, Ximena, I love, and love one of my country's foes!"

"I have long feared it, sister, but you must banish such feelings. Let pride conquer them if nothing else!"

"Nothing can conquer love! Pride, all things must yield to feelings such as mine. Long, long have I tried to control them, this single interview with him proves how vainly!"

"But, dear sister, such love is hopeless. Our father has decided that you shall marry Colonel Alfrede; besides, this war—"

"This war will not last forever: when it is over, *he* will come to honorably claim me; and for Alfrede, I would sooner die by my own hand than give that hand to him whom I detest!"

Ximena saw that it was of no use to combat feelings like these, and she went sorrowing to her couch. Little did Magdalena sleep on that night; yet when she met her father in the morning, he thought that he had never seen her looking so bright and beautiful, and when he remarked upon it, she smiled and said,

"I am glad my looks please you, my father. These are kinder words than you have been wont to use to your poor daughter lately!"

"Ah, child, if I have been harsh, it was for your own good—your happiness and that of Ximena is all that I have to live for now!"

"But, my father, that which has been the plea of your severity, would be anything but happiness to me. I cannot love the man whom you would *force* me to wed!"

"Say not *force*, Magdalena, rather say him whom I *implore* you to wed!"

"You said I *must* wed him, my father, in yester-eve!"

"Oh, my daughter, if you knew all you would not think me severe. Much depends upon this marriage, and I have set my very heart upon it!"

"While I have set my very heart against it, father!" said she, playfully, and then in a touching tone she added—"Can it not be delayed till this dreadful war is over—now do delay it till then, and see if I do not become more reconciled to it before then!"

The father regarded his daughter sternly for a moment, but his look softened as he gazed upon her beautiful and innocent face, so like that of his lost Seberina, and he answered:

"I will see Don Gustave, my child, and I will to try to gain his consent; but he has my promise, my sacred honor is pledged to him, and if he persists then you must—"

"Die, sir, *die!*" interrupted the passionate girl, "for know, that before I will wed him with my present feelings, I will bury this dagger in my heart!" and she once more showed the pearly hilt of her bosom companion.

At this moment a servant announced that Don Gustave was riding toward the house, and the excited girl at once retired to her chamber.

In a few moments the colonel was announced.

Don Ignatio had not quite recovered his equanimity, but received his guest with his usual urbanity.

"The ladies are well, I hope?" said Don Gustave as he seated himself.

"Quite well—that is, Ximena is, but Magdalena is a little indisposed this morning!" said the father hesitatingly.

"Nothing serious, I hope?" said Don Gustave, with great apparent anxiety of manner.

"No, senor—but I believe that the idea of this hasty marriage is injurious to her. Can it not be delayed till the close of the war?"

"Delayed, senor! Have I not wooed your daughter for years, have you not at last set the day which was to see me united with her, and now you ask for delay!"

"Don Gustave, I have passed my word, but she insists upon delay—it is a painful thing for me to force this marriage!"

"Is she more averse than usual to it?"

"Yes, this morning she threatened her own life, preferring death to an union with you!"

"Will you send for her?—there is some mystery in this. I ask for a few words with her in your presence!"

"I will have her called, Don Gustave," replied the father.

In a few moments the maiden made her appearance, and certainly she never had looked more beautiful than she did at that moment. Her face was flushed with a rich and rosy hue; her eyes were full and bright; her form seemed to dilate, and swell into perfection with the air of queenly dignity, which seemed so natural to her.

"Lady, your father informs me that you wish our marriage delayed for a time!" said the colonel, in a soft and pleasant tone.

"I do, sir, I wish it delayed for *all* time! You surely cannot wish my hand, if my heart goes not with it!"

"Has that heart been given to another?" As the cunning officer asked this question, he intently gazed upon her countenance, as if he there could read the truth. Nor in this was he mistaken, for a deep blush overspread her fair face. She seemed to know this, and scorning all subterfuge, boldly answered,

"I have, sir, and who shall dare deny my right to do so!"

"Is it my rival the traitor—the horse thief?" asked the colonel, sneeringly.

"Did you call him by those names when you saw him at Monterey, and turned from his conquering blade to seek safety by a timely retreat!"

"Ha, lady! How knew you of this? The traitor must have met you, perchance he is even now lurking in the vicinity!"

"If so, than you had better keep well on your guard. Remember his mother and sister! Remember the oath of revenge!" The tone of the maiden in saying this was as cold and sneering as his own had been, and as she repeated the threat of the ranger, the villain quailed beneath the flashing glance of her dark eyes.

But he replied not to her remark, his brow grew darker as he drew a packet of papers from his breast, and handing them to her for perusal, remarked in a firm but fiendish tone:

"I trifle no longer with you, lady. We must be wed! There read and see if your father dare to refuse to urge the marriage on the appointed day!"

One by one the maiden read each document, and then reread their titles aloud. "An agreement for my marriage in two weeks from yesterday—a mortgage upon my father's estates, and a certificate of debt to the amount of thirty thousand dollars—the last two to be null upon the accomplishment of my marriage!"

For a moment the maiden looked upon her father, but his face was hidden in his hands. With wild energy she rushed to his feet, and as she held the papers before him, she cried:

"Are these true, my father? Oh, are you thus in his power?"

The father was dreadfully agitated and seemed unable to answer. The colonel saved him this trouble, for in a colder tone than ever, he said:

"Look upon the seals and attests—each document is true and perfect. You see that there is a debt heavy enough to make you all peons for life. The fate of your father and sister is in your hands. If you would see him, her, yourself, all *slaves*, then persist in your refusal to be mine!"

The fearful truth seemed to strike home to the very heart of the poor girl. One only hope seemed left to her, and that was delay.

"Oh, if it *must* be so, let me have time to be reconciled to my lot," she asked, in touching tones, "give me one year more of freedom!"

This stern answer came like ice to his soul.

"Lady, the agreement names two weeks, less one day. It must be fulfilled, or its forfeits shall be put in force!"

"Heartless monster, you know the love I bore my father, else you would never have brought me to this alternative! Be gone from my presence: if I must be yours at the end of two weeks, at least let me be freed from your hideous attentions during that time!"

"Lady, you shall have your own way in this, but at the hour appointed, I shall stand before you with a priest at my side, ready to make you mine!"

As he said this, he took again the papers from her hand, and turning short upon his heel, strode heavily from the apartment. She shuddered when she heard his words, but she heard not his low mutterings as he left the room.

He said:

"I go, lady-fair, but you shall have a keen watch kept over your motions! Nothing shall foil me now!"

The father only raised his head after Don Gustave was gone, and then it was to look upon his daughter, with an expression of unutterable agony. She saw his look, and throwing herself into his arms, said tenderly:

"Do not grieve, my father, your Magdalena blames you not; for your sake she will be at least equal to her fate!"

Still the stern old man could not speak the feelings which choked his very heart: he simply sobbed, "my child!" then burst in a flood of tears.

It was late in the afternoon of that day before Donna Magdalena found herself free from her attendance upon her father; but the moment that she could do so, she hurried to a well-shaded arbor in the garden, and beckoning an Indian boy, of nineteen or twenty years of age, to her side, asked:

"Zalupah, do you love me enough to risk your life to serve me?"

The young Indian, who was a delicately but active formed youth, with eyes dark as a thunder cloud, and bright as the lightning within it, answered:

"Let mistress try Zalupah; he will kill other men—he will kill himself for her!"

"I want no blood shed!" said the fair girl—"but I want you to take a long ride for me, and to deliver a message!"

"Zalupah is ready!" was the simple but all-expressive answer of the youth.

Donna Magdalena then described to him the location of the ranger camp, gave him the whistle, and severed a lock of her jetty hair, and bade him ride to the ranger's camp, and deliver it to him, whom the Indian well remembered as the wounded prisoner, and to tell him that the lady Magdalena was in peril, and wished him to meet her at midnight, on the second night from then, at the garden gate.

"Zalupah will go!" was all that the Indian said, as he left her side; yet Donna Magdalena knew that in his simple promise she could put more dependence than in all the oaths of more *civilized* men.

CHAPTER IX

Within the dense shade of a thick forest near Saltillo road was the ranger's camp, the location of which he had described to Magdalena. Brackett, with a chosen band of twenty well-armed and well-mounted friends, had been sent thus in advance by General Taylor to watch all of the motions of the enemy and make frequent reports; and he had chosen his general hiding place and rendezvous, because it was a convenient center, and an excellent spot for concealment. It was so near the main road that the tramp of any heavy body of men on the march could easily be heard, and still sufficiently distant for the trivial sounds of their own carefully-kept camp not to be noticed.

Within a small cleared space in the bushes, which was entirely surrounded by the thick undergrowth, the party clustered around the dying embers of a little fire, which had been built in a hole dug in a ground, in the Indian way, when they are on a war-party. Their horses were tied also within the circle, with bags, in which perchance corn had been, hung like muzzles below their mouths. There were only eighteen men by the fire; two, therefore, were acting as sentinels, or were absent on duty.

The party were all conversing in a low tone, and a little apart from the main body sat Brackett, with one other only by his side, this person from his dress appeared to be also an officer.

He was, and we will introduce the reader to Lieutenant Allen, a tall, finely-formed, fair-haired, light complexioned man, of about twenty-three or -four years of age. At the moment of introduction, Allen had requested Brackett to relate to him that portion of his history which had caused him to join the "bloody rangers" of Texas. To this Brackett sadly acceded, and thus ran his story:

"I was but a youngster at the time the Texans rose and declared themselves independent of Mexico, yet I well remember each era of that struggle. My father came into the country and settled upon the Austin grant just before that time, but he had been but a few days in the country when he died, leaving my mother, sister, and self with a small but comfortable property.

"I used daily to ride upon a little pony to school, about five miles from where we dwelt, going in the early morning while the dew lay upon the grass and flowers, and returning when the sun went down behind the forest.

"We thought little of danger when the war began, for we lived in a retired and a quiet spot in the country, and though we heard of many a fearful outrage at a distance, we little expected the enemy at our own door. One morning as I went forth to school, a bright, cloudless morning it was, one of those cool clear days when the birds sing louder than usual, and the flowers look brighter than ever, my dear mother and beautiful sister kissed me tenderly as they ever did, and I was never happier in my life, than when I rode away from the sweet little cottage which held them.

"I came back at night. The cottage was not there. Smoke arose from smoldering embers where it had stood. Oh, God! The agony of that moment! I rushed to the side of the expiring fire—I called upon the names of my mother and my sister, yet no answer came. I ran madly through our little garden, and saw the flowers had been trampled down—I reached my sister's favorite bower, the lattice of which I had myself made; the vines which shaded it, I had planted. Before I reached it, I heard a feeble moan, this hastened my steps, and soon I saw—oh, God of Mercy! such a sight as never—never will leave me. My mother lay dead upon the ground—my sister by her side, with just strength enough to tell me the fearful fates which she and her wretched mother had endured, and to say that the hellish wrong had been perpetrated by an officer whom she described, and who had commanded a scouting party of lancers.

"She told me this—and then she died."

While the speaker related this dreadful story, the big drops of perspiration gathered upon his pale face; the agony of a life-time's misery seemed to be centered in his soul. After a moment's pause he went on:

"I buried them—there on the ground where they died, there I buried them with my own hand. Then I knelt down over their corpses, and swore by the holy love which I had borne for my mother; by the almost idolatrous regard which I held for my sister; by the noble blood which coursed through my veins; by the almighty God who made me to be revenged! To live for nothing but to avenge that fearful, nameless wrong which all the blood of Mexico could not wash away!"

"And that oath?" asked Allen.

"Has not yet been fulfilled. I tracked and traced the fiendish officer till I secured his name, and knew his person. Gustave Alfrede yet lives, but his time is coming!"

"Is he not a colonel of lancers? Was he not at Monterey?"

"He is and was. He is now quartered but a few miles from here. I am watching him as the falcon eyes his prey. I will make him swoop when I am sure to reach him!"

"By heavens! Captain, in this, as in all things, I am doubly yours. Whenever the time comes let me aid in his punishment."

"You shall, my friend. His time is near. He is now endeavoring to force a marriage with one that I love; but he will find himself forestalled in all his aims."

The other was about to speak, when a low whistle was heard in the direction of the road. Both started, but they sat quietly down again as they saw that it was the absent two of the party. These rode up to the fire and dismounted.

One of them hurried to Brackett and handed him several papers, saying:

"I just took these, sir, from a courier beyond Saltillo. He seemed in a hurry, but I sent him a request from my rifle to stop, which he *red*-dily complied with, and then I *rifled* his pouch of these papers."

"They are valuable dispatches. General Taylor must have them immediately!" said Brackett, who had hastily looked them over while the other was speaking. "Take fresh horses," he added, "and ride at once to the camp with them!"

The man hastened to obey these orders. The excitement of the moment had produced a flush upon the ranger's face, which now faded away as he continued:

"After all this had passed, you need not ask *why* I joined the rangers. When and how, I will tell you. The battle of San Jacinto was raging, the foes were ten to one of the Texans.[26] Just at the moment when the latter were preparing for their last desperate charge upon the enemy, a boy—a mere boy, dashed into their lines, mounted on a small black Indian pony, which was white with foam. In the hand of the boy was a long hunting-knife—he had no other weapon. He arrived just at the moment when the gallant Houston had ordered the charge, and without touching bridle, or looking to the right or the left, that young boy led the way in the charge which won that day. On—on, amongst the flying foe, riding close to their sides, and driving his long knife home to the hilt in every Mexican whom he could reach, the boy rode. The Texans looked upon him as a supernatural being. Unharmed, unscathed, he dashed into the thickest of the fray, and his shrill cry—'revenge, revenge!' rung sharp and loud amongst them; yet no one knew who or what he was. He continued amongst the foremost in the chase, until not a foe could be found, and then sunk exhausted from his pony. The rangers who had seen his actions on that day, now picked him up, and bore him carefully to their camp. He soon recovered—his simple but dreadful tale was soon told, and from that hour he became one of them. He was at Mier—he was at Resaca—Monterey—that boy is now by your side!"

So much had Allen become excited by this strange and thrilling recital, that he could not give utterance to his feelings. He could only grasp his friend's hand and say:

"By heaven! It is too much! I am yours for revenge, soul and body—now and forever!"

The ranger was on the point of replying, when again a low whistle was heard in the direction of the road; in the next moment a horseman was seen slowly pushing through the bushes, peering around as if he knew not exactly where he was going, or what he was searching for. Seeing that in his dress and appearance he was decidedly Mexican, nearly half of the rangers sprang to their feet and raised their rifles. One moment more and the imprudent stranger would have met his death, but Brackett who thought that he had seen that dark face before, bade his men drop their pieces, and stepped out from the thicket where he could be seen.

Uttering a cry of pleasure when he saw him, the dark rider advanced to the ranger, holding out in his hand a long tress of jetty hair.

The face of Brackett turned pale as he saw it, and paler still when the Indian boy of Magdalena, (for it was he,) said:

"Zalupah has found El Senor Americano! Mistress wants you tomorrow night at the garden,—bad times for poor mistress!"

"What is the matter—is she in peril?" asked the ranger, trembling with anxiety.

"Zalupah was told to bring lock of hair to Senor Americano, and to tell him mistress wants him. Zalupah knows no more."

"Ride back, good boy, and tell the lady that I will be there, and beware how you speak upon the road or elsewhere of having met me."

"Zalupah understands," said the Indian, and in a moment his bridle was turned again toward the road.

When the ranger returned to his companion, he said:

"Allen, I shall have to leave the camp in your charge again, tomorrow. I have duty to perform which requires my personal attendance."

"Has it anything to do with that lock of hair which you have wrapped so carelessly around your fingers?" asked the lieutenant.

"Yes, this is a sign that I had agreed upon with one who is persecuted by Gustave Alfrede, the murderer of my mother and sister. She needs my assistance, and I must hasten to give it."

"You surely will not go alone?"

"Yes, for I think that she is in no immediate danger, else her messenger would have known it. She probably wishes to inform me of some change in her prospects."

"It is dangerous for you to ride about alone, through a country filled with foes."

"I fear little for such danger while I've a good horse under me, and trusty weapons in my hand," replied the ranger.

"Where do you go on this mission?"

"Even I cannot tell you now. I will return before the day after tomorrow," replied the ranger, "in the mean time keep up the surveillance of the road. All reports of importance must go at once to the general."

In a short time the young commander of the spies was in his saddle, bending his way through the forest cautiously, his horse's head turned to the southward.

CHAPTER X

It was nearly midnight, the night when Donna Magdalena expected the ranger to meet her at the garden gate. Zalupah had returned home and told her that he would be there and now, with all the impatience of a new-born love, and all the anxiety which her situation had inspired, she was upon the spot, awaiting his arrival. Her beating heart often misled her and caused her to think that she heard his horse's galloping hoofs, but she had looked out many times in vain.—The moon had not arisen yet, had it she might, perhaps, have seen that her every motion was watched, and that her father's house was surrounded by spies, the chief of whom, Don Gustave himself, was within a few feet of her, so near that he could hear the sighs that ever and anon broke from her heaving bosom. But she knew it not.

At last the hour approached, and as she bent her ear eagerly forward, she indeed heard the sound of a courser's hoofs borne upon the breeze, and in a moment more he—her lover was by her side. Springing from his horse he folded his arms around her beautiful form and for the first time in life their lips met in the warm touch of love. She did not turn from him with any cold mock modesty: she did not try to hide the natural blush which came and went like the flushes of sunset on a summer sky, upon her cheek: she returned both the embrace and the salute with an ardor which, while it spoke her own feelings, was like burning fire to the heart of him who stood crouching in the shade near the gate, the cunning Alfrede.—When he had threatened to watch her motions he had been in earnest, and if she had but heard his threat she might have been more careful. He had seen the Indian boy returning from the direction of the mountains, with a horse evidently jaded by travel, and he at once felt suspicious that something was concealed in this boy's unusual ride, especially as he knew the boy to be a favorite with Magdalena. Hence the cause of the watch which he had set around her, and which he headed in person.

"You are kind, senor," said the blushing girl—as she withdrew herself from the embrace of the young ranger, and led him to a seat close to the gate—"You are very kind to come so promptly to me. I little thought that when you gave me the whistle and bade me send for you in case of need, that the necessity was so near at hand!"

"What is your danger, dear lady?"

"My father has given a written agreement to that detestable wretch, Alfrede, that I shall marry him within less than two weeks. He has, I know not how, got my father completely sworn to force me to the dreadful sacrifice!"

"Ha—ha, *sworn* did you say? I too have sworn, and the hour is drawing nigh when my oath shall be fulfilled—but why do you start to tremble?"

"I thought I heard a sound as of someone breathing heavily near us!" responded the girl.

"It is only my horse panting—I rode rapidly, for I had to make a circuit to avoid some new outposts, and I feared to be late to our tryst!" said the other, and then added: "Do you know the day when he proposes to attempt this marriage, and where he will try to have the ceremony performed?"

"In two weeks less four days now, and he said that here to my father's house he would bring the priest who should rivet the chain which would make me far, far worse than a slave!"

"I will attend the wedding party, and I will not come alone! I will bring goodly company to assist at the feast, men who will bring their own knives and forks and be their own carvers!"

"How, senor, do I understand you?"

"I will be here in time to forbid the banns lady. He shall have a bride on that day, but it shall be such a bride as the villain deserves. Cold steel shall be all that he shall hug to his breast."

"Hark—I surely heard footsteps.—Oh, I fear that we are watched!" said the timid girl.

"Oh no, 'tis but the breeze rising as the moon comes up; you can see the limbs are beginning to move. None would be astir about your father's house this hour."

"No, yet I know not why, but my heart is filled with an involuntary dread, a kind of unconscious warning that an enemy is near, or danger in our vicinity!"

"You are too timid, dear one—I apprehend no danger. And now let me ask one more question. When the villain Alfrede brings hither his priest, and I come to render the services of that priest useless to *him*, it would be cruel to cheat the reverend gentleman out of a job. Will you not promise then to be *mine*?"

"While our countries are at war? While we are foes by nationality? Oh, no— wait till the war is over and then—"

"Why do you hesitate, say all!" cried the young ranger, trembling with anxious suspense.

"Then, if you still desire it, then I will be yours!"

"It will not be long then, dear one, for soon a peace must ensue, and when the happy day arrives—"

"You will not be alive to see it!" said a harsh but well known voice at his side, and ere Brackett could move or lay his hand upon a weapon his arms were pinioned from behind, and several stout men held and surrounded him.

"Oh God, it is *he*! All is lost!" cried Magdalena, as she sprung still closer to his side, and clasped her arms around him.

"No, not lost yet"—he quickly whispered, "the boy—let him fly to my band with news!" The noise of the struggle had served to conceal that he had spoken to her, and when Don Gustave tore her from the side of the ranger he knew not that already had one way of rescue been thought of and planned.

Her shriek as she found herself and lover surrounded, had already aroused the inmates of her father's house, and soon they began to gather thickly into the garden, and in a few moments the voice of the old don was heard as he inquired what was the meaning of the alarm.

"I have only been interrupting a little love-chapter in which your virtuous daughter has borne a prominent part!" said Alfrede, rudely pushing the pale girl toward her father.

The latter looked one moment at her, then at the prisoner, whom he recognized by the light of the torches which the domestics had brought out, and then in tones deep, and low, and sad, he asked:

"Is it true, Magdalena? Have you held a midnight meeting with yon traitor, one who is an outlaw and a foe?"

"I have met yon noble cavalier, sir," replied the girl, her color returning with her pride—"I met him at midnight, and have been watched over by the low spy and villain who disgraces in a thousand ways the uniform which he wears, him to whom you would wed a *Valdez,* one of the proudest names in Spain!"

"A *Valdez*?" repeated Brackett, while a shade of astonishment seemed to cross over his brow. No one, however, heeded this remark, but the father responded to the daughter:

"Girl—I little thought this of you! I have ever treated you kindly—I have been ever lenient to you, but now it is time to adopt more severe measures.—When you can disgrace the name of Valdez by holding stolen interviews in the shadow of night with an unknown vagabond, you need not object to linking it with that of any cavalier who will do you the honor to look upon you!"

Again the prisoner repeated slowly the name of Valdez. There was something in it, which seemed to touch upon his ear with singular effect.

"Don Ignatio, once more I shall have to make a temporary prison of your house—and this time I will see that no escape will take place!" said Alfrede.

"My house is at your service, Don Gustave, and that the prisoner may not again receive aid from my recreant daughter, she too shall learn the use of bolts and bars. She has said that she wished to be freed from your presence until the day of her marriage. She shall have her will, for until that day, she shall enjoy the solitude of a prison!"

"Let her room be one that looks out upon the road, if you please, Don Ignatio. There will be a court-martial held here on the morrow, and if I err not in my judgment, the next morning's sun will rise for the last time upon yon low-born spy!"

"Low-born, did he say? Is the name of Valdez that of one of the proudest of Spain's families?" His tone was too low to be heard, yet when Brackett thus spoke, there seemed to be a deep meaning in his words, and while he gazed steadily upon the face of Don Ignatio, he murmured:

"It must be so—he is very like!"

While all this was going on, Magdalena had not been seen; she had bent her head down as if it was to conceal the feelings which overcame her, but while her head was bound so low, she had torn even up by the roots, a tress of her jetty hair, for she had no chance to sever it, and then having caught the eye of her faithful Zalupah, who stood among the crowd of servants, she had dropped it upon a bush where he could reach it unobserved, and then looked toward the gate. The faithful boy knew the meaning of the glance and sigh, and at once divined the wishes of his mistress.—While the others moved slowly on toward the house, he dropped behind, unobserved, and as soon as the garden was clear, took up the jetty token which the maiden had left upon the bush, then mounting the ranger's splendid horse, was in a few moments riding at full speed toward the camp of the latter, to bear the news of his arrest.

Don Ignatio was somewhat surprised when he heard the prisoner request a private interview with him, as they led him away to the same room which he had formerly occupied, but as the colonel had no fear of treason in him, and made no objections to the interview, he consented to it.

The door of the prison room was closed upon them. Then Brackett, whose arms were still pinioned, seated himself upon the settee, which had before time been his couch.

"Well, sir, what is the reason of your desire to see me alone; what can you have in common with the father of her whose affections you have inveigled, and whom you come to see by stealth, at midnight, like a common thief?"

"Senor," replied the ranger, "I asked not for this interview to hear reproaches—but to satisfy my curiosity upon one point."

"Well, sir, go on, let me know the point."

"You heard that cowardly colonel of lancers, call me *low-born*!"

"Well, sir, I know not that he was in error there."

"Did you not speak of the name and family of Valdez being ranked amongst the noblest of Spain's chivalry?"

"I did so speak, and I shall even so maintain!"

"And yet I am *low-born*!" said the ranger in a tone of bitterness.

"What has your birth to do with the name Valdez?" asked Don Ignatio, haughtily, and as he saw that the other hesitated in his answer, he added—"speak, sir, and say that which you have to say speedily; I have little time for dallying here!"

"Did you ever know Isabella Marin y Valdez?" asked the ranger, and as he spoke he regarded Don Ignatio with a searching look. But it need not any searching gaze to detect the surprise which came over the haughty Castillian when he heard that name.

"Know *her*?" he cried; "say where *you* have heard that name; oh! What know you of her?"

"She *was* my mother; she is now an angel in Heaven!"

"Your mother? Oh, man—man! Prove that you speak the truth; prove it, else I will curse you for bringing up her memory in vain to me. It is many years since I have seen her. Our father opposed her marriage to a foreigner; she eloped with him, and I have never seen my only and dearly loved sister since, or had a trace of her. Prove that you are her son, or I will curse you for a base liar!"

"Look upon this ring," said the ranger, showing a massive seal graven with a coat of arms, "here is her family arms!"

The old Castillian looked upon the ring, then looked long and steadily upon the face of the ranger. For long minutes he regarded each feature, then, as if speaking to himself, said:

"The ring must have been stolen—but *her* features never! Yes, you are, you must be my nephew. Your name—what is it?"

"Charles Brackett!"

"What was the name of her husband—yes, Brackett was the name! Is he dead?"

"Yes, father, mother, sister, and *all* gone, and the last—oh! ask that fiend Gustave Alfrede how they died!"

"He—has he ever seen them?"

"Go ask him, ask him how they died. He is their murderer, their worse than murderer!"

The young man bent low his head, and whispered but a few words to that old man, yet these words were like the blighting frost of death unto that hearer. His face blanched, his form quivered, his eyes seemed as if about to start from their sockets, his whole appearance changed. He gasped for breath; then in tones husky with horror he groaned:

"Oh! Holy God; can all this be true! Is he the fiend that would shame the very thing of hell! And he would wed my daughter. By the God of justice, he shall die!"

The horrified Don Ignatio was about to rush forth from the apartment, when he was met at the door by the villain himself, who had again played the part of a spy and listener.

With a cold sneer, the colonel said:

"You need not trouble yourself to change your quarters, Don Ignatio; you had best stay here to console your new-found nephew, for he is near the end of his days!"

"What mean you, base dog? I surely am not a prisoner in my own house?"

"You certainly are, and likely to be for some time, if you address me in terms so exceedingly flattering!"

"Sir, I demand my release instantly!"

"I regret that it is not convenient for me to accede to your request!" said the colonel, still in the same bitter and contemptuous tone.

The exasperated Castillian was about to rush upon the villain, who opposed his path, but a glance beyond him showed a line of sentinels with presented lances, and he only gasped:

"Oh, God! My poor daughter—what will now become of her?"

"She will be my bride in twenty-four hours. I shall give her that time for preparation, and no longer. The hour that makes her mine, ends the life of yon *high-born* braggart, for he shall witness the ceremony before he dies!"

"Oh, God, protect us all!" gasped the unhappy father, while with a fiendish laugh the demon-like Alfrede heavily closed the door upon the prisoner, and, after bidding his lancers guard it at the peril of their lives, he turned away to seek the unhappy Magdalena, and to inform her of his intentions.

"Twenty-four hours," murmured Brackett, after the door closed—"twenty-four hours—if the messenger has gone, there will be yet time; but oh, God, if his path should be intercepted, if he should not reach Allen, then indeed are we in this fiend's power!"

CHAPTER XI

The second night had arrived—the night of doom for Magdalena and her unfortunate lover. It was a strange bridal party that. The father was present, but he stood a prisoner between two lancers; Brackett was there, but he still was pinioned; the maiden alone stood free unbound, and never, never had she worn a look of greater dignity, a more beautiful appearance. Strange as it may seem, she was comparatively calm, though her eye ever and anon wandered with a quick, anxious glance toward the door.

Alfrede, too, looked often toward the door, and the reason could easily be told, for he stamped his spurred boot heavily upon the floor, and in tones which betokened his impatience, cried:

"Curses on the head of that laggard priest, why comes he not?"

The domestics of the house, with pale countenances, stood in a corner of the apartment, near the door, wondering what next was to happen, for, though devotedly attached to their master, they were completely overawed by the superior force of well-armed soldiers, who guarded the house.

Toward this group the eye of Magdalena turned, as she saw a slight bustle amongst them, and that eye brightened with joy as she saw a new addition to their number, and in him recognized her faithful Indian boy. A look of intelligence passed between them, the Indian in it signified that all was right; but the keen eye of Alfrede was already upon him, and darting into the cowering crowd of servants, he caught the slight form of the boy in his grasp, and dashing him to the floor, placed his sword's point at his throat, shouting:

"Where have you been, you black dog? What treason have you and your mistress been hatching now? Speak, or by the God who made you, this moment is your last!"

The Indian neither moved nor spoke. The sword of the enraged officer was raised to strike the fatal blow, when at the instant he was nerving his arm for its descent, his weapon was dashed from his hand by the heroic Magdalena, who had snatched a weapon from a soldier who stood near her. At the same moment the two doors of the apartment were burst open, and Allen and his rangers with presented rifles filled the room. The lancers saw these dreaded weapons and in an instant dropped their arms. Aflrede alone would have resisted, but his weapon was gone, and in a moment he was pinioned, while Don Ignatio and Brackett were once more free.

At this moment the priest arrived, and now Magdalena, with all of the arch mockery of manner which she could assume, walked up to Alfrede, and asked him if he was ready to have the ceremony proceed.

The discomfited villain would not answer, but his face was a picture of all that was working within his breast, hell itself would have been a paradise to it.

But it seemed now as if his cup was not full, for Don Ignatio, who had been conversing in a low tone with Brackett, turned to his daughter and asked:

"Magdalena, do you love this cavalier?"

"I do, my father," answered the blushing girl.

"Wilt thou wed him? My consent is given, for he is thine equal in birth, he is thy cousin!"

"My cousin?" asked the bewildered maiden.

"Yes, my child; thy father's nephew—Charles Brackett, the son of my sister!"

Pale turned the face of Gustave Alfrede as he heard these words, and paler still when Don Ignatio approached him, and hissed one word in his ear. It was but a word—"*remember*!" and yet it sounded like a death knell unto him.

Again he heard it, louder still from the lips of Brackett, that fearful word—"remember!"

Oh, there is to the guilty something more terrible in *memory*, than in all other things. It gives a double terror, for it links the past with the present and the future.

At this moment the gentle Ximena appeared, having been informed by the domestics of the happy change which had ensued in her family's situation, and after her father had feebly explained to her and Magdalena the relationship of Brackett, he once more proposed that they should be united upon the spot, by the priest whom Alfrede had sent for.

To this no objections were made, and then, at the still, solemn hour of midnight, before all those witnesses, Charles Brackett was united to his beautiful cousin. While the ceremony was being performed, the firing of cannons was heard in the direction of Saltillo, and Allen hastily dispatched a couple of his scouts to see what it meant. The ceremony had been over but a few moments when these returned, and reported that the garrison of Saltillo was in full retreat along the road toward the house, thus showing that the American force under Worth had arrived in the town.[27]

For a moment only, Brackett paused to consider how he should act. The scouts reported that the enemy were several thousand strong; he knew that resistance would be useless; therefore he determined at once to retreat with his prisoners, leaving Don Ignatio and his family at home, for he knew that they, of course, would be safe, and he could rejoin them on the morrow. To this plan Don Ignatio gave his assent, and snatching a hasty kiss from his bride Brackett, and Allen, with his rangers, left the house, taking with them Alfrede and his disarmed band of lancers. In a few moments, all were in their saddle, and Brackett started with them up a ravine which, by a circuitous route, led to the rear of Saltillo. The moon had now arisen, and it was a beautiful sight to see those armed men file silently along, now in shadow, then in light; now hidden in some little glen, then emerging over some little hillock where horse and rider would lay their shadows upon the rocks beyond them. And it was a beautiful sight, but not a very romantic one to them, at least not a pleasant one, when they saw ahead of them, riding down the same ravine, a body of the enemy's lancers; and as they knew that, encumbered as they were, it would be impossible for them to break through this force, they determined to turn rein and seek another and safer route.

This was done; but soon Brackett found that the danger in his rear was greater than that in front, for the main body of the retreating army occupied the road, and it was now impossible to avoid one or the other of them. He held a rapid consultation with Allen, as to how he should dispose of the prisoners. The advice of the latter, was to free all except Alfrede, and to kill him upon the spot, then to cut their way through the lancers in the front. But all of this did not suit the too noble mind of the young ranger captain. His foe was in his power, but he could not *murder* even him in cold blood. "Oh, that I had but five minutes left to us on a fair field, I would let God prove the right!" he cried; "but I cannot kill him without a weapon in his hands. I had intended to have tried him regularly, by a jury, and to have hung him for a murdering dog as he is; but I cannot slay even him in cold blood, when he is entirely in my power!"

The party had in this time come to a halt and Alfrede, who was bound upon his horse and rode between two of the rangers, cast uneasy glances around him, for he seemed to know that the conference between Allen and Brackett concerned him, especially as Allen had used several pantomimic actions, such as laying his hand upon the hilt of his heavy bowie knife, pointing to his throat, and so forth; and the villain feared that the ranger would act as would *he* have done, had the tables been turned and they in his power.

Brackett, at last, with a singular smile, said to Allen:

"I have formed my plan, George, we cannot afford to be hampered with prisoners!" Then riding to the center, where they were sitting, bound upon their horses without arms, he bade his men turn the prisoners' reins to the south, and, speaking to them in their own tongue, he bade them ride to the army and thank their stars that he did not slay them on the spot. But when he reached the side of the black-hearted Alfrede, his look was fearfully dark and ominous. The lancer officer turned pale as death, when he saw the ranger deliberately draw his large bowie knife from its sheath, and as the latter approached him, he shuddered, and gasped:

"For the love of God, sir, do not murder me!"

He trembled more than ever, as he saw the unrelenting expression of the ranger's face, and when he saw that bright, broad-bladed knife raised in the air, he closed his eyes, for he thought that his time had come.

The next moment he felt its keen edge, as Brackett, with a quick and skillful hand, cut a gash into the bone, down the center of his forehead, from the hair to the spot where his dark eyebrows met, and then he thought he was to suffer a most painful death, and again gasped:

"If I must die, oh, kill me outright, do not torture me!"

But the ranger spoke not a single word to him, he again raised the blade, now darkened at its edge with blood, and with the same skillful touch, drew a gash horizontal to the other, thus making upon his forehead a large red cross.

"Now, thou dog of hell, I've marked you, so that when we next meet, be it in the smoke-cloud of battle, or in the glimmering light of a starry night, I may know you; and when next we meet, remember that I will fulfill the oath of revenge! Think not to escape me—you are *marked*, and if I should die, every friend I have on earth would dog you by the sign of the bloody cross upon your brow!"

With a groan of mingled pain and rage, and fear, the marked villain heard these words, then saw Brackett turn his horse's head to the south, and drive his pointed knife deep into the tender flank of the animal. With maddened speed the horse bounded off toward the Mexican army, bearing his helpless rider along with him

When this was done the ranger quickly formed his little band into a solid phalanx, himself taking the head, and Allen, much against his will, but in obedience to orders, closing up the rear.

"You must ride and fight for your lives now, men! Keep close, support each other, and follow me!" said Brackett in a low tone.

For a moment there was a tightening of each man's grasp upon his rein, a movement to fix his seat firmer in the saddle; then again their commander's low tone was heard:

"Spurs will avail you more than your blades. Draw only a revolver, press close upon me, and drive through their ranks! It is your only chance, we are but twenty, they at least a thousand!"

Then, as the moon's rays glanced down upon bright lance-heads, and a forest of waving pennons, which were now close upon them, their brave leader shouted:

"*Forward*!"

With one wild cheer, they sank their rowels deep into their horses' flanks, then on, on they dashed like one huge black wave rolling up singly and alone over a thousand lesser breakers on some rugged shore. One moment more and they were upon their foe, and then their leader shouted again:

"*Fire—give them lead*!"

And the little band poured in a rapid volley from their unerring revolvers. Had the foe met this charge boldly, like men, it would have been much easier for the heroic little band to have cut its way through them; but they reeled back in confusion, and the foremost of them attempted to fly. This threw their whole column into a medley mess, and made it impossible for the rangers to ride through them, though they succeeded in penetrating to some distance, but this, in the narrow ravine, made their situation still worse.

"To your knives, boys,—give them steel now!" shouted their captain, and then the fearful bowie knife began its murderous work. But the Mexicans were not idle now, for they saw how few were their enemies in number, and they fought for very shame. The rangers now began to drop one by one, by the side of their gallant leader, yet for every one of them fell many of the foe.

The commander of the lancers, a noble looking, gray-headed man of the uniform of a general, now shouted to Brackett, begging him to yield, promising, on his honor, to treat him with the courtesies of a prisoner of war.

Brackett looked around him—more than half his men were gone, the rest were fighting gallantly; but he knew it was in vain that they struggled against such fearful weight of numbers, and he asked to whom he must surrender, if he yielded.

"To General Vasquez, of the regular army!" was the reply of the gray-headed officer whom we have above alluded to. Brackett knew that this officer, by reputation, was one of the most gallant and brave in the Mexican army; he also knew that gallantry and honor in a soldier, are inseparable; therefore, to save the lives of his gallant comrades, he surrendered his sword to Vasquez.[28]

The rangers were then surrounded by a strong guard, and their horses' heads turned toward the southward. The Mexicans were on the retreat to San Luis Potosi, where Santa Anna was collecting an overwhelming force, with which he had pledged himself to the "magnanimous Mexican nation," to drive "the perfidious Yankees" beyond their utmost borders.

CHAPTER XII

*I*t was morning. The "flag of the free" waved on the battlements of Saltillo. Not an armed Mexican was to be seen in its streets, all was quiet and orderly, more so than perchance it ever had been before. But few of the houses were closed, the citizens seemed perfectly at their ease as they opened their shop doors to trade with the new comers, or perambulated the streets to gaze upon them at their different posts. Saltillo had been taken—bloodlessly, noiselessly, and now not a sound of rejoicing over an humbled *foe* was heard from the lips of the victors; they were quiet, orderly, as well behaved as they would have been here in our own cities.

Oh noble—noble has been the conduct of the American victors in this war. Let their conduct at Monterey be held up as an example to a whole world. For weary days they fought before that rich city—hundreds of their best and bravest fell before their eyes, yet when the victory was gained and a rich city lay open before them, when the temptations of uncounted wealth came and knocked at their hearts, though they were suffering for clothes and food, not one of our noble little army was known to commit a single outrage upon the vanquished foe, even though there were men there whose relatives had been butchered in the "Alamo," or whose families had been robbed and murdered on the gory plains of Texas.

Oh, let such conduct be written in letters of gold on the fairest pages of our country's history, that every American heart in ages yet to come may proudly point to the starriest spot in all our glorious escutcheon.

It was morning, and not a Mexican soldier was in sight from the casa at Buena Vista.

Yet there was mourning and sorrow in that house, for they had heard the firing on the night before, immediately after the departure of Brackett, and knew by this that he had been intercepted.

Sleep came not to the eyes of the newly wedded bride on that night and soon as the dawn came to light up the east, the servants were dispatched up the ravine to see if they could gather news of the rangers.

Soon they returned, bearing with them one of the rangers, whom they found still alive upon the battle-field. The rest who had fallen were all dead, but they lay amid a heap of fallen foes, enough in number to have hidden them from sight.

The one whom the servants brought in was dying, yet he lived long enough to tell the fate of his comrades, and to say what had become of Alfrede and his lancers, and to tell how the latter had been marked for vengeance.

Pale turned the cheek of poor Magdalena when she learned that her husband was a prisoner in the hands of her countrymen, and that Alfrede was again free, and had now a double incentive for revenge.

The fears of Don Ignatio, too, were excited, and he determined at once to communicate with General Worth at Saltillo, and inform him of the fate of the rangers, in order if possible to have them exchanged or rescued in some way.

Magdalena, too, formed a determination, bold as it was sudden, and one that showed well what a *true* woman's heart is capable of when she loves and her beloved is in danger. To let the reader into the secret of this, we must give them the substance of a scene which occurred in the favorite arbor of Donna Magdalena in the garden.

She had gone hither, taking with her Zalupah, the faithful Indian boy, whom the reader already knows.

When they were secure from observation, she said:

"Zalupah, do you love your new master, the noble cavalier to whom I was married last night?"

"Zalupah loves all who love his mistress!" replied the boy.

"Your new master is a prisoner!"

"Zalupah is sorry; he will go help to get him away!"

"You cannot go alone; he has many guards!"

"Zalupah can crawl like a snake in the grass, get close to guard, stab 'em, and let his new master out of prison!"

"If they catch you they will kill you!"

"Can't die but once, Zalupah isn't afraid to die. His father died long time ago!"

"But you will need help. I will go with you, Zalupah,"

The boy's black eyes dilated with wonder and astonishment as he heard this. Shaking his head, he said:

"Mistress go? Oh no! feet too small, road too long. Bad man see her, bad man treat her cruel. Colonel Alfrede not dead yet—Zalupah will kill him when he catch him, but mistress must stay here. Zalupah will go alone!"

"No—I shall go with you!" replied the maiden bride firmly—"You must get me a dress like your own, Zalupah. I shall stain my hands and face dark, and dress like you. Nobody will know me then!"

"Foot and hand too small—shape too pretty!" said the Indian, and again he shook his head.

In a tone now so firm that he dared not disobey it, however so much he wished, Magdalena bade him provide her with a dress like his own, with good weapons, and to have two of her father's best horses saddled and ready for the journey as soon as darkness came over the sky. She had determined to follow her lover and to effect his rescue, or to perish by his side.

We will now follow the fortunes of the unfortunate ranger and his companions, who were retreating with the Mexican army toward San Luis Potosi.

They halted not until they had reached Guadalupo on the next evening, for they thought that the whole American army was in pursuit.

It was not until this halt took place that Colonel Alfrede, who, with a patch over his forehead to conceal his disfigurement, had ridden on in moody silence, at the head of his corps, learned of the capture of Brackett and his comrades, for his wounded and frightened horse had borne him far beyond the sound of the pistols, ere the combat began, which had resulted in their capture.

Our pen cannot paint the fiendish joy which filled his breast when he heard that Brackett was captured, and he at once flew to General Vasquez, and demanded that the prisoner should be turned over to him.

"On what grounds do you claim him—what right have you to him?" asked the general, sternly.

"He was an escaped prisoner from me—I had captured him but the evening before!" replied the colonel, who in his eagerness betrayed his enmity.

"Then in losing possession of him, you lost also all right to him!" replied the old general.

"He is a spy and a traitor! I demand that he be tried and treated as such!" cried the colonel, now excited beyond the bounds of prudence.

"He surrendered to me as a prisoner of war, after gallantly fighting till half of his men were slain, and as a prisoner of war, as a brave and honorable man shall he be treated till he is exchanged for some officer of our own his rank, who meets with a fortune similar to his!"

"Exchanged!—What, shall he escape me! Sir, he is my enemy. Look here!" and the enraged officer tore the patch from his forehead—"look at this, sir! This is his mark,—shall a man live who dares to treat me so? Think you that I shall let him escape my vengeance? No—by the high God of Heaven! *No*!"

"Sir, if you threaten thus the life of my prisoner, perchance you may find yourself placed beyond the power of harming him! Use but one more tone or gesture so disrespectful as your last, and I place you under arrest!"

The colonel saw that he had gone too far, and in a lower tone, said:

"I beg your pardon, General Vasquez, but he is an ancient enemy of mine, and that, with this last damning insult, is enough to drive me beyond all bounds."

"Have you never given him cause for enmity, sir; have you never injured him?" asked the general still speaking with unbending sternness.

The colonel's face flushed and darkened as this question was asked, and the general, noticing this, turned to an orderly near him and bade him bring Captain Brackett before him! The colonel now endeavored to make an excuse to leave the spot, but his countenance had paled too suddenly to allay any of the suspicions of the cunning old general, and in a tone more severe than before, he ordered him to remain until the prisoner had confronted him.

In a moment more the sworn foes stood face to face.

When General Vasquez asked of Brackett the cause of this terrible enmity, and while he listened to the harrowing tale of wrong, frequent and loud were his bitter tones of condemnation; and when Brackett related the scene where he had affixed the Cain-like mark upon him, the honest hearted general cried:

"'Tis well that he is thus marked! It and its cause shall be known throughout the army, and no worse punishment can be inflicted than that which draws down upon him hissings and the universal scorn of the whole army: the contempt of all honorable men!"

Then turning to the colonel, whose face was livid with mortification and rage, he added, in cold and bitter tones:

"Go, thou disgrace to a soldier's name; go, and if I ever find you near my quarters again, you shall be whipped from the vicinity by the scullions of my camp!"

The colonel attempted to speak, but the choleric old general burst out with a fresh volley of invectives:

"Begone, thou Cain; begone from my sight. I hope that soon I shall have a chance to exchange or free my gallant prisoner; for I sigh for the time when I may hear that he has met thee once more upon a fair field!"

The colonel, now completely discomfited, turned away, his face presenting a picture which would well have suited one who wished to make a painting of a devil in hell.

"I can reach you yet!" he hissed, in tones that, from the fearful import of the threat which followed, went like ice to the heart of Brackett, who alone heard them—"I can reach you yet, my revenge shall be the deeper that it is through another, and doubly shall it fall upon you: for *she* shall *now* be mine!"

These words were indeed fearful to the ranger. He knew that his virgin bride and her family were without a protector now; he knew the fiendish feelings and wild lust which filled the heart of his enemy, and he trembled for those whom he could not now protect.

He would have given worlds now to have recalled the act of mercy, the feeling which induced him to spare the villain when he had him in his power. These feelings were only the more increased when, to his utter agony of heart, a short time afterwards, he saw the fiend ride off to the northward with a small body of lancers in his train, and his tortured mind was left to paint a thousand horrors. He saw his helpless bride shrieking in the lustful villain's arms, shrieking in vain for aid from others; for mercy from him! Oh, God! Who—who can paint the feelings of a husband's heart in such a situation. It is far—far beyond our feeble powers.

CHAPTER XIII

*N*ever did mortal suffer greater agony of mind than the unhappy Brackett in his prison at San Luis Potosi. His only friend amongst the enemy, General Vasquez, was now too intently engaged in drilling his brigade and preparing for the next contest, to visit him. Amongst the group of officers whom he could see among the Plaza which fronted his prison grates, he never could see the hated form of Alfrede, and his mind was left to imagine all kind of horrible possibilities.

The few days he had been confined there had been to him as months. If he would have given his parole not to attempt to escape he would have been allowed the freedom of the city; but this would not do, for he ever hoped for some opportunity to escape. He was confined separately from the rest of his band: therefore had nothing to cheer his mind up, or to drive away the fearful visions which continually rose before him.

We will now take the opportunity of chasing Colonel Alfrede on his mission of revenge.

True to his threat and purpose, he had bent his course back to Buena Vista; but when he arrived there he found that not only Magdalena was absent, but also Don Ignatio and Ximena. From some of the frightened domestics he gained the information that Donna Magdalena was missing, her father and sister knew not where, and that the latter had fled to the city and placed themselves under the protection of the Americans. His first act was to set fire to the building, and soon all, save its massive walls of stone, was destroyed. With a fiendish smile of exultation, he watched this scene of devastation; but when he saw that troops were dispatched from the city to reconnoiter it and its cause, he hastily withdrew with his forces.

On learning that Donna Magdalena was not with her father and sister, and had suddenly disappeared, he at once conjectured whither she had gone, and at once retraced his course to San Luis Potosi; not, however, proceeding far in his own character, but soon assuming a disguise which enabled him to conceal the scar which not only disfigured but marked him so singularly. This was the cowl and gown of a Dominican priest. He gave his lancers orders to return to their camp, and, under the security of his disguise, pursued his journey alone. Every desire of his heart, every thought of his mind, every energy of his soul and body was bent upon one object, that object—*revenge*. He was now determined to forgo all things else; and his revenge embraced a wish for the death of Brackett and the possession and ruin of poor Magdalena.

The disappearance of the latter caused the unutterable misery to Don Ignatio and Ximena; for they knew not whether she had fallen into the terrible hands of Alfrede, or had taken the dangerous resolution to follow her husband and to share his perils and captivity. When they found that their dwelling was destroyed by Don Gustave, which they learned from the frightened domestics, they for the first time learned that the villain was as ignorant as themselves of the whereabouts of Magdalena, and in this they had some comfort, though they feared much that she yet would fall into his hands; for now they had no doubt but that she had sought her husband in the Mexican camp.

The reader, especially if that reader be a descendant on the side of Eve, undoubtedly has a great curiosity to know where and how the lady is situated. We will accommodate him or her, as the case may be.

In the suburbs of the town of San Luis, are a vast number of little mud cottages. These are mostly inhabited by peons or slaves, or by the lower classes of society. In one of them, a few days after the destruction of the house at Buena Vista, were two persons. Both were nearly of a size, both dressed similarly, both nearly of the same hue, being fully as dark as a New Orleans quadroon, or a Seminole Indian; yet there was a vast difference in the points of the two. The eyes of both were large and jetty black; yet the eyes of one were fierce, and sharp, and flashing, as are those of a serpent; the eyes of the other were soft, dewy, and mournful in expression. The hands and feet of one were small and perfect; while those of the other were coarse and clumsy. Both were habited in the usual costume of the peons of the country. The reader, of course, recognizes Magdalena and her faithful Indian.

The latter had just come into the hut and was speaking to his mistress.

"So you saw him, Zalupah?" asked the latter.

"Yes, mistress. I sold soldier some *aquediente*, and when I took him the bottle, I saw my new master!"[29]

"How did he look? Was he sad and sick?"

"He looked like the lazy cloud in summer—white. He looked as if his heart was dry, and no blood for his face."

"Did he see you?"

"He didn't know me—Indians all look the same—he not know Zalupah when he did see him!"

"He would know me, and yet I dare not go near him in the daytime, for fear of discovery!" sighed the poor girl, "and yet I must see him. How can you get him out?"

"Creep up to guard in night time—stab him in the throat, so can't make noise, then break open door!"

"It is a fearful risk, yet something must be done, and that soon!" sighed she, sadly.

The faithful Indian knelt by her feet, and, looking up in her face with his usual expression of devotion and respect, said:

"Zalupah try to-morrow night—dark come soon, no moon now!"

"God bless thee, my faithful boy! If you succeed, you shall have your freedom and a rich reward!" said the lady, while her eyes filled with grateful tears.

"Zalupah don't want to be *free*—he never want to leave his mistress!" said the boy, earnestly.

When this conversation was going on in the hut, not a far different scene was enacted in another hut near there, but the motives and the feelings of the party were far different.

A man in the habit of a priest was conversing with another dressed as an officer in the Mexican army. The latter was a captain in the brigade of General Vasquez.

"It will be your guard-night tomorrow evening, will it not, Captain Morelo?" asked the one who was clothed as a priest. We forgot to note above that his cowl was drawn almost entirely over his face.

"I am officer of the night for tomorrow eve!" answered him whom the other addressed as Captain Morelo.

"And you are willing, on certain conditions, to give orders to admit me to the American prisoner's room—Brackett's I mean!"

"On certain conditions, Don Gustave!" replied the other.

"And those conditions are—"

"That you first give me a sufficient sum to fit myself out completely for the war with a fine horse, arms, and all equipments; second, that you have me advanced to a majority in your own regiment; third, that you give me means to bribe my sentinel not to divulge my orders; forth, that in killing him, you leave the dagger in his own hands, as if he had committed suicide!"

"Well, sir, you have quite a string of them, but they are all such as are within my power; therefore I accept them all, and at the mid-watch, on tomorrow night, I shall be upon the spot, robed as I now am, and then *he* shall *die*!"

CHAPTER XIV

*I*t was night—the night when Zalupah had promised to attempt to free his master; the night when Alfrede had vowed to murder the helpless and unarmed prisoner.

Brackett was not asleep—seldom did sleep visit his eyes. He had just heard the sentinel for the mid-watch relieved, and was listening to his heavy footsteps as he paced to and fro before the dungeon door, where he heard the soldier hail some one who was approaching.—To the cry of who comes there, the answer was given:

"A father of the church!"

The countersign was demanded and given, then the prisoner to his astonishment heard the new comer demand to be admitted to the cell. The sentinel, who played his part well, demanded the usual order; it was shown to him, and, apparently satisfied, the soldier opened the door to admit the holy "father of the church."

Brackett was about to demand the reason of this singular and untimely visit, when the stranger, who was indeed habited as a priest, whispered:—

"Be silent and on your guard. I am a friend!"

Thinking that he had heard the voice before, and that perchance this was some messenger from his bride, the ranger made no objection to the visit of the stranger, whose form he could but dimly distinguish by the feeble glimmering of his prison lamp.

As the door was but partly closed, he in a low whisper asked:

"Who are you, and for what purpose come you hither?"

"I come from her you love—from Magdalena; my object is to rescue you from this prison!" replied the stranger.

"Oh, my darling bride—is she well? Has she not been persecuted by that fiend in human form, Alfrede?"

"She is safe, and soon will greet you with all the warmth of her fond heart!" replied the stranger. Brackett was so much excited that he did not notice how the pretended friar's voice trembled with passion as he answered the last question.

The reader of course recognizes the villain under the priestly garb, and now Alfrede had found out one thing which he was anxious to know; that Brackett had not seen his bride, nor knew where she was. He could now have at once proceeded to put his fiendish purpose into execution, but he determined his refinement of cruelty to torture him before he put him to death.

While he had been engaged in the conversation which the reader is already possessed of, a strange scene was enacted on the outside of the cell. Immediately after the pretended priest had been admitted to the cell, a figure might have been seen cautiously creeping along in the shadow of the wall, toward the sentinel, stopping whenever the latter was faced toward him, again creeping forward when his back was turned.

At last the Indian boy, for it was he, stood so near the soldier, that had he not held his breath he surely would have been discovered.

The soldier paused a moment, as if he wished to listen to what was passing within the cell. That pause sealed his fate—that moment was his last, for quick as a flash of lightning from a storm cloud, the Indian sprang noiselessly upon him, and while one hand was placed over the poor soldier's mouth to prevent his giving the alarm, the other drew the keen blade of a broad, double-edged dagger across his throat with a force which severed at once all the arteries, and even the wind pipe. The Indian was so cautious that he did not even let the dead soldier fall to the floor, but gently and cautiously eased the body down, so that the whole deed was entirely unheard except by those two who were within the dungeon.

Zalupah now noticed that the dungeon door was opened, and creeping cautiously to the door, saw all that was passing within. A grim smile came upon his face, as he recognized through his disguise the person of the infamous Alfrede, and he wiped his bloody knife, and examined its edge carefully, as if to see that it was ready for another victim.

This was done at the moment when Alfrede, in the refinement of his cruelty, determined to reveal himself to his intended victim, and the smile of the Indian turned into a look of deadly hate, as he saw the pretended priest cast back the cowl from his face, revealing to Brackett the red cross upon his forehead.

"Oh, fiend of hell, is it indeed thou?" said Brackett as he saw his foe once more before him.

"It is, noble cavalier, and I am sent by your bride to inquire how you like your present quarters?"

"Oh, God! She is not in your power?" moaned the unhappy man.

"She is very comfortable at my quarters!" replied the inhuman fiend in a sneering tone, "but is extremely anxious to know how you bear your present life of inglorious ease. She sends her regrets that she has been able to enjoy so little of your company since your hasty marriage, but wishes me to tell you that your place is filled entirely to her satisfaction!"

"Dog of hell!" cried the tortured husband—"thou liest; if she is in thy power, it is by no will of her own."

"Oh, no, gentle cavalier, you err; she is a very willing companion, I assure you—nay, do not approach me so fiercely," he added, drawing a dagger from his breast, as the miserable ranger showed evident intentions of springing upon him—"stand back, else I may make a widow of her before the time for the honey moon is past!"

"Oh, God! Can it be that she is in that fiend's power!" groaned Brackett.

"If you do not believe it now perchance if I walk arm in arm with her upon the Plaza tomorrow, you will be convinced of it!" replied the cruel villain, in taunting tones of triumph—and then changing his tone to one still more bitter and fiendish, he added:

"However, you need not wait here to see her. She has desired me to set you free, and I will comply with her request!"

"Her request?" asked the half-bewildered man.

"Aye, her request and my will!" replied the heartless torturer, "and the key which I shall use is this dagger to your heart!"

As he uttered the last words, Alfrede raised his hand to strike his helpless victim, but at the same instant the dagger was dashed from his hand—another as broad and bright gleamed before him—it was raised above his breast, and descended swift as thought, aimed at his very heart. But alas, the blade shivered in the grasp of the brave hand which held it; a secret coat of mail was hidden beneath the priestly gown, and the blow of the faithful Zalupah was not only lost, but his only weapon was broken. Still he did not falter. Without uttering a word he closed with the villain, and in a moment more, both fell to the ground, each clenched so closely that it could not be discovered who was likely to be the victor.

Brackett supposed that his timely assistant was the sentinel, and the first thought of his heart was to rush to his assistance, but when he saw that his prison door was open, his thoughts rushed to his bride, and he determined to effect his escape while he could. With a wild bound of joy, he sped through the open portals, and snatching as he went the dagger of Alfrede from the floor, where it had been thrown in the struggle, hastened from the vicinity of the prison. Mounting a horse which was fastened near, he dashed at full speed along the deserted streets of the city, toward the northern gate. Here only one guard stood, and as Brackett saw him, he felt in the bolster of his pockets at his saddle bow and found a brace of pistols. The sentinel fell back in surprise before the dashing rider, and it was not before he had ridden far beyond the reach of its ball that he fired his musket to give alarm. On—on at the utmost speed of his horse rode the freed ranger—his course toward Buena Vista.

When the Indian saw that his master had left the prison, his next thought was to get free from Alfrede and to follow the ranger, that he might tell him where he could find his mistress. But ere he could succeed in this, the ranger had fled, he knew not where. He instantly bent his steps at full speed toward the hut where he had left her, to acquaint her with the result of his adventure, unconscious that at nearly the same speed he was followed by Alfrede, who had regained his feet almost as soon as the Indian.

The former followed the Indian unseen, until he saw and noted well the hut where the latter had entered, then turned rapidly to his own quarters, where, quickly resuming his uniform, he hurried to call a small party of his band, and bade them follow him.

Meantime the whole city was in alarm, the report the sentinel's musket having caused the roll to beat and the guard to turn out.

Zalupah, when he rushed into the hut where he had left his mistress, found her trembling with anxiety, and when she saw him, pale as death grew her face, for she saw that her husband was not with him.

"Where is he? Oh! Is all lost?" she shrieked, but the color returned to her face when she heard that he was *free*, and she at once thought that as he had not probably recognized his deliverer, he would hasten to Buena Vista in search of her.

She at once bade Zalupah make preparations to leave the city on the same route, and in a few minutes was ready to mount.

She was alone in the hut—trembling with anxiety, for she knew by the alarm that her husband's escape had been discovered. Zalupah had gone for the horses, and as she heard a step at the door, she supposed it to be him, and hurried to open it and go forth.

To her horror, she saw the hated form of Alfred before her.

"Mine—fair bride! Mine and forever!" he shouted as he rushed toward her. One wild shriek, then she gasped, and she fell senseless to the floor. The rude villain raised her form in his arms and turned toward the door, where stood his band of lancers. At this instant Zalupah arrived, and seeing in whose arms his beloved mistress was clasped, with a wild yell of despair, dashed toward her in a vain attempt to rescue her. With a fiendish laugh, Alfrede drew a pistol from his belt and fired as the youth sprang toward him. The youth reached the form of his mistress, but it was only to cover it with his noble heart's blood. The ball of the fiendish lancer had sped but too truly on its errand, and the brave Indian fell dead at his feet. Yet that shot was the salvation of his mistress.

The hurried tramp of the night guard was heard the next moment, and in an instant Alfrede and his band was surrounded by a much larger body of infantry.

At the head of these men was General Vasquez, who had turned out upon hearing the first alarm, and was now on his march to ascertain the cause.

When his eye fell upon Alfrede, and he saw the form of the beautiful female, (for the hair of Donna Magdalena had burst from its fastenings, and her dress but feebly concealed her form so perfect,) in the arms of the villain, and saw also that she had fainted, his brow grew dark with anger and suspicion.

"Who is that lady? What means this scene of blood and outrage? Is that her defender who lies dead at your feet? Speak, villain!"

Alfrede returned no answer, but looked around as if he fain would attempt to dash through the guard, but Vasquez, who saw his look, bade them stand fast.

Magdalena, who now began to recover, heard his words, and seeing him a protector, burst with one desperate bound from the hated arms which held her, and casting herself at the general's feet, cried—

"Oh, senor, for the love of heaven save me from that monster! Oh, save me, and take me to my husband's arms!"

"Your husband?" asked the general. "Your husband, who is he?"

"A prisoner, an American, senor; he has but now escaped from an attempted assassination by the hands of yon fiendish wretch!"

"Is his name Brackett?"

"It is, senor; oh, is he re-taken?"

"No, lady, I but now learned of his escape. You need not fear any further outrage from the hands of yon dog. I will protect you and restore you to your husband's arms, whether he escapes or is re-taken! You are as safe in the hands of General Vasquez, as you would be in your father's house!"

The lady looked down upon the corpse of her faithful Zalupah, and tears fell like the rain of a summer shower from her eyes, as she gazed upon him, and thought that his noble devotion had cost the poor boy his life.

"He shall have an honorable burial!" said the general, who noticed the direction of her gaze, and then added:

"You shall now retire to my quarters; tomorrow our army advances to meet the Americans. You shall proceed with us in safety, and as soon as it can be effected you shall be restored to your husband in honor and security!"

The guard still remained around the foiled Alfrede, but after giving orders for them to attend to the corpse of the poor Zalupah, he bade them let the colonel and his men depart, simply saying, that in the future his own eye would be upon his actions.

CHAPTER XV

*M*any and fearful were his perils; heavy and painful were his toils; narrow and providential his numerous escapes; yet at last Charles Brackett arrived safely in Buena Vista. It was almost sunset when he arrived there; the golden rays of the declining god of day were sleeping upon the hill tops, but had departed from the vales, where the twilight shades began to gather.

Yet there was light enough left for him to see how desolate was the spot where his virgin bride had dwelt—he saw the blackened walls of the mansion, and his heart sunk within him as he thought she too might have perished in those flames—that her ashes perhaps were scattered beneath those ruined walls. The thought was as the very fire of agony in his heart. He had passed the outposts of the army at Agua Nueva, some miles in advance, but he had not paused to make inquiries, but had urged his jaded steed to the utmost in hopes to meet her. But to a cruel disappointment was he doomed. Buena Vista was indeed desolate. Not a person was there to inform him what had become of the family of Valdez, not one to relieve his almost crazed mind from its terrible load of anxiety and suspense.

His horse was worn down, and darkness had gathered upon the earth long before the tired animal could bear him to the city of Saltillo. On arriving there, however, he learned that General Taylor had already arrived, and hastened to his quarters to report himself.

Warm was the greeting which the ranger received at the hands of the noble old general.

"Why, sir," said the hero—"I had supposed that you were lost; that in some daring reconnaissance you had fallen into the hands of the enemy and had been massacred!"

"I have suffered all but death, sir," answered the ranger, "and am now suffering a suspense which is worse than death!"

With his usual kindness, the general inquired the cause of this anxiety, and when in the course of his story the ranger mentioned the name Valdez, he muttered to himself:

"Valdez?—Surely I have heard that name before—oh, yes, I remember—here, orderly!"

The soldier whom he called appeared, and the general then added:

"Captain Brackett, let the orderly show you the way to a house which stands in the Calle de Obra-pia, where it opens out from the grand Plaza, second house, right hand. I think you'll find some one there to give you news. Saw an old, soldier-like looking man there this morning, leaning upon the shoulder of a pale, sorrowful-looking little girl of eighteen or nineteen—asked who they were—some one said Valdez."

The ranger had not heard more than half of this. Upon hearing the first part of it, giving the location, without even waiting for the orderly, he had rushed from the presence of the general.

"Poor fellow, he seems half crazy, and he has suffered enough to make him so!" said the kind general, without taking any offense at his abrupt and unceremonious leave-taking, and then added:

"I must do something for him; he deserves well!" He bent down over some papers, which had been absorbing his attention before the ranger had entered.

The latter in the mean time had hastened to the location spoken of by old "Rough and Ready," and now knocked at the door, with a hand trembling with impatience.

It was opened in a moment by a domestic who did not recognize the person of Brackett, but as the voice of the latter was heard inquiring for the name of Valdez, a wild, glad shriek was heard from the hall within, and the next moment he clasped a female form to his bosom—not that of his bride—but her sister, the gentle Ximena.

"Where is Magdalena, oh, where is my beautiful, my own?" he asked, as he pressed his lips to the pale brow of his fair sister-in-law.

"Alas! If you know not—if she is not with you, then we are still unhappy!" replied Ximena.

"I have not seen her since the night we were wed!" was the sad remark of

the ranger, and then Don Ignatio, who hurried forth, having heard and recognized his voice, said:

"And we have not seen her since the next evening, or heard from her. On
that night, she and Zalupah, her favorite Indian boy, disappeared, we have
ever supposed, with the intention of following you to share in your captivity!"

"Oh, God! Then indeed she may have fallen into the hands of the cursed
Alfrede. His words might indeed, have been true, when he boasted that she was
in his power!" moaned the unhappy husband, and then added,

"I will return to the Mexican army camp; if she is there I will find her, and
if, oh, horror, the thought is death to my soul! If *he* has wronged her, deeper
and darker shall be my vengeance than ever mortal plotted or fiend executed
before!" Then a new thought seemed to have come into his mind; he remembered to have seen the Indian boy regarding him attentively on the day before
his escape, he also remembered to have caught a glimpse of the face of the
person who saved him from Alfrede's dagger on that night, and the thought
of a resemblance to Zalupah passed in his mind, and once more hope reanimated his soul.

"She may yet be safe!" he cried, "and has heard of my escape, and will soon
rejoin me. Should she fall into the hands of Vasquez, she will be safe; but, oh,
holy God! Save her from the power of Alfrede!"

"She may yet be safe," said the gentle Ximena; "as for her honor that I know
is safe, for she wears not a dagger on her bosom for nothing. She never can be
in the power of her infamous persecutor, while she is alive, for I know well that
her own hand would use that dagger, even upon herself, should it become
necessary!"

Brackett shuddered as these thoughts were suggested, but he had quickly
formed a plan of ending his dreadful suspense. Telling Don Ignatio and
Ximena that he would soon return, he hurried forth, and soon had again entered the quarters of his general. He found the latter in a high state of glee. A
booted and spurred courier was standing by his side, who had come in express from the out-posts.

"Good news! good news, Captain Brackett" said the general as soon as he
saw him—"the enemy is advancing, and we shall have a brush within a day or
two at farthest. There will be plenty of work for you. I shall want his motions
constantly watched. If reports are true, his force is, at least, three or four times
greater than our own!"

"I can ascertain his force exactly, sir, if you will grant me a favor, which I
come hither to ask."

"What is it?" asked the general.

"It is that you permit me to go under a flag of truce to the enemy's camp
to make inquiry after one whom I am very anxious about!"

"True—true, a very good chance to find out his force—yes, sir, you can
take a flag with you to serve as your escort—but return quickly, and let your
report be accurate!"

"Your orders shall be obeyed, general!" was the reply of the ranger whose heart was once more reanimated with the hope that he might see or hear from her in the enemy's camp.

In a very short time he was in the saddle again, all of his fatigue forgotten in the one hope which alone buoyed him up, that of seeing or hearing from her whom he loved with all the elevated strength of his wild, enthusiastic nature.

CHAPTER XVI

*T*he flag of truce borne by the ranger met the column of advance of Santa Anna and his vast army near Agua Nueva. The American forces had already fallen back from this point by order of their general, and now were choosing their positions amongst the hills and ravines in advance of Buena Vista.[30]

As he rode rapidly up toward the enemy, with his truce-flag flinging out its white folds upon the breeze, Brackett saw another hoisted on a lance shaft in the columns of the enemy, and fearlessly rode up to it, while the Mexican column came to a halt.

On inquiring who was the officer in command of the advance, Brackett learned to his joy that it was General Vasquez, and at once requested to be led to him.

As the general saw him, and the flag which was now his protection, he smiled, and frankly extending his hand, said:

"You were lucky in effecting your escape, brave cavalier, in time to take part in the struggle which must take place, for it would pain a soldier's heart to be held a helpless prisoner while his countrymen were upon the battle-field."

"I believe I have to thank Colonel Alfrede for my liberty," replied the ranger, "and I hope that I shall soon have an opportunity to return my thanks upon the battle-field!"

"You will, probably, but you have more to thank him for, than you are aware of!"

"Oh, it is more to curse him for, I fear!" replied the ranger—"my business here in your presence is to face him and force him to answer me one question."

"I know what your question would be, and, thanks to him, are able to answer it!" said the general. "You seek your lost bride—and you seek not in vain!"

"Oh, God—where is she? Is she safe—not in *his* power?"

"Safe, under my protection now, but shall be in yours, soon."

The general gave an order to an aide—the officer rode back to the center, and in a few moments returned with the beautiful Magdalena, who rode upon a mule. She was pale and faint with fatigue, but her face reddened with a rich glow of delight as she saw her beloved once more, and she flew to his arms with a wild cry of joy.

For a moment the two embraced in speechless happiness, then turning to their noble friend Vasquez, they poured out the expressions of their full hearts to him who had proved so nobly kind unto them. The gallant old soldier was almost as much excited as were they, and the great tears of pleasure rolled down his bronzed cheeks as he gazed upon their tender meeting.

"My mission is completed!" said Brackett, a moment after—"I have found my bride, and must now return to my duty!"

"Go, and God's blessing follow thee!" exclaimed Vasquez, and then more sadly he added: "Send your bride far into the rear of your army, for ere another day, I fear that army will be on the retreat!"

"General Taylor does not know how to order a retreat; he may fall, his army may perish, but never will you see his back!" said the ranger proudly.

"I know that he is brave," replied Vasquez—"but we number five times more than his force. Our very weight must crush him!"

"Heavy weights are unwieldy—the lightest men are the most active," replied the ranger with a smile.

"I fear that you will find us too much for you this time, and I fain would see blood spared, for life is precious to men—if your general would surrender Saltillo and fall back with his army, I could almost agree that he should not be pursued. Bear a message to him from me!"

"Were I to bear a proposition to him for a surrender of one inch of ground which he has gained, he would drive me from his presence with scorn and contempt!" said Brackett.

"You Americans are very strange people. You never count numbers or cost, when you go into a fight. You seem to shut your eyes when you rush to the battle-field!" said the old general.

"We always keep them open, when we are there!" rejoined the ranger, "but I must not longer delay. Once more thanking you for preserving my precious bride, I must take my leave. I pray that *we* at least may not meet upon the battle-field hand to hand, and if we do, other foes shall receive my blows."

"And mine—but beware of Alfrede—he will be there, surrounded and followed by his desperate lancers—beware of being overpowered, for he is a fiend, and will fight now, for his hate is like a bursting volcano."

"I only ask that we may meet!" replied the ranger, then bowing low in his saddle to his courteous and magnanimous foe, he turned again his rein to the northward, bearing with him his now happy bride.

Darkness was again coming upon the earth, when he placed Magdalena in the arms of her father and sister, and then was forced again to part with her, for the distant firing told that the combat had already begun, and that soon the heavier shocks of a regular battle must follow. Therefore he at once hastened to the quarters of his general, whom he found surrounded with officers to whom he was giving orders of battle.

The firing which the ranger had heard, was only the meeting of the outposts of the two armies, and the general knew that the actual ball would not open before morning. Yet now, under cover of the shadows of night he was forming his line to receive the foe, preparing with all his energy, to fight one of the most desperate battles that the pen of history has recorded since the days of Leonidas the Spartan.[31]

"Well, sir, how many are they?" asked Taylor quickly, as his eye fell upon the ranger, who had joined the group of officers who surrounded him.

"Full twenty thousand, if I am to believe their own reports and my own observation,"

"Just enough to give us a good day's work—we need exercise, I'm afraid we'll forget how to fight if we lay idle so long a time!" said the old general with a smile. Such a smile and such tones as his were well calculated to reassure the hearts of his officers, some of whom felt that the odds between their *five*, and the enemy's *twenty* thousand men, was indeed desperate.

But it was not numbers, that the old general thought of, it was that he knew what kind of material his little army was composed of, which gave him the confidence to risk this battle.

He had the surviving heroes of Palo Alto—Resaca de la Palma and Monterey, still with him—men whom he knew to be as true as the steel which they carried—men whom he had seen climbing the hills of Monterey amid the sheets of fire and storm of balls which thinned their ranks as the hail cuts down the green blades of the young corn,—men who had with him endured heat and thirst and hunger, and the weary toils of the march, without a murmur, and he *knew* that they were invincible.

"I wish a thorough reconnaissance of the enemy's line, and a full description of the ground between them and our own lines, Captain Brackett!" said the old general. "You will perform this duty, and return to me as soon as possible. Your place tomorrow will be by my side."

The ranger hastened off to perform his duty, pausing but one instant to kiss the pale cheek of his virgin bride, and to bid her await fearlessly the result of the morrow's conflict.

And she,—wept she when saw him ride forth? Oh, no—a Spanish bride never sheds a coward tear when goes her lover, brother, or husband forth to battle.

She may pray on bended knees for his preservation and success, but she weeps not for his danger.

During all that long night the troops were moving about on Buena Vista, gaining in column and in line, by squadron and by company, the posts which their general had chosen.

Few eyes closed on that night—each motion was conducted in almost perfect silence. Calm and ominous seemed the stillness; it seemed as if the elements were suspending their usual duties to witness the fearful conflict which was soon to ensue. The wind moved not through the trees, or stirred a ripple on the bosom of Juan's gentle river,—neither rain or thunder-cloud came to disturb the slumbers of such as chose to cast them down upon their arms to wait in slumber, for the tongue which with the dawn's early light was to awaken them—the hoarse tongue of battle.

Officers rode here and there, conveying orders to the different divisions, and thus ere the dawn of day came to light up the battle-field, all was ready for the conflict.

There they stood, Washington's battery of the gallant 4th in the road which led to the south, the volunteer regiments to his right and left, the mounted men of Arkansas and Kentucky close at the mountain's base.

Thus with the narrow valley walled across with ardent and gallant men, the sun arose upon the field of Buena Vista on the 23rd day of February, 1847.[32]

CHAPTER XVII

The day dawned upon the serried lines of both friend and foe, and while yet the gray of twilight was over them, the rattling of musketry along the mountain side to the left told that the combat was begun. Soon Marshall's rifles began to ring sharp and loud amid the echoes of the heavier guns, and foes began to fall before them thick and fast.

Then up along the road where the gallant Washington was posted with his artillery, came a heavy column, moving steadily and fiercely on to the attack. On, like a huge black cloud coming to cover over a single star, they marched, but as they came within the range of his guns, he poured out a shower of iron hail among them. Still they pressed on, reeling and staggering, but yet moving forward. Then again he poured forth his shower of death, and now, confused and shattered, the massive column fell back, and his smoke-darkened artillerists had time to take momentary rest.

Now, while yet the smoke of their guns arose in heavy wreaths toward the sky, a group of officers came dashing down at full speed from Saltillo; amongst them one dressed plainly, but mounted on a large white horse, whose presence had a strange effect along the whole line. Loud cheers arose from every lip as "Old Rough and Ready" took his station in the center, and now began the fray in real earnest. Wherever a gun could be brought in play, its deadly fire was opened, and murmurs alone arose from those who had not yet been brought into a position to share in the conflict.

A select band of aides and chiefs were by the side of the general, amongst these Brackett held a place. He had been in the saddle all the night, and had traversed every part of the battle-field, therefore could inform his general of every favorable point where his troops could act with the most effect.

The sight now was grand, terrific beyond the power of description. The enemy's artillery had all opened their fire—their infantry was engaged in pouring in a deadly fire of musketry, and under cover of all this, his immense cavalry force was preparing for the charge.

Oh it was a gallant and yet a fearful sight, to see thirty-nine squadrons of Mexican horsemen, seated with their bodies bent forward upon their war-steeds, their lances all in rest, each pennon glistening in the sunlight, each bright spear-head glittering and as yet unstained with the red life-stream, all ready for the trumpet's blast to charge. And it was a thrilling sight to see how silently and calm their foemen stood to receive them. There in square, as stood the English at Waterloo, they were planted, firm as the rocks beneath them.[33]

On—on came the glittering line of lancers, and with thundering hoofs and clattering of steel, like a mighty wave rushing upon a pebbly beach.

But see, as on they sweep, see that fearful sheet of smoke and flame, hear the rattling lead and iron as it hisses through flesh and crushes bone—oh see the dark mass of foremen reel and quiver—see riders tumble from their saddles—see steeds mad with affright bounding still on toward the fearful line—crushing alike the dead and the living.

See the survivors of the unsuccessful charge wheel and turn them from the band. Then hear the wild hurrah which rises unbidden from every American lip.

General Taylor had watched that charge—his face was pale, not with fear, but with excitement, as he saw the Mexicans advance like a huge ocean wave rolling up against a dark and moveless cliff. But when as that wave dashed against the solid rock shivers into foam and nothingness, he saw his noble troops meet and repel the terrible shock, his eye brightened, his color returned, and he shouted:

"Nobly—nobly done! With such men, who can fail!"

But again he saw that in another part of the field a still more desperate struggle was about to ensue.

In front of where O'Brien's well served artillery was stationed, supported by the second Indiana regiment on foot, the enemy had concentrated an immense mass of infantry, and against our center they seemed disposed to make a desperate effort.

In one solid mass the enemy advanced upon O'Brien's battery. As they came within range, his guns opened and every discharge swept windows of dead through his ranks, but the dreadful lanes were instantly filled with the living, and on, on still came the foe, pouring in as they advanced, a most terrible fire, sweeping down the artillerists and cutting down the front ranks of the American infantry.

In vain did the noble O'Brien pour in the grape amongst them; the foe seemed to feel that in their numbers they must conquer, and still on they pressed. They were almost upon the guns, still the gallant O'Brien, though wounded, kept up his fire, depending on the support of the Indianans at his back, but when all of the men at one of his guns was killed, not one horse left to drag away a cannon, then he saw to his agony, the regiment which should rather have fallen, man by man, than then to have deserted him, he saw the second regiment of Indiana volunteers turn and flee! Oh, shame! shame! But yet it was, and here while he in vain strove to recall the fugitives to a sense of their duty, while in vain he bade the cowards rally to his side, fell the noble Lincoln.[34]

When nearly all of his men were slain, when all support was gone, then and then only did the noble O'Brien turn and leave the guns which he had so well defended.

With feelings that we may not describe, General Taylor had watched this scene, and now saw with pain, that his flank was turned and that a portion of the enemy had gained his rear. The enemy, now cheered by its success, poured down in full force upon the Mississippi and Illinois regiments.

These met them as none but they could meet them, and the shouting foe who but the moment before had been victorious, and were met breast to breast by men, who knew not how to yield, whose only cry was victory or death.

"Oh, my brave Mississippians!" cried the excited Taylor, as he saw them, supported by the gallant Hardin and a portion of his men, force back the foe-men at the reeking points of their bayonets. Back they reeled, and then again they gained a step upon the foe, like the trees of a forest in a mighty storm they seemed to reel to and fro, and hard was it to tell which should conquer.

Meantime the eagle eye of Taylor was scanning all parts of the field. He saw now that the enemy were concentrating a force of cavalry at the base of the mountain, evidently intending to attack his wagon train and baggage, which was stationed near the ruined walls of Don Ignatio's former residence.

The eye of the general brightened. He turned to Brackett, who had been panting to join the conflict, and cried, as he pointed to the cavalry of the enemy:

"Ride, sir, to May's position; the colonel has been foaming to make a charge; tell him that with his squadron, Bucker's company, and Pike's Arkansas boys, he must 'head off' those lancers! You know the ground, you can show him the way!"

Oh, gladly leapt the heart of the young ranger then in his manly breast. He knew that his time for action had commenced, and he hoped to meet his marked foe among those lancers.

Driving his spurs deep into the flanks of his snorting steed he dashed off to the spot where May sat upon his large black horse, chafing madly at not receiving orders to join in the fray.

When he saw Brackett riding toward him in hot haste, his face brightened, for he felt that his general had "cut out some work" for him.

"Where now?" he asked as the ranger rode up to his side.

Quickly, the general's orders were given; then, almost as quickly as the squadrons were formed into column, and May shouting his usual cry:

"*Follow!*" dashed on side by side with Brackett. On, through ravines, over hills and rocks they sped, till they saw the enemy before them. It was not the main body of the Mexican cavalry, but a force of a single regiment, yet this regiment was treble in number to the force of May.

This he regarded not, nor did Brackett, who saw the hated Alfrede at the head of his regiment, pause to think of the odds. The charge was sounded and on—on they dashed amongst the foe. The latter stood for but one moment and then, with their colonel at their head, they turned and fled. In vain did Brackett strive to reach the recreant villain whom he had sworn to meet; in vain did he call upon him to turn and meet him steel to steel.

The lancers fled to rejoin the main body of the Mexican cavalry, which was now preparing to charge upon the hacienda, more to the left, where, also, Marshall's Kentucky and Yell's Arkansas cavalry had prepared to meet them.

May and his gallant men hastened to rejoin the latter, and once more the horsemen of either army were opposed in front of each other, each seeming determined on victory or death.

This time Brackett determined that he would reach his enemy, and carefully watching the spot where Alfrede's regiment took post, he placed himself to front it. This left him by the side of the gallant Yell.

Soon the charge was heard from the Mexican bugles, it was echoed from our side, and in a moment both masses of horsemen were dashing on at full speed, each to meet the other.

On, waving his saber in the air, rode the noble Yell, close upon his left was Vaughan of Kentucky, and equally with them in the advance rode young Brackett. They were met, Brackett parried a lance which was one of the perfect hedge that was lowered to meet them, and at the same instant saw Vaughan upon his one side, and Yell upon the other, fall pierced through and through. A thousand points seemed aimed at him, but sweeping a wide circle with his heavy saber he sped on, knowing by the shout close to his rear, that he was not alone.[35]

Oh, those were fearful sounds to hear—the shouts of the excited men, the groans of the wounded and dying; the yells of the wild horsemen of the west. Clash of steel, and pistol shots; the cries of wounded horses; the crashing of heavy sabers as down they clove through flesh and bone; oh, these, indeed, were fearful sounds.

On—on, wheeling in pursuit of these broken squadrons of the enemy rushed the American horsemen; and close in the rear of the squadrons of Alfrede, which again had turned and fled, rode Brackett supported by a few of his own rangers and some gallant Kentuckians, not more than twenty in all. He was fast gaining upon the flying lancers, and his voice reached the ears of his foe as he fled.

Casting back a hasty glance, Alfrede saw how few were the men who were with the ranger, and he began to blush at flying with five hundred lancers from so few. Giving the order to wheel, he suddenly swept around with his squadrons, and in a moment had, completely encircled the little band, and now closed around them, separating them entirely from the rest of their force, and hiding them from the view of their busy comrades, in the cloud of dust, and by his superior numbers.

CHAPTER XVIII

We know that it is painful to the reader, not to be permitted to see all the scenes of this terrible contest at once, and to know the result of the peril in which we have left the young ranger, but we must for a moment return to Saltillo.

Upon the flat roof-top of the house in which Don Ignatio had taken up his temporary residence, and from which a view of the battle-field and all of the surrounding country could be obtained, stood Don Ignatio and his two daughters, watching every distinguishable maneuver with deep anxiety. Donna Magdalena was pale, but her lip did not quiver, her eye dropped no tear, though her face was marked with the deep shades of care and anxiety. In her hand she held a spy-glass and while she gazed upon the battle she told the result of every movement which she could see, to her father and sister, but much was hidden from her view by the smoke which at times completely shrouded both armies.

She had been able in the early part of the battle to see the position of the commanding general; she had also recognized her husband by his side. She had, however, lost sight of both long since, and his situation was left entirely to her imagination. She could only see the rolling wreaths of smoke and hear the discordant sounds of battle, save now and then indistinct masses of moving men, whether friend or foe she could not tell.

While the tides of battle were thus mingling in the direction of Buena Vista, her attention was called by her father to a moving body in the rear of the town.

"What see you there, beneath the mountain's base, my girl; my eyes are dim, but methinks I see the waving pennons of lancers, amid the thick growth of trees that grow upon the side of the Rio Juan."

The maiden wife turned her glass in the direction noted by her father, and paler yet turned her cheek, as she exclaimed:

"It is too true, my father! There are mounted men, and they are many in number. They are lancers. Oh God! Is not this some movement of Alfrede!"

"Seem they bent to attack the rear of the American army, or act they as if they would attack the town?"

"They ride toward the town, my father!" replied the maiden; and then she added: "all of the forces nearly are drawn from here to the battle-field, the town must be taken, for the force that is approaching cannot be less than two or three thousand!"

"Much I fear that the day is lost to General Taylor," said Don Ignatio, "for this battle of near a day's length must have worn down his little army, and in such a terrible fire many must have fallen."

The gentle Ximena spoke not but silent tears coursed down her cheeks as she gazed toward the battle-field. She was thinking of the death and carnage there, of the dying sons, brothers, and lovers who had no gentle hand near them to cool their burning lips with water, or to whisper a kind word in their ears.

Meantime Magdalena was watching the approach of the cavalry.

"See!" she cried, "they reach the road between us and the battle-field; they are placed to intercept the retreat of the American army if it is defeated. Ah, I see even now, some horsemen and footmen flying this way along the road from the army, and while yet I look they are intercepted and hewed down by the cavalry.

"Ah, the lancers now ride toward the city, but see, a gallant band of cannoneers advance with but a single piece of artillery to meet them. Others join this little band, and now they fire upon the advancing column of horsemen. Ah, see how they fall, horses and their riders before the iron hail. Another small band join the first, but even now they are not more than an hundred men with but two guns.

"The lancers are about to charge them; oh, look, they dash down at full speed upon them. The brave cannoneers do not shrink back; they are calm and steady as if they were about to fire at a target instead of a mass of living beings.

"The horsemen are near—they shake their pennoned lances in the air, but look again, the iron hail rains in its fearful shower upon them. Down go their foremost ranks. I see men and horses struggling on the ground. They are all in confusion. Again the cannoneers pour into their fire, and now the lancers turn and flee.

"Oh, the cowards! Three thousand fly before an hundred, see! the little band pursue them still, sweeping down their flying ranks with fearful effect.

"Now they fly along the mountains, base, and another battery from Buena Vista opens upon them—Oh, heaven! it is a sickening sight to see them falling there like grain before the reaper's sickle!"

The excited maiden shuddered as she spoke, and for a moment withdrew her gaze then again she looked, and now more pale than ever was her look:

"Oh, my father, I see men flying hitherward from the battle-field. They are few, but they fly; oh, if all is lost what will become of him—of my husband!"

"A strange transformation has love worked in your heart, my daughter!" said Don Ignatio. "A few days since and on bended knees you would have prayed for the success of the Mexican arms, now you seem only to fear for the defeat of the Americans!"

"It is true my father, but when I wedded him, I became an American. We are not Mexicans. Spain alone has a right to our allegiance. Why should we hope for the Mexicans to conquer in this battle? That this now quiet city should be filled with troops of rude and licentious men, who respect no law, and are governed by no principles?"

"You are right, my child, but look again and see if you can see how runs the tide of battle now!"

"Still the smoke cloud is too thick to see; the night is coming on; oh, that mine eye could pierce the gloom!" replied the maiden, as she in vain sought to descry the position of the still conflicting armies.

We left young Brackett and his little band entirely surrounded by the desperate lancers of Alfrede. The ranger saw his situation, but he blanched not at the danger, he only thought of the enemy who was so near him, and bidding his men keep close, hewed a broad and bloody path toward the spot where he heard Alfrede shouting to his men to give no quarter.

"We ask none, you cowardly miscreant!" shouted the ranger, "only fly not again from before us!"

The intention of Alfrede was not now to fly, nor cared he to cross swords with his antagonist, when the death of the latter could be accomplished by others, within his sight without danger to himself; therefore he simply cheered his men on to the combat, bidding them give no quarter to the heroic little band. We know not how long they could have withstood the fearful odds against them, had not an officer rode up to Alfrede and communicated some order to him, which evidently forced him to continue his retreat, for shouting to Brackett:

"The fight is not yet over—we will meet again!" he turned his horse's head again to the south and bade his bugler sound the retreat.

The next moment Brackett and the remnant of his little band were alone among the dead and dying, for they were neither in force or strength able to pursue the enemy.

The body of lancers under Alfrede were seen to rejoin the main body of the army, which, now strengthened by a large reserve, was preparing to decide the fate of the day by one overwhelming and universal charge.

Taylor, seeing this, had also concentrated his forces, and now both armies paused for a moment as if to gather strength for the fearful struggle.

Brackett and his few companions hastened to rejoin the main line, which now needed every man that could lift a weapon.

The day had nearly passed, the sun was just sinking into the western sky, and at this moment the heavy line of the Mexicans, infantry, with cavalry at their backs, moved on toward the Americans.

Taylor saw that the battle would depend on this one movement, that if the enemy was repulsed now, the day was his own, and promptly ordered Bragg's battery of flying artillery forward.

They came up at a gallop within a few hundred yards of the advancing body of the enemy, and unlimbering their pieces opened a dreadful fire upon the enemy. At first the Mexicans recoiled, but led on by officers who knew that the day hung upon the crisis, they again pushed forward. Perilous then in the extreme was the position of Bragg; infantry had been ordered up to his support, but it had not arrived, and his little band of scarce a company was the isolated object of the attack of the thousands who pressed upon him. His fire had been rapid and destructive; but his men were worn down by the long day's toil, and though they seemed determined to die at their guns, still their fate seemed inevitable and their fire began perceptibly to flag.

At this moment, when the heroic Bragg was leading a gun with his own hands, a cheerful voice was heard close behind him:

"Give 'em a little more grape, Captain Bragg, and the day is our own!"[36]

Like the sound of magic were those words, and that voice to the fainting artillerists; "Old Rough and Ready" was there to share their peril and their fate. Never before, perhaps never again, will guns be worked as was then that battery. The "grape" hailed upon the enemy, and completely held them in check, while now the regiments of Mississippi, Illinois, and Kentucky came gallantly to the charge.

Oh, what a fearful conflict then took place. Hand to hand, mingled and mixed up together, the foes met in the last desperate struggle of the day. Now fell men as thick upon the ground, as ripe fruit from the shaken tree in autumn. There in the very van fell the noble Hardin, the brave McKee, the chivalrous Clay; there fell hosts of brave men on either side. To and fro waved the lines now advancing, now retreating, victory seemed uncertain, but still hailed Bragg's battery its iron storm upon its foe.

General Taylor was now with the advance, and every man felt as if the eye of "Old Rough and Ready" was upon him. We need not then so much wonder at the deed of that hour.

The sun went down, and the gray twilight came on. One more struggle did the Mexicans prepare for, before they would yield their ground, and to support this they moved up their cavalry. One more charge from them—it was met by our horsemen, the Kentuckians, dragoons, and rangers. Brackett once more saw the deadly enemy before him, he was so near that he could see the red cross upon his brow, and when he with the rest dashed on in that terrific charge, he swore not again to lose sight of him whom he had *marked* for that hour.

The charge was made—the foe reeled before the terrible shock, their lines were broken, and the day was won. The charge became a pursuit, the battle a massacre, though until darkness came over the earth, the struggle in detached parties was kept up.

At last the sounds of clashing steel and echoing guns were still—nothing could be heard upon the battle-field except a hoarse murmur, like the hum of a busy city heard at a distance by the quiet peasant. And this sound arose from the moaning lips of more than three thousand wounded and dying men. Oh, God, how long did that night seem to many a suffering being, who felt that his life was ebbing fast away, and yet no friend near to make its last moments more comfortable. And yet there were kind and ministering angels there, such angels as a noble poet of our own land has alluded to in a poem which we here give to the reader—only hoping that this little story may have but half of the immortality which will make this poem live when the heroes of Buena Vista are all passed away.

We make no excuse for copying this beautiful poem into our story; it, like the fame of the gory field whose name it bears, is public property, and the soul which could conceive verses so beautiful and grand, the mind which could give them into light, could never be possessed of one feeling which could receive offence at a liberty which we know will gratify our reader.[37]

The Angels of Buena Vista
By J.G. Whittier

A letter writer from Mexico, states that at the terrible fight of Buena Vista, Mexican women were seen hovering near the field of death, for the purpose of giving aid and succor to the wounded. One poor woman was found surrounded by the maimed and wounded of both armies, ministering to the wants of Americans as well as Mexicans with impartial tenderness.

I.
Speak and tell us, our Ximena, looking
   Northward far away,
O'er the camp of the invaders, o'er the Mex-
ican array,
Who is losing, who is winning? Are they
   far, or come they near?
Look abroad and tell us, sister, whither rolls
the storm we hear?

II.
"Down the hills of Angostura, still the storm
   of battle rolls;
Blood is flowing, men are dying, God have
   mercy on their souls!"
Who is losing, who is winning?—"O'er hill
   and over plain,
I see but smoke of cannon clouding through
   the mountain rain."

III.
Holy Mother! keep our brothers. Look,
   Ximena, look once more,

"Still I see the fearful whirlwind rolling
    darkly as before,
Bearing on, in strange confusion, friend and
    foeman, foot and horse,
Like a wild and troubled torrent sweeping
    down its mountain course."

IV.

Look once more, Ximena. "Ah, the smoke
    has cleared away,
And I see the Northern rifles gleaming down
    the ranks of grey.
Hark! that sudden blast of bugles! There
    The troop of Minon wheels;
There the Northern horses thunder, with
    cannon at their heels!

V.

"Jesu pity! How it thickens, now retreat
    and now advance!
Right against the blazing cannon shivers
    Puebla's charging lance!
Down they go, the brave young riders, horse
    and foot together fall:
Like the ploughshare in its fallow ploughs
    the Northern ball."

VI.

Nearer came the storm, and nearer, rolling
    fast and frightful on,
Speak, Ximena, speak and tell us who has lost
    and who has won.
"Alas! alas! I know not, friend and foe to-
    gether fall,
O'er the dead, rush the living, pray, my
    sister, for them all.

VII.

"Lo! the wind the smoke is lifting, blessed
    Mother, save my brain!
I can see the wounded crawling slowly out
    from the heaps of slain.
Now they stagger, blind and bleeding: now
    they fall and strive to rise.

Hasten, sister, haste and save them, lest
   they die before our eyes.

VIII.
"Oh, my heart's love, oh, my dear one,
   lay thy faint head on my knee;
Dost thou know the lips that kiss thee?
   Do you hear me, canst thou see?
Oh, my husband, brave and gentle! Oh,
   My Bernal! look once more
On that blessed cross before thee! Mercy!
   all is o'er."

IX.
Dry thy tears, my poor Ximena, lay thy dear
   one down to rest.
Let his hands be meekly folded, lay the cross
   upon his breast;
Let his dirge be sung hereafter, and his
   funeral masses said;
To-day, thou poor bereaved one, the living
   asks thy aid.

X.
Close beside her, faint and moaning, fair
   and young, a soldier lay,
Torn with shot, pierced with lances, bleeding slow his life away;
But, as tenderly before him the lorn Ximena
   knelt,
She saw the Northern eagle shining on his
   pistol-belt.

XI.
With a stifled cry of horror, straight she
   turned away her head;
With a sad and bitter feeling, she looked
   back upon her dead.
But she heard the youth's low murmuring, and
   the un-lagging breath of pain,
And she raised the cooling water to his lips
   again.

XII.

Whispered low the dying soldier, pressed
   her hand, and fondly smiled;
Was that pitying face his mother's? did
   she watch beside her child?
All his strange words with meaning her
   woman's heart supplied!
With her kiss upon his forehead, "Mother,"
   murmured he, and died!

XIII.

"A curse came upon them, poor boy, who led thee
   madly forth
From some gentle, sad-eyed mother weeping
   lonely in the North!"
Spake the mournful Mexique woman, as she
   laid him with her dead,
And turned to soothe the living, and bind the
   wounds which bled.

XIV.

Look once more, Ximena. "Like a cloud
   before the wind
Rolls the battle down the mountains, leaving
   blood and death behind.
Ah! They plead in vain for mercy: in the
   dust the wounded strive;
Hide your faces, holy angels! Oh, thou
   Christ of God, forgive!"

XV.

Sink, oh night, among the mountains! Let
   The cool grey shadows fall:
Dying brothers, fighting demons, drop the
   curtain over all!
Through the thickening winter twilight,
   wide apart the battle rolled.
In its sheath the sabre rested, and the can-
   non's lips grew cold.

XVI.

But the holy Mexic women, still their holy
   task pursued
Through that long, dark night of sorrow.

Worn and faint and lacking food;
Over weak and suffering brothers with ten-
    der care they hung,
And the dying foeman blessed them in a
    strange and Northern tongue.

XVII.
Not wholly lost, oh Father, is the evil world
    of ours;
Upwards, through the blood and ashes, spring
    afresh the Eden flowers:
From its smoking hills of battle, love and
    pity send their prayers,
And still Thy white-winged angels hover
    dimly in our air.

CHAPTER XIX

*A*ll of that long, weary night passed away, and it was a night of misery to Magdalena. The news of the victory had reached her ears—but her husband came not, nor sent he any message to her.

She had inquired of all whom she could see who had been in the battle, and learned from these that he had been seen up to the last fearful charge, at that then he was the foremost in the onslaught upon the enemy's lancers. As our army slept upon the battle-field that night, she hoped that her husband was safe, though when she heard that the field was strewed with the dead and the dying, her heart sunk within her.

All of that night she heard the moans of the wounded as they bore them in by wagon loads to the hospital, and the distant hum from the battle ground came cold and awful upon her ear.

Morning came at last, and then she learned that all of the Mexicans had fled, that there were none for our army to pursue—none for them to fight. Still her husband came not back with the victors—still he was not borne along among the maimed and wounded.

She asked every officer whom she could see, if they had seen him, and all that she could learn was that he had fought like a lion in the fray, and had been foremost in the last desperate charge which had won the victory,

From that moment he had not been seen by any one from whom she inquired.

"Oh God! this suspense is too much!" she cried; "I must know the worst."

"Be patient, sister," said the gentle Ximena, "he may soon return."

"Yes," replied the other, "and yet he may now be upon that battle-field, dying, or maimed and helpless, suffering for water or help. Oh, I cannot stay here; I must go and search for him!"

"Oh, no, sister, go not to that scene of carnage—Oh, it would be too terrible to pass over that harvest-field of death—to wade through pools of clotted blood—to pass over the disfigured corpses of the dead, Oh, stay, and go not there!"

"Ximena, I must go; you paint horrors, but there amongst them, perchance, is the body of my husband—perchance he lives; I must—I will seek him!"

Almost crazed with her heart-sickening fears, the unhappy bride rushed from the house, and bent her feeble steps toward the battle-field. She was not alone in the way, for hundreds of tearful women were wending their way sadly to the spot, perchance to look for husbands or lovers, fathers or brothers. As they went, they would gaze with mournful anxiety on the maimed and wounded whom they met, for hundreds were being carried from the open field to more comfortable quarters at Saltillo.

When Magdalena arrived upon the battle-field, she found that the scene of horror which poor Ximena had painted was far below the dreadful reality. Her soul sickened, as she saw strewed here and there, every where the bodies of men, some disfigured by ghastly wounds; others with scarce a mark upon them. Horses and men—arms and accoutrements were every where strewed. The burying parties had already commenced their heavy labors, and in huge pits dug where the dead lay thickest, they laid all whom they did not recognize as officers of rank: friend and foe laid they side by side.

Still, among the dead and wounded, she saw not the face of her husband. Almost frantic, she flew from one spot to another of the field, calling upon his name as she went, now pausing by a heap of the slain, and gazing upon every form, then turning shuddering away from a sight which was too much for her to bear. Her feet were slippery with blood—her dress was red with its stains.

For hours, weary, miserable hours, she wandered over the heart-sickening plain, asking every one whom she met for her new husband, and when, at last, she met one who had been with him in the last fearful charges, and had been wounded in it, she learned where he had last been seen, far in the advance of the others, engaged in a furious running combat with an officer of lancers. Then she hurried in the direction which she had been told that he had taken, and still, though she walked far along the mountain gorge beyond the battle-field—she saw not his corpse.

Yet, even there—all along the narrow pass, lay dead and dying men. Ever and anon she would turn as she heard the groans of men in misery—and at times she would almost fancy that she heard her name called, and would start and rush toward some wounded and groaning man, and looking in his face, would find him—*a stranger*.

Oh, who can tell the agony of that fearful hour to her. Faint and weary, half dead with suspense, at last she sank upon a rock by the road side, and burst into a flood of tears. She felt that indeed hers was a widowed heart.

Then she heard the merry rush of the fountain which bubbled out from a rock but a little way beyond her, and she staggered toward it, to dip her burning brow into the cooling flood. While she bent her head to the stream, she heard a voice faintly moan the word "*Water*," in English near her. She thought that it was her husband's voice, but as she sprang to the side of the feeble sufferer who was laying near the water, toward which he had vainly tried to crawl, she again found but a stranger. Yet she turned not in coldness away from him— like a pitying angel of Mercy, she raised his cap from the blood-stained ground beside him, and rushing to the fountain filled it, then returning, placed it to his parched lips, and when he had drank, slaked his burning brow with it.

"God bless you, lady—this has been a dreadful time!" murmured the man—"I was at Palo Alto, Resaca, and Monterey, but this has beat them all."

While he spoke, Magdalena saw that his was the uniform of the rangers, and once more, though now without a hope of hearing from him, she asked after her husband, giving his name.

"What!—Captain Brackett your husband, lady? Yes, I saw him, he was the last I saw, for I received this wound in defending him from a brace of lancers who were attacking him as we rode close upon their flanks. I shot one, he lies by the side of yonder-rock. Your husband was close in pursuit of the other when a shot aimed at him, missed him and tumbled me from my saddle. He may be but a little farther on, or he may have been taken prisoner by following the enemy too far!"

"Did you see the face of the lancer whom he was pursuing?" asked Magdalena.

"Yes," replied the soldier, much revived by the water which she had given him; "he was a singular looking man, with a red scar or cross on his forehead, and such an eye as few men have!"

"Oh God! it was Alfrede, and if my husband is a prisoner, then is his fate worse than if he had fallen upon the battle-field!"

Then another thought struck upon her mind. He might have fallen farther on—he might still be alive. Telling the wounded soldier that she would again return to him, she arose and hurried along the rocky ravine.

She had been but a few moments when the soldier heard a scream so wild and thrilling, that it racked his very soul. Feeble and wounded as he was, he crawled slowly along the ground toward a slight bend in the path behind which she had disappeared, and when, at length, he passed it, he saw her,— but she was not alone. Her fair arms were spotted with blood, and were clasped around the cold form of her husband, who, with his broad knife blooded to the very hilt, lay upon the earth, with his face toward the sky.

Near him lay the form of a Mexican officer with a horrid gash in his breast, and he, too, was dead—stone dead. His face, too, was turned toward the sky, and upon his dark forehead was the red scar of a cross. In his hand was a pistol, but its bullet was in the heart of the ranger—both had fallen in the death-struggle.

The soldier spoke to the lady—but she raised not her head to look upon him—she opened not her lips to answer his words. Feebly and slowly he crawled along to her side, and when he again spoke without receiving a response, he reached out his coarse hand, and touched hers, so fair and delicate.

He shuddered when he found out that it was cold and pulseless, and then he wept as he saw her so beautiful and good, laying there a corpse upon her brave, dead husband's bosom.

Yet he, too, was helpless—he could do no more than weep. All of that long, weary day the poor man lay and watched those dead bodies; but when it was near the sunset hour, he saw an old man and a fair girl riding slowly along the ravine, searching into every nook and shade as they came on. He saw them slowly approach the spot where he lay; he saw the old man's eye fall upon the cold group which lay beside him, and heard him groan in a tone of agony:

"Our search is ended! They are here!"

Then he saw the feeble girl and the aged man alight from their mules and kneel beside the bodies of the dead lady and her noble husband, and he heard their moans of sorrow as one called upon the name of her only sister—as the other looked up to heaven and said—"Oh God! give me strength to bear this loss! My Magdalena, the image of my lost Seberina is dead—the virgin bride sleeps by the side of her husband!"

And thus lived—thus died the noble "Magdalena, The Beautiful Maiden of Mexico."

THE END.

'Bel of Prairie Eden

George Lippard was one of the most popular writers of the 1840s and 1850s. During the early 1840s, he worked as a journalist and fiction writer for the Philadelphia *Spirit of the Times* and the *Citizen Soldier*, but after his first novel *The Quaker City; or The Monks of Monk Hall* became a phenomenal best-seller he was able to support himself as an author without writing for other papers. As a result, he devoted his energies to using literature to promote the interests of the white working class and the cause of land reform in his weekly story paper, the *Quaker City*, and in his many novels. Before his untimely death from tuberculosis in 1854, Lippard published several mysteries-of-the-city novels with titles such as *The Empire City; or New York by Night and Day*, *The Killers, a Narrative of Real Life in Philadelphia*, and *New York: Its Upper Ten and Lower Million*. He also wrote several war novels, including one entitled *Washington and his Generals; or, Legends of the Revolution* and two about the U.S.-Mexico War: *Legends of Mexico* and *'Bel of Prairie Eden*.

Lippard believed that if lands in the West were opened up for settlement rather than being monopolized by the wealthy, many of the problems of the white working class would disappear. This helps to explain why he promoted the U.S.-Mexico War, but *'Bel*, which was published in 1848, also reveals many of his doubts about the war, especially his fears that slavery would extend to the new lands taken from Mexico. As he does in many of his novels, Lippard makes women's bodies symbolically central by using sensational narratives of seduction and revenge to figure larger conflicts between classes and nations. In *'Bel*, Lippard aims to mobilize readers' sympathies on behalf of the U.S. colonizers by focusing on the Mexican villain's seduction of the Texas heroine, 'Bel. But after 'Bel's brother, John, avenges her by seducing the sister of the villain, Don Antonio Marin, and by orchestrating Marin's murder, the bleak conclusion suggests that U.S. colonizers are implicated in the sensational crimes that the war provoked.

'BEL OF PRAIRIE EDEN.
A ROMANCE OF MEXICO

BY GEORGE LIPPARD, ESQ.,

Author of
"Washington and His Generals, or Legends of the Revolution,"
"The Quaker City," &c., &c.

"You see, it is a sad and yet a beautiful story, stranger, and it begins on the wild prairie—goes on in the city of Vera Cruz—winds up in Philadelphia. A sad story, and I'm loath to tell it; but as we're here alone by the camp fire, and may never see one another again, I'll tell it to you. But first, your word, stranger, that you'll never tell it again, until I am dead!"

—FROM THE MSS. JOURNAL OF A SOLDIER OF MONTEREY.[1]

CHAPTER I

"They are strangely superstitious, these wild men of the prairie, who, with rifle in hand, and the deep starlight of the illimitable heavens above, wander in silence over the trackless yet blooming wilderness. Left to their own thoughts, they seem to see spectral forms, rising from the shadows, and hear voices from the other world, in every unusual sound. Among their superstitions there is one which has often struck me with its singular interest and beauty."

—Mss. of a Texan.

"Come, brother, it is a beautiful view—look yonder."

The boy advanced from the shadow of the oak and gazed upon the prairie, bathed in the light of the setting sun. He was but a boy, slender and girlish in form, and yet he grasped a rifle in his hand and carried a knife in his belt.

His brother did not seem to heed him, but stood leaning against the trunk of the oak, his arms folded over his rifle, while his downcast eyes were fixed upon the sod. The sun in its last glow cast a warm light over his broad chest and muscular form, and invested with a golden flush, his fine aquiline features, shaded by a dark beard and flowing black hair. It was altogether a striking face; the eyes, somewhat sunken beneath the well-defined brows, were large, black, and strangely brilliant. He would have been observed and gazed at in any company, and even now, as he stood beside the oak, the boundless prairie around, and the Great God above, there was something noble in his look and bearing. It is true he wore a plaid gray frock, reaching to the knee and edged with fur, yet this unpretending garment displayed a broad chest, supported by a waist, at once slender and pliable, and revealed the iron outline of his sinewy arms. Its color, pale gray, gave a richer luster to the sunset glow which bathed his face.

On the sod before him lay his hat, a rude thing of gray felt, with skull-crown and wide slouching brim. It was decorated with a single black feather.

"Come, brother John; look! is it not a beautiful view? Our men, the Volunteers of Prairie Eden, encamped on the prairie; near this knoll, their horses grazing on the rich grass, as gathered in a circle, their rifles near them, they build the camp-fire and prepare for their evening meal. Look at the sky, John—not one cloud! Yes, one; a little cloud, hovering like a bird, in the west, just over the setting sun, and turning, blue, purple, and gold, as the light grows brighter ere it fades. The prairie, John,—the grass moving like waves at sea, with all kinds of beautiful flowers, starting from the sod. Come,—don't stand muttering there; come I say."

And the slender boy laid his hand upon his brother's arm, and playfully sought to raise his head.

The brother, still absorbed in his thoughts, did not heed him.

"Here we are, thirty miles from San Antonio. Shall we go forward?—shall we return home?"

"Home!—pshaw! Did we not leave Prairie Eden this morning—we—"

"*We!*" echoed the older brother, raising his eyes and surveying the girlish form before him.

"Yes, *we!*—the Volunteers of Prairie Eden—composed of Mr. Jacob Grywin's two sons, forty white laborers,—some civilized people from the States, other German emigrants—and ten black slaves; not to mention Ewen McGregor, who now comes up the knoll to speak with *Captain* John Grywin."

John raised his eyes, surveyed for a moment the smoke of the camp fire in the prairie, not one hundred yards from where he stood, and then his gaze rested upon the newcomer.

You will observe that the knoll on which the brothers stood was one of those delicious green islands which dot the rolling surface of the wild Texan prairie, and are seen by the wayfarer sometimes at the distance of thirty miles. It was crowned by a solitary tree, a green oak, whose trunk three men could not have spanned with their extended arms. Broad and wide above the brothers' head, stretched out the rugged branches, clad in a glorious drapery of silvery moss, which floated like a shining shroud, among the deep green leaves.

"Captain John, while the boys take their supper, I've come up here to have a little talk with you."

It was a harsh, grating voice. The figure was that of a giant, so towering in stature, so massive in the bull-like chest, and formidable long arms, whose corded sinews were impressed upon the folds of the gray sleeves.—The face was like the form, huge and burly. A red visage, with white eyebrows and eyelashes, short stiff red hair, and an immense red beard, matted like the mane of some wild animal. It was not the most prepossessing form in the world, nor the prettiest face, yet an air of bluff, hearty frankness, seemed to pervade each feature—even the mouth, with thick lips and the large eyes with yellowish balls—and govern the movement of every limb, as Ewen McGregor drew near the oak.

"Well, Ewen, or rather, Lieutenant McGregor—" said John.

"You see, when we left Prairie Eden this morning, bound for San Antonio, in obedience to a proclamation of the president of Texas, which summoned 'all good citizens' to the western frontier, menaced as it is by a fresh Mexican invasion—when we left, I say, there was some things which we *did* know, and some things which we *ought* to know, but *did not* know, by—!"[2]

"Well, Ewen?" said John, calmly surveying the bluff form before him, while Harry looked on with a sort of comical wonder dilating his clear blue eyes.

"We are going to San Antonio," resumed Ewen, resting his rifle on the sod. "For days there has been a rumor of the approach of the Mexican general who commands at Presidio del Rio Grande. How do we know that at this very moment this general, Don Bascus, is not in possession of San Antonio?"

"If we don't know we can easily ascertain. A ride of thirty miles after dark will bring us to San Antonio before midnight."

This cool response seemed to disconcert the bluff Ewen.

"But, Captain John, suppose the town should be occupied by some thousand Mexican devils—"

"That would make us equal. Fifty white men of Texas are equivalent to one thousand Mexicans, any day. That computation is in some degree unfair, for it gives one Texan and his good rifle for twenty Mexicans. You see, Ewen, General Bascus and his thousand men must not stand in the way of fifty volunteers from Prairie Eden."

"Not mentioning the ten niggers," laughed Harry, as he mischievously pulled Red Ewen by the beard. "We'll fling the darkies in, and not make any charge for them."

Was it a flush of anger that crossed Ewen's face? He was silent for a moment, and then in a voice and with a manner which indicated a man of some education, he resumed—

"Let us dismiss all jesting on the subject, John. General Bascus, whose approach is indicated by a rumor that grows more like truth every hour, has not merely a thousand men, but ten thousand incarnate devils with him. Suppose you go on to San Antonio tonight and fall into his clutches? Just think of it, John—you and your brother, and all your laborers and slaves, dragged away to rot in a Mexican prison, while your *father* and *Isabel* await your return at Prairie Eden."

This picture touched John with great force. Harry's smile died away and tears filled his blue eyes.

"O, John! Ewen speaks the truth! What would become of father and Isabel, in case we were taken prisoners?"

"Yes, I see it now; I was wrong this morning to leave them so utterly unprotected at Prairie Eden. To be sure, our home is isolated; there is not much danger from the Indians, and as for the neighbors, the nearest is ten miles from Prairie Eden. But what would you propose?"

"Remain encamped here tonight. It will be time enough for us to go on our way tomorrow morning. And in the meantime—but look to the east; do you see that knoll, distant some ten miles?"

They followed the direction of his brawny hand, and saw the knoll, rising dim and vague among the mists, which began to whiten the eastern prairie.

"I know Ben Davis, the scout, who has pitched his cabin there. If any one can give us any news of the Mexicans, he's the man to do it. By your leave, I will take my horse, ride over there, and have a talk with him. I can be back long afore midnight."

John's face manifested some thought. "It seems about the best course."

"Oh let him go—think of father—Isabel!" cried Harry, seizing his brother by both his hands.

Ewen smiled at Harry's earnestness, and smiled until his thick lips parted, and his decayed, irregular teeth were visible.

"Well, Ewen, you'd better go; and mind ye, let your return be as speedy as possible."

"Trust me for *that*!"

And Red Ewen turned away, without a moment's delay, and descended the knoll, bending his steps toward the encampment. They saw his broad knife glistening in the sun, as he crushed the grass with his long heavy strides.

"Do you remember Ewen in Philadel—" Harry began as he surveyed the peaceful group of the encampment of rugged hunters encircling the fires which sent their volumes of pale smoke into the sky.

"Hush!" and John's brow grew dark; his eye flashed with sudden intensity; "we never mention that name in the prairie."

"There he goes, the Giant with Red Head and Thick Lips! Look how he rides!"

Wishing to drive his brother's thoughts from a painful topic, he stretched forth his small white hand and pointed toward Ewen, who was seen dashing toward the east, mounted on one of those fiery horses, peculiar to the prairie, with eyes like coals, and long, black, matted mane.

John stood buried in thought. The twilight was gathering over the prairie, and in the broad west glowed the last flush of the departed sun. A fresh breeze arose and came tossing the grass like waves, as it gathered perfume from the innumerable flowers.

Henry gazed with some awe in the face of his older brother, and saw his brow grow darker, his eye more wild and absent in its glance.

"It's always the way with him when I mention that name," he said and turned away to the western edge of the knoll.

It was a very beautiful thing to see the last flush of the day imparting its soft golden warmth to that boyish face, whose white brow and clear blue eyes seemed animated with a deep, tranquil delight.

The boy was gazing to the west, far, far over the boundless view, as the night seemed hovering above the prairie, pausing for a moment ere it came down to kiss the flowers and sleep upon its breast.

Far in the north-west, the level line of the horizon was broken by an almost imperceptible elevation which shone like a golden point, from the shadows which sheltered around and beneath. Henry gazed upon that elevation, earnestly and long, until his breath came in gasps, his blue eyes acquired a light, well-nigh as intense as his brother's.

"That must be *Prairie Eden*," he said, as sinking on the sod, he crossed his hands upon his knees, and thought, while the night came down, of home, of father and Isabel.

The night came slowly in its starlight drapery, and still the boy Harry sat in silence on the edge of the prairie knoll, his slender form couched artlessly on the tall thick grass, while his eyes were raised to the heavens, and an indefinable emotion stole over his face. Believe me, it was a face to love, so much of woman in its every outline, and yet a firmness like that of tried manhood, manifested in the sudden flash of the blue eyes, the quick nervous compression of the warm lips.

And the breeze tossed his soft brown hair, and it floated in glossy masses over his forehead, but could not hide the tears that came imperceptibly into his eyes, and made them shine the brighter in the deep starlight.

"I know what they are doing now at Prairie Eden. I can see the wide hall lighted up, and father sitting near the table with the Bible on his knee. Sister is near him, bending over his shoulders as he reads. Yes, yes; I can see her black ringlets touching his gray hair, and floating upon his forehead. It is a happy home, and—"

His fancy dared not look upon the picture of the future, for a vision of war and battles rose up before him, and while his young blood danced with the raptures of a soldier's life, he seemed to hear a voice which said,—"*And that home you will never reach again!*"

Long he sat there, absorbed in his own thoughts, while from the other side of the knoll, the songs and merry voices of the encamped Volunteers of Prairie Eden, broke unheeded on his ear. At last his waking thoughts melted in a dream, and sinking on the sod, with the rifle in his hand, he slept the sound sleep of boyhood—that sleep worth all the gold and power in the world, for angels watch over it, and fan the sleeper's cheek with their invisible wings.

He unclosed his eyes at last, and started up half-dreaming and but half-awake. The morn was rising over the prairie. Far in the east a globe of pale gold was seen on the verge of the horizon, gleaming a sad and solemn light, as it was about to launch away into the great ocean of the sky.

As Harry started to his feet a dark object interposed between his sight and the moon. He passed his hand over his forehead, and with the peculiar nervous fear of one suddenly aroused from a sound slumber, uttered an ejaculation that broke with startling emphasis on the dead silence of the prairie.

For all was dead and still. The camp fires had gone out, the song of the hunters died away. Not a voice nor sound—no vision but the great prairie stretching forth in the light of the rising morn, with that unknown object towering black and dark before him.

"Who comes there?" He stood with the rifle in his grasp, his finger on the trigger.

A voice answered him—could it be his brother's, so changed and hollow?— "Harry, it is I!" It scarcely rose above a whisper—"Hush!—not a word. Our horses are ready at the foot of the knoll—come!"

Wondering whether he was awake or dreaming, he suffered that extended arm to lead him silently down the knoll. He saw his own horse and his brother's standing there, the saddles on the horses, the reins flung over their necks, and for the first time recognized his brother in the dusky figure.

"Mount!" And his brother's face was turned to the moon; Harry saw with indefinable fear, that the features were changed, his eyes unnaturally vivid and glaring, the broad forehead marked with swollen veins.

"Brother—" he faltered out as he placed his feet in the stirrups.

"Not a word! Turn your horse toward Prairie Eden and ride as though a thousand deaths were dogging at his heels. Do not spare the spur,—follow me!"

John's horse plunged beneath the merciless iron, and dashed through the grass, as though possessed by a devil.

Henry saw his brother's form, rising boldly in the moonlight, and urged his own horse forward at the top of his speed.

"But, the volunteers, brother," he cried, as he grasped for breath.

"Ride, I say! That star in the north-west—you see it? Don't take your eyes from it. On, in the name of God! That star shines above Prairie Eden."

Away they dashed without a word, their horses maddened by the sharp steel points, bounding over the sod with an accelerating speed that seemed rather like the flight of a bird than the pace of an animal.

Not a word passed between the brothers, for Harry, panting for breath and racked by the plunging gait of the horse, looked on the form of John with an unknown feeling, something between wonder and awe.

Once or twice a word trembled on his lips—but still his brother, without turning his head, muttered between his teeth,—

"Ride!—spur! It is thirty miles to Prairie Eden—we must reach it in two hours or we are accursed for ever!"

There was something terrible in the sight!—these black horses, with snorting nostrils and starting eyeballs, plunging over the prairie, while their riders dug the spurs into their flanks until the blood spouted forth and mingled with the white foam.

The moon shone over them as they dashed away, and flung their shadows far and black upon the waving grass. John never once turned his head, but kept his eye fixed on the *star*. Harry could not keep his gaze from his brother's changed and ghastly face,—it held him like a spell.

At last—it was when the moon was high above the horizon, and an hour and a half had passed away—Harry's horse stumbled and fell, the blood pouring in torrents from his nostrils.

Severely bruised and half-stunned, Harry struggled from beneath the flanks of his dying horse, and saw John reining his steed back on his haunches.

"Your horse is dying—come! Give me your hand! Spring up before me—now then! Yonder is the island knoll of Prairie Eden—only five miles distant."

Harry felt his brother's strong arm around his chest, and saw his eyes—almost touching his cheek—flash with the same unnatural fire—he felt that his brother was mad, and grew cold as ice, although the breath that fanned his cheek was like the air of a furnace.

"Only four miles—do you see the knoll, Harry? The house among the trees—ah!"

Down came the horse upon his knees—he made an effort to rise, trembling in every nerve—it was in vain. With that desperate effort he rolled upon the sod, the brothers half bruised beneath his quivering flanks. It was scarcely an instant before John had gained his feet and rescued his brother from his perilous situation.

"Harry—are you hurt? Have you strength left to run those four miles? Take your rifle and come."

He clutched his brother in an iron grasp, and hurried him away, rather dragging him along than running by his side.

"It may have been a dream," he muttered; "but, no, no!—I saw *him*! With my eyes—before me!"

"Saw *him*?" Harry gasped, as all the blood in his body seemed rushing to his eyes.

"Yes; I saw *him*—no vision—reality, my brother, horrible reality! My God! the moon fades, the day is breaking. We've at least four miles to go. Do not fall, Harry, do not faint—a firm heart, my boy, and God will bless us! You know I am not superstitious, but tonight, as I stood beside the oak, while you lay sleeping near me, I saw *him*, with his white beard and spectral eyes, and—he was dressed like an old hunter, Harry,—you have heard the old prairie hunters tell of him,—how he walks the prairie at dead of night, and starts suddenly upon you, from the earth, at your horse's side, or even from the sod, where you lay sleeping. He wakes you with an ice-cold hand—so the hunters tell the story. But you know they are superstitious. I believe in nothing of the kind—I—but tonight I saw him at my side! Look, Harry, the sun is rising, and we're three miles from the knoll!"

Thus gasping these incoherent words, as he dragged his awe-stricken and fainting brother along, John kept his eyes upon the knoll and his face grew even yet more pale, his eyes more frenzied, as the first ray of the rising sun shot like a golden thread, across their path.

"Saw whom? Speak, John! Your face frightens me—I believe I'm dying—" he sank on one knee.

"Harry, my dear boy—my child!—Oh do not faint now! in a little while and we are there! You are strong, Harry, it is but fancy—come, I will carry you! But I saw him tonight, and talked with him, *The Old Man of the Prairie*! that specter of these horrible solitudes, who comes to the dwellers in the wilderness, and tells them of coming evil—nothing but evil. He told me— look, Harry, the sun is shining on the knoll!"

Ere we record the full history of the eventful night—it was in the spring-time of 1842, that these incidents occurred,—let us, in order to understand the history in all its details, gaze on a scene which occurred some ten years before.

CHAPTER II

Prairie Eden

A lone Indian stood on the summit of the mound.

It was in the center of one of those prairies which, in their boundless view, their vast horizon, remind us of the ocean, only for waves of foam, we behold emerald grass, tossing with gentle undulations, their summits crested by the roses of the wild rising into view, like sea foam, tinted by the last glow of a setting sun.

These prairies, like the ocean, have their islands—green mounds, that rise above the boundless level, blossoming on their banks, with flowers and vines; crowned on the summit with aged trees, that stand in circular groups, like the solemn mourners over the dead centuries.

A lone Indian, leaning on his rifle, his muscular form, attired in a panther's hide, which left his sinewy arms and broad chest, bare to the light, stood on the summit of a green island, in the center of that boundless prairie.

His head was drooped, his dark eye, fixed by strange emotions, glared with an immoveable gaze over the glorious view.

Around the prairie that rolled away, far into the distance, until it became lost in the hazy line of the horizon, above the blue sky of a summer's day, dimpled only by a group of snowy clouds, that seemed to undulate in mid-air, the clear azure gleaming distinctly through their feathery folds, even as a virgin's bosom looks more beautiful through a veil of lace; by his side, a massive oak, the broad green leaves almost touching the tuft on his shaven brow. Alone that Indian stood, his body turned to the west, while, with his face over his shoulder, he gazed long and sadly upon the eastern land.

It was a sad gaze, eloquent as a smile upon the lips of a dying man, whose veins are racked by superhuman torture.

The trees of the island grove were all around him. Giant oaks, not more than twenty in number, circled on a space some three hundred yards square. Their trunks were like the huge pillars of some temple, reared in the wilderness to God; massive as blocks of granite, and encrusted with the thick bark, that had been hardening for centuries. Three hundred years had written their dusky memories upon that rugged rind of the ancient oaken trees. White moss clothed their far-spreading branches, and graceful vine blossoms trembled among their leaves of luxuriant green.

A hundred men might have encamped with ease beneath each grand old oak, and found shelter from the sun and rain, in the shadow, the silence, the fragrant air of the green island of the boundless prairie.

The sod, smooth as a floor, and covered with dark green moss, was sprinkled with flowers, whose unnumbered shapes of graceful beauty and dyes of rainbow loveliness, neither pencil nor pen can ever paint. Upon the foliage quivered the drops of last night's shower.

And in the center of the island, a spring of clear, cold water bubbled into light, between two huge rocks, and without a visible outlet, kept murmuring and sparkling forever, always clear, cold, and pure.

The Indian gazed to the west, and the silent eloquence of his deep eye found vent in his rude Indian tongue.

"My fathers dwelt here, when these giant trees were saplings, not higher than my rifle, Where are they now? Before this knoll itself was reared, as the grave of warriors, Red Men were upon this soil, the Kings, the Prophets of their people. Where are they now? The bones of the mighty men rest in the bosom of this knoll—but their children, where are they? Look for them far away by the great Salt Lake, in the land of the setting sun!"

Once more the Indian turned his eye to the east, as though in the dim line of the horizon he already discerned the banners and bayonets of White civilization, and then turning sadly away, he sat him down by the waters of the island spring.

"Water, that comes from the caverns where my fathers sleep, I drink from your fountain, once more, and drink for the last time, ere I depart forever!"

Bathing his hands and brow in the pure element of the island fountain, he went on his way toward the west and came back no more.

Years passed on, and that prairie of the wilderness was left to solitude and God. In the tall grass the deer, with branching horns and mild eyes, moved over the flowers, the roses, the dahlias, and the lilies of the desert, without a fear. Along the summit of the island came herds of wild cattle, drinking one by one at the pure spring—gazing for a moment at the boundless view, and then dashing away through the sea of undulating grass, like a cloud hurled by a thunder storm. Sometimes the wolf, gaunt and lean, and treacherous as a hypocrite, stole over the sod of the island grove, and the jaguar, with its flashing eye and sleek fur, dipped his blood-streaked jaws, in the clear wave of the island fountain.

But man came nevermore along the prairie. The Indian—search for him toward the west, in the land of the setting sun. The White Man—yonder, in the region of the rising sun he dwells. His footsteps have never pressed this virgin soil.

Ten years passed, and a strange sight was seen one summer morning upon the summit of the island grove.

A large mansion, reared in the space between those circling trees, and built of massive logs, disclosed its lofty hall door, its many windows, and its steep roof, varied by numerous chimneys, to the beams of the rising sun.

The huge trees stretched forth their boughs above its roof, and the vines trailed in festoons about its windows. Its black timbers looked out from the graceful drapery of the white moss, hanging like a silvery shroud from branch to branch and from tree to tree.

Altogether, this huge mansion looked like a baronial fabric of the Middle Ages, invested as it was with the tokens of a barbarous luxury, something between savage grandeur and refined civilization. It was two stories in height, with four spacious rooms on a floor. These rooms were divided on the first floor, by a spacious hall; on the second by a corridor.

Instead of paint or plaster, the walls of log were concealed by hangings of various hues and devices, some of dark green Cordovan leather, edged with gold, some of the richest silk. The chairs, the tables, the fire places, and the stairway, were all on the same scale of antique grandeur, mingling luxury and rudeness in every detail.

From the center of their island grove, this spacious mansion rose, with the green sod all around it, the trees half closing it from the sun and rain, the cool fountain bubbling near it, some few paces to the west.

Yonder, north of the grove, you behold fields of emerald corn, with small huts, built of logs, rising from the quivering leaves. On the prairie graze herds of sleek cattle, their dappled sides contrasting with the rich grass around, the quivering beds of wild flowers beneath. And at the morning time, a column of blue smoke rises over the tops of the trees, and glows, like the white breast of a bird turned to the rising sun. It is incense from the fireside of the prairie home.

Who is it that dwells within the prairie home?

A father and his three children.

That father, a man of slender form, gray hairs, and sad aspect. He was known by the name of Jacob Grywin. The nearest neighbor—who lived only ten miles from the island grove—looked with wonder, mingled with some awe, upon the sad, stern man, who had so suddenly erected his home in the wilderness.

He came—no one knew whither. In the year 1840, after the young Texas had struggled into Independence, through the bloody clouds of Goliad, the Alamo, and San Jacinto, the emigrant first appeared on the prairie, and with his family of three children, his retainers—some fifty in number, and mostly from the "States"—some dozen German colonists, and as many slaves, reared the mansion, known by the appropriate name—*Prairie Eden.*[3]

Two years had passed, and the unknown emigrant, living in a kind of barbarous splendor, beheld his children rising round him, like fruit and flowers, nursed into vigorous bloom by the air of the wilderness.

His sons presented a strong contrast. John, aged twenty-one, was a man of stalwart, yet graceful proportions, with a dark brown visage, strongly marked with aquiline features, and shadowed by dark hair and beard. He was a magnificent horseman and a fearless hunter. As he mounted his dark bay horse, with his rifle, "Old King Death," as he quaintly called it, slung over his shoulder, his long hair floating in the wind, and his eagle-like features, marked boldly out against the sky, he looked for all the world, like a true knight of the chivalric age.

Harry, his brother, a mere boy of sixteen, with girlish form, and beardless face, along whose smooth outline flowed his curling brown hair, compared with John, reminded you of the quivering sapling beside the hardy oak.—And yet there was a volume of daring in the glance of his dark blue eye. John loved him, as though he was at once father, brother, and friend to girlish Harry,— even as David loved Jonathan, with a love passing the love of women.

The third child, three years younger than John, and of course, one year older than Harry. I see her now, standing upon the porch of the mansion, her dark hair, plainly turned aside, from the warm beauty of her face, while her round arms, full bust, and passionate eyes, attest an impetuous, nay a voluptuous woman.

She was indeed one of the women, whom we call "queenly," especially in case our knowledge of queens is limited. Her stature was commanding. Her complexion, a clear, deep olive, burning with red bloom on each cheek. Her lips, full and warm, and tinted with dewy vermillion. Her forehead, white and high, with the jet-black hair, shadowing its outlines.

These words may give you some idea of 'Bel Grywin, but no words can describe how suddenly her face changed its expression, now glooming like a thunder storm, the eyes armed with lightning and the brow gathering blackness; and in a moment, soft and yielding and tender, as the face of a slumbering child.

When the eye of the father rested upon the faces of his children, the cloud passed from his brow. But when he was alone, either striding along the porch of his mansion, in gazing silently over the great prairie, or passing, with cat-like step, from room to room, there was a gloom upon his features, which, to say the least, was not pleasant to behold.

That sidelong glance toward the window, or the door, that involuntary start at the sound of a footstep, what did they mean?

What need Jacob Grywin fear? Centered in the midst of this prairie, afar from civilization, and yet surrounded by all of its comforts—nay, its luxuries; his children blooming round him, and his slaves and laborers ready to do his will, what had he to fear?

There came a day in the spring of 1842, when the Proclamation of the Texan president summoned all good citizens to the western frontier, in order to defend the soil of the young state from a threatened invasion.—Mexico was, of course, known to be the invader, and the impulse of the invasion, Santa Anna.

Vague rumors floated over the prairie, telling of outrages on the frontier, and it soon became a settled opinion that Santa Anna, like the Bourbons, could neither forget nor learn. It became evident that the horrid butcheries of past years were again to be enacted on Texan soil. That Santa Anna, who had been dragged from a swamp, clad in the garb of one of his lackeys, after the battle of San Jacinto—presenting a rather contemptible image of despair, had not forgiven the Texans for sparing his life. In a certain view of the matter he was right, for if ever a murderer forfeited his life, by a series of cold-blooded butcheries, that murderer was San Antonio Lopez De Santa Anna.[4]

Among other rumors it was announced that Don General Something, from the Presidio del Rio Grande, was approaching the western frontier, in formidable force, his object, the possession and plunder of San Antonio, near which still arose the blackened walls of the Alamo.

These rumors reached the solitude of Prairie Eden. One morning,—it was when the spring of 1842 was melting into summer,—John had a mysterious and energetic conversation with his father; and ere an hour had passed, the entire population of Prairie Eden, numbering nearly seventy men of all colors and nations, had taken horse and rifle, and ridden away in the direction of San Antonio De Bexar.

Mr. Jacob Grywin and his daughter 'Bel, alone remained on the island knoll.

At the head of the Volunteers of Prairie Eden rode the brothers, John and Harry. By their side, the overseer of the plantation,—Red Ewen McGregor, a man of gigantic frame and rude aspect, who seemed connected with the old man by some mysterious and indefinable tie.

It was John's object to advance to San Antonio, with all his disposable force, join his men with other bands of volunteers, and make a Texan resistance to the approaching Mexican army. He did not contemplate an absence of more than one week from Prairie Eden. The isolated position of his father's mansion—so they all said—was its surest defense against any predatory attack.

Let us now return to this night in the spring or early summer of 1842.

CHAPTER III

The Chamber of 'Bel of Prairie Eden

"A hideous alternative,—your honor or *his* life."

—Texan Mss.

It was deep night, and the stars shone with their calm, sad light over the mansion and the grove of Prairie Eden.

In the mansion all was still as death. The old man slumbered in his chamber on the ground floor; his daughter slept in her room on the second floor.

All the other chambers were tenantless, and a silence like a tomb brooded over the corridors of that prairie home. The wind sighed mournfully through the tops of the trees, as their mossy branches swept the roof. The sound of the island fountain, making low music, as it bubbled from its cavern source, was heard in every pause of the breeze.

Yet within the mansion—tenanted only by the old man and his child—all was darkness and silence.

The chamber of Isabel!

A large room, lighted by a lamp that stands upon a table near the bed, and sheds a feeble and flickering ray. It is shadowy here, in the bower of virgin repose, and yet you may discern the luxurious details of the place.—Soft matting on the floor, whose down-like texture would not return too rudely, the presence of an infant's naked foot. Curtains of pale crimson silk, hanging from the ceiling, and imparting a warm roseate glow to the face of the sleeper. Yonder an image of the Divine Virgin, a marble shape, elevated on its snowy pedestal, and over the mantle a picture of a wild-wood scene in far-distant Pennsylvania.

The bed, with curtains, and coverlet, and pillows, all like a snow bank freshly fallen from the sky, so pure, so white, so spotless.—The curtain is slightly parted; through the interval gleams the vision of that face, framed in the darkly flowing hair, and pillowed on right arm, that bosom, which now is lost to view, and now quivers into light, above the tremulous lace of the night robe. A beautiful woman slumbering; with her lips, so ripe in their red bloom, gently parted, until they disclose the white teeth; the eyes closed, with the long black fringes resting on the cheek—It is a sight for angels to behold and love.

She tosses in her slumber—you see a full round arm, with its small hand, all beautiful as an arm and hand of alabaster, tinted by the daybreak flush extended from the curtains. You hear a whispered word. Then the sleeper sinks into repose like death, and a single black tress, curves over her neck and nestles on her bosom.

At this moment a faint, creaking sound is heard, and all is still again. The door slowly opens, and a face, leering with a hideous smile, appears in the dusky interval. A cautious, cat-like footstep, and a form advances to the maiden's bed, and the light of the taper reveals a strange picture.

That face, with short stiff hair and shaggy beard, alike scarlet red in hue, the bleared eyes and the thick lips, laughing the same brutal scorn upon the sleeping woman, that almost giant form, clad in the costume of a Mexican ranchero, white pantaloons, ornamented with glittering buttons, green jacket, tawdry with gilt trappings and a stout leather belt, girdling two pistols and a long and quivering knife.

Who is this ruffian that dares intrude upon the sanctity of a maiden's bed chamber?

He sweeps aside the curtains, his breath pollutes the cheeks of the slumbering Isabel.

You see his thick lips parting in a brutal grin, his huge arms extended, his colorless eyeballs—so white, and bleared, and glossy—fire with a gloating intensity.

The white breast, the round neck, the warm countenance of Isabel lay open to that gaze of pollution.

He turns to the door—listens. All is still! The hand of the ruffian plays upon the hilt of his knife, but it is for a moment only. Extending his brawny arms, he grasps her form and tears her, half-naked, from her virgin bed.

In a moment the room is vacant. The outline of that pure woman's form is still traced upon the pillow, the lamp yet burns on the table, but the room is silent and tenantless.

But did you see that unconscious form, bound in the ruffian's arms; did you—even as he left the room—see that face, turned over his shoulder? The long, black hair showering down his back, as the eyes unclosed with a frightening glance?

There is a gasping, half-suppressed cry in the corridor without—a hurried footstep and all is still again.

When Isabel, thus rudely torn from her bed, unclosed her eyes, she beheld the dark green hangings of the eastern room on the ground floor.

Pinioned in the ruffian's arm, she gazed around with the frightened glance of one suddenly aroused from a dreamless slumber, and beheld that wide room crowded by the forms of armed men, attired in the half-bandit, half-soldier costume of Mexican rancheros.[5] A solitary ruffian stood alone in the center of the group, his slender form and bearded face, revealed by the light of the blazing pine knot, which he raised above his head with his right hand.

That light flashed strongly over the green jackets and tinsel trappings of the soldiers, and played upon the blade of every long and quivering knife.

For a moment the maiden trembled with fright as she beheld that swarthy face, scowling all around her, but that moment passed, the warm blood coursed over her face and bosom; with a sudden movement she flung herself from the ruffian's arms and confronted the assassin band.

"Why this outrage?" she cried, dashing the clustering hair aside from her face, and fixing the glance of an indignant eye upon the foremost of the group. She looked very beautiful, that half-clad woman, whose clasped arms were dressed upon her tumultuous bosom, with her unbound hair streaming over her white shoulders.

There was dead stillness, and then a deep groan from the dark recesses of the room.

The bandits parted, and in the interval made by their movement to either side, appeared an old man, whose slender form was clad in plain black, while his strongly marked features were rendered ghastly by a livid paleness.

"My father! You here, bound too, and in these ruffian arms?"

The old man, Jacob Grywin, replied by wringing his pinioned arms and uttering a low, deep moan.

"My sons! my sons! why did I suffer them to depart to San Antonio? My men, too—all are gone, and here I am. Would to God I had only faithful Ewen here!"

He spoke of the overseer of his plantation, that brave hardy fellow, who had left for San Antonio in company with his sons.

A hoarse laugh echoed round the chamber—at once Jacob looked up, and Isabel turned as though a viper had bit her heel.

"Your 'faithful' Ewen is here!" said the voice of the ruffian, who had torn Isabel from her bed.

There he stood, dressed like the rancheros, his stiff red hair and matted red beard imparting new hideousness to his bleared eyes and grinning lips.

The old man was speechless. You see Isabel survey the ruffian from head to foot, while her face changes color, now red as daybreak, now white as a shroud.

"Aye, it's me:—Ewen McGregor, Red Ewen, or whatever the boys choose to call me! I *am* here! This band of trusty spirits are mine. I have come here at dead of night to secure this traitor to the Republic of Mexico.—We had hard riding to reach the place in time—a great many weary miles since nine o'clock. Somewhat in a hurry, you know; for tomorrow morning your sons will be home—bye-the-bye, I left John and Harry at sunset. They were quite well."

He drew his knife and playfully felt its sharp edge.

"My God! can this be real?" moaned the old man.

"I tell you it can be, and it is."

"But you were my friend—my overseer—you followed my fortunes into the wilderness—Ewen a traitor! No, no! I will not believe it."

The ruffian advanced, confronted the old man, and glowered upon him with his bloodshot eyes,—

"You talk of traitor—*you*. The broken bank director of Philadelphia, who turned traitor to the trust of some thousand widows and orphans, and then fled the city, seeking refuge for his guilty wealth in the prairie of Texas, sixty miles from San Antonio. Oh, Jacob! Pshaw, man! I know you. You forget that I was your clerk."

It was a hard blow; the old man felt it to the heart.

As for Isabel, she stood like a thing of marble, frightfully pale, her clasped hands pressed nervously against her bared bosom.

"You here too, my pretty one!" the ruffian sneered, as he turned upon her. "In my power! You were once the *aristocratic* lady of the aristocratic mansion, in Philadelphia. *Now*—"

A movement was observable among the soldiers and a form advanced into the glare of the pine torch.

It was a young man slenderly made, with an olive cheek and long flowing curls of jet black hair. His beard and mustache, all curling and as soft as silk, imparted a chivalric appearance to his delicately cut features. His eyes were very large and bright, and withal intensely black. Their expression was peculiar, indefinable.

A close-fitting uniform of dark green, relieved by a single row of gold buttons, displayed the elegant proportions of his form.

"Isabel," he whispered, "we did not anticipate this moment when we last met."

He bowed low before the half-clad maiden, and looked on her with upraised eyes.

"Don Antonio!" was all that trembled from the lips of the wondering girl.

It was a strange group. The central figures—that handsome soldier with the olive cheek and smooth silken beard; the beautiful girl, whose flowing hair but faintly concealed the fluttering of her bosom; the light held overhead by the brigand soldier, the livid face of the father and the brutal sneer of Ewen, distinctly revealed by its glare—the encircling rancheros and the dark background of the curtained walls.

A strange group, now shown in red light, again darkened by the shadows as they went and came.

Don Antonio drew near to the maiden, extending an elegant cloak of rich, purple velvet, edged with golden fringe. Gently he flung it over her shoulders, and as her bosom was veiled beneath its folds, he whispered,—

"Isabel! for the sake of the Holy Trinity, let me see you *alone*—alone, for one moment only."

He spoke in English, somewhat fluently, though with a decided Spanish accent. There seemed a more eloquent language; so thought Isabel, in his large lustrous eyes.

"Come!" she whispered and led the way from the room.

"You must be in a hurry, I tell ye," they heard the coarse tones of Red Ewen, "for we have got a heap of justice to do, and little time to do it in."

Up the stairway she led him, and scarce knowing whither she went, entered the bed chamber from which she had been torn only a moment past.

There, by the light of the taper, which stood upon the table, near the bed, there, in the silence and gloom of that virgin retreat, they confronted each other.

Isabel, very pale, with her white arms, appearing from the folds of the purple cloak, her naked feet touching the soft matting on the floor; Don Antonio, with his brow uncovered, his head drooped, his upturned eyes, resting on the half-shrouded form before him.

"Speak," she gasped; "this outrage—"

The words died on her tongue.

In a voice tremulous with delicate modulations, Don Antonio spoke, still maintaining that respectful bearing.

"You are in danger, Isabel! Last Thursday, at our nearest military post, sixty miles away, this ruffian Ewen appeared, denounced your father to the colonel of our regiment, stated the unprotected situation of Prairie Eden, and offered to lead a picked squadron to the place."

"Ah! I remember he was absent two days last week. But what charge could the traitor prefer against my father?"

"You know, Isabel, that our Government has decreed a new invasion of the rebellious Province of Texas. Our armies, even now, are encamped on its southern border. Ewen stated that your father's house was often used as a rendezvous for the rebel Texans. Nay, that his sons, his laborers, his very slaves, within a few days depart to join the army of some Texan general at San Antonio. I fear me it will go very hard with your father.—This Ewen is as cruel, as brutal, as traitors always are."

"But you can save us! You whom we knew in our prosperous days."

A meaning smile crossed the face of the Mexican.

"I am only a subordinate officer. Red Ewen met us after sunset, at a designated point, and took command of this squadron on horse."

"And my father?"

"May be put to death within an hour. Red Ewen seems to have some secret purpose of revenge."

Isabel sank to the floor; not prostrate, but kneeling with her white arms upraised, her eyes streaming tears!

"My God! it seems like a hideous dream."

The Mexican raised his hand to his eyes—was it to hide a tear?

"But you can save us, Don Antonio!" And with a bound she passed the distance between them, and knelt at his feet. "You *will* save us! I see how it is— you only accompanied this expedition to do us service. O remember how my father's home in Philadelphia was once your home; remember—"

"How the peerless Isabel scorned the suit of Don Antonio Marin, the attache of the Mexican legation, at Washington. Is it so, Miss Grywin?"

Was that a sneer upon his dark-red lip?—What meant that sudden lighting up of his large eyes?

Isabel trembled, shuddered as she beheld the sudden change of the Mexican's face. In an instant that expression was gone; he was composed and respectful again.

"O, you would not be so ungenerous as to revive that memory now! I was but young—vain, frivolous then. I refused your suit it is true; my father to that refusal added some words, at once needless and bitter; but now, we are in danger; you will save us!"

"Rise, lady! On one condition I will peril my life to save you."

He raised her gently from the floor. She stood there, erect as a queen upon her throne. Around her neck waved her glossy black hair. You could see her young bosom pant and writhe beneath the velvet cloak.

"One condition!" she murmured; and waited for him to speak.

He spoke it with his eyes. With his parting lips. With that sudden gaze which devoured every outline, every tint of her voluptuous form, from the head framed in the black hair, to the feet as white as marble.

She shrank back as though a bullet had pierced her brain.

"No! No! No! You cannot be so base as to think it!"

"Isabel—" the whisper, husky with passion, fell on her like a torrent of boiling lead. "The case is plain. I love you—have loved you for years. Be mine, and I will sacrifice my rank, my honor, to serve you!"

"Be mine!"—she echoed his words, and looked at him with a dumb, wandering stare.

He beckoned her to the window.

"Look yonder!"

She looked, but would not believe her eyes. There rolled the prairie, silvered by the rising moon, but she saw it not, nor dwelt on the solemn beauty of that boundless sky.

But a pine torch flung its ruddy glow over the sward in front of the mansion. That light revealed the bandit soldiers, the form of Red Ewen in their midst. There, with his neck bared, his brow uncovered, his face livid as death, stood her father.

There was a rope about his neck, and that rope swung loosely, as it was tied to the oaken branch above his head.

Isabel beheld that hideous picture, and sunk like a crushed flower, on the floor. All sense, all consciousness were gone. Her white arms, relieved by the purple cloak, dropped by her side, a glimpse of her pulseless bosom gleamed over the golden edge of the garment. She lay like a dead woman, her face like marble, her eyes wide open and glassy.

Don Antonio bore her to the bed, and stamped his foot thrice upon the floor. A burly ranchero appeared in the shadows of the doorway; it was Red Ewen, in his hunter's garb.

"Wine, slave! Search the cellars of the old heretic, and bring me a goblet of his rich old wine!"

This, it must be confessed, did not look very much like respecting Red Ewen as the *superior officer.*

A few brief moments passed—the lady still lay swooning—and Ewen, the newly fledged ranchero, appeared with a massy golden cup in his hand, its glittering flowers contrasting with the purple gleam of the liquid trembling against the brim.

"Begone! And mark ye, *Don* Ewen, *commander of the squadron of Mexican horse!* do as I have commanded you. Begone!"

The ranchero was gone. Don Antonio was alone with the unconscious woman. What means that scowl glooming over his handsome face? What means that hand lifted over the goblet—that white powder, pouring from the paper in his fingers down into the red current of the wine?

He gazed upon her, his black eyes dilating until they assumed a tiger-like glare. So helpless she lay beside him, unconscious, upon her virgin bed, with her dark hair wound about her round white throat; so like an image of purity, carved out of Parisian marble, with her glassy eyes turned toward heaven!

Ah, that was a coward act, Don Antonio! To sweep the cloak aside and gaze with gloating eyes upon the shrine of purity—her white and pulseless bosom.

Ah, that was a traitor's kiss; that kiss from your burning lips pressed upon her lips as cold as clay.

"Awake! Isabel, my love! I will save your father!"

His arm is around her waist—he presses his bearded cheek against her cheek of velvet softness, and his lips, pressed with passion, quiver against hers.

Dreamily she unclosed her eyes, and all unconscious as she was, drank from the goblet which he held to her lips.

Then her countenance glowed, a blush like living flame overspread her face, her eyes seemed on fire with liquid light.

"Where am I?" she gasped. "Ah, these forms that glide to and fro in the dance, these fountains that murmur drowsily in mine ears, these gardens, where a thousand lights break from the shadowy trees over groves of flowers."

"Her mind wanders!" and Don Antonio smiled until his white teeth shone like ivory under his black mustache.

The maiden rose, spread forth her arms like one struggling with a fatal sleep. The cloak fell, and that form, which combined all that is beautiful in the physical and intellectual organization of woman, glowed in the light, from its trembling veil. The drugged potion was in her veins—you can see it in the voluptuous dimness of her eyes, in the deeper red of her lips.

Even in this moment her soul shone out, from the clouds which had begun to darken it.

"Ah! Where am I? Don Antonio, is it you? My father—oh save him!" such were her incoherent words.

Don Antonio started to his feet, and at once there gleamed from his eyes a strange light—there broke over his lips a stranger smile.

"Listen, Isabel,—but two minutes of consciousness, of volition are yours! In those brief minutes I will lay your fate before you—aye, and you shall read it. Two years ago, in the city of Washington, you scorned my suit. Scorned! Your father heaped insult upon your scorn. My time has come!—Unless you become mine—mine at this hour, mine without priest or vow, I swear to leave your father to his fate—"

"Mercy!"

"That fate, death by the rope, at the hands of the ruffian, Red Ewen! Your brothers will return by morning light, but it will be too late—we will then be far on our way; but your father will swing on that tree, before the door of his home!"

"You cannot be human! Not one drop of pity, not one—"

"Reflect! I do not force your wishes.—You may swoon, but unless you say 'yes' to my proposal, your father shall hang, and you will not feel my kiss upon your lips! Say 'yes,' and I will save him. I that love you with a love that is merciless in its every pulsation. I that adore you so much that I will wreck every moment of your existence unless you consent to become mine!"

He shook his small white hands above his head in the impulse of the fiery thought which corded every muscle of his face, and gleamed like an undying vengeance from his eyes.

"One moment only remains! Think—I will not speak to you until that moment and consciousness are gone!"

He turned away into the darker corner of the room.

Standing near the bed, her form erect, her black hair tossing on her brow, she felt that the drugged potion was working in her veins, and that the next minute would fire her heart with the mad dream of voluptuous passion.

Her mind was very clear—like a lake enshrined in the hollow of a mountain top, its glassy surface unruffled by a breeze. But the next moment!

Slowly, she glided to the window. Again that sight.—The livid face, the dangling rope. With a creeping shudder she turned away, and turned her eyes upon the tempter.

In the dim corner he stood; his finger pressed against his lip, his dark eyes blazing upon her even through the gloom!

Pity her now, all good angels!

She felt the blood rushing to her brain; she heard gentle voices singing songs, as in the air; she saw soft masses of light playing over the uncovered forms of dancing women. Like a sleep that dream, born of opium, possessed her nerves, her brain, her soul!

"Yes!"

It is morning, and a faint ray of light trembles through the darkness of the corridor. Let us await, in this silence and gloom, with our eyes fixed upon the massive panels of yonder door. That door leads into the bed chamber of Isabel.

Forth from that door, as the rising sun streams through the window, glides a wild figure, with unbound hair, and livid blue circles under each glassy eye. The bosom is bare, and naked the feet,—you see the air play with the scanty robe,—but the feet are cold, the bosom white, pulseless, like the frozen breast of a dead woman.

Is it a ghost? Can it be the warm and blooming Isabel, who last night said the evening prayer with her father, and went singing to her virgin bed?

Along the corridor she glides, one word quivering from her lips—"Father!"

No reply,—the mansion is deathly still.

Down the stairs, and out upon the porch. The rolling prairie, with the sun rising over its waves of grass and flowers—the blue sky and the grouping clouds, who hang above the path of day, catching his freshest kiss upon their bosoms.

She saw it all—felt on her cold cheek the fresh breath of morning. But the soldiers! where are they? Ewen—Don Antonio—where? They are gone, all gone. She is left alone with her father. How can she meet his gaze! She, the—but pity her good angels, and weep fiends, as you behold your darkest work!

"Father!" she cried, and listened. No reply. She turned from the sunrise, and shuddered as she anticipated the withering gaze of that parent, whose life she had bought with her—soul.

She turned, and saw her father. He did not frown upon his child, nor smile. There was a cold, calm look upon his face, and his eyes were steadily turned to the rising sun. But those eyes were glassy, that face was discolored, for the father dangled in the air, as the rope was about his neck, and the tree branch quivered with his weight.

Two forms were seen toward the east.—She saw them, as they came rapidly on, and greeted them with a shout of horrible laughter.

"Welcome, John—Harry, welcome home!"

CHAPTER IV

The Rancho Salado

"There came an order from Santa Anna, stating that as these Texans, who had honorably capitulated at Mier, were pirates and robbers, every tenth man of them should—"

—Texan Mss.

It was a dreary rancho of dark stone, one story in height, with a stunted and withered tree before its low and narrow door. To the east extended a wall of stone, of the same hue as that which formed the rancho, only that a few miserable shrubs struggled into light between the solid blocks.

Around that rancho all was one monotonous waste of sand, as far as the eye could see, and far in the east and west rose a range of barren hills, their rugged peaks rushing into the sunset sky.

A view more desolate cannot be imagined. The rancho, with its wall, encircling a space some hundred feet square, was the only object that met the eye in all that waste of dreary sand and barren cliffs.

A single black cloud, with rugged edges, spread over the tops of the western hills, and veiled, as in a pall, the last beams of the dying sun.

The air was hot, stifling, like the atmosphere of a furnace. It was the close of a long and sultry day. A flock of vultures were perched upon the flat roof of the rancho, folding their sluggish wings, as they seemed to scent the smell of human blood.

Before the door waited a half-robber form, dressed in the tawdry green jacket and wide trousers of a Mexican ranchero. There were pistols in his belt, as leaning on his rusty musket, he cast his sleepy eyes to the setting sun.

This lonely farm house, or military post, call it what you will, was situated in the heart of Mexico, some hundred and fifty miles south of the city of Saltillo.

It was called the *Rancho Salado.*

Within the court yard, hidden by the impenetrable wall, a scene of peculiar interest was in progress.

One hundred and seventy men, chained in couples, their faces worn by famine, and rendered more hideous by the uncombed hair and unshaven beard, were grouped in a circle. Their shrunken forms, wasted by long days and nights of thirst, hunger, and cold, were miserably clad in rags that fluttered to every breeze.

In the center of that circle was a massive log, and on that log an earthen vessel resembling an antique funeral urn.

Around these gaunt and famine-stricken forms was grouped a solid mass of Mexican steel. At least three hundred soldiers attired in green, gazed on the chained men, and raised their muskets in the light of the setting sun.

Near yonder post, the colonel of the detachment, a man of some thirty-five years, with a dark olive face, rests his arms against the wall and turns his face away from the group of prisoners. This colonel has seen much bloodshed, and washed his blade on many a Texan field, but now the tears stream freely down his battle-worn cheeks.

His officers, young men and aged, clad in the gay Mexican array, gaze on the group with wet eyes and quivering lips.

Only one man,—you see him slightly advanced from the others—gazes upon the miserable men, with an aspect cold, stony, and unpitying as Death. He is by no means an unhandsome man, for his beard is dark and silken, his hair glossy as a raven's pinion, his eyes full and lustrous.

He gazes upon the prisoners and the urn and smiles, until his teeth glare out from beneath his mustache.

Have we seen this man before?

The colonel advances; as if choking down his emotions, he surveys the group and speaks. The priest, by his side, with dark brown and rotund face, translates his words into English.

"Texans! Taken prisoners in an attack made by you, last Christmas day, on the town of Mier, situated in the Republic of Mexico, you were brought, some months since, to this rancho, on your way to the city of Mexico. You rose on the guard, shot and stabbed our sentinels, and escaped. After days and nights of starvation and misery, worse than death, you were re-taken, and again you stand upon the scene of your mad adventures. Texans! By the order of Don Antonio Lopez de Santa Anna, president of the Republic, you are declared pirates and robbers, out of the pale of all international law, and stripped of all the rights of civilized communities. You are worthy of death, in the most sudden and ignominious form, but, *in mercy*"—there was a convulsive movement in the brave colonel's throat, which well-nigh choked his voice—"in mercy, I say, the president decrees that only one out of every ten men shall be put to death."[6]

He paused, and as though embarrassed by his emotions, played for a moment with the hilt of his sword. You see, his officers stand weeping near yonder wall, and still, with his uncovered brow, glowing in the light of the setting sun, stands that solitary and unpitying cavalier, with the dark hair and silken beard.

"Within that urn are deposited one hundred and seventy beans; seventeen black ones, among the hundred and fifty-three white ones. You will advance two by two, and draw each of you, from the urn a single bean. If it is white, you live,—black and you die before sunset."

He turned away, and the Texans looked silently in each other's faces. The unpitying officer—did we ever see him before?—advanced, passed through the prisoners, and took his seat on the log. The priest handed him a large blank book, with pen and ink. This man was to enter the names of the living and the dead, as one by one, they raised the death urn.

The air seemed to grow more sultry, and a strange silence descended upon the scene.

While the colonel and his officers were moved to tears—while even the rough soldiers wept, as they grasped their muskets—while that solitary, unpitying man, seated by the urn, looked coolly in the faces of the Texans, they advanced two by two and chained as they were, inserted every man his hand into the urn of death.

The first couple—a man with sinewy form and hair like snow, and a man whose robust figure indicated the wreck of Herculean strength.

At once they inserted their hands: there was a pause. Sobs were heard from the group of Mexican officers. The register of the dead—so let us call the handsome officer, who, seated on the log—coolly watched their movements, as though he had wagered a few dollars on the result:

The old man drew a black bean.

"Death!" cried the register, as he entered his name on the book.

The old man, whose features, covered with a snow-white beard, belied not one trace of emotion, whispered to his comrade—

"Should you ever return to Texas,—I have a daughter,—you will bear to her my blessing?"

The Herculean Texan could not reply.

The manacles were loosened, and the aged man calmly stepped aside, and stood erect on the spot allotted to the doomed.

The horrible lottery went on in solemn silence, only broken by the sobs of the Mexican officers,—the sneering laugh of the gallant register, who cried, "Life," or "Death," as though he was but marking the result of a game of cards.

You may believe me, that it was a sad scene. The sun never shone on a sight more harrowing. Two by two they advanced, these heroes of Mier, who had mothers, wives, sisters in the sunny land which they had bought with their blood—the beautiful land of Texas.

Not a groan from their lips—no! not even a sigh. Half naked, unshaven, and miserable to look upon, they came, two by two to the urn, raised their faces in the sunset glare, and calmly took their places in the ranks of life and death.

At last, when the setting sun trembled on the hill-top, his red disc seen between the cliff and the black cloud above, there stood sixteen men, side by side, on the spot assigned to the condemned.

Two Texans only remained to fulfill the conditions of the lottery; there was but one black bean in the urn, and one of the twain must die.

Every eye was fixed upon them as they advanced.

You see the tallest of the two, a man of sinewy form, and aquiline face. His broad chest quivers beneath its covering of rags—ah! unmanly spectacle—there are tears in his large dark eyes.

Why these tears?—for himself? Look at the prisoner chained to his wrist, and answer!

A very boy; scarce sixteen, with a girlish form, and smooth, beardless cheek, and strangely lustrous blue eyes. His face, too, is worn by famine; but there is a calm, almost holy light upon his soft features; he looks up into the face of the robust man, and a sad smile wreathes his lips.

"Fear not for me, brother—I'll not play the coward!" he says, in a distinct firm tone.

"Fear not for *you*," and a hoarse groan swelled the broad chest of the bearded Texan. "By—I swear, I do not fear for you; you shall not die. No—no! That would be a little too hard for the devil himself to think. Hark ye, Harry"—this in a hasty whisper—"let me draw first: the black bean is smaller than the white—I can tell one from the other by the touch. I will—"

The younger brother replied by thrusting his hand into the urn.

There was one groan thrilling from every lip in the courtyard. The chivalric register alone regarded the scene with a pleasant smile, and politely asked,—

"The color of the bean?"

"*Black*!" cried the heroic boy, turning with a triumphant smile to his brother. That brother wrung his manacled hands and bowed his head upon his breast—it would have made your blood run cold to see that strong man weeping like a child.

"Name?" added the polite register, smoothing his silken mustache.

"*Harry Grywin*!" replied the boy, in a firm tone.

The register started, his face became pale, almost livid for an instant, but recovering his composure he coolly entered the name. Murmuring, "Harry Grywin—*Death*!"

This scene did not pass unobserved. No! The doomed sixteen men saw it, the Mexican officers shuddered as they beheld the black bean in the hands of the girlish boy, and ten Texans stepped from the ranks of the living exclaiming incoherently,—

"I will take his place."—"By—you cannot kill that boy!"—"Behold us! We will die in his stead!"

But a voice deeper than all rung through the court yard,—

"Who talks of dying for Harry Grywin, when his brother, I, John Grywin, am here? Look you, he is but a child—you cannot put him to death. The foolish boy saw the bean before he drew it—he denied himself the shadow of a chance. Take me!"

His tall form swelled in every fiber as he towered erect, the red glow of the setting sun lighting up his aquiline features, framed in masses of hair and beard as black as jet.

"Take! Look you, my Mexican friends, I do not owe you much love. I have cut and carved you in battle, as I would cut and carve again, had I free field and a good knife. But now I will stoop to you, kneel to you. Come, priest, tell it to them in Spanish, only so that you will let me die in place of Harry here, for as there's a God, he looks the very image of his mother."

The tones of that strong man, his tears, his gestures, had a language which went like a fiery arrow to every heart.

"This must not go on," shouted the veteran colonel, rushing forward,— "These men shall not die! And the boy; Holy Trinity! it would be sacrilege to kill him."

The register sprang upon the log, with his fine form and handsome face revealed against the sunset sky.

"Fall back, colonel; I command here," he said, quietly waving his hand.

"But your Excellency,—Don Antonio Marin—"

At that name, John Grywin looked up and surveyed the handsome form of the register, Don Antonio Marin. It was horrible to remark the strange pallor of the Texan's face, the iron impression of his bearded lips.

"Don Antonio Marin!" he exclaimed; "Oh sir, I am glad to know you!"

"Separate these heretics," shouted Don Antonio with rapid utterance and violent gestures. "Quick, I say! The sun is setting and it must be over before he is below the horizon. Soldiers, advance by platoons; to your duty— present—fire!"

It was done like a lightning flash. Harry was separated from the brother's side, hurried away into the ranks of the Doomed; there was a report like separate claps of thunder, mingling on one awful peal, and a mass of blueish smoke rolled over the scene.

Groans, prayers, low-muttered curses mingling in chorus! Do you see the smoke-shroud roll aside for a moment? That old man on his knees, lifting his hands in prayer? The red blaze pours into his face and the smoke cloud rolls over them all. Peal on peal, volley on volley, and now the whole courtyard is veiled in smoke.

An awful silence.

The smoke slowly rolls aside. Ah, those mangled forms, with here and there a limb quivering with the last impulse of life, a hand raised, but to fall stiff and frozen to the ground, a face uplifted, with the blood pouring over the hollow stomach, which but a moment ago were eyes.

There, on the log, beside the fatal urn, stands Don Antonio Marin, gazing coolly on the bloody heap of dying and dead, while his curling hair, and silked beard, and smooth olive cheek glow richly in the sun, as he lights a cigareto and emits volumes of perfumed smoke from his vermilion lips.

Near him, John Grywin, frozen into a dead stupor, his hands clasped, and his vacant gaze rolling from the mangled forms to the soldiers and last of all resting on that prominent figure.

Don Antonio, standing on the log and puffing his cigareto with infinite relish, his face and beard encircled with clouds of fragrant smoke—as the sun dips below the horizon and night rushes on the scene.

CHAPTER V

The Lady of Vera Cruz

"It was on the ninth of March, 1847, that Winfield Scott, landed with 12,000 Americans, on the very coast where Cortes, with 300 Spaniards had landed three centuries ago."

—Texan Mss.

The white arm of a woman, thrust through the staples of that massive door, with the iron pressed against the delicate flesh, supplied the place of a bolt and held the panels firm.

It was a fearful thing to behold that arm, quivering and almost crushed by the sturdy blows which fell against the opposite side of the door. And yet the arm was firm, pressed by the heavy panels of the door, against the rusted staples, into which it was inserted, it trembled like a withered reed, the small fingers straightened with intense agony, the skin was rent by the overwhelming pressure, but it was still there—the only bolt of the iron-bound door.

The scene was a narrow room, with a lofty ceiling and floor of dark gray stone.—From the tapestry on either side, marked with the figures 1716, the portraits of grave Hidalgos, encircled by heavy frames, and manifesting in their steel armor, their bearded faces and helmeted brows, distinct traces of the age of chivalry, frowned gloomily on that brave and lonely woman.[7]

The only light which imparted its faint glow to the place was a small lamp uplifted in the left arm of the maiden. Her right arm was inserted in the place of a bolt. For some two or three feet around her the rays of the lamp fell warm and glaring; beyond that circle of light in which she stood all was gloom, and the extreme end of the apartment was enveloped in thick darkness.

For a single moment all is still as death. While this dead silence broods on the place, while the thick darkness hangs over its distant extreme, and the faces of warrior Spaniards from the tapestried walls, we will gaze upon this brave yet delicate girl.

Her half-naked form is pressed quiveringly against the dark mahogany panels. That massive door supplies a black background to the lithe outlines of her shape, and strongly relieves the alabaster whiteness of her shoulders, her feet, her arms and bosom.

A solitary garment, hastily gathered around her waist, falls in careless and loosening folds to the floor. Her young bosom heaves freely in the light. You may trace the agitation which swells her heart to bursting, in the almost imperceptible quivering of the nostril.—You may read it in that silent compression of the warm, red lips. It brightens wildly in those dark eyes, dilating in their sockets, and gleaming a steady luster from the shadow of the long black lashes.

A single vein, swollen as though it was about to burst, shoots upward from her brows and mars the pale beauty of her forehead.

Her hair—there is not a breath to stir it into motion—falls in one mass of glossy blackness over her right shoulder.

Her form is neither tall nor masculine.—She trembles before us, one of that diminutive shapes which supply in grace and lightness what they lack in height and majesty. A slender form, yet blooming freshly in the full bosom; warm, almost voluptuous, in the flowing outline of the broad shoulders and rounded arms; beautiful in the stainless whiteness of her small feet and hands, wild and flashing with the light of large deep eyes that seem to burn as they dilate. Altogether one of those small yet impetuous daughters of the South, who resemble the tigers in their stealthy tread, and not in each movement only, but also in their love and their revenge.

What means this picture, framed by the dark mahogany panels of the massive door? This solitary room, gloomy with tapestry and moth eaten portraits, floored with stone, and with a single doorway, at either extreme?—the white arm, thrust through the iron staples, the enlarging eye and bared bosom, throbbing with death-like emotion?

Wherefore, with a picture, so mysterious and yet so beautiful in its very danger and mystery, commence this new page in this legend of the golden and bloody land?

From this dim room, faintly illuminated by the lamp that quivers in the uplifted arm of the maiden, we will go forth, on our pilgrimage, through the dusky battle-gods and sepulchers of Mexico. It is in the Home that the bolt of war descends in its most terrible glare and reaps its most precious harvest of blood; in the Home we will raise the curtain, and lay bare the awful theater of revenge, over whose blood-stained bounds glide the phantoms of human passion.

Hark! this silence, so death-like, is broken by the sound of repeated blows, hurled against the opposite side of the door. Deep voices are heard in the interval between each blow.

"Open, sister! Your brother demands entrance into this chamber!"

"Open, Isora; it is your betrothed that calls!"

One quick and intense glance toward yonder door, almost hidden in the gloom—it is the door of her bed chamber; and the girl silently withdrew her arm. The blood starts from the white skin, and a livid streak deforms its alabaster loveliness.

The door swings slowly into the room;—two figures are disclosed, half-advanced from the shadows of the doorway. A monk and a soldier; the monk with his pale face sunken on his folded arms; the soldier with an unsheathed sword gleaming in the light.

"Sister!" said the monk, in a voice at once sad and reproachful, "this dishonor is too great to be borne. An American—aye, a heretic, a spy, is discovered at dead of night, in the streets of Vera Cruz. He is pursued by Mexicans; his accursed life is in their power; and lo! a Mexican girl, the orphan child of Don Antonio Marin, gives shelter to this spy—a shelter in the home of her dead father, shelter in the secrecy of her bedchamber!"

"Where is he?" hissed the soldier, as his bearded face and tinselled form were disclosed in the light; "this sword shall anticipate the vengeance of the giblet."

The half-naked girl stood like a thing of marble, the light raised in her uplifted arm.—

Silently she gazed with her large eyes on her brother and her betrothed.

That brother, a man of some thirty years, whose pale and beardless face stood out distinctly from the long and flowing robe of his order. There was a silent scorn about his colorless lip; an agony of shame, in the glance of his eyes, as they dilated in his death-like face.

By his side, his drawn sword grasped in a firm hand, stood the soldier, quivering with silent rage. Clad in a green uniform spangled with ornaments of every shape and device, his wide trousers glittering with gold lace, a pistol in his belt, and his small eyes twinkling from a mass of dark hair and beard, he presented an effective contrast to the pale face and somber attire of the monk.

"Brother," replied the girl, in a tone that was firm in its very tremulousness, "it is false; there is no spy here. Yonder is my bed chamber, search it."

Her red lip curled in quiet scorn, and with her blood-stained arm she silently lifted her loosened robe upon her bosom, blushing like a beautiful sunset in that action of maidenly modesty.

"But we saw him enter;" vociferated the soldier. "We traced him along the corridor—aye, to this very room! He is here and his life is ours."

You should have seen the girl turn the silent scorn of her large dark eyes upon his face.

"It is Don Augustin, then, who enters like a robber, at dead of night, the bedchamber of his betrothed. My brother may hold himself excused; he is a monk, and knows but little of the respect due a woman, a maiden. But you, the soldier, the cavalier, the gallant. O! chivalric Don Augustin."

Her lip curling, her head thrown back, she flashed the light of her dark eyes upon his lowering visage.

His head drooped, the point of his sword touched the floor. The scorn of that half-clad and lonely maiden cut him to the very quick.

Meanwhile the monk, with his arms folded, his head sunken, regarded his sister with a silent look—long, searching, and full of agony.

"We traced the spy to this apartment," he said in a voice that scarcely rose above a whisper. "There is but one door, besides this through which we have entered. The other door is yonder, and it leads into your bed chamber. Sister, we will reach that room."

What means that head turned hurriedly over her shoulder, that glance toward the distant door? Does the maiden fear the search?

Her face was very pale, as she turned once more, and with flashing eyes, besought her brother "not to profane with his midnight intrusion the sanctity of her chamber and her couch."

The monk stood silent and confused—ashamed to advance and unwilling to recede—but the tinselled Don Augustin sprang forward, sword in hand, toward the door of her bed-room.

With one sudden and impetuous bound, that slender girl darted before him, and shielded the door with her outspread arms. She shone very beautiful in the action. Again the dark robe fell, and with the darker hair, relieved the soft loveliness of her virgin breast.

"Back! It is not for *you* to enter here!"

And as the flash of her indignant eyes met his cowering gaze, he started back, ashamed of the meanness of his purpose.

"Brother, advance! It is for you to commit this outrage, alone."

Slowly, as though every step was clogged with a leaden weight, the brother advanced and laid his hands upon the dark panels of the door.

"Why do you hesitate?" said the maiden, as her bosom throbbed in long and deep pulsations. "Are you afraid?"

Her words were brave, but the pallor of her face, the unnatural brightness of her eyes, told the story of her intense agony.

It was a picture, to live upon the memory forever.

The room so dark, and the dusky faces frowning from the tapestried wall; these three figures near the doorway,—the maiden, with her bared bosom and uplifted light, shining down upon her pale face; the monk, with one foot advanced, one hand laid upon the panels; the soldier with his head bowed, his sword lowered, gazing with upturned eyes upon the sister and the brother, his chest heaving with suspense.

The strong light upon these figures, and the gloom all around—it was a most impressive scene; and a silence like the grave, added awe to that moment of anxious hesitation.

"I will enter," said the monk.

He pushed open the door and disappeared at the same moment. The sister sank on her knees, while a groan of intense agony swelled her bosom. Yes, with her hair, falling over her face, she covered her eyes with one hand, and the other, grasping the light, drooped by her sides.

Don Augustin, like a statue of surprise, stood as if chained to the floor, gazing in mute horror upon the kneeling woman. He was a soldier, and he had done brave work in many a battle, done hideous butchery in many a memorable Texan field; but now the damps of fear started from his cold forehead. He was afraid.

He listened to the sound of footsteps within that chamber, he heard a deep-toned ejaculation, and then all was dead silence. The sword of Don Augustin shook as the tremor of his arm agitated the gilded hilt.

"Thou are false, Isora!" he whispered, as his parting lips disclosed his white teeth firmly set together.

She did not raise her head. Cowering on the floor, her robe, her hair, mingled in wild disorder, she pressed her left hand against her forehead and laid her head against the panels of her chamber door.

And thus they kept their fearful watch; the maiden and her plighted husband. She, the orphan child of an honored race of old Castile, now trembling in fear and shame, as her brother searched her chamber. He, a brave and cruel soldier, quivering in fear of that dishonor which seemed glaring in his face from the somber panelling of the fatal door.

Within the chamber!

We will follow the footsteps of the monk.

He entered, and the sanctity of his sister's bed room lay open to his gaze. It was a cool and quiet place, hung with faint crimson curtains, a single window opening on a garden to the north, a solitary light placed in a niche before an image of the Virgin Mary. The perfume of flowers imparted a delicious sweetness to the sultry air. Beautiful in their rainbow hues, they were clustered in a vase near the window. In one corner stood the maid's couch, yet bearing the outlines of her shape on its silken pillows.

The monk advanced—trembling he took the light and searched the room. There was no one there. All was silent and deserted. That light fell over the bed, revealed the folds of the silken hangings, the flowers by the window, and the Virgin smiling from the recess, but it did not disclose the form of a living thing.

"The spy is not here!" he gasped, and approached the window. "He cannot have escaped in this way; the leap were certain death!"

He looked down into the garden, where flowers and shrubbery were grouped, in a wilderness of perfume, and then, through the interval of the vines which clustered round the window frame, he saw the mild, sad light of the stars.

"This is strange," he murmured, as he approached the image of the Virgin. "As I live, he entered this room, and yet I can discern no trace of his footsteps."

As he spoke, a dim, distant, murmuring sound, like the tramp of ten thousand men on a sandy shore, came through the thick walls of that ancient mansion. The monk groaned as he bit his lips in impotent rage.

"*They* come, the heretics, the invaders!"

But what is the sight that fixes the glance of his burning eyes? The statue of the Virgin has been moved from its place in the recess: the monk remembers the old-time legends of his paternal mansion, and at a glance discovers the entrance to that secret stairway, leading from the bed-chamber to the roof.

"Ah!" he groaned, with an oath in pure Castilian, "I have tracked the wolf to his lair!"

It was the work of a second to spring forward through that holy image, open wide the narrow door, and glide into the darkness of the secret stairway.

Ten steps upward—steps of stone, built in the thickness of the walls—and he stood upon the flat roof—, amid the battlemented walls of the mansion, with the light of the stars upon his brow.

A hand was laid upon his arm; the stern, stern gripe of these iron fingers forced an involuntary murmur of pain.

Fiercely the monk turned, his lip compressed, his brow scowling—it was his impulse to hurl the intruder from the roof.

But the scowl passed from his brow ere he drew another breath. His lips parted, the indignant flash of his eye was succeeded by a vacant stare.

He felt his blood curdle in his veins. For there, in the pale light of the stars, rose a tall form, swelled to gigantic proportions by the gloom, and a voice low and deep, which thrilled to the inmost heart of the monk, whispered these words,—

"Remember the Rancho Salado, and look yonder!"

While that death-like clasp tightened on his arm, the monk recognized the voice, and trembled like a frightened child before the specter of some goblin story.

Quivering with a fear more terrible to behold because its source is unknown to us, the monk beheld the sight which spread before him.

It was a sight to swell the heart with a vague yet overwhelming sense of the sublime.

Let us stand beside him on the roof of the mansion which overlooks the main square of the town, and gaze upon the vision which he beheld and feel its dusk sublimity rush thro' the eyesight to our souls.

CHAPTER VI

The Landing at Vera Cruz

"Winfield Scott in the footsteps of Cortes."

—Texan Mss.

*A*bove, the sky of night, that dome of deep and tranquil blue, shining with the gleam of the stars. Beneath, the town of Vera Cruz, its roofs and towers, rising indistinctly in the gloom, with the Grand Plaza, right before us, encircled by noble structures, and the sandy shore, stretching as far as eye can see, to the north and south, in dreary barrenness.

Yonder, to the north-east, above the waves, glooms the castle of San Juan de Ulloa; a dark pile, rising sullenly into night, with the Mexican flag, waving from its loftiest tower. Toward the east the waves break in low murmurs against the barren Isle of Sacrificios, barren to the sight, yet bearing in its bosom mysterious chambers, stored with relics of six hundred years ago.[8]

Beyond the Castle and the Fort spreads the illimitable waste of the trackless gulf, a world of waves, reaching out into the vague night, until it kisses the world of sky.

Landward we gaze: beyond the waste of sand and the dark line of forest and hill, a colossal mass, white as snow, towers serenely into the western sky.

That white mass, rising in its lone magnificence from the distant horizon, its sublime summit rushing proudly into heaven, is the Peak of Orizaba; the altar of this glorious temple which has the waste of sand and forest and the sweep of the vast ocean, for its floor, the sky for its dome, the stars of God for its sacrificial lights.

It is one of those scenes which glide into the soul and fill it with a sublimity that has no speech. No word escapes our lips, no sudden ejaculation give vent to our awe. Here we gaze, the ocean is before us, the gloomy castle rising from its waves,—there, and Orizaba glares like the ghost of past ages from the western sky.

For a moment we turn our gaze, from the ocean and the mount, to the city that sleeps before us, that home of plague, nestling on the low and sandy shore, called Vera Cruz.

The mansion, on whose roof we stand, lies east of the Plaza. Yonder, to the west, with its front to the eastern sky, towers the Cathedral, a noble structure, whose dome and cross are lost to view in a vague mass of blackness. What means this blackness that seems to undulate, like a cloud as we gaze upon it? That dome is black with vultures—look! Upon the cross, rising high in the serene air, crouches the sentinel of the band; an omen of death and blood, nestling upon the emblem of Jesus and Peace!

He will have a brave feast ere many days, that gory vulture, rest tonight on the highest Cross of Vera Cruz.

There, on the south of the square, rises another church, or mass of churches, swarming with buzzards, black even to the cross, with those birds of death.

Ere a month has passed, those churches will be blasted into ruins; the bodies of the dead will darken their altars; the vulture pick his ghastly meal even in their most holy places.

Before us, on the east of the square, we behold the National Palace, surmounted by the tri-colored flag of Mexico.

And from this Plaza, shadowed in deep night, by those noble forms of architectural grandeur, extend the smooth-pebbled streets of Vera Cruz, overhung with balconied windows, gay with many colored awnings, and rendered uniform by a wide extent of level roofs.

It is indeed a beautiful town. Far out on the sea—like a gleam from Italy or Asia,—the voyager beholds it, with its towers and cupolas, rising from the waste of sand; while far above smiles the serene Orizaba. In the calm evening hour when the white peak blushes in the sun, and the smile of the dying day is upon wave, castle, and shore, these balconies are crowded with beautiful women whose white fingers gleam through the intervals of flowers, while their gracefully gathered mantle cannot altogether hide the glance of their dark eyes, the red warmth of their lips, the passionate heaving of their veiled bosoms.

And yet from this town, so sublime with its distant Orizaba, so beautiful with its warm southern women, its tropical flowers, so grand with tower and dome, the Plague every year hurls two thousand people to their graves. One-third of its houses are ravaged every year by that pestilence, which wings its deadliest dart where the verdure is freshest, the sky most serene, the flowers most beautiful.[9]

Tonight another, a deadlier plague threatens Vera Cruz.

What mean these batteries erected everywhere about the city, hemming its houses in a wall of latent flame? Wherever you gaze, not an inch of ground beyond the walls of the town but is commanded by some deadly engine of war. To the North, you behold Fort Conception, to the left Fort Santiago, one mile from the city, with a belt of water between, San Juan de Ulloa all formidable with cannon, all prepared for the hurricane of battle.[10]

What foreign enemy will dare assail the impregnable castle, the city of the Gulf, defended by a wall of steel, by the invisible barrier of the Plague?

Hark! There is a strange sound to the south—that waste of sand is black with shadowy forms—the tread of ten thousand men fills the air with a sound like the first moaning of a thunderstorm.

Gaze upon the channel which glides between the castle and the Isle of Sacrificios.

Even as the light breeze crisps the waters into tiny ripples, we behold glooming through the night the dark forms of ships of war, some white with sails, some sending the smoke of their steam-engines into the starlit sky. The night is dark, we may not trace distinctly the shapes of these vessels, nor count their cannon, nor estimate the awful power of their death machinery, but they are there, gently undulating upon the smooth waters, their decks black with warriors, the banner of the stars waving over all, as if to hash back unto heaven the smile of the cloudless sky.

What means the banner of the stars floating over the Gulf of Mexico?

Look! There are barges upon the waters, gliding as noiselessly as any gondola of Venice, that bears the lover to his mistress's smile, gliding from the ships to the shore, and bearing armed men to the plague-smitten shore of Vera Cruz.

Does not the scene rivet your gaze—fill your heart.

You see those boats extended in the form of a crescent, approach the sands, while the water breaks in foam around their prows—the bayonets twinkle like fireflies through the darkness, a vague murmur stealing over the waves, swells along the shore like the hushed whispers of ten thousand men!

They come on, those death-boats, bearing many a true heart to the hideous grave of the pestilence, they grate upon the pebbly beach, there is a flag waving through the gloom, and the forms of armed men start into view far along that drear, that barren shore.

Where is now the thunder of San Juan de Ulloa? Look!—that slight elevation of sand commands the shore, a single cannon planted there would hurl a thousand men back into the waves, and redden with blood the ripples as they gurgled over these mangled "falls"?

Is there not one true-hearted Mexican, only one, to place the cannon and fling the lighted match to his fatal work? Not one?

For there is a doom upon the land, the hardy children of the North are here, the soldiers of the new crusade throng the waters and the shore, at least twelve thousand strong, and there is not one Mexican to meet them on the beach with the warm welcome of a warrior's steel.

At sunset you should have beheld the scene, for if it is impressive now, at sunset it was most beautiful!

It was a calm afternoon, on the ninth of March, 1847. The glow of sunset was upon the waveless waters of the Mexican Gulf, upon the city of Vera Cruz, with its roofs and towers, centered on the sandy shore, upon the dark castle, glowing to the north, and those beams so vivid in their tropical glare hung in a baptism of life around the far-off Peak of Orizaba.[11]

There, in that sweet, sad calm of the evening breeze, which makes the stranger in a foreign land dream of home, a strange sight was seen by the light of the setting sun.

The roofs of Vera Cruz were black with people. The soldier sprung to the battlement and held his breath as he gazed. From yonder castle the gay group of Mexican generals looked forth upon the tranquil waters. Every eye was centered upon the channel, between the castle and Sacrificios, and every heart beat quicker at the splendid panorama, warmed by the sunset rays.

For the huge Princeton came gliding over the waves, urged swiftly on by her tremendous machinery, with the smoke curling over her masts, and melting into the serene gold of the upper sky. The dark form, the white sails of the other vessels, swept black and glittering in the center. She seemed, that fearful Princeton, renowned for the bloody tragedy once enacted on her decks, like the head of a huge serpent trailing its sinuous way over the calm waters.[12]

As the feet approached the Isle of Sacrificios, the armed men crowded on the decks, their weapons flashing back the glare of the sun, cast their gaze to the west, and saw the desolate shore spreading wide and dreary as the waves broke over its sands. The city crowded on its every roof with the men, the women, the mothers and daughters of Vera Cruz are there—the vessels of other nations anchored in the harbor, their masts alive with silent spectators, and in the distance Orizaba seemed to woo them on. Orizaba, that soon would see them hurled by hundreds into the plague-pit, or crushed in bloody heaps upon the battle field!

In the shrouds of the steamer Massachusetts, at this moment of intense expectation, stands a man of some sixty years, his form unbent from its stern majesty by the toil of battle or the frost of age, clad in a costume magnificent in its severe simplicity. Blue, relieved by gold,—a broad chest heaves beneath that uniform, a kingly form supports that warrior head. His brow was bared: you could see the gray hairs curling round it; the sunset glow upon those firm features, every line glowing with a warrior soul.

Over his head, and around him, throwing his expressive form distinctly into view, waves in slow undulations the banner of the stars.

His eye brightening as it expands, roves over the scene, and he remembers that bloody field fought years ago, with the thunder of Niagara, and looks forward with a quickening pulse to these words, which history will soon write in characters of light—"Winfield Scott, in the Footsteps of Cortes!"[13]

With twelve thousand men, their lives, their honor, hanging on his fiat, this man of Niagara sees the American army approach the land of Mexico.

Hark!—the thunder of a signal cannon breaks the silence, a volume of blue cloud sweeps over the form of Scott.

That is the signal gun!

And parting from the vessels' sides, as they swing anchor near the isle, a line of barges, crowded with soldiers, sweep toward the shore. It is a beautiful thing to see them come spread forth in the form of a crescent, which flings the glitter of four thousand bayonets over the waves.

On toward the sands—nearer and nearer—in sight of the city and the fort, the object of the gaze of thousands, these veterans of Monterey, these men of Louisiana and Kentucky, approach the hostile shore.

That form, standing erect in the foremost barge, with the light playing upon the muscular chest; the uniform of blue glittering with gold, the deep eye, gleaming beneath the waving plumes, as white as snow.

Over all he towers; the American Flag grasped in one hand, the unsheathed sword flashing in the other. Behind him, the fleet; before him, the shore; far above, the white altar, Orizaba.

Look upon that banner and read in its blood-stained folds the single word, "Monterey!" Gaze upon that waving plume; it gleamed like a beacon through the three days fight of the Mountain City; it waves above the brow of Worth, whose eye flashes again as he prepares to spring from the barge, and plant the banner upon the sands of Mexico.[14]

Silence reigns, only broken by the sweep of the oars; now hearts are beating impetuously beneath their warrior covering; the setting sun shines over compressed lips and woven brows. A moment of fearful suspense!

Nearer to the shore glides the foremost barge.

You see Worth lift at once his sword and banner; with one hurried glance he surveys the hostile beach—the city is five miles distant, the harbor white with sails; and then casting his face, so chivalric in its ripe manhood, to the glow of the setting sun, he springs upon the shore.

In silence he plants the banner staff upon the sands and uncovers his brow.

Ten thousand eyes behold the picture.

That solitary soldier, standing alone upon the beach, the waves curling at his feet, the Banner of the Continent waving over his head. The golden sands relieve his form, the evening breeze lifts the banner into light.

Then, and not till then, the ominous silence is broken by a thunder shout. It is the heart-warm cheer of our thousand brave men. Look upon them as they come! With one impulse they plunge into the waves and dash onward, lifting their glittering arms into the light,—they cannot wait until the barges grate the sand, but springing into the water, mid-breast deep, they hurry forward, and encircle with a guard of hearts and steel, the noble form of Worth.

The last gleam of the setting sun disclosed that barren shore, clouded by the firm array of six thousand men, with the gloomy outlines of cannon and mortar, seen distinctly even amid the flash of these long belts of dazzling steel.

Darkness gathers on the ocean and the shore; one by one the prominent points of the picture went out in the gloom. First, the shore faded; and the soldiers, in their beautiful array, became a vague mass of moving blackness, their presence known by their thunder tread alone. The domes of the city glittered for a moment and then were dark; the huge castle sank into the bosom of night; the ocean reached forth its waves and melted through the dusky air into the distant horizon.

And when the shadow was upon the ocean and the shore, like a mantle of tangible darkness, still, in the west, Orizaba lifted its white altar into heaven, and while all was black below, the last rays of the departing day hung round its glossy pinnacle like a smile from God.

Now it is dark night, illumined only by the stars. While the American legions are hurrying from the battle ships to the shore, and extending in silent and terrible array around the slumbering city, our souls are hurried by the stern emotions of the hour, back into the bosom of the Dead Ages.

Three hundred years ago, and the same lone Orizaba, that towers serenely now, flashing its calm scorn upon the petty broils of man, smiling calmly on, whether he marches to battle in glittering array, or sinks disfigured and horrible, into the loathsome pit of the plague—that same Orizaba beheld a far different scene.[15]

Then, the great woods sent forth their arms of foliage and flowers even to the ocean shore. The palm grew near the waters, a straight column, towering into upper air, with a coronal of broad leaves and luscious fruit around its brow. The cypress, too, that stern monarch of dead centuries, rose here, with all manner of rainbow flowers, blooming round its massive trunk, and vines of various beauty hanging about its branches. Then, the desert sand, where San Juan de Ulloa glooms, was a fair green isle. Sacrificios yonder, was the Temple Isle of a strange and mysterious religion. Upon its sands, among the gay glory of the tropical vegetation, the horrible altars rose, dripping with the warm blood of the human sacrifice. Beneath its surface were chambers reared in the barbarous yet impressive architecture of the people, whose name has for thousands of years been lost to human lips.

Wonderful chambers were those, hidden beneath the sand, gloomy with images of the devil, God; and burrowing far into the caverns beneath the ocean waves.

Then, it is of the time, three hundred years ago we speak: a wondrous people dwelt in this land, amid gorgeous cities, or in the silence of the beautiful valleys, their dusky faces, glowing with the same passions that fill our bosoms now, the fury of war, the avaricious lust of traffic, the magnetic tenderness of love.

Yes, besides this shore many a great lord, clad in garments that were woven with feathers of rainbow dyes, and dazzling with ornaments of solid gold, strode proudly along, followed by the innumerable column of his half-naked and dusky warriors. Yes, beneath yonder cypress, in those days that are now almost forgotten, crouched the dark-cheeked but impetuous daughter of the South, looking with her large deep eyes upon the brown child that slept upon her bosom. Yes, upon yonder isle the chant of prayer was heard, the altar smoke arose, the yell of the victim—forced to the altar, his heart torn from his living body—shrieked in horrible cadence upon the still air, and died far along upon the waves.

The ruler of this land dwelt in a valley, some hundreds of miles to the west, in a tranquil valley of blossoms, whose gardens and lakes were guarded by volcanic mountains.

At once the High Priest of the awful religion and the Emperor of the people, he was called the "Sad Warrior," or in the Aztec language, *Montezuma*.[16]

Wherefore called the Sad or Doomed Warrior? It is a strange story, and I will speak it in a few words.

The religion of this vast people, which raised its altars in every city, and sent its sacrificial flames into the sky, from every mountain, comprised the worship of two deities. Like all the religions, or rather forms of religion in the world, it adored two gods,—a God of Blood, a God of Peace.

The God of Blood, in some lands, demanded the offerings of an Inquisition, pledged to do the works of hell on earth, on the victims of persecution, slain without mercy on the battle fields of bigotry.

In Mexico, this God of Blood demanded merely the palpitating heart of a solitary victim, who was stretched upon the altar stone, amid the gaze of thousands, and torn to death with his livid brow crowned with blossoms.—This victim was slain on stated occasions of solemn ceremonial, not in the gloomy hall of an inquisition's dungeon, nor in the Molock–sacrifice of a Genevan stake.[17]

In all lands of the world, the God of Peace received the worship of the purest hearts.—The brutal man, swayed by the bigot's lust, into a hellish frenzy, loved Him not. But His name was written in serene skies, in waveless lakes, in all that was tender and beautiful in the world, as much in the bared beauty of a stainless woman's bosom as in the lone majesty of the mountain top, smiling in the last gleam of an unclouded sun.

After ages of darkness, this God was clearly written in the Bible—He shone an image of Time joined to Eternity, in the serene Jesus.

In the land of Mexico, three hundred years ago, this God—only revealed to the Aztec people in the language of external nature, or the voiceless eloquence of the heart—was seen in the blossoms, in the cloudless skies, in all the tenderness and sanctity that whispers in the syllable *Home.*

In their traditions, which called Him *Quetzalcoatt,* it was taught that He had lived in the Mexican land, some thousand years before; that He had been banished, in His golden reign of peace, and driven from His very shore by the God of Blood.[18]

But a glorious hope lived in their traditions that He would return and bless the land again, and reign the Messiah of the Heart.

In this hope lived Montezuma; but priest and king as he was, of a despotic government and a barbarous religion, the hope soon became to him a nightmare fear; he looked for the return of the good God with trembling, and saw the coming of the blessed age, with the terror of self-convicted guilt.

He was doomed to destruction from his birth, by Prophecy, and the coming of the blessed Quetzalcoatt was to ripen his doom into judgment. Therefore, from his birth, he was called Montezuma, or the Doomed Man.

Did the Messiah come?

Yes, but not the God of Peace, nor the apostle of the God of Peace, but a stern Messiah, whose crucifix was the hilt of his sword, whose black banner bore a red cross, with the words,—"In this Sign We Conquer."[19]

A single picture from the life of this Messiah of Blood.

CHAPTER VII

Three Hundred Years Ago

"In order to estimate the present we must look upon the past. 'I will tell you,'
said the veteran, 'a story of the days of old, in order that you may understand that
which I have to state of,—the ninth of March, 1847.'"

—Texan Mss.

*U*pon the sandy shore a white tent arose, shadowed by the deep-green
leaves of a cypress tree.

Around that tent were grouped a band of warriors attired in linked steel,
their bearded faces surmounted by iron helmets, an iron sword in each sinewy
hand. A deep murmur thrilled the group, and the last gleam of the fading
light revealed the various passions,—anger, despair, hope—contending for
the mastery in every warrior's face.

While they were surrounding the tent, flinging their mailed hands in fierce
gesticulations, in the air, the light of sunset mellowed the waveless ocean, and
the waters melted without a sound upon the pebbled shore.

Around was the glowing panorama of fruit and flowers: from the thickly
clustered foliage the purple grape, the fragrant fig, the golden orange, were
seen, while over all arose the melancholy palm, so lone in its majesty; or the
strong cypress, so big, in every inch of its rugged bark, with the history of past
years.

And over all, far away to the west, the cloudless blue of the evening sky was
broken by a colossal mass, white as sunless snow.

It was a wild and yet a beautiful scene.—That group of warriors, bearded
from the mouth to the throat, and clad in mail of iron, clustered about the
white tent, their war-horses, also iron-clad, standing near; the golden sand
stretching far to the north and south; to the east, the ocean, vast, calm and
trackless; in the west, the serene peak of Orizaba.

Attracted by the sound of those earnest voices, speaking deeply, in pure
Castilian, we enter the group and start back, wondering and dumb, as we behold the two figures that form the center of the circle.

A man of thirty-three years, clad in glittering steel armor, his form at once
agile and athletic, is seated there, upon a rock; his helmet laid aside, his hands
clasping that sword whose hilt pierces the sand.

A face, high and bold in the forehead, thoughtful, almost sad, with the light
of those eyes, so unnaturally large and dark; firm in the silent compression of
the bearded lip—altogether the face of an enthusiast and a warrior. Were it not
for the air of practical energy which invests the face we should say, at the first

149

glance, that we beheld in that mail-clad man, a dreamer, cased in armor instead of a cowl.

While all are moved by the tempest of passion, he alone is calm. Yes, while the monk at the right surveys the group, and clasps his crucifix in prayer, while the splendid warrior on the left, whose battle steel shines with drops of gold, seizes his sword, and with a scornful lip, confronts the group, this man, with the uncovered brow, is firm and cold as marble.

"The ships which bore us to this accursed land, *you* have destroyed!" shouted an athletic man, whose dogged features, half-hidden in his hair and beard, announce a reckless nature. "By the Holy Trinity, we are here in a heathen land, at the mercy of the savages—our bones will bleach upon their altars before many days!"

And a chorus of fierce ejaculations disturbs the silence of the evening hour.

"Pity us, Mother of God! We shall never see Castile again."

"Never! Our ships, torn to pieces, rot beneath yonder wave; the madness of this man hath undone us all!"

"Conquer a nation like this, a nation of millions, ruled by a great king! It is madness to think it."

The man with the uncovered brow heard it all, with his large eyes fixed upon the sand. Not a word passed his lips.

"Back!" shouted the splendid knight, who with drawn sword stood by him; "dare you menace the captain?"

"For the love of God, my children, be calm," besought the priest, lifting into light the holy Cross.

By this time you have doubtless discovered that the name of the priest was *Olmedo*, the splendid knight, *Alvarado*; these mailed forms, the adventurous Spaniards, who landed a few days ago since on this unknown shore; the central figure, so calm, while all around is storm, *Hernan Cortes.*[20]

He has destroyed their ships. They cannot go back—the ocean is between them and home; before them the wondrous land of Montezuma, swarming with its millions of people, and glorious with its unmeasured stores of gold. This man, Cortes, not long ago an obscure planter of Cuba, has sworn with this little band to conquer the empire of Montezuma!

It is indeed madness.

At last he lifts his eyes and surveys the angry group. You see the madness of his dream in the deep flush which reddens his cheek, in the unnatural glare of his eye.—That flush, that glare, says more to the warriors than a thousand words, for they tell us that the soul of this man is up within him,—that alone he will accomplish this deed, if not a single arm moves with him.

He rises, lays his left hand upon the banner staff—above him the Gonfalon of black velvet, with its red cross; and with his right he raises the blade of his sword slowly over his head.

"Be it so!" his deep, indignant voice is heard to exclaim. "You all desert me. I will go alone."

Silence! The genius flashing from this man's eyes begins to work upon every heart. Silence, hesitation, suspense!

"There is a land to conquer—it is yonder!"—he pointed to the setting sun—"There is gold to win—it is there. There are millions of heathen, whom we can convert to the true cross; they, too, are there. You are afraid to conquer, convert, or win—afraid!—you desert me. It is a crime that I have destroyed your ships. I am guilty; I confess it.—Take your way where you will; as for me, with this sword in my hand, this banner over my head, I will cry to God and his saints and go forth to conquer, alone!"

The silence deepens. Heads are drooped, upraised arms sink with their swords; with wondering eyes they gaze upon the form of Cortes.

Alvarado, so splendid in his knightly array, advances silently to his side,—

"Not *alone*! for I am with you."

"And I!" exclaims the priest Olmedo, advancing from the other side.

"And I!" exclaims a soft, low, musical voice in Castilian, broken by a strange accent it echoes from the tent and pierces every heart.

Two white arms are wound around the neck of Cortes; and pillowed on his right shoulder is seen a warm face, framed in flowing hair, and lighted by large eyes that burn with the religion, the love of a true woman.

Who is this beautiful woman, from whose brown cheeks glows the ripeness of fiery blood? So queenly is her form, so voluptuous in every out line—her young limbs trembling beneath a robe of spotless white—so like a passionate woman in her ripe lips, so like a spirit in her large, eloquent eyes?

Every Spaniard knows her at a glance. The child of the heathen people, she has forsaken home and altar for the Christian; she has linked her fate with Cortes, saying to him in the beautiful language of the Hebrew maiden to Naomi,—"Wherever thou goest, I will go; thy people shall be my people— thy God my God!"[21]

Now spreading forth her arms she looks upon the stern soldiers, with that glance, so sublime with woman's faith, and utters the broken words,—

"I, too, will go!"

Had you turned your eyes for a moment from this group and then looked again, you would have seen the sand crowded by kneeling men, their eyes gleaming with the frenzy of enthusiasm, their swords lifted toward the holy banner, their voices joining in the shout—"Mexico and Montezuma! Lead us on—we will conquer with you, Cortes, or with you, Cortes, we will die!"

Orizaba glowed in the setting sun, and the Indian maiden, Mariana, held over the dark hair of Cortes a crown of orange blossoms, with a single blood-red flower in the center.[22] As the night sank over the scene, she fluttered it gently in the air, and it sank, like a good omen on his brow.

CHAPTER VIII

The Avenger of a Three-Fold Wrong

"Whenever he tried to pray, one word, written in letters of fire,
flared between him and God—Remorse."

—Texan Mss.

"Remember the *Rancho Salado* and look yonder!"

That voice, we say, curdled the blood of the monk.

There, beside him, on the roof-top of the old mansion of Vera Cruz, rose a somber figure, which, in the dim light of the stars, resembled a phantom rather than a man.

It was some moments ere the monk could gather nerve to raise his eyes and look upon the shadowy form. At first he saw only a tall figure, attired in gray, with a rifle in his hand, a pale face, encircled by masses of dark hair, with a long black beard clothing the lower part of the visage, and descending to the broad chest.

Then, as he saw more clearly, he beheld that white forehead, the dark eyebrows, the aquiline nose, firm mouth—curving with a smile that was almost Satanic—and a rounded chin, appearing from masses of black beard. A frock coat of gray hues, edged on the skirts with dark fur, and girded by a belt of black leather, displayed the sinewy proportions of the stranger. Over his white brow arose a cap of dark fur, with a single long and slender feather, quivering in its front.

"You tremble, *Father Pedro*,"—the voice sounded like a death-knell to the monk—"and yet there is no reason to fear! Come, while the stars gleam above us, while San Juan frowns yonder, and the tramp of ten thousand heretics resound from the sandy beach. Come, I say, sit by me on the battlements, and let me tell you a story—an amusing story, as there is a God! Do not wonder that I speak Spanish with such a glib tongue—I learned the language in an excellent grammar school—rather rough though it may be, but still excellent—the castle-prison of Perote!"

Father Pedro sank backward on the battlement, his hands hanging motionless by his side. He trembled as with an ague chill—but then the air was so cold.

Taking his seat beside the monk, and resting one arm on his rifle, the stranger began his story,—

"Did you ever, Father Pedro, in your priestly wanderings, behold a picture like this? A lonely rancho, centered in a valley of barren hills, and illumined on every stone with the dusky glow of a clouded sunset? In the courtyard of that rancho a handsome soldier, standing on a log; shrieks to his bloodhounds, and bids them to put to death seventeen men, rebel Texans, who await their fate near the wall—a boy, mark ye, a smooth faced girlish boy, standing in their midst? There is a crash, Father Pedro, a smoke, and horrible groans, rise from that heap of palpitating forms, which writhe, struggle and die, even on the spot where a moment since, stood seventeen living men. Not a Mexican eye is but wet with tears, not a soldier but pities the miserable men, who are butchered thus in cold blood. Yes: there is one! Cold, relentless, unpitying while all are weeping round him, stands that handsome officer, Don Antonio Marin!"

The monk shuddered.

"But near the gallant officer is seen the brother of the smooth-cheeked boy, waiting until the smoke clears away, so that he may recognize the mangled form of Harry Grywin. That brother is a strong man, Father Pedro, yet he bites his lip until the blood comes—weeps! O, every one of his tears is worth a Mexican's life; and all the while the handsome officer stands smiling at his agony. Come, man, you are dull—why don't you laugh? When the smoke clears away, John the elder brother advances, searches for his girlish brother's body. There are sixteen carcasses on the sod, but Harry's is not there!"

You may see the head of the monk fall slowly on his breast.

"The scene changes to Saltillo, a beautiful city, some hundred miles and more from the Rancho Salado. Two months have elapsed since the handsome officer halloed his bloodhounds to the slaughter. It is a festival day in Saltillo, the Church lines the street with her banners, her crosses, her glittering robes, extending in a gorgeous procession. Above all, above the points of encircling bayonets, shines the Host—'the body and blood of Jesus' shrined in a golden cup. But who comes here, along the streets—this ghastly figure clad in rags, the face thinned by famine, the blue eyes hollow and ghastly? It is a Texan, aye the very boy who, two months since was doomed, shot, in the Rancho Salado, he escaped, wandered among the mountains for two months, and now rushes into the ranks of the procession, screaming for bread! for water! For you see, he is maddened by thirst and hunger! Like a hunted deer, that can drag its bloody trail no longer he turns to his hunters and beseeches mercy! Bread! water! Behold the mercy which is given to him. A file of soldiers separate from the procession, at the command of their leader.—A ghastly figure is kneeling on the center of the Plaza, the Cathedral before him, the host gleaming above his head. 'Present!—fire!' There is a quivering mass of flesh and blood on the stones of the street, and the officer advances, contemplates the form of his victim, or, to put it in plainer words, Don Antonio Marin looks quietly, and with his most winning smile, upon the mangled corpse of that boy of sixteen, girlish Harry Grywin."[23]

The monk lifted his eyes and muttered the name of the Holy Trinity.

The voice of the stranger echoes clear and deep through the silence of the night,—it pierces the soul of Father Pedro, yet he dare not gaze upon the eyes nor look upon the face of the unknown man. Unknown?

"Look yonder, monk."

So careless, so conversational was the tone of the stranger's voice, that the monk raised his eyes.

"Yonder, Father Pedro! Not upon the star-lit sky, nor upon the dreary shore of sand—not yet the wooded hills; but yonder to the north-west. What is this that we behold? A Texan home. Reared on an island knoll, some sixty miles from San Antonio, amid a grove of oaks, venerable with their waving festoons of silver moss. It is not beautiful? The fountain bubbling in the center of the grove, the rich masses of sun and shade chasing each other over the sod, the world of prairie and sky, spreading around and above that home of Prairie Eden. A father and his three children dwell there, in the wilderness, the free canopy of God above them, and the breath of God blowing freshly over the prairie, into their dear home of the blossoming desert. But mark ye, Father Pedro, the brothers are called away to San Antonio, called, with the laborers and slaves of the plantation, to defend the frontiers of Texas from Mexican outrage. They are gone only a few brief hours; warned by a supernatural messenger they leave their men encamped and hasten home. They do return home—behold them, after journeying all night, approach the island grave, in the dimness of the daybreak. John is mounted on his black horse, Harry on his ambling bay; and you'll remember John was a muscular man, sure as Death with his rifle; and Harry a mere boy, with such laughing blue eyes that went right into his rude brother's heart.

"They are coming home—alone!—for they have left their soldiers on the prairie, thirty miles away. They are in sight of Prairie Eden. Their horses have fallen, but still they hurry on. How beautifully the morning sun shines over the mansion, with the oaks grouped around it, and the white moss quivering in every breath of air. Coming home! They hear the sound of the fountain, see the porch, ascend the knoll with a merry hurrah; for John begins to think that his presentiment was false—the words of that awful messenger a lie! But what is the sight that meets their eyes as they reach the porch? Where is the father to welcome the children home, where the sister to press her lips upon her brother's lips? Look!—ha! ha! the father hangs to the tree before his own door, his dead face gilded by the morning sun—the sister crouched in the porch, a mad, *a dishonored woman*!"

The monk fell on his knees,—"Mercy!—for the sake of the Holy Trinity! No more, no more!"

"But the brother, even John, bends over his lost sister. 'His name?—the author of this double wrong, the doer of this devil's work?' Hark! that voice from the white lips of the wrecked woman,—'*Don Antonio Marin!*' "

As he hissed the last words through his compressed teeth—the monk crouching all the while before him—the stranger dashed his rifle on the flat roof and beat his forehead with clenched hands. The groan which came from his lips was not human; it resembled the howls of a dying tiger.

"You will confess, Father Pedro, that John Grywin and Don Antonio Marin have a long account to settle whenever they may chance to meet. You admit that even if John should discover Don Antonio under the cowl of a monk, his chivalric name, transformed into Father Pedro, that it would be a very amusing thing for the said John to stab the good father at dead of night, and pitch his bloody carcass over the battlements into the streets of Vera Cruz. This would be amusing, I say, but very, very far from just. Let me picture a little piece of justice for you. After the lapse of long years, John Grywin finds Don Antonio under the cowl of a monk, his only care, the charge of a beautiful and orphaned sister. The monk loves that sister, adores her, even as John adored his sister. Yes, the monk wishes her to marry the chivalric Don Augustin, bestow her wealth on a convent, and live happily for long years, encircled by blooming children. At this crisis of her destiny, John Grywin comes to Vera Cruz, finds entrance into the home of the sister, and night after night, sitting by her side, with her soft hand within his own, tells her the moving— somewhat melancholy—story of his life, and wins her heart forever. In this story, mark you, he leaves the names a blank—does not tell the voluptuous Isora, that the name of the assassin and ravisher is Don Antonio Marin. Well, after all his plans are laid, John Grywin, being still in pursuit of justice, brings the threads of destiny together on the night of the 9th of March, 1847. Look yonder, Father Pedro! Behold the barren Isle of Sacrificios! There, in the sepulchers of the Aztec race, my bridal bed is waiting for me now. Your sister is pure at this hour—when morning dawns she will repose in my arms, in yonder bridal bed, sacrificed—her honor, purity, all, offered up to the ceremony of my sister! Come, monk, unfrock yourself; I want your cowl. It will serve me as a disguise to pass the guard—or stay—ha! ha! Isora shall wear the monkish gown, and I will assume the handsome uniform of Don Augustin."

The monk, Father Pedro, otherwise called Don Antonio Marin, lay prostrate on the roof—prostrate and helpless, as though a palsy had possessed his once vigorous limbs. His eyes were riveted on the face of the stranger. He suffered him to strip the gown from his form, saw him wind it about his form, and for a moment all was silence.

Slowly, heavily the monk raised himself into a sitting posture. The form of the stranger was half lost to view in the aperture of the stairway leading from the roof to the room of Isora.

That face, framed in its dark hair and long beard, glared from its large eyes full in the face of the monk.

"One word before we part! Your turn will come; it is not yet time. Do you remember walking some three months since, just before you assumed the cowl, in the Alameda of Mexico, your white-haired father on your arm? It was a beautiful evening; the valley of Mexico glowed with its groves and spires in living light, while far above rose the volcanic mountains, sending their smoke, like incense-clouds into the evening sky. And you, with your white-haired father, were walking amid the blaze of rank and beauty which floated along the Alameda of the gay city.—A bullet from an unknown source, pierced your father's brain. He fell at your feet, his white hairs bathed in blood. Whence came that bullet? You could never guess; in remorse for your crimes, you deemed it a vengeance dealt by a supernatural hands, and immediately assumed the cowl, Ha ! ha! it is indeed amusing!—that bullet came from the rifle of the escaped prisoner, John Grywin!"

"Oh God! my poor father!"

"Thus, one by one, I will sweep your family down to death. First your father falls; to-night Isora sinks in the embrace of pollution! Last of all your turn will come, yours, Father Pedro, otherwise called Don Antonio Marin, hero of the Rancho Salado; hero of the mass at Saltillo; hero of Prairie Eden."

He was gone.

It was some moments before the monk recovered his consciousness. He tottered to his feet, and the mild light of the stars shone over his shaven face and revealed his broad forehead and wildly-glaring eyes; there was a damp like death upon his brow; he wiped it away with his chilled hands; but the cold dross started forth again and bathed his clammy flesh.

Then gazing toward the ocean, Don Antonio contemplated, with a shudder, the dark history of his life.

"I thought it was but revenge when I dishonored Isabel and slew her brother—revenge for the scorn which the proud girl flung in my teeth long years ago, in her Philadelphian home! But now, my father murdered, my sister on the verge of dishonor—I learn at last, that the devil who urged me to my revenge, brings home to me the poison which I distilled for others! My sister, she is pure, what harm has she done?"

But Isabel? Ho, ho! Sir Monk, thou hast forgotten the beautiful and sinless girl of the prairie?

"I will save her! So aid me God and all his saints!"

With that trembling vow upon his lips, he rushed down the stairway, and found himself in the darkness of Isora's chamber.

The door, he tried it, with the nervous force of despair, but it fastened, and the echo of voices came through its thick panels!

He listened!—the voice of Isora, Don Augustin, and the Avenger, mingling in chorus. Again, the monk, driven to frenzy, tried the door, but his attempt was hopeless. He sank back upon the bed of Isora, and a hand, cold, clammy, was laid upon his own, thrilling his veins, as with the touch of the dead.

"Fear not, Don Antonio," said a soft, mild voice, "for I, Isabel, of Prairie Eden am with you!"

CHAPTER IX

The Threads of Destiny

"It matters not how brave, how ferocious the criminal may be when in the act of his crime, let but Destiny weave its threads about him and the hero of vengeance come and lo! your criminal is but a child in strength and an idiot in intellect."

—Texan Mss.

*A*t the same moment, on the opposite side of the door, in the gloomy chamber, frowning with the portraits of the Castilian hidalgos, Don Augustin maddened by blind rage, stood prepared to lunge his sword into the heart of his unknown enemy.

That enemy stood near the door, his arms folded over the rifle, while a smile of cold contempt played over his lips.

Kneeling by his side, the light held in her extended arm—it seemed frozen into marble, Isora wound the dark robe around her breast, and looked with vacant terror into the face of her betrothed husband. Her bosom is now stilled like death, now heaving suddenly under the dark robe, her rich olive cheek, chilled into a dull, lifeless hue, her eyes gleaming a light at once vivid and un-natural—all betokened the violence of the emotions which threatened her reason with utter annihilation.

Indeed she seemed sinking fast into a stupor, a dull apathy worse than death.

Calm and sneering, John Grywin—his cold smile rendered sinister, aye, Satanic, by the upward direction of the light—looked into the face of Don Augustin, as though he would read his soul, through his small and restless eyes.

"Heretic! never do you leave this room alive! You have poisoned the mind of this pure lady—*pure*! ha! ha!" He laughed bitterly. "You have outraged the honor of a Mexican. Come,—I am hungry for your blood!"

"You talk like a hero! Bravo! I really begin to admire you, Don Augustin."

Such was the reply of John Grywin, delivered in a quiet tone, his arms still folded about his rifle. Not a muscle of his face moved—not one sign of agitation was visible in his tall form or bold, white forehead.

"Dog! coward! I spit on you!"

Don Augustin grew grotesquely eloquent.

"I say you are afraid to measure swords with me! I call you poltroon!—and scorn you."

"You are ungentlemanly, Don Augustin," quietly remarked the Texan. "Now I have but one word to say, and that is to request the loan of your coat for a few hours. I wish to pass the guard at the Mole, and to pass in your uniform; you understand? Will you strip?"

There was a sneering consciousness of superior power, not only physical but intellectual force, in his look and tone, and yet Don Augustin was not a man at all to be despised.

With an impetuous bound he hurled the point of his sword at the unprotected breast of the Texan.

It was a deadly lunge, a moment of quivering suspense.

Then occurred a sudden and sublime sacrifice.

This woman, Isora, kneeling on the floor, the light extended in her palsied hand, was only clad in the solitary robe which trembled on her heart. Yet she did not remember this nor call to mind that modesty which is the most sudden instinct of a pure woman.

There was a wilder instinct in her breast; call it fascination, magnetism, love; and it taught her that the sharp point was hurled against the Texan's heart, that she must save him at every hazard.

Quick as the tigress, maddened by the slaughter of her young, she darted from the floor, raised the light in one hand, and with the other flung the robe from her breast and hurled it upon the point of Don Augustin's sword.

Then panting and glowing—her form brave as the form of sinless Eve, she flung back her head, and with the eye flashing, the nostril quivering, she entangled the sword, and with a sudden movement, hurled it and her robe together, on the floor.

The light was still in her uplifted left arm, and in its beams she stood revealed, glowing from head to foot, on bosom, cheek and brow, with the fiery impulse of that heroic deed.

Don Augustin started back and shrieked her name, coupled with a word too foul for manhood to repeat.

Maddened as the Texan was by the wrongs which had goaded him for years, until his very life became one brooding revenge he felt his blood boil at that unmanly word. Look! You see his clubbed rifle circle his head, you see Don Augustin hurled senseless to the floor.

Then the beautiful girl, roused once more into her woman's modesty as the impulse of her action passed away, blushed in every pore, tossed her dark hair on her form; it fell, it waved, it streamed over her bosom and down her limbs, and sinking on her knees wept aloud.

Methinks I see some sensualist of the pulpit or the press read this passage, and as his foul imagination, incapable of anything but that which is born of the kennel of his own heart, covers this heroic deed with the atmosphere of his sensualism, and gravely groans "Immoral! Damnable!"

I write this scene, first of all because it is true, and next, as a defiance to those poor earth worms, who crawl over all that is pure and beautiful in the earth of God, leaving their slime wherever they writhe along.

I paint this woman, with the bared form, and look upon her unveiled loveliness, blooming in such roseate hues, flowing in such waving outlines, as a type of all that is pure in the wide earth, an incarnation of that love which hallows a man's soul, when he thinks of a mother or a sister, a love stainless as the snow-flake trembling from the parent cloud, and bathed as it floats in the ray of a setting sun.

But the sensualist, whether he whines in the pulpit, or croaks in the press, or howls in the brothel, what message has the statue or picture, or the wood-painting, which embodies a woman's unveiled form, what message has this purity enshrined for him? Nothing but earth, for he is of the earth, earthy; nothing but filth, for he is born of filth, filthy; nothing but lust, for the impulses of his heart are like the bubble on the Dead Sea, stagnant and pestilent excretions fomenting on the very dregs of rottenness and decay.

Such a sensualist have I seen, talk with prim utterance, in his demure journal, about immoral books; quoting garbled passages to prove his point, claiming sympathy from the *moral* public, because he had slimed over some sentence or chapter that was pure before he touched it; and all the while the victim of this *chaste* editor's perjury—a broken-hearted and wronged woman, lay mad and howling in the cell of an insane hospital.—This was a moral editor of a Moral Newspaper.

An expression of mingled character passed over the Texan's face, as he gazed upon the kneeling girl. His large eye dilated, and flashed with unusual light, while a smile played over his lip. Veiled in her luxuriant hair, the snowy skin gleaming through the interval of her tresses, she still grasped the light, as her tears fell like rain on the half-revealed bosom.

"Come, Isora," said John of Prairie Eden—and believe me, his voice was low and deep, and thrilling with that music of passion which always steals to the heart, and makes it beat more tumultuously—"we must away! Assume this monkish gown and wind the dark robe over it, while I put on the handsome dress of Don Augustin. Or stay! your purpose is changed; you will not fly with me and share the fate of the outcast and the stranger!"

Isora raised her eyes. John was standing with his head drooped, his hands clasped, his wild and singular face mellowed by a shade of overwhelming sadness. The strong man seemed melted into very womanhood as he talked to himself—it was his manner when wrung to the heart by sudden emotion.

"Outcast! Yes, I have no home, nor father, brother, sister—not one friend on the wide earth of God! Poor Harry! I see your boyish face and clear blue eyes—your voice, O Harry, how it comes back to my soul!—And in cold blood they put you to death. I saw you—yes, now I see your face dabbled in blood, a smile quivering on your lips, and they are cold forever! Isabel, dishonored—*dishonored*! The father hanging before the porch of his own home; his ashy face glowing in the morning sun! Isora deserts me too! Isora—this dear flower which I found blooming in her Mexican home, and wound to my heart—Isora leaves the outcast to his fate!"

No wonder that voice, whispering its wild soliloquy, pierced the maiden's soul.

She rose from the floor, and winding the robe once more upon her form, laid her right hand upon his muscular chest, while her eyes, shining through the intervals of her hair, burned with emotion too deep for words.

Their eyes met; the maiden seemed to grow into his heart, even as their glances mingled in one; a rosy red stole over her cheeks and bloomed in dewy freshness on her parted lips.

"I have no home but with thee!"

She did not tell how he had won her heart, how, appearing at first in her lonely home, with an atmosphere of mystery and romance about him—he had besought shelter from his pursuers. This was many days ago. She listened to his story, won by the melody of his voice, the strange light of his eyes, but more than all by that absorbing story, which spoke of the dear Prairie Eden, circled by the trees of the island grove; the gentle brother Harry, the dead father, and the beautiful Isabel.

From that hour she loved him, and many a time, in the gloomy chambers of the mansion, secluded from her brother's eye, and from the gaze of the Argus-eyed Duenna, this young and passionate woman suffered her unknown lover to kneel at her feet, to thread his fingers in the masses of her silken hair, and looked the magnetism of his soul into her eyes.[24]

She did not tell him in words this story of her love, but it shone in her eyes, it spoke in the brief sentence, uttered with dewy lips and panting bosom.

"I have no home but with thee!"

Let us pass once more into the shadows of Isora's bed chamber, where the monk shrinks back from the touch of a death-cold hand, as he hears the well-remembered voice.

CHAPTER X

The Voice of Isabel

"How like a voice from the dead comes up that voice of the wronged and dishonored, speaking through silence and darkness to the heart of the wronger."
—Texan Mss.

"Fear not, Don Antonio, for I, Isabel, of Prairie Eden am with you!"

The chamber was dark, and that voice, breaking suddenly from the gloom, sounds like hollow accents from the lips of death.

"It is her ghost," groaned the miserable man, as remorse began to rend every fiber of his soul. "From the shadows of the grave she comes to haunt me."

"Not Isabel the ghost, but Isabel, the living, blooming—fair as when she won your heart at Prairie Eden."

The cold hand pressed close within his own, and thrilled its ice to his heart.

"Nay; shrink not from me, Don Antonio. You loved me with an idolatry so wild, so mad! Loved me even when my father hung writhing on the tree, before his porch, his last groan gurgling up to God, as your kiss was on my lips. Long years have passed since then, Don Antonio; would you like to look upon my face once more? Or do you fear to behold those eyes which once filled your soul—those lips which once clung to yours, when the heart was maddened by a foul drug—the soul lost in the dreams of opium?"

Don Antonio started from the couch and struggled nervously to free himself from the grasp of the cold hand. But it held him as with the clutch of an iron vice, and the cold fingers seemed like the bony hands of a skeleton.

"Would'st like to look upon my face, Don Antonio?"

Not a word from the lips of the trembling man. Alone, in that dark room, with a woman, who had come from her grave to haunt him, he grew icy cold and heard his heart throb like a death-watch. Yet he was a brave man, and he had done a butcher's work on human forms in many a battle.

All the while the sound of voices, in the next chamber, came indistinctly to his ears, and added to his frenzy; for he was frenzied now, cold and hot by turns, now burning with fever and now chilled into ice.

Suddenly all was still in the adjoining chamber, and Don Antonio felt the cold hand and heard the voice again.

"Come, you shall look upon my face!"

The door swung open; Don Antonio had missed it in his nervous frenzy, and the cold hand led the shuddering man into the next chamber.

Holy Trinity! It is the novice, Brother Paulo.

Retreating with a shudder, Don Antonio beheld, in the center of the chamber, the form of a monk, whose dark cowl was thrown over his head and face, suffering only a glimpse of the features to be visible.

The lamp stood on the floor, and flung its upward rays over that dark, motionless form with the marble-white hands appearing from the folds of the shapeless robe. Around were the walls of that desolate room, the grim portraits and tapestry that flapped against the stone which it concealed, with a slow and hollow sound.

John of Prairie Eden, Isora, and the brave Don Augustin, all were gone from that gloomy chamber. The cowled figure and Don Antonio were alone in the silence and shadow.

"Yes, it is the novice," said the well-remembered voice from the shadow of the cowl. "The novice who three months ago entered the monastery of San Francisco, as a lay brother, and soon became the secretary of the reverend monk, Father Pedro. You have never seen this face, good father,—at least, never in a cowl—never since *the night*. Oh you remember it?—*the night of Prairie Eden!*"

Don Antonio, even with his shaven crown and cheek, was by no means an unhandsome man. His dark olive features, the boldly chiseled nose, the ponderous brow, overarching large and lustrous eyes; the mouth, around whose lips scorn and love, and the power of a dauntless will, played by turns—all resembled some antique head molded in rich bronze.

He was, we say, by no means an unhandsome man; his springy step, his graceful form, the monkish robe could not altogether hide. But now he was hideous, livid in the face, and stricken down as by a pestilence in every trembling limb; a fear, a horror worse than death possessed his veins; for before him, in the cowled form of the novice, or neophyte, Paulo, who had glided by his side for the last three months, he beheld not a living shape, but a ghostly image from the regions of the dead, sent to haunt his perjured soul.

Falling on his knees he crossed his brow and cried to God for mercy!

The neophyte raised that marble-white hand; in a moment the cowl would fall from the face. Don Antonio dared not turn his eyes away, and yet shuddered as he anticipated the disclosure of the ghastly features of the dead.

The cowl fell—O, what a ghastly vision broke on Don Antonio then!

That face, whiter than alabaster, with the delicate veins traced on the colorless brow, and a single spot, deep red, burning like a flame on each cheek; those lips, pale vermillion, moving without a sound; the eyes, unnaturally large, spreading with their strange light from the brow to the cheek-bone, and shining with an unfaltering glare upon the kneeling monk.

Around this deathly face, like a crown of ebony, was a mass of jet black hair, making the pale features yet more pale, and giving additional fire to the glaring eyes.

There are no words in language to picture the sad reproach, the overwhelming melancholy of that face. Around it, like a veil, seemed to hang the very atmosphere of despair.

"You think it sadly changed, Don Antonio, that face, which once won your *love*? Yet we are all changed, Father Pedro! Five years ago you were the handsome cavalier, pressing the drugged goblet to the lips of a weak girl, who sank at your feet, her soul wrung in every fiber, her brain whirling in madness. Now, you are the monk; and before you stands the girl whom you dishonored, while her brother bears your sinless sister away to his bridal chamber. Bridal chamber—a sweet word, father!—bridal chamber!—without one priestly rite or marriage vow—a meaning word, Father Pedro."

She raised herself erect, in all the pride of her fallen majesty, and stretched forth her white hand, as though she scattered the ashes of her curse upon his brow.

It was pitiable to see the agony of the monk, whose heart seemed crushed by his remorse.

"Holy Trinity! My sister—pure and stainless—what has she done to merit this wrong?"

"She is guilty even as Isabel of Prairie Eden—guilty of her innocence and beauty."

It was now the moment, when the cup of Don Antonio's degradation filled even to the brim. Before the woman, whom he had wronged five years ago—basely wronged, with an outrage that has no forgiveness, this side the grave, no revenge save the outpouring of blood—this proud man now grovelled like a slave beneath the lash; yes, like a hound beneath his master's scourge.

"Lady! be you a living woman, or be you a spirit from the grave, listen for a moment before you pour the last drop into this bitter cup. I confess my crimes, my baseness. I acknowledge this on my knees, thus crouching at your feet! I murdered the father—the daughter I dishonored—the brother I put to death, even as he begged for a crust, for a drop of water. No tears, no prayers, not one writhing of my victim's soul swayed me aside from my course! Can I confess more? Yet my sister—in the name of God and his angels, do not suffer wrong to visit her, and of all wrongs, that outrage which has no baptism of redemption but blood. For she is pure, she is innocent! Take my life, but do not, O—listen to me—do not harm this child whom my dying father bequeathed to my care!"

Cold and calm the cowled woman listened to his prayer. Not one feature in her marble face indicated emotion; her lip was firm, her eye unfaltering in its withering scorn.

There was no answer from her lips, but the monk read it in that silent vengeance of the pale, beautiful face.

Bowing his head on his hands, the cowl dropped over his face, and a silence ensued, unbroken by a sound.

At last it was broken by the echo of a footstep, and a half-clad figure rushed wildly into the room.

It was Don Augustin, his face red with frenzy; stained on the brow with a hideous wound; his form divested of his handsome coat of green and gold.

"You linger here—you!—shame! Has the *monk* robbed you of all that belongs to the *soldier*, to the *man*? You linger here, and the accursed heretic has borne your sister away, passed the guard, disguised in my coat, and now, perchance—but what mummery have we here?"

For the first time he beheld the disguised woman.

"Don Augustin,"—the voice of the monk was husky as he raised his livid face—"in that cowled form you behold my fate—the destiny of my house—the woman whose honor I crushed without remorse, five years ago, in her home of Prairie Eden!"

The small, ferret eyes of the Mexican twinkled with rage.

"Can I believe my eyes? Is it Don Antonio Marin whom I see kneeling here? Arise, be a man! Let us pursue the heretic! there is a boat by the mole; we will pass through the American fleet and track the robber to his den in the Isle of Sacrificios. It is a work of danger, I know—you are afraid—afraid! when the honor of the home of your father is at stake!"

He paced the floor, rubbing his hands together, as he cursed some dozen excellent oaths in pure Spanish.

"Come, I will go with you!"—and Don Antonio sprang to his feet—"but who will lead us to the den of the heretic?"

A low, sad voice, unbroken by a tremor, was heard echoing far along the gloomy chamber,—

"That will I!"

And Isabel, with her pale face turned to the light, her full eyes fixed upon her betrayer, pointed with her white hand toward the door.

CHAPTER XI

The Isle of the Sacrifice

"Near Vera Cruz, in the Isle of Sacrificios—where the Aztecs offered the sacrifice of human blood—subterranean chambers have been discovered and images of the forgotten religion, with the altar stone on which the victim was slain."

—Texan Mss.

The Isle of the Sacrifice!

We stand upon its sandy shore, with the dark waves, breaking in low murmurs all around us, the deep night gleaming upon us from the dark dome, overspread with stars, San Juan's castle frowning over the waters, and white Orizaba lowering from afar into the great temple of the midnight universe.

A strange isle, with its rocks, and sands, and scattered herbage, stretches before us.—Three hundred years ago the altar of sacrifice smoked with his blood-red incense here, and the groans of the victims echoed far over the waters, as the anointed priest of the faith of Murder, tore from the mangled breast the quivering heart.

Even now, beneath this soil, strange chambers lie hidden, stored with the gods and altars of the Aztec faith.

Still, from yonder shore, echoes the tramp of armed men, and through the night the sails of the American ships gleam like white mists, hovering over the waters.

Suddenly a half-naked form springs from the waves and stands erect upon the sand.—By the dim light of the stars you may discern the iron outline of that figure, with loose trousers clothing it below the waist, while the sinewy arms, the firm, broad chest, are bared to the night breeze.

Had you but one gleam of light you would behold the flesh along the back severed with many a hideous welt, mangled into one clotted mass of sores and blood.

This unknown man, springing from the waters without one sound or word to warn us of his approach, shakes his huge arms in the air, and with clenched hands and groaning utterance, disturbs the silence with words like these,—

"By ___ I am free! You shall not scourge my back again, nor dig your lash into my flesh once more, though I am but a common sailor in the American Navy! By ___ I would sell my soul to the devil, could I but have the brave captain of the _____ here, on this barren shore for five minutes! Curses upon that flag, curses upon its stripes and stars! The stripes for the common sailor's back—the stars for every petty tyrant who may buy a commission by crawling around the avenues of the city of Washington. I swear as God sees me, to hate and fight against that flag forever! May the devil catch me this minute if I would not like to have it here, and grind it into the sand beneath my feet."

The escaped sailor turned from the waves and steadfastly fixed his eyes upon the barren isle.

"'Twenty paces from the shore, a small rock of peculiar shape rises from the sand.—Near that rock your freedom awaits you.'—What can it mean? To-night, as I lay in my irons, a paper was pressed into my hand by a strange man, who whispered, 'Take this file—read the paper—and swim to the Sacri-ficios'—I am here, but where's the rock?"

Even as he spoke there rose at his feet a small rock, triangular in shape, with its surface covered with uncouth figures, discernible by the light of the stars. He examined the rock with a careful and searching scrutiny.

All was silent around: no trace of a human form was visible.

"I'm prettily fooled!" growled the escaped sailor with an oath; "but it's my only chance—here goes."

With a strong effort he raised the rock from the sand, or to speak more correctly, lifted it on one end, and a warm light, streaming from a square aperture at his feet, bathed his face, with a ruddy glow. Then it might be seen that his hair and beard were alike fiery red in hue, his face embrowned by the sun and rain, his eyes bleared and swollen, his teeth revealed by his parting lips—black, broken, and irregular—altogether a hideous visage.

At his feet, as from a well, streamed that hidden light, disclosing a ladder, whose top rested against the side of the aperture. In an instant his huge form was concealed in the passage, and with his brawny arms he drew the rock back to its original position and descended the ladder. Seven steps he counted, and turning his head over his shoulder, he saw that he had entered a small room or cavern, with a blazing pine-knot attached to its rocky wall.

In that light, like the crude horrors of some nightmare dream, he beheld the details of the place. Three obscene idols, formed of porphyritic rock, and six feet in height, supported the ceiling of the cavern. Between these idols, three black spaces appeared, evidently passages, leading deeper down into the subterranean chambers of the Isle of Sacrifice. On the wall, near the eastern idol, the pine-knot was hung; by its light the sailor read the crumpled paper which he drew from his trousers's pocket.

"To-day you were lashed like a dog, your flesh peeled from your bones, at the command of a petty tyrant. Would you be free? Tonight a file will be placed in your grasp, and with it directions which will enable you to seek the company of a jovial band who acknowledge no lord nor master, save

The Chief of the Free Rangers
Isle of Sacrificios, March 9th, 1847"

It was an interesting thing to observe the face and form of this escaped sailor, while he stood by the torch, engaged in deciphering the somewhat mysterious epistle which we have given above.

The light streamed over his red hair and beard, disclosing the sinews of his gigantic chest, and revealing his broad back, with the blood oozing slowly from its welts and sores.

At first his countenance wore a gloomy scowl,—

"I have been fooled," he murmured, with a blasphemous oath, and tossed the paper to the ground.

"Ha! what is this?" he cried, as he beheld a piece of paper, some ten inches square, affixed to the wall by a knife,—"Beyond the eastern idol lies your way; pursue it in darkness for some hundred paces, descend a stairway, and await further orders from the

C.F.R."

Without a second thought, the sailor passed beyond the eastern idol, and measuring his paces through the darkness—while a chill air swept against his cheek—soon came to the stairway, which he descended, and discovered a light shining around the angle of a rock, distant from where he stood and not more than ten yards.

He soon reached the rock, and started back with a shout of wonder, mingled with delight. The rock, a huge and irregular crag, with a similar crag opposite, formed a doorway to a chamber some twenty feet square, in the center of which stood a table, stored with the most luscious fruit and viands, mingled with flasks of wine.

This much, at a glance, the escaped sailor beheld, but entering the chamber he examined its minutest details with something of a cold shudder thrilling every nerve. For around that table, with a chair at either end, and spread as if for a banquet, were grouped the most hideous forms of the ancient Aztec theology, sculptured in every variety of ugliness, and looking altogether, with their uncouth shapes, stony eyes and distorted features, like the attendant devils of some infernal festival.

The light in the center of the table, standing amid fig and oranges, grapes and flowers, imparted a ruddy warmth to the prominent points of the idols, while everything beside was wrapped in misty gloom.

"A devilish queer company," cried the sailor as he flung himself in a chair; "but the wine bottles look tempting, and the cold ham is not to be 'sneezed at'—particularly by a common sailor, who has not tasted food for twelve hours! Ha! champagne, as I'm a sinner—pop! How the sound of that cork makes them stare—these respectable gentlemen, with the stony eyes and peculiarly ugly faces. A slice of ham, a biscuit, and another pull at the champagne bottle. I feel quite comfortable, by—"

It would require the pencil of some artist who delights in the grotesque and horrible to picture this scene.

Relieved by the dark background, the burly face of the sailor, framed in red hair and beard, stood boldly out in the light. In one hand a champagne bottle, in the other a slice of ham inserted between two biscuits. His huge form is comfortably disposed in the arm chair, and his broad chest begins to swell and heave with the fiery impulse of the wine.

Above, the rocky ceiling, and around the table those distorted forms and uncouth faces, looking like living things as the light flit to and fro over the dusky outlines.

One figure towers above the rest; a dim shape of dark-red stone, with a knife of obsidian, or volcanic glass, extended in its deformed right arm. It is the Aztec war-god, *Mexitili*.[25]

And here, where the priests of the forgotten creed administered their bloody rites 300 years ago, now sits the escaped slave of the American Navy making merry, with the wine bottle in his hand, while his roystering catch is echoed far along the gloomy recesses of the cavern.

It was a strange song that he sung, and seemed to have some bearing upon a murder done at sea by a captain of the American Navy,—

"They hung at the yard-arm, swing so gay,
    Their feet in the air, their faces to heaven.
The captain wiped his lips, and said,—'Let us pray!'
    And then three cheers for God were given.
The stars and stripes and the tyrant's law!
    Let us merrily, cheerily sing,
For God let us now my boys hurrah!
    As we merrily, cheerily sing."

With some dozen more doggerel verses of blasphemous tenor, the escaped sailor plied the wine bottle until the Aztec gods seemed dancing round him and leering in his face with their stony eyes.

Then crowning his brow with a wreath of blossoms snatched from the table, he gravely drank to the health of the idols, one by one, terming them "all good fellows of the right stripe, though, d—n it! they needn't make such ugly faces."

The wine which he drank seemed not so much to cheer as to madden him. He felt it, burning like molten fire in every vein, and encircling his brain as with a mass of liquid light.

Whether from his long fast or the peculiar effect of the wine, we cannot decide, but wherever he turned his head he saw the cold face of a dead man, who glared upon him, with eyes like glass, as his body hung suspended to an oaken limb.

That quivering oaken limb, that cold white dead man's face was everywhere, now among the idol forms, now moving slowly overhead, now seen in the center of the table, the limb always trembling, the face always white, dead, and ghastly.

Yet this sight did not strike the drunken sailor with anything like fear. He drank only the more, shouted the louder, and trolled as he danced around the table, his doggerel song, until the nooks and corners of the cavern-room seemed yelling on with the echo of a hundred voices.

At last, whether it was a reality or but part of his drunken dream, we know not, but he suddenly became aware of the presence of a new guest, a tall man, dressed in deep black, a veil upon his face, shrouding his features from view.

"Would you," said a voice of full and manly intonation, "would you become one of us?"

"That depends pretty much on who you are and what you follow."

And the drunkard staggered to the chair, endeavoring to clear his eyes from the fiery mist which danced before them.

"We are a band of brothers, who, gathering our taxes from the land and sea, have turned this war to our own uses. We have gathered our members from the oppressed in the army and navy of the United States. We have a three-fold object—security, plunder, and revenge—will you join us?"

"I will, hoss!" cried the sailor, falling into the slang which he had acquired, years ago, in the prairies of the West. "Jist show me a chance now."

"But you are afraid to take our oath? You will shudder at the initiation of the Independent Order of Free Rangers."

The sailor started to his feet, leaned over the table, and while his bloodshot eyes rolled in frenzy, grinned until his discolored teeth were visible, as he uttered an oath too horrible for repetition.

"I don't care much what yer oath is; I'm a Royal Arch Curser myself—I am. And as to yer Initiation, tell me, what kin a man fear who has been lashed like a dog on board a free American ship of war? Show me a chance I say, and let me but stand free to face with the captain of the ___; only for a minute—, only for a minute!"

"Wait here, and in one hour you will be summoned by a brother of our order. He will lead you to the altar, where your courage will be tried; for as our lives will hang upon your fidelity, it is important that we know what manner of man you are before we admit you into our brotherhood. Remember—in half an hour prepare."

The figure in black disappeared behind the image of the war god, Mexitili.

Half an hour passed away. The cavern no longer rang with shouts of boisterous merriment; the viands were no longer eagerly devoured, nor the bottles emptied with mad rapidity.

Along the table, heaped in inextricable confusion, were scattered wreaths of blossoms, slices of ham, biscuits, bottles, oranges, figs, and flowers; but the drunken sailor, who with the print of the Free American Lash on his back, reeled here an hour ago, singing blasphemous songs, where is he now?

In the arm chair at the head of the table behold him, his shock of red hair and beard presenting a frightful contrast to his face, which is now pale as a corpse.

He is a very strong man, and yet now he trembles from head to foot, his bloodshot eyes neither turn to the right or left but glare fixedly before him.

Why this paleness, this trembling, this unknown fear?

A deep groan is heard.

"I believe that my heart is burning to a cinder within me. My temple throbs as though the pendulum of a clock were enclosed in my skull. I cannot drink any more—I tremble; I am hot and cold by turns. Ah! who's there?—who's that repeating my name?"

"*Ewen McGregor!*" called a voice from the recesses of the cavern; "do you still desire to enter the brotherhood?"

"I do," faltered the sailor.

"Then come hither."

He arose, tottered along the cavern until the darkness enclosed him. A cold breeze swept against his cheek. There was a hand pressed upon his own—why did he turn cold as that hand touched his fingers?

"Advance twenty steps with me. Take this knife and obey."

He took the knife and was led forward in the darkness until the folds of the curtain brushed his face.

"Within the chamber, shrouded by the curtain, lies your victim, bound to the altar of the Aztec faith, as they bound their victims three hundred years ago. Do not fear—do not tremble, but think of the lashes you received this day, and, without lifting the veil which conceals the face, strike home. Enter and obey."

Why did the brain of the stout-hearted sailor suddenly feel as though all the blood in his Herculean frame had rushed into his skull?

He grasped the knife and dashed the curtain aside.

CHAPTER XII

The Monk Beholds the Revenge

"It was a bitter drop in his cup, no doubt; but he had to drink it."

—Texan Mss.

We will return to the chamber of the three idols.

Not ten minutes had elapsed since Red Ewen the sailor left its confines, when three figures stood revealed by the light of its pine torch.

Here Isabel, her pale face framed in the cowl, which increased the strange luster of her eyes and made her features both spectral and ghostly; by her side, Don Augustin, his form shrouded in a dainty brown mantle, varied with silver trappings and glittering with a single jeweled star. Under the torch, his bronzed visage distinctly disclosed in every vein and nerve by the downcast rays, stood Father Pedro, otherwise called Don Antonio, clutching his hands in nervous intensity, as his livid lips trembled with a soundless motion.

The cowled lady was calm and cold!—Don Augustin red-faced and fiery about the eyes.

Don Antonio a picture of remorse, carved in black and bronze.

Around them the obscene images seemed to live and move, as their forms were now darkened by a sudden shadow and now illumined by so ruddy a light.

Don Augustin dashed the sheath of his sword against the hard floor of the cavern, in a gesture of extreme impatience.

"Come!—the devil and all his imps seize this night and all its works"—he was choice in his cursing was Don Augustin—"we have lingered long enough, dared danger enough, good lady it is time for you to fulfill your promise. Lead us to the haunt of this Texan—heretic and pirate as he is, and we will force the lady Isora from his grasp."

"My sister! as my father poured forth his blood at my feet he consigned thee to my care!" murmured the monk.

"The brother alone may thread these passages with me," broke in the sad tones of the cowled Isabel, "Father Pedro alone may rescue his sister. Nay, scowl not, Don Augustin, nor curl your lip with scorn—it must be so, or I will even leave the poor girl to her fate."

"Await here, Don Augustin," hurriedly exclaimed Father Pedro. "I will track these solitudes alone; if I do not return within an hour, follow and avenge."

Why that smile on the pale red lips of Isabel, as she surveys their parting embrace—the cheek of the monk laid against the face of the soldier—the firm clasp of each other's hands and the meaning glance of their eyes.

"I will await you—if need be, avenge you," Don Augustin laid the point of his sword to his lips.

"Come!—your sister calls you." And Isabel led the way into the darkness beyond the western idol.

Saw you that pale face turned to the light, the moment ere it disappeared, the eyes and lips wearing the same expression. Cold, relentless, ghostly?

Now came the moment of Don Antonio's triumph. Through these dark passages, where the air was hot and stifling and chilled with subterranean draughts by turns; down these rude stairways, hewn three centuries, aye,—perchance ten centuries ago, in the solid rock—up these rugged ascents where the footstep became unsteady as it encountered the stony fragments flung over the dark path; on and on, in darkness, the monk followed his silent guide.

The darkness was dense, palpable, it seemed to shut him in like the boards of a coffin; the silence was dead and appalling, unbroken save by the echo of their footsteps.

Isabel was silent; for a quarter of an hour no word passed her lips, but her cold hand was damp with a clammy moisture that chilled the hand of Don Antonio throughout every nerve.

How the consciousness that he was alone with the woman whom he had so foully wronged, pressed like a sentence of Death on his soul!

Still, in all the wilderness of his baseness and crime, there bloomed one beautiful flower—more lonely from the very blackness that encircled it—the love of a pure and stainless sister.

At last—oh, how gladly—with what an involuntary cry of delight he beheld it—a light shone from afar over the darkness of their way.

Isabel spoke for the first time,—

"That light shines on your sister's face!"

The word touched Don Antonio's heart with new life.

"On on!"—he shuddered—"it may be too late."

Nearer and larger grew that light until it resembled a sun, so round, and full, and blazing it broke upon their eyes, an unearthly sun glancing over the darkness of these Aztec vaults.

Why linger on each moment of stifling suspense?

At last they stood near the light. It shone out upon the rock bound passage, from a circular space, framed by rocks and lighted up the roof, the floor, the walls of this lone corridor, with a red, glaring glow.

"The passage ends here," whispered Isabel. "That light shines from a chamber, from which we are separated by a solid wall of rock."

"Let us enter the chamber; my sister is there," gasped the monk.

"Your sister, indeed, is there, but you cannot enter the chamber, unless you retrace your steps, and from the chamber of the three idols depart by the eastern passage. It may be well for you to do this, but first advance, and through this crevice behold your sister."

Don Antonio saw her look—saw her face lighted for a moment by a smile—oh, how wild and unearthly—and was afraid to advance. He feared to behold the secret of that unknown chamber.

She took him by the hand and dragged him to the aperture in the solid wall of rocks.

This was the sight which he saw:—

A small room, circular in form, whose wall was formed by one undulating curtain of faint crimson, which was supported by three slender white pillars. From the ceiling—it was like a dome, and painted to resemble a midnight sky; blue, spotted with stars—hung a fiery globe which bathed the place in dazzling light.

This light, which seemed to float and wave in waves of liquid flame, was tempered and softened by clouds of snowy incense smoke, which emerged from the thousand apertures of the globe, and wrapped the room in intoxicating odors.

Beneath the globe, in the center of the rich matting which supplied the place of a carpet, was a cushion or couch of rich scarlet velvet, fringed with gold; and near it a sofa or divan of the same rich texture.

On the sofa, half seated and half reclined, was a man of some twenty-five years, he did not seem more; his dark hair and beard, curled and perfumed after the manner of the luxurious Sybarites of old.[26] His broad chest heaved beneath a garment of purple velvet, flashing with gold and jewels. Fine linen about his bold throat, and around his bronzed hands; a broad belt of rich embroidery across his chest; a dagger quivering by his side.

His face glowed; it shone in every feature with a mad delight. It was a face that could not easily be forgotten.

Behold that downcast head, those large eyes, whose intense gaze grows soft with moisture, those parted lips, which seem unclosed in the act of murmuring words of passion.

His right arm was extended, it held aloft a golden goblet, curiously carved and brimming with deep purple wine.

But there was a fair hand laid upon the wrist of that extended arm.

Well might Don Antonio gasp for breath!

A woman's form was couched upon the velvet cushion, her head resting upon the knee of the man, as with an intoxicating langor stealing over her face she gazed upward through the intervals of her soft, silken hair, and lifted her arm, clutching his wrist as if to seize the goblet.

She was clad in an azure tunic, or loose frock, which fell, without a girdle, from her shoulders to her knees, revealing by the soft gradations of every fold, the gentlest undulations of her shape. Below the knees her limbs were bare, their snowy whiteness contrasting with the scarlet rubiness of the cushion; a delicate sandal of pink satin was bound to the sole of each foot, leaving all beside, in its unveiled loveliness, the delicate azure veins, perceptible beneath the softly flushed carmine skin.

A diamond sparkled on the tunic, where it half and only half concealed her bust; it sparkled with every pulse of her bosom, shone as that bosom rose, and glittered softly like a fading star as it fell.

No more beautiful, no more delicate contrast can be imagined, than that which was presented by the soft whiteness of her half-revealed shoulders, and the mazes of her silken hair, as black as a pall.

One tress fell over her rising bosom, as if in shame, and veiled it as it heaved, like a creamy billow, into light.

The face told the full story of that mad intoxication which thrilled every nerve of this beautiful girl—this Sultana of the rock-bound bower.

Through the lips—they were slightly parted—glowing with moist vermillion, gleamed the ivory teeth. Over the cheek, soft, rounded, downy, burned a rose-bud flush, which now contracted in one intense heat of passion and again seemed to spread forth its rosy leaves over the whole face.

The eyes, bright and dewy, and shining languidly from the heavy lids, which seemed weighed down by the intoxicating odors of the place, were centered upon the face, glowering down upon that beautiful form with a glance not to be mistaken.

"Wilt drink, Isora? Wilt drink to our merry life upon the broad ocean, where I, thy lover-husband, will gather spoil for thee—for *thee*—from every flag, and win diamonds for thy white brow from every clime? And after the battle is over, the good ship, with its royal Black Flag will tranquilly glide into the green cove of our island home. Thou wilt stand upon the shore, waving thy white arms as thy Rover comes up the steep cliffs, comes home to thee, covered with laurels and spoil! Drink, Isora, to the days when we shall dwell on our island home!"

She raises her white arms, the goblet is in her hand, its golden rim is pressed against her red lip, the purple wine glides slowly, in a rich, mellow current, through that quivering portal.

"I love none but thee—thee only, Juan!—Wherever thou goest, upon sea or shore, I will go with thee! In battle"—her slight nostril quivered—"I will bind on thy sword and laugh as the red mist waves over thee; in peace, when the fight is over, this bosom shall pillow thy head, as we sit at the porch of our island home and gaze upon the young moon rising over the waveless sea."

She twined her white arms upon his sinewy hands and dashed her silken hair over his arms. All the while her bosom, veiled by that solitary tress, rose like a creamy billow, bearing on its crest a dark and glossy burden.

The incense smoke, agitated by a current of air, descended and swept over them like a veil.

Don Antonio could not withdraw his gaze from the aperture. Oh, what fiend but would pity him now, as the crushing agony of his soul glares in his glassy eyeballs, and quivers in his parched lips. He cannot withdraw his gaze from the aperture; his eye is fixed upon the undulating veil of the incense smoke—he hears those kisses, those words of passionate transport, but cannot withdraw his gaze.

Isabel—is she still cold and calm? Does no relenting throb pulsate in her ice-cold bosom?

The light glaring around that passage revealed that motionless form, resembling a marble image of vengeance, veiled—all save the face—in a monkish cowl.

Once, only, there was something like a burning tear upon her colorless cheek—a tremor on her lip. It was for an instant—she was marble again.

Don Antonio turned, he seized her death-cold hands,—

"Woman!" he fiercely shrieked, "Have you no pity? Look! my sister, my only sister's senses drugged by maddening draughts—her honor torn from her in a moment of delirium. Pity—mercy—not for my sake, but for hers!"

Isabel was silent; one word, after a pause, she gasped; one only, and that with an evident effort.

"*Prairie Eden!*"

The monk fell backward, as if blasted by a thunder stroke. But those sounds in the curtained chamber, those kisses of mad passion, those raptures of voluptuous transport—he heard them still, and was nerved with the savage strength of despair.

"You must save my sister! By the Holy Trinity I swear your life shall pay the forfeit of her outraged honor. Your life! I swear it!—"

He had grasped her wrists, and all the devil of his soul shone from his features, horribly distorted by passion, rage, madness.

With but a single phrase she answered him,—

"*Rancho Salado!*"

The hands of the monk fell. He beat his forehead against the rocks, grappled the cold surface until his nails were splintered at the finger ends; and in the pauses of his frenzy he shouted aloud her name—his sister's name,—

"Isora!—'tis your brother who calls.—Isora, in the name of your dead father,—hear me!"

The incense smoke waved aside, the monk looked through the aperture.

"Oh God! this is worse than eternal death—she hears me not—kisses! His arms about her neck—the goblet! Isora! O shame—despair! Villain, I defy you—proclaim you coward—monster! Will meet you face to face in combat.—Isora!"

And like the chorus to his broken ejaculations, were heard those whispering voices,—

"Mine?"

"Thine only!"

"But my poor brother Harry, with his pale face and blue eyes, we'll drink to his memory—drink to him as he kneels in the presence of his murderer, the prayer yet warm upon his lips, as he falls cold—cold—dead! Vengeance to the murderer of poor Harry!"

"Give me the goblet. Thine eyes madden—thy voice whirls my soul as on a billow of flame. I drink, Juan—death and shame to the murderer of thy brother!"

"Isora!" groaned—not shouted—the monk as he fell back from the fatal aperture in the rocks, his soul stupefied by the voluptuous frenzy which burned his eyes as he beheld it!

Isabel hears this, and does not relent? Ah, the cold, remorseless vengeance of the dishonored woman fails her at once. You see a vivid flash brighten over her face; she veils her eyes, beating the hard earth all the while with her tiny foot.

"He murdered my father—I see his cold face—oh God! how it glares in the rising sun. Harry, too, went forth from home, and came back no more. There stands the murderer. My honor—that which is the world, heaven, life to a woman—he crushed into the dust, as the poisoned cup whirled its frenzy through my brain. I know it all—confess it my God; but his sister, she hath done no wrong; her ravings, uttered in the madness of passion, they madden me. I can bear it no longer!"

She turned aside from the glare of the light and her footsteps echoed along the caverned passage.

The monk raised his eyes—she was gone. His despair was now complete. It was a horrible sight to see him tear the flesh from his face with his splintered nails.

Suddenly three forms veiled in blue robes, appeared in the light, their faces lost to view in the folds of their garments.

With one movement they seized Father Pedro, bound him despite his frantic resistance, and held their sharp knives at his bared throat.

With the bandage across his mouth, the corns on his arms, these veiled forms lifted him to the aperture once more.

He looked.

Those who held him were thrilled with the cold shudder that pervaded his form.

Once more!

He lay motionless in their grasp, his proud spirit broken, his face changed and fallen, as though the ice of death had been poured upon it.

"You have beheld only the beginning of justice as administered by the Free Rangers. Now comes the end!"

Like an inanimate burden they bore the conscious but palsied monk into a dark passage which suddenly opened near the bright aperture in the wall. Whether it was a secret door or only a hollow in the rocks, which had evaded his search, he knew not, but suffered them to bear him unresistingly along.

CHAPTER XIII

Red Ewen Is Initiated

"A singular rite was the initiation of the Free Rangers. A dead man was
placed upon the Aztec altar and—"

—Texan Mss.

Red Ewen grasped the knife and pushed the curtain aside. It was a wondrous sight that met his gaze. He was a man of giant strength and superhuman nerve, infernal beyond the fancy of a devil in his remorseless cruelty, but within half an hour a strange coldness, succeeded by a burning sensation, as sudden and as strange, had robbed his iron sinews of their vigor.

The knife trembled in his grasp.

He stood in a room, or cell, or vault, as you may please to term it, hollowed out of the living rock, not more than five yards in diameter. The floor was level, the ceiling shaped like a dome, but all was solid rock.—In the center of the vault, a square form of stone arose, a block six feet long and three feet wide, with its sides sculptured into every variety of obscene or hideous hieroglyphic.

At the head of the block—it resembled an ancient altar of sacrifice—towered a shape of brownish rock, veined with bright scarlet and representing in its ferocious eyes, embruted features and upraised war club, the Aztec god of war.

Around the altar were grouped four living forms, clad in long robes, with a mantle falling over every face.

The mantles were blue, the robes bright scarlet. From every robe was extended an arm grasping a lighted torch. Their mingling rays filled the vault with light and scented the air with grateful perfume.

Red Ewen stood like a statue, dumb with amazement.

To understand his feelings we must call to mind the incidents of his life, which took place upon this eventful 9th of March, 1847.

This morning he writhed beneath the hang man's lash, on board a ship of war bearing the banner of the Stars.

Only a few hours ago he lay in his chains, when a veiled man appeared in the darkness, and taught him the way to freedom.

An hour ago he danced in drunken madness in the Aztec banqueting chamber, his veins fired by something more than champagne, some deadlier poison than the venom of alcohol.

Now a change had come over him. The madness was gone. Cold, hot, fire, ice by turns, he stood under the door of this strange vault, knife in hand, and shuddered as he beheld the four veiled forms whose heaving breasts told that they were living, the solitary shape whose horrible deformity spoke of the dim ages, long since departed, when the quivering victim, a strong man full of life, was hewn to pieces in this very cell.

One by one, the living figures addressed the escaped sailor,—

"Could you become a Free Ranger, admitted to all the privileges of our Brotherhood?"

"The right to spoil and slay, wherever a sure foot, a true steed, a good ship may bear you?"

"To gather tribute from all nations, on land and sea alike, and select from the loveliest women of the earth the woman who you shall call wife so long as it may please you and no longer?"

"A short life and a merry one! A life with the outcasts and oppressed of all nations, a jovial band, who know no laws save those proclaimed by their chief, who reward the traitor's deed with the sharpest knife and the strongest cord."

Then their voices joined in chorus,—

"Would you, Ewen McGregor, escaped slave from the American Navy, become a free ranger of the land and sea?"

"I would!" faltered Ewen, as the light played over his enormous chest and his broad back seamed with weltering stripes.

With his brutal form and animal face, he stood in the vault like the appropriate demon of the scene, his burly face, with blood-shot eyes and thick lips, disclosing black and broken teeth, encircled in his short, stiff, red hair and long, matted beard.

His face was pale, his lip quivered as he uttered the response.

"Then take the vow."

Far be it from me to repeat that eloquent liturgy of blasphemy.

It was loathsome enough, horrible enough, in its crowded imprecations to satisfy the Demon of Blasphemy himself. Even Ewen shuddered, but that was the fire and ice which possessed his veins by turns.

"And if I fail in this to obey the commands of my leader, or betray the secrets of the Free Rangers, may the knife of the suicide sever my heart, may earth deny me a grave when I am dead, and the beasts feed on my senseless corpse."

So ran the mildest part of the loathsome ritual.

On his knees, before the altar, he took the oath, "to obey the commands of *the Leader,* whatever they might be,"—and knife in hand he rose.

"Advance!"

The voice sounded deep and hollow as it echoed back from the dome.

Red Ewen drew near the altar, his animal visage growing deathly pale.

"Uncover the form of the dead!"

At the word one of the figures robed in scarlet, his face mantled in blue, extended his hand and lifted the altar cloth, until a small space of flesh, evidently a glimpse of a human chest, on the left side, near the heart was visible, the veins distinctly marked beneath the clear olive skin.

"Prepare for the last act of initiation! Behold this dead man—raise your knife and strike deep into his chest. Do this,—prove your defiance of all obligations, imposed by what pious fools denominate morality—prove that you fear nothing, either living or dead, and we hail you as a brother."

"Yet, I swear by—he lives!" faltered Ewen, as an indefinable fear palsied his arm. "Look—he is not dead—this man upon the stone—he breathes."

"Folly! your fancy deceives you—he is dead—aye, dead. He was a traitor and he died according to our laws. Advance and strike."

The blood rushed to Red Ewen's face, filling every vein with the sudden and ferocious instinct of carnage. Each starting eyeball was filled with ejected blood; his thick lips became dark purple; he grasped the knife with all the vigor of his Herculean arm, and came nearer to the altar.

Still it seemed to move, that chest, concealed by the cloth, nay, the bared spot of brown flesh seemed to glow, as with the sudden impulse of strong emotion. True, the face of the dead man was veiled in the altar-cloth yet still the bosom seemed to quiver with life.

Look—Ewen stands over the dead, the knife raised—it is ten inches long— the point poised over the bared flesh.

A hissing sound—it descends—it is buried to the hilt in the breast of the dead man.

There was a pause, while Ewen with his hand clutching the hilt, exerted all his strength to withdraw the blade, *and in the action, he felt the body of the dead man writhe beneath him.*

At the same moment the altar-cloth was partly raised and the face disclosed.

Ewen, the giant with an appetite for carnage like the tiger's, staggered from the altar as though the knife had pierced his own bosom, instead of the bosom of the dead.

For that face was a fearful thing to look upon.

The cloth bound around the jaws of the uncovered face did not conceal the horrible working of the features, nor hide the slow, rolling motion of the eyeballs, terribly bright with death, as they turned from side to side.

A moan was indistinctly heard.

"Don Antonio Marin!" shouted Red Ewen, as his veins seemed filled with an intolerable heat, and staggering back, he gazed stolidly upon the writhing features of the dying man.

A figure dressed in blue and gold, stepped lightly over the entrance of the vault, and approached the altar.

The torch light which shone over the contorted features of the dying— hark! that gurgling moan!—played upon the broad chest, the firm features of the intruder.

"John of Prairie Eden!" shouted Ewen, as he stood rooted to the floor. "Hey! what's this! By the living—there is some plot in this! You here! Who lighted this vault with those hellish flames, and sent the devils dancing around that dying Spaniard?—Ah!"

He fell, writhing in horrible convulsions, to the floor, the foam frothing round his lips as his fingers clutched the hard stone.

By the altar's head, his brow uncovered, and his broad chest glowing with purple and flashing with diamonds, stood John of Prairie Eden, his features wearing a marble calmness, only disturbed by a slight movement of the nether lip.

There was a Satanic beauty about his face, whose broad forehead, shaded by dark hair, firm, aquiline nose, compressed lips—appearing in the midst of his mustache and beard—and large eyes, deep sunken beneath arching brows, now wore an expression not the less infernal because it struggled with a look of quiet composure.

He bent over the uncovered face of Don Antonio, and whispered—even as his beard touched the brow of the dying man—as his eyes, blazing with rapture, shot their glance into the starting eyeballs of the wretched victim— whispered in a soft voice, and with a pleasant smile, these words—

"When I withdraw the knife you will die, my friend. Hold, you will injure yourself if you attempt to speak again, for that bandage on your mouth makes it difficult for you to breathe, much less speak. Be perfectly calm, my dear friend, for I have much to say to you ere you die. Do you know me? Do you know me? Do you recognize these features? Whom"—his breath swept the cheek of Don Antonio—"whom do I resemble, brother Harry—eh? Or do I look like my father? Or, hold—do you not trace a resemblance in my smile to the gay laugh of Isabel?"

The cloth over the mouth was agitated by a convulsive motion, as the dying man made a horrible effort to speak.

He knew the face. Look how his starting eyeballs glare into the eyes of his Dooms-man!

This scene seemed even to affect the forms in robes of scarlet with blue mantles over their faces. By the light of the torches which they grasped you can see their robes heave, as from the impulse of horror,—agony.

On the floor, his giant form distorted into a shapeless heap of deformity— so horrible was the fire which gnawed his intestines—Red Ewen lay, the foam gathering in white beads upon his swollen lips, the white surface of his eye- balls suddenly turned to scarlet.

"Oh, it was horrible"—he raved—"to force me to drink that goblet of melted lead, hot, hissing hot! It burns!—it burns! O, water—water! You have covered my brain with hot coals! Take your knee from my breast, old man of Prairie Eden; for you are a dead man; your eyes are cold—I hung you myself to the tree—"

"That is Red Ewen's voice, my dear friend." And John smiling pleasantly, bent over the face of Don Antonio. "Do you know his voice? A pleasant voice! You heard it once in Prairie Eden, I am glad you know it. It was Red Ewen that stabbed you. Ungrateful dog, to turn his fangs against his master. My God!" he cried, with an air of chagrin, "this man is dying—he has not more than one minute's life in him, and I have so much to say to him. So many important things!"

Look yonder, where the curtain hangs over the narrow entrance, and do not breathe lest you disturb the beautiful vision. A lovely face, with glossy black curls waving around it, appears amid those curtain folds; the eyes, dancing with wild light, gazing with wonder and fear upon the strange group of this cavern vault.

It is Isora, whose brother, pinioned and gagged, the knife sunken to the hilt in his breast, lies writhing in death agony upon the altar.

One movement of John—the mere change of his position, for a single inch to either side will reveal the horrible face of the dying brother to his sister's gaze. But John does not move—all good angels be thanked—there is a belt of shadow between the dying face and the lustrous eyes of the sister,

"Ha!—that footstep! Isora!"

Without moving one inch, John turned his smiling face over his shoulder and whispered gently,—

"My love, you have come. It is well. Remain where you are, for a moment only, beautiful Isora! How I love to linger on the music of that name—Isora!"

The name rung through the vault in mellow cadence.

She remained there, trembling on tip-toe, in the narrow entrance of the vault, her azure tunic relieved by the dark curtain which touched her shoulder as it fell; her snowy right arm raised upon her panting breast, and half mantled by her unbound hair.

"Juan, I will stand here until you bid me enter."

How musical the low tones of that voluptuous woman's voice! It broke like a whisper from some blessed spirit upon the stillness of the vault, and right upon it an infernal chorus after angel music, clashed with the howl of Ewen, writhing on the floor; the faint moan of Don Antonio gasping from the cloth that bound his mouth.

He heard that voice, knew that his sister was there, almost within an arm's length, and yet he could not speak to her, she could not see him.

"Isora is here, my dear friend—Isora!"—He whispered in the very ear of Don Antonio—"Would you like to speak to her? She loves me, the beautiful girl; and is mine—mine without marriage! Are you perfectly sensible, Don Antonio? Have courage, man, for you will need it. I am about to place the cloth over your face—it will never be lifted while you live. Never will you look upon a human face again. And you will die, with the voice of your own sister in your ears; that voice, which you love to hear, invoking vengeance on the murderer of the father and the brother; eternal vengeance on the betrayer of the sister."

It was horrible to see the effort of the dying man to unpinion his arms and make one intelligent sound through the thick cloth which bound his mouth. Once from side to side rolled his glassy eyeballs. John beheld and smiled. Once, the nerves of his face twitched like the nerves of a corpse agitated by galvanism; and then—

John quietly placed the cloth upon his face and shut him from the light forever!

Turning from the altar, his face beaming with a smile, he wound his arm around the lithe waist of the young girl, and led her gently forward.

Did the dying man hear that tripping footstep?

"Love—my own Isora!" he gazed his gaze upon her face, glowing so rosy red, on the lip and cheek, shooting such voluptuous languor from the eyes. "You know my wrongs—have heard me tell of the incarnate fiend who hung my father, in his gray hairs, to the felon's tree; who had no pity for poor Harry, though he knelt to him in the Plaza of Saltillo, and implored mercy with his blue eyes.—The fiend, Isora, who bought my sister's dishonor with the price of a father's life, and bade her rise from his arms that she might behold the dead face of that very father, glowing in the rising sun. Isora, you have heard it all!"

"Juan, speak of it no more—no more! Woman as I am, weak and trembling, there is yet the blood of old Castile burning in my veins! I will roam the world with thee, Juan. Come—we will find this wretch, and will look upon his agonies while you avenge! Yes, I will pray God to nerve your arm, as you strike deep, exclaiming with every blow,—for my brother, for my father, for my sister!"

Eye flashing, bosom panting, she laid her white arms upon his shoulder and looked up into his face.

Did the dying man hear that voice? Look! the cloth on his breast quivers in the light.

"You need not roam far, my love. Look! upon the altar lies the incarnate fiend, the remorseless destroyer of my race."

"There?—Let me look upon his face."

She started forward; John held her by the arms, but lightly, as though he hesitated; his dark eye perusing all the while the passionate warmth of her face.

"No, Isora! You must not gaze upon him," he said; "but hold.—Wretch, now quivering on the altar, I see your chest heaving with its last pang, and know that your moment is near. I ask you now, in this moment whose flight will leave you cold, would you like to look on a woman's face, and hear her beautiful lips curse you as you die? If your answer is 'yes,' utter but the slightest moan and your face shall be uncovered."

The wretch moaned.

Yes, rather than die thus in the dark, cut off from sight of a human face forever, he would look upon his sister and hear her curse him as he died. Little did he imagine that this beautiful sister was unconscious of his presence; that she did not know him as the "incarnate fiend." If there was one thought darker than another in his dying heart, it was the thought, "to be cursed by my own sister, the beloved of my heart, as I die!"

In that thought he felt, horribly felt, the full retribution for his crimes.

"No! By the fiend whom you have served, you shall not look upon a human face again. Die in darkness, in the name of the father, the brother, and Isabel!"

That movement of the altar-cloth.

"This form upon the floor, Juan, it frightens me—this monster with the white foam on his lips?"

"The accomplice of the fiend, who blindly struck the blow which killed his master, and now dies near him, his heart eaten by poison. Ewen, I say; do you know me? Champagne is a glorious drink, but arsenic—ugh! Rise man, and die with some courage—only brute courage, if you will—don't writhe here like a dog."

The voice, thrilling in cold tones through the vault, seemed to rouse Ewen from his stupor.

He rose heavily into a sitting posture and brushed his brawny hand across his bloodshot eyes; the whole scene seemed to undulate before him—the altar, the silent figures, the beautiful Isora, and the calm, smiling John of Prairie Eden—all seemed to glide slowly to and fro.

He brushed the white foam from his lips; it was evident that his hour was near, for his finger nails were blue, and the ruddy hue of his face began to deepen into purple. The change of death was on him.

"John, I know you," he gasped, as though every word was wrung from him by infernal tortures. "A bad man, John—I've been. *In Philadelphia—my boy!— have mercy on him!*"

With those incoherent words, uttered with hands clutching each other, and bloodshot eyes rolling in death, he sank slowly into a shapeless heap on the floor.

There was no groan—not even a gasp.—His purple face became black, his swollen lips the color of bluish clay, his broad chest was frecked with crimson spots. Not one quiver disturbed his sinewy form, nor did a single tremor announce that a spark of life yet lingered in his own muscles. He was dead— horribly distorted, and blackened, and swollen—dead as the rock upon which he laid.

Why does that sudden paleness cross the face of the Avenger? Does his heart quail now?

When he taunted the poisoned man, and bade him rise and die like a man, he anticipated a volume of curses from his foamy lips—he believed that Ewen would yell forth his last breath in blasphemies.

But those incoherent words, uttered with his last breath, in the voice so strangely softened and with a look of horrible entreaty, "My boy—in Philadelphia—have mercy on him!"

John of Prairie Eden, so remorseless in his Satanic revenge, felt a sudden shudder pervade his form, a horrible gulf, black, fathomless, yawned before his eyes; he trembled and sank on his knees, his face buried in the bosom of Isora.

Her soft hands played upon his forehead; her dark tresses waved over his shoulders.—He could feel her heart beating warmly on his cheek, but that voluptuous pulsation, could not still the prayer of the poisoned wretch which shrieked forever in the Avenger's ears—"In Philadelphia—my boy—have mercy on him."

The figures in blue and scarlet are motionless, the torches still burning in their extended hands; Ewen is blackened and dead upon the floor; Mexitili glares in horrible grotesqueness at the head of the altar; John is kneeling, his head pillowed upon Isora's breast, and for the last time heaves the altar cloth, as a hollow sound, the death-rattle, echoes round the vault.

Then over the threshold comes the form of a woman, clad in a monkish gown, her bosom panting, her breath trembling in gasps, her pale face flushed in every pore. You see her as she stands over the strange scene, her white hands clutching the robe to her breast, and her eyes—each pupil surrounded by a white circle—glare in silent agony from face to face.

Her dark hair, gathered like an ebony crown around her brow—swollen in every vein with intense emotions—burst its cincture and waves in glossy tresses over her shoulder. Glossy and dark, and yet, amid its blackness, there are streaks of silver gray.

Then to the altar advanced the miserable woman, whose life had been an ante-part of hell since the dark day when her honor was wrecked; she saw the clothed form on the altar and lifted the cloth from the face,—and—

But there are emotions of the heart, agonies of the soul, which angels fear to behold, and devils dare not look upon, and we will drop the pall over the scene, over that sight which we cannot witness,—

Isabel of Prairie Eden gazing upon the dead face of her betrayer!

CHAPTER XIV

From Vera Cruz to Philadelphia

"The Vengeance was complete, but now came the turn of the Avenger."
—Texan Mss.

It was in the Walnut-Street Theatre.

I hear the snarl of the critic, and thus he barks,—

"Here's a pretty transition—from the Aztec vault of Vera Cruz to a Philadelphia theater! Horrible! Here we have a story commencing on the prairies of Texas, suddenly dashing away to a desolate rancho in the heart of Mexico, then to Vera Cruz and the vaults of Sacrificios, and last of all to a Philadelphia theater!"

This is truly horrible, and the author who is guilty of the deed, should be condemned to solitary confinement for one day, with a dozen critics, selected at random from the newspapers and magazines of the large cities. Such a punishment could make the warmest blood run cold.

Just fancy it in all its details. One poor author among a dozen critics. Here a critic from Boston, brimming full of cant, breathing it, talking it, living in it—cant from head to foot, all cant. By his side, distinguished by a jockey coat and dirty brown mustache, a Cockney critic from New York, talking alternately of Progress and Pennies, wanting very much to know—in one breath—when the human race will take passage in the Progressional Steam Car for this Millennium, and how much you will give him for a first-rate puff in his paper?

Far in the corner of his cell where our author is confined, behold the magazine critic of Philadelphia; a jaunty thing, delicate in perfume, with oysterish eyes; the scissors in one hand and the scrap-book in the other.—A prim gentleman altogether, who pities our author in yellowish tears for—horrible!—being "popular with the *many* rather than the *select*." That "many," the rouge, hardy people of the workshop and plow; that "select," some dozen newspaper and magazine editors of Philadelphia, who hate each other most fraternally, and yet keep saying, all the year round to one another,—"you are a great man!" and "I am a great man!" and "we are all great men!" So, Allah Bishmallah, there is but one Literature; it is in Philadelphia, and Humbug is its prophet!

Or yet; to go from small things to smaller, a critic south of Mason and Dixon's line—a Baltimore critic. The drollest of all kinds of critics; the very friskiest of all kinds of insect, crawling and biting around the skirts of literature, and growing fat as it crawls and steals. Look at it; a critic, whose whitish hair, eyelashes, and beard, and tallow complexion, all indicate a human thing, gone to seed, and sweltering in decay, long before it has enjoyed one moment of healthy ripeness. It publishes a large sheet, called soundingly, "the Universal Hemisphere," and in the agonizing effort to be witty or die, takes some such slang name as "Major Tomkins," and writes in bad spelling, bad grammar, and bad decency; all being very humorous and quite original.[27]

Imagine a poor author condemned to be crawled over and bitten, for one day only, by vulgarity and indecency, impersonified in a Major Tomkins, a Baltimore critic.

My kind readers in the country, you will pardon me for this digression, about critics, when I assure you that it was undertaken entirely for your good. Call this digression a preface to my story, if you please, and I will explain.

You very often see a ferocious attack in some city periodical, which cuts into ribbons a book which you have been pleased to buy, read, and love. You wonder at this, and perchance take the attack as an honest expression of prejudice, although you, of course, deny its fairness and truth. Your opinions would be somewhat modified were you aware that criticism is in the cities—pretty generally, and with some honorable exceptions—a mere matter of dollars and cents, a business contract between booksellers and critics—so much praise for so many pennies—an honorable understanding between those who sell books and who notice them; that genius is a thing made altogether of puffs, and that he who has most dollars can buy most puffs, and is, of course, the most extensive genius.

You will pardon me if I have the smallest opinion of these magazine and newspaper critics, for in a circle of twelve, I have in my time seen one critic who had forged another man's name; one who was a clergyman, and took his "brandy and water," and was often led by his sympathies, with virtue, of course, into places better known than named; one who had issued counterfeit notes in his time, and finding this kind of paper rather unprofitable took to newspapers; one who had been convicted of swindling; and some three or four who had divided among them the shattered fragments of the Decalogue, broken into pieces and trampled under foot.

Rather a jovial band of moralists, this?

These critics will be the first to attack my story and pronounce it a combination of improbabilities, when from first to last it is founded on published facts, which I have varied, to avoid the imputation of an unjustifiable personality.

When they blow their blast, and snarl their snarl, you will understand at once what they mean. That I am either too poor to buy their praise with money, or that I have nothing of the Egyptian in me, never looking with favor on that creed which taught you to worship apes, lest they would do you a mischief; and go down on your knees to vipers lest they should bite you.

It was in the Walnut-Street Theatre.

Look over this thronged house, swarming from the ceiling to the cellar, with life—life in every shape—tapestried in its three tiers of boxes with human faces, a sea of ragged humanity boiling over in the pit—and tell me it is not a very solemn sight? Solemn! You laugh.

Yes, solemn as the air of a grave vault and more impressive than the black skull of death. Look at the scene.

Here, in the first circle, the most elegantly dressed men, the most beautiful women,—whose silken garments glow in the dazzling light, as their lovely faces are turned toward the stage; whose eyes outsparkle the jewels on their heaving breasts, and all the while, right before those sparkling eyes, in the overflowing pit, you see the hardy sons of toil mingled with the ragged vagabonds of the good Quaker City.[28]

And all the while, in sight of those sparkling eyes, in full view of those grave mothers and beautiful wives and sinless sisters, you behold the third tier festering with the painted prostitution of the good Quaker City!

Delicate contrasts these.

What is the sight that enchains the gaze of the sinless girl and the painted outcast of shame? That rivets the eye of yonder white-haired man in the first tier and the ragged boy in the pit, right before him, within reach of his golden-headed cane? On what vision of moral or intellectual beauty is centered those thousand eyes, flashing and sparkling in the red gas light?

A half-naked woman whirling over the stage, her form clothed in flesh-colored hose that clings to the skin, a piece of white gauze fluttering from her waist, her arms and bosom bare! A half-naked woman, whirling over the stage, now standing on one limb, while the other is poised in the air, on a line with her shoulder; now trembling along on tip-toe, as in the ecstasy of lascivious frenzy; now crouching near the foot-lights, her head bowed until her naked breast is revealed to the universal gaze—to the eyes of the sinless girl, the painted outcast, the old man, and the ragged boy.

This is the sight which rivets the gaze of the crowded theater—a woman floating along the stage and trafficing her nakedness for bread.

For her, the poor moth of the foot-lights, now fluttering in their glare only to be the more surely withered in their blaze, there is some excuse. It is her livelihood—perchance the head of an aged mother, nay, the life of a sister, depends on her dancing limbs. Every twirl of her naked limb is one tear less on her dying sister's cheeks.

But for these beautiful women, these gray-haired men, who, in the presence of the painted prostitute and the ragged outcast boy, gaze on this spectacle with trembling delight, what is their excuse?

Come, I do not place it on the ground of religion or morality, but merely as a matter of common decency—decency so common that it can only raise one blush and die—I ask you, my reader, whether the world can furnish a sight of more disgusting and heart-rending shame than this?

A half-naked woman showing her limbs for bread to feed a sick mother or dying sister, perchance, while gray-haired men look on and gloat; and beautiful women, made by the same God who made the dancing woman, going down to the same grave-worm, which will feed on her form—gaze on their sister's shame and do not blush.

Do not charge me with a prejudice against the drama. That miserably prostituted drama may be made the voice of genius, the music of religion.

But these half-naked women on the stage, tossing in lascivious transport; these painted ones in the third tier, bargaining in pollution, while their pure sisters may look on and up, from the Aristocratic circle—these elegantly decorated bars, where drunkards are educated and poison sold—will you tell me what all this has to do with a pure and intellectual drama?

Must William Shakespeare forever be made the cloak of loathsome appetites and nameless pollutions?

It was in the Walnut-Street Theatre. The curtain had fallen and the dancing woman was gone. The ragged boys were fighting in the pit; the traffic of shame was going on in the third tier. In boxes, handsome women were conversing with fashionably attired men, and here and there a puppy, with something like a human face, dressed, at all events, in the garments of a man, was staring those modest women out of countenance, and fastening its obscene gaze upon the face of the pure maiden or the virtuous wife. Of all puppies in the world, the most impertinent is the puppy of the theater, with an opera-glass in its hand.

It was in the midst of this confusion, between the acts, that two persons entered the central box, and at once riveted every eye. A tall man, attired in plain black, with the slight form of a woman, supported by his right arm.

They quietly took the unoccupied seat, and as if by an instantaneous impulse, the thousand eyes of the theater were turned upon them.

The man was, or appeared to be, some thirty-five years of age. There was nothing peculiar in his dress. Black dress coat and satin vest, black neckerchief, loosely tied, a faultlessly white shirt bosom, sparkling with a small diamond. Yet his face enchained every eye by a kind of irresistible fascination.

The features were bold, his complexion, a pallid sallow olive, indicated the traces of strong physical or mental suffering, and the eyes, so unnaturally large and dark, seemed not so much to gleam as to burn in their sockets. There was no mustache upon his lip nor beard upon his chin, but masses of dark hair fell carelessly over a bold, white forehead.

He leaned his elbow on the edge of the box, and gazed upon the curtain with a vacant stare.

By his side the slight form of a woman, whose face appeared among the folds of a Spanish mantilla. The dark hues of the graceful robe gave an unnatural paleness to the colorless cheek, and increased the burning light of her large black eyes, which shone from the shadow of their long and quivering lashes.

As she raised her hand to adjust the folds of her mantilla, a bracelet was visible, dazzling with the radiance of a solitary diamond.

Altogether, the pair would have attracted the eye in any place, and became at once, in the street, ball-room or parlor, the universal topic of conversation.

In the theater the sensation was universal. Eyes were turned, glasses leveled; the house buzzed with a thousand whispers.

"They are the strangers who have attracted so much notice in Chestnut Street lately."

"He is very, very rich—a millionaire."

"No; a soldier from the Mexican war."

"I tell you that I have the right story,—a Mexican general taken prisoner at Cerro Gordo."[29]

"How odd! That mantilla—bad taste."

"I rather like it. It gives quite a charm to her face."

"What a splendid bracelet!"

"Do you observe that diamond upon his bosom?"

Whispers like these from fair ladies and fashionable men created a buzz-buzz murmur in the dress circle. The third tier was somewhat eloquent in its remarks, rather too much so; the second tier quite boisterous; and as for the pit, it seemed to hesitate between a cry of "boots!" and "chuck 'em over!"

A single instance will serve as an illustration of the public opinion of the pit,—

"I say, hoss," screamed a ragged newsboy, raising himself on his toes, as he stood within the reach of the stranger's arm, only separated by that barrier which confines the whirpool of the pit within its limits; "Wot did yer giv' for that ar' di'mond? Jimini, boys, wot a scorcher!"

Still the stranger, with his cheek resting on his hand, stared vacantly upon the drop curtain. Not a movement manifested his consciousness that the eyes and impertinence of the theater were turned upon him and the lady at his side.

The lady seemed surprised. Her cheek flushed, her dark eyes dropped their glance.

But the mantilla, which half-concealed her smooth black hair, and floated over the outline of her small but lovely form, could not be forgiven.

It was an unpardonable sin, in a Philadelphia theater, where everybody must dress like everybody else, or be pointed at and "put down."

"How odd!" trembled all over the dress circle.

At last the lady whispered a word in Spanish,—

"Juan!"

He turned his gaze upon her with a look whose mingled meaning it were in vain to guess, and exclaimed with an evident effort,—

"You seem melancholy, Isora? In a moment the curtain will raise and the play begin. It is indeed a very dull place, a crowded theater."

He leaned back in his seat, and the lady, with a single red spot glowing on each cheek, murmured in almost inaudible tones, still speaking in Spanish, you will remember.

"But the *letter*, Juan?"

A sudden, nervous start shook the stranger's frame. He turned quickly, as though he had been bitten by an adder; a cloud rushed over his brow.

Mastering his agitation he composed his pale features in a smile,—

"I cannot show it to you now, Isora. It is postmarked New Orleans. Your brother is now in that city; he is on his way to Philadelphia—he will be here in a few days."

How her face flushed from its sad hue into a rosy life.

"Oh, I am so happy, Juan! He will be here in a few days; he has forgiven his wayward sister for her wanderings—he will be your friend, Juan. Is it not so? Blessed Virgin! we will all be so happy!"

Juan smiled; and then his eye flashed, his brow was corrugated, the expression of his sallow face was horrible—it passed like a cloud—he smiled again.

"This letter, Juan, is from my brother?"

Again he started, once more that expression, and then the calm smile,—

"No more now, Isora, when we return home I will tell you all. For the present,—your brother, Don Antonio Marin, will be here tomorrow—perchance to-night."

He said no more, but while the curtain rose and the play went on, and the audience laughed, and hissed, and stamped, he sat with his cheek upon his hand, his large eyes fixed upon the stage with an absent stare.

It cannot be denied that his face was invested with a cold, pallid beauty; the firm, aquiline features stood out in the glaring light, like the head of an antique statue, darkened by the dust of ages. Yet never once, during all the play, did he turn from side to side, or change his fixed, unvarying glance, though Forrest was on the stage and the play was Richlieu.—Forrest and Richlieu after the shameless display of a half-naked woman's limbs![30]

The play was over, and the audience, pouring from the various boxes of the theater, swarmed through the outer corridor, and swept like a torrent into the street.

Amid the crowd descending the stone steps in front of the theater, the form of Juan and the lady were marked, prominent; his head rising above the crowd, her mantilla contrasting with the rainbow dress of the other women.

The other women! Yes—courtesan and fine lady mingled together in the crowd that poured from the doors of the theater, and the flaming gas-lamp on the pavement disclosed, with impartial light, the face of the sinless girl and the painted visage of her sister-woman, the child of shame.

Suddenly, even as Juan and Isora were descending the steps, a cry was heard; the crowd rocked to and fro—a strange wave of human faces—and universal clamor and confusion tossed the strongly contrasted mass together.

It was shouted that the stranger had been robbed, his pocket-book stolen; four or five men, with red faces and noses of extraordinary development, were seen rushing toward him, making with their fists an extemporaneous lane through the center of the crowd.

They were known at once as police officers.

"I say, mister," cried the foremost, a rotund man, on whose rich-colored visage brandy had not been showered for nothing; "I saw the fellow hook your pocket-book—will know him again. What's the figure? Damage very ser'ous?"

Juan bent his lips to the ear of the red-faced man, as his brow manifested deep vexation and chagrin,—

"Five thousand dollars were in that pocket-book; if you reclaim it by to-morrow morning *without touching the papers which it contain, one thousand shall be yours.*"

"Won't I! Why I've had my eye on the feller these three weeks and know'd he was up to mischief. Your residence, sir? The pocket book 'ill be in your hands before nine o'clock to-morrow morning!"

"Enough! We understand each other.—Here is my card"; and supporting Isora with his arm, he pushed down the steps, and presently stood on the edge of the pavement, where stood a glittering carriage with a coat of arms on the panels; a liveried footman holding the open door, and a coachman, also in livery, snoring on the box.

"Rather aristocratic!" murmured voices from the crowd.

"Splendid turn out!"

"Just look at them blooded bays—and that darkey, with one eye and a blue coat!"

"Isora, you will enter and go home alone! Urgent business demands my presence elsewhere, for an hour or more. Nay, do not look so reproachful."

From the folds of the mantilla her pale face appeared, as her lustrous eyes were raised to meet his glance.

Her delicate foot was upon the carriage step—her hand upon the door.

"The letter, Juan?"

It was but a whisper and yet her bosom heaved as she spoke the words.

"Within two hours I will return home and tell you all!"

He lifted her gently into the carriage, closed the door and spoke to the lackeys.—In a moment the coach was seen dashing away through the hacks and cabs that lined the street.

Juan turned up Ninth Street, murmuring as he hurried along,—

"She fades every hour—I can see her fade—withering, drooping into the grave. 'My brother!' her only word, from hour to hour. She dreams, even now, that I have gone to bring *him* home!"

At the corner of Ninth and George streets, in the shadow of that immense pile known as the Museum, a dark horse stood saddled, the bridle held by a liveried servant. Juan spoke to the servant, and with a bound sprang into the saddle and dashed away, as though his own spirit had maddened the veins of his horse.

Up Ninth Street, into the Ridge Road, and out into the country.

It was a gloomy night in May; the air was damp and misty; the sky one mass of leaden cloud.

Along the dark road—the trees on either side appearing like a shapeless mass—bounded the horse, striking fire with his hoofs as he flew, while his master applied the spur and chafed and maddened him to the utmost stretch of his speed.

Through the misty atmosphere, a huge white mass arose; looking somewhat like a mountain of snow, shaped by superhuman hands into the form of a Grecian temple. It was a magnificent sight, that College of Girard, looming through the misty night, but Juan did not see it.[31]

His head upon his breast, his dark eyes glaring straight ahead, he kept his mettled horse at the same arrow-like speed, and soon left the college three miles behind.

Down the steep hill, into the hollow, where an old tavern stands—somewhat retired from the road—its lonely sign creaking on rheumatic hinges.

A light shone out upon the porch as the foaming horse, bounding aside from the road, attracted by the echo of his hoofs, the tavern keeper, lantern in hand, came to the door.

"I wish you to take care of my horse for an hour or so," said Juan, as he bounded from the saddle upon the road.

The sleepy host rubbed his eyes, and surveyed the stranger, with as much amazement as though he had been rained from the clouds.

"You don't live here about, it may be?" he drawled. "Hello! He's gone. Don't much like him—very pucooliar eyes! Not a bad horse, though!"

While the tavern keeper stood wondering, Juan had crossed the road, leaped the wicket fence, and was now threading a westward path that led along a broad and gently undulating meadow.

In the day-time, when the bees fill the air with their music, this meadow is very beautiful—a broad mantle of trembling green stretched in sight of the dusty road. But now there was a mist upon it; a floating shroud hung over its gentle undulations and veiled its moist verdure.

Soon the path terminated, and before the wanderer rolled the Schuylkill, its beautiful hills and picturesque bridges and island of glorious foliage, all shrouded by that misty veil.

To the north over those rude cliffs and down into the wilderness where the herbage and trees are locked in one woven mass of leaves and flowers. Up the steep rock that rises like a wall, stone heaped on stone, and mass piled on mass, with vines twining all about it—like little children around a harsh old warrior—and saplings starting from every cleft, then exuberant foliage clothing the granite heap with a girdle of summer green.

The wanderer stands upon the summit and feels the night breeze from the river on his hot brow, and sees the mist gliding among the trees and over the graves of Laurel Hill.[32]

CHAPTER XV

Laurel Hill

"Two coffins in that solitary vault—two only."

—Texan Mss.

*L*aurel Hill! Did you ever see it by daylight—on a Sabbath day, when the crowd who come here to gape about the graves, are locked out—on a Sabbath day in June, when everything was silent, save the bees, and all things motionless as death, save the gentle blossoms, trembling above the grass.

It is very beautiful then, with its white monuments and winding walks, its high wall and entrance gate, shutting out the hot dusty road; its chapel, with stained windows, where prayer is said before the coffin is laid away, in the dismal vault, or planted in the fresh, smoking earth; altogether a place of perfume, bees, and flowers, graves burthened with sculpture and marbles rich in epitaphs.

Yet I like it not. It looks to me, with its dainty monuments burdened with flowers, like an attempt to be elegant with Death, and decorate his fleshless skull with the ribbons and millinery of the fashionable world.

There is too much mockery, too much mimicry of woe, in this elegant cemetery. Too much of—

> "Here lies my husband Jean,
> Whose affectionate widow still sells ribbons
> and laces,
> At the old stand,
> No. 29, Rue Jacconot."[33]

Give me an old graveyard, where the graves are hidden among tall grass and wild flowers, where tombstones peep modestly above the blossoms and the verdure, and a holy air of repose, as if from God, imbues the place where the dead people sleep, and brings sweet messages of immortality home to the soul.

But these fashionable cemeteries, Mount Auburn, Greenwood, and Laurel Hill. Could you not, my dear friends, keep Fashion in your ball rooms, and leave the grave as it was in the days of our fathers, a holy altar, where none came to look save those who had friends among the dead?

"Come boys, we've had our dinner and our wine at the United States Hotel—lobster and champagne, and all the et ceteras—let's take a cab and go out to Laurel Hill and have a jovial chat as we smoke our cigars amongst the graves!"

Does that sound very sweet! Think of a mother, or a sister, or a wife, sleeping in the sod, while a party of half-drunken dandies stroll over their graves, venting their obscene souls in jests that taint the very air. I have even seen one of those wretched manikins, from Chestnut Street, whom the tailor makes, stand on Laurel Hill, plying his opera glass among the homes of death.

Laurel Hill is beautiful without all this garniture of sculpture and millinery of fashion—it was beautiful long ago, before they made it a "fashionable cemetery."

Down by the river where the trees grow thickest, dipping their leaves in the waters, and the bank arises, rugged with huge old forms of rock, there is many a solemn walk among the quiet nooks shrouded in foliage, or over the steeps shaded by the sighing pine. The sunlight comes in stray gleams, and through the trees the river glimpses on the sight. Gloomily in the shadows the dark vaults are seen, their iron doors sunken in the clefts of the rocks, while, overhead, a leafy canopy waves like a pall.

It was down among these haunts of gloom that the wanderer bent his steps at dead of night.

No sunlight now upon the vaults, no gleam of moon or star to light, with a solitary ray, those paths leading to the river, those wind-winding ways that climb the granite rocks.—Like the spirits of the dead, the mist glides about the rocks, and winds—so white and cold—among the trunks of the centuried trees.

Juan paused before an iron door, sunken beneath a mass of rock, with a pine tree shooting away from the sod in front of it. He took from his breast a key, and the harsh sound of the yielding lock echoed like a shriek through the silence.

He advanced, and in the very air rushing from the charnel, felt that death was there. Closing the door he stood in the darkness of the vault; a horrible intense darkness that seemed to shut him in its stifling folds and bind him like a cloak.

Silence, darkness, thought!

With a phosphorescent match he produced a blue and vivid light which glared at once upon the darkness, disclosing the narrow walls of the vault and shining upon those coffins—there are two—placed side by side on the floor.

That bluish light burned for a moment, glittered on the silver plate upon each coffin's breast, and went out.

The darkness was more horrible from the glare of that sudden, phosphorescent ray.

That ray revealed the features of Juan, working with fearful agony, and revealed the names inscribed upon the coffins.

These were the names, glaring for a moment and then gone,—

"*Isabel.*"

"*Don Antonio Marin.*"

For the first time the Wanderer spoke,—

"I was in the room when John Randolph died, and saw him trace upon a card, with his skinny finger, a single word—'Remorse'—and saw him die, with his eye glazing as he gloated on it. That word I never knew what it meant till now."[34]

He was silent; there was no light to show the hideous writhing of his face.

"Isabel! Isabel! You answer me not, for you are cold and dead—the worms upon your brow, the shroud upon your breast—dead. You who shone so beautiful in the Home of Prairie Eden."

"Isabel, when you were dying you told me that 'there had been too much blood shed,' too much even for the hideous ruin which the betrayer worked for you. You besought me to bring his body from the vaults of Sacrificios and lay it by your side, to show that you forgave him even in death. I have obeyed, today Don Antonio arrived—he is here, my sister; by your side, and I, your brother, feel *remorse* for the revenge which I hurled upon his dying hour—*remorse.*"

Silence and thought.

"Speak to me, Isabel, tell me, is there a hope for me beyond—there, across the black grave? Speak, is there one hope? Isabel, here, beside your coffin, in the cold, dark vault I kneel, and repeat your dying words, '*The blessed God forgave his murderers even on the Cross*! John, there has been too much bloodshed—too much too much. *Vengeance is mine, and I will repay*, was spoken by God himself, and we John, have taken from God his own time and manner of justice—we have done much wrong; let us now forgive.'"[35]

"I see your dying eyes, my sister, and hear your voice,—

"'For forgiveness is such a beautiful blossom to bloom upon our shrouds when we are dead.'"

A pause once more—sobs—tears.

"'Let us forgive, and make such recompense for our wrong as is in the power of man to make. Be kind, very kind to Isora—let her never know her brother's fate. Bring hither his body and let it be placed beside mine when I am dead, in token, that after much wrong and horrible crimes, we sleep in death together, and sleep in forgiveness.'"

"These words on your lips, you fell back and grew cold in my arms."

A sound as of a strong heart breaking in agony.

"I kneel, Isabel; I place my hand upon his coffin—I—I—Oh God!—*I forgive him*!"

Again the silence of Death upon the dark vault.

"Behold me, Isabel! My Free Rangers, those outcasts of the land and sea, no longer know that their leader lives. I am alone.—There is no living breast into whose recesses, I may pour the agony of my soul—may pour my horrible secret and my remorse. For Isora—oh God! she is dying—every moment she dies before my face. I cannot tell her that it was her brother whom she cursed in the vaults of Sacrificios—no, no! I come to you—speak to me—let me know whether beyond this dark grave there is a hope, whether there is one star in the midnight sky of death?"

And shaken from the proud might of his vengeance, the strong man grovelled beside the coffins, and laid his brow upon the slimy floor of the vault.

"*Remorse!*"

CHAPTER XVI

The Perishing Heathen of Philadelphia

"Ten thousand in a Protestant city, who have no church, no Bible, no God."
—Texan Mss.

One night, not long ago, I stood in a crowded church and saw three missionaries consecrated for a great work. They were about to cross the globe and preach the gospel to the poor of Hindustan. To aid them in this work some thousands of dollars were showered upon the altar; nay, beautiful women tore the bracelets from their wrists, the pearls from their bosoms, and said,—

"Take these and carry the Gospel to the perishing heathen."

Within a stone's throw of that magnificent church, at the same hour, there occurred a scene of somewhat different kind. Behold it.

Leaving the church we will enter this narrow alley which branches from the main street. In this narrow alley, the only light that shines is from the dingy windows of the Rum-shop. In this narrow alley, at least one hundred houses or huts are huddled together, some of frame, others of brick, all with their windows stuffed with rags.

These houses yield a handsome rent to their owners. You imagine that one family of three or four persons occupies each house?

You don't know Philadelphia. That is evident.

Let me show you how a single room in one of these huts—that one next the tenth rum-shop—is occupied.

Through the narrow door, into this room with low ceiling, black walls, and floor some twelve feet square. What have we here? By the light of a penny candle, stuck in a porter bottle, you may behold the scene.

Close to the wall, side by side, their knees drawn up to their chins, are crouched at least twenty human beings, from the half-naked girl of fifteen to the old man of eighty; here the mother with the baby on her breast, there the negro, with his rum bottle, and along the square formed by their huddled forms, you see everything that is miserable in nakedness, disease, and rags.

These are the rum-shop keeper's lodgers, but not all.

All day long they prowl the street, picking rags, or begging cold victuals, or stealing a morsel, and at night, they repose here for one cent a head.

The porter bottle, which illuminates the room, is held by a huge negro, who, with rags upon his chest, is playing cards with a white woman, who also crouches upon the floor.

As the greasy pack passes from the white hand to the black hand, you see a woman—only a miserable rag upon her form—stretched stiffly out in the center of the room, her bosom, and arms, and limbs disclosed by the light.

That bosom is wasted, those arms shrunken to the bone. As for the face, you cannot see it, for her black hair, streaked with gray, falls over it.

Does she sleep?

Lift the hair from her face and behold those stony eyeballs. She sleeps— and sleeps all the better that she has had no bread for three days.

My good Missionary friend permit me to take you by the bow of your white cravat, and lead you from the crowded church into this room—and don't think me impertinent when I tell you, that the Lord Jesus will smile more blessedly upon you if you sell one or more of your handsomely bound Bibles and buy a little bread, a little shelter for these heathens of Philadelphia.

Excuse my freedom, friend; I have an odd way of saying things, but as there is a God, you need not go all the way to Hindustan to find perishing Christians.

The breath left her body an hour ago. She is cold now.

The door opens; a boy, half-naked—for his only dress consists of trousers that reach to the knee, and a check shirt with one sleeve—a boy comes forward to the light. You see his freckled face, concealed by a mass of matted brown hair, from beneath whose uneven ends a pair of bright eyes gleam with steady luster.

He may be twelve years old, and he may be fifteen; but in sober truth you cannot guess his age from his face, for its lines are sharpened into premature manhood, by a course of severe study.

Poverty and starvation are great thinkers.

"Mother!"

He kneels beside the dead woman, and places his lips to her ears,—

"Mother, come! I have that which will buy us bread."

She does not answer him—he shakes her gently by the arm—feels that it is cold.

"Mother!" arose the shriek of that poor wretch's agony. "You are so cold—so hungry—you can't be *dead*? Come—quick I say." He whispered the last words "*I have money, mother; come!*"

The gambling negro turned from his game,—

"Look yer, young gemmen, ef you don't stop yer dam noise, I'll break yer dam jaw!"

The boy did not disturb the negro any more. He felt his mother's hands and bosom and knew that she was dead, and then went out into the alley and leaned his face against the wall, and his tears fell without a sound.

She was the only thing that cared for him in the world; she was dead. The little boy looked up into the misty sky and along the alley, and wondered where he should go now? The watchman from the neighboring street yelled,—"Two o'clock, and a cloudy mor'n," and a dead silence hung over the slumbering city. Where could he go, that motherless wretch?

Approaching the light which fell from the rum shop window, over the gutter, the boy drew from his rags a pocket book of dark morocco, which he opened, and spread forth the soft silken notes in his dirty hands.

"Money—it must be money—and I can't read—mother could have read 'em. Mother!"

His tears fell afresh, and he was turning from the light when a rude hand pinned him by the shoulder:

"Come, my larkey; I'll take care of that money for you. O, you're a precious one—ain't you! I say, Charley, give us the 'barkers'; we'll fix this lively youth so that Judge Cant'll be pleased to see him. A very fine judge is Judge Cant; though he makes temperance speeches on the bench, he can take quite as big a brand-and-water as any of us."

The boy was surrounded by some half dozen men, with red faces, well-developed noses, and flashy guard-chains.

They were dragging him along the alley, with some force and a few kicks, when a figure advanced from the shadows and confronted the party.

He had evidently been attracted from the main street by the cries of the child.

"Hello! It's the gentleman that was robbed. Well, sir, you see we've got him; we follered him up, watched him, and found the property on his person."

"Give me the pocket book," said Juan, as he gazed steadily in the face of the police officer. "Here is your reward—one thousand dollars. Now, what will you do with this poor boy?"

"O, as for him, Judge Cant 'ill fix him.—Nothin' pleases Judge Cant so much as to get hold of a young shaver. Oh my! doesn't he give 'em fits!"

Juan, or John of Prairie Eden, as you please, drew near the scared and sobbing child, and swept back the matted hair from his forehead.

"Have you a name, my little fellow?"

"Never had a name. The boys calls me Young Rags an' my father's gone away, an' my mother's dead, an' them men have been a kickin of me."

Blurting his many sorrows in a breath, he rubbed his fists in his eyes, and sobbed as though his heart had broken.

"If you want to know anything about him," said the police officer with the reddest nose, "I kin tell you, for I've had my eye upon his mother and father for this five years past.—His father 'listed this spring in the Navy and haint been heered on since. He was a poor devil enough, but once was rayther respectable, that is afore he first left the city, some years back, with the runaway Bank Director. You see McGregor was once this Bank Director's clark—"

"McGregor!"

John started as he echoed the word.

"Y-a-s, Ewen McGregor."

"Ewen McGregor!" John whispered as he took the boy by the hand. "Prove this to me, and I'll make your information worth money to you."

His voice was tremulous; he laid his hands on the police officer's arm.

"Prove it!—Why we all know it. You see McGregor went away to Texas, then jined the Mexican army, and last winter came back to town a poor, miserable devil, without one cent to rub against another. He found his wife, whom he'd deserted years before, in a 'bad place'—you take, eh?—an jined the American Navy an' hai'nt been heered on since."

"That wife?"

"About an hour ago, when we first set our watch in the alley to catch this shaver, we found her dead in yonder hole. Guess she ain't got alive sence.—ha, ha!"

"Come! show me where your mother lies dead."

The ragged boy looked up into those large dark eyes, saw them filled with tears, and took the stranger's hand.

"Come, I'll show you. Ye see I was hungry and mother was cold—"

But John of Prairie Eden did not wait for the boy to finish his incoherent ejaculations.

The police officers with some wonder and a few extra-judicial oaths, beheld that tall stranger, disappear into the shadows, led by the child to the dark hut where lay his mother's corpse.

Into the hut, where the negro holds the light, and thumbs the greasy cards.

John bent down, lifted the black hair, sprinkled with gray, beheld the wasted face and stony eyes.

Years before he had known her, so young and beautiful. Even amid the wreck made by starvation and disease, he knew her, and traced the outlines of what she *had been* in the withered thing which lay before him stiff and cold.

"You see, we hadn't any bread"; the boy whimpered. "That is, mother hadn't; for what she could git she give me; an' I watched by the theater, an'—"

John took the little outcast by the hand:

"Come home with me. While I have one crust left you shall never want."

CHAPTER XVII

*D*ay is breaking in the east, and the morning mists glide like phantoms over the broad Delaware. The gray light of the dawn steals through the curtains of the chamber, struggling with the beams of the lamp which stands near the bed on yonder table.

A sad sight awaits us.

True, the chamber is luxuriously furnished: the richly papered walls bloom with the warm creations of the artist's thought; the curtains of the high windows are of satin and gold; the carpet from the looms of Smyrna; the bed itself with hangings of white satin and pillows of down, presents an image of voluptuous repose; it is imbued with an atmosphere of luxury and quiet splendor, and yet another atmosphere is stealing slowly into the place, and covering all things with its vague, chilling mist.

It is the atmosphere of Death.

Beside the bed—the damps of Laurel Hill yet fresh upon his attire—is John of Prairie Eden, his face wearing a dead stupor, an apathy of despair, which blunts its well defined outlines, and covers his eyes as with a glossy film.

The sorrow is too crushing for him to feel it now. He cannot feel it, cannot believe, the air seems but a mass of whirling phantoms, it is not a reality, but a dream.

A dream; and yet tomorrow.

Isora lies upon the snowy coverlet of that bed. Her form but half-clad, she rests with her hands folded, her white bosom gleaming in the light, her eyes closed, the fringes reposing on the colorless cheek, her hair descending over her shoulders, and resting in glossy curls upon her arms.

Does she breathe? Ah, the bosom seems pulseless, cold.

A faint trembling of the lower lip, alone attests that the soul is quivering there, ere it departs forever.

So gently she dies, that it but seems like gliding into a pleasant sleep. So softly passes her soul away, that it seems a lily torn from its stem and cast upon a smooth lake that bears it tenderly upon its breast and ripples in low music round it as it floats along.

At last her lids unclose; how black, how flashing, how beautiful those death-dewed eyes.

"Juan!"

She knew him and reached forth her hand.

He took it, pressed it to his lips and bosom; it was wet with moisture from the kiss of Death.

"Juan, I am going. Ever since the day when the rite of the church blessed our union I have felt a burning here—"

He laid her little hand upon her naked bosom.

"Last night, when I came home, I laid me down to sleep, and felt that in that sleep, my soul was going fast away; yet I could not, until now unclose my eyes, or manifest by any sign I knew you were here. I heard your groans, Juan, your prayers, I felt your tears upon my cheek, but could not speak to you. A few moments now are given to me, and let me lay my head upon your breast, and wind my arms about your neck, and die. My heart shall beat against yours when it flutters its last; my last breath mingle with your kiss. I am so happy, so much peace! Do not weep, Juan; there is a bright angel at the foot of the bed, who lifts his white wings and says, 'Come!'"

He had taken her to his breast and wound her arms about his neck—ah! they were so cold!—and covered his eyes with her silken hair. But he could not speak.

"When you see my brother, for he will come, Juan—tell him that I spoke of him to the last, and died so happy because I knew that he had forgiven me! Tell him—ah! Juan, my arms are cold, I cannot move my fingers. Is it dark, Juan, or have my eyes been covered by a veil?"

Over his shoulder she raised her head, glaring around with her large, deep eyes.—They were glassy—a misty film shrouded their dazzling brightness.

How her slight form rocked as his broad chest heaved, and struggled, and fell, with the overwhelming agony of that hour. Yet he spoke not, but grasping her hair, swept its glossy masses over his eyes, and wept aloud.

"It is dark, Juan—I cannot see you. Holy Virgin! Mary, Mother of God, pity and forgive me, a weak, weak child! Closer, Juan; kiss me. Ice upon my heart,

Juan, ice; but I can feel your lips; your breath warms my cheek; my brother, Juan, tell him—ah! the white angel lifts his wings—I see him now—*It is light again*! Come! come!"

A trembling flutter of the lips, and the white angel has borne a spirit home.

Those icy arms are round his neck, that icy breast against his own; the glassy eyes, how cold, how dead they glare; the lips that are pressed to his, are chilled and colorless forever.

Still he tries to dry the tears with the soft masses of her silken hair and kisses her cold lips, as if to win back the departed soul.

Little did the proud, revengeful man imagine this hour, when in her home of Vera Cruz, he cruelly planned her shame. That he should ever weep hot, scalding tears for the sister of Don Antonio; that he should love her better than life, or what to the proud heart is worth all, revenge; and press her dead breast to his heart, and drench her silken hair with the baptism of her agony.

Maybe some white angel had changed his breast, and turned the blight of his revenge into a blessing fresh from God.

She died, the victim of a rapid and imperceptible decay, but died without knowing that her brother was the writhing wretch of the Aztec vault of Sacrificios; the Destroyer of Prairie Eden, its beautiful maiden, white haired old man, and blue-eyed boy.

For that ignorance which hailed her dying hour, let us bless the white angel, who lifted its wings as she grew cold and whispered "Come!"

THE END.

A Thrilling and Exciting Account of the Sufferings and Horrible Tortures Inflicted on Mortimer Bowers and Miss Sophia Delaplain

In 1851, E. E. Barclay, along with M. B. Crosson, published *A Thrilling and Exciting Account of the Sufferings and Horrible Tortures Inflicted on Mortimer Bowers and Miss Sophia Delaplain*. The author remains unknown. The story is set in New York but ostensibly published in Charleston, South Carolina, suggesting that Barclay understood the Narciso López campaigns were popular with both Northerners and Southerners. A career military man, López appeared in New York in 1847 after his plot to overthrow Spanish rule in Cuba was discovered. He organized several clandestine campaigns to invade, liberate, and annex Cuba to the United States, mainly to maintain the island's slave economy. The U.S. Navy stopped his first filibustering effort in July 1849. His May 1850 expedition landed at Cárdenas; the filibusters took the city but retreated the next day under fire from Spanish reinforcements. The Cárdenas expedition made López a popular name in the press. In August 1851, the Spanish army captured López and his men during their third invasion. The volunteers were imprisoned and López was garroted on September 1, 1851.

The Delaplain narrative seems to have been written after the 1850 expedition but before López's September 1851 execution. The story's transvestism and tortures capture the ambivalent excitement Cuban filibustering generated for Southern slave interests, eager with the possibility of gaining a slave state or two with Cuba, and for Northern capitalists, enticed by Cuba's propitious location for overseas trade. As with the Siddons narrative, though, which Barclay also published, the Delaplain account seems to warn against expansionism by suggesting that filibustering and Cuba threaten white masculinity, undermine genteel femininity, and raise the possibility that, rather than liberating Cuba, U.S. whites might become enslaved by torturous Spaniards.

SUFFERINGS AND TORTURES
OF MORTIMER BOWERS AND SOPHIA DELAPLAIN

A Thrilling and Exciting Account of the Sufferings and Horrible Tortures Inflicted on Mortimer Bowers and Miss Sophia Delaplain by the Spanish authorities, for a supposed participation with Gen. Lopez in the invasion of Cuba; together with the plan of the campaign of Lopez. It is supposed that the Spaniards ventured to maltreat the two innocent persons spoken of in this narrative, on account of their isolated condition, on a remote part of the island, and owing to the impression that their incarceration and treatments would never be made known in the United States,—the tortures being inflicted to elicit information relating to the expedition against the island by Miss Delaplain.

The invasion of the Island of Cuba by General Lopez, is fraught with many incidents which never have been, and I presume never will be, laid before the eye of the public.

On my return from that island, on effecting my escape from the worse than demons who held me in bondage, the relation of my strange abduction, and the tortures and privations to which I had been subjected, excited such an interest in many of the most influential citizens of Baltimore (Baltimore being the place at which I landed on my return) that, at the earnest solicitation of those citizens, I have been induced to transcribe an account of my adventures, for the benefit of all who choose to read them.

My narrative will be found to contain many things characteristic of human nature, and it will prove in the highest degree salutary to the young and inexperienced.

In order to give a just idea of the sacrifices which I have made, and the extent to which the confiding and unsuspecting female is capable of being wrought upon, it is necessary that I should begin with my early life and habits.

My father was one of the most wealthy merchants of the city of New York, and I an only child and daughter. Our family residence in town was in Broadway, and the house in which we resided is familiarly known as the Broadway Mansion.

As a matter of course, I was the pet of my parents, and of all their acquaintances who sought to win their favor. My smallest wish was immediately gratified, and thus I was petted and fondled until I arrived at the age of six years.

When I had turned my sixth year, it became necessary to take measures to provide for my education. A governess was procured, as ordinary in such cases, but so great was my waywardness, that she was under the necessity of paying implicit obedience to my commands,—and thus, the one who by right should have governed, was converted into the most pliant subject. I have since looked upon her in the light of a fawning sycophant, for not sometimes checking me in my headstrong willfulness. Considering, however, that she was under no injunction from my parents on that point, and that my parents did not themselves subject me to any restraint, I am inclined to the opinion, that, perhaps, she was excusable.

When it pleased me I attended to my lessons, and when I was otherwise inclined, it was necessary to coax, or hire, or hold out some inducement to me, stronger than the inducement to remain idle, or not to attend to my ordinary task. I would never subject myself to a command.

Among other things, as was perfectly natural, I was exceedingly fond of the society of the neighbor's children, and the play with them, of "All the way to Boston," or "We're marching forward to Quebec," was decidedly more agreeable than the dull monotony of "Webster's Easy Standard of Pronunciation," or "The Child's Instructor." It is not to be wondered at, then, that I sought the romp of these agreeable playmates in preference to the dull routine of study.

Among my youthful associates was a boy, a year or two older than myself, and residing next door to the Broadway Mansion. This little fellow was my particular favorite, on account of the mildness of his disposition, and the beauty of his features. His hair was of the pure auburn, and fell in natural glossy ringlets upon a neck whose lily hue told that the sons of Africa, the Spanish Moor, the Eastern Celestial, or the Aboriginal American, could claim no affinity. Nothing but the pure Circassian blood flowed there.[1] And then he was so kind. Even at that tender age, he was always ready to administer to my slightest wish, and to do every thing to please me. His eye, the index of his soul, told that his mind was in perfect accordance with the beauty of his person.

The parents of this youth were in circumstances very different from my own. They were poor, and under the necessity of prosecuting business energetically, in order, as the saying is, "To keep themselves up in the world."

As the youth to whom I have alluded is to occupy a conspicuous place in this narrative, it may be well to announce to my readers that he was known under the name of Mortimer Bowers, or, familiarly at that time, to his playmates, "Little Mortimer."

Time thus passed on, until I arrived at the age of twelve years, when it was deemed advisable to send me to a boarding-school. After some consultation, it was determined to send me to St. Ann's Hall, located at the romantic village of Flushing, on Long Island—then under the superintendence of Rev. Dr. Schroeder.[2]

Strange to relate, my state of mind was such that I felt not the least regret on leaving my home, although I kissed my playmates affectionately when I bade them adieu, and even condescended to shake hands with my governess.

My parents accompanied me to the Institution, at which I was destined to finish my education, and we met with a very gentlemanly reception from the superintendent. I was so well pleased with the deportment of Dr. Schroeder, who was to be my future guardian, that when my parents took their leave, I kissed them with a merry laugh, although my mother dropped a tear, as she resigned me to the doctor's family.

Although I was well pleased with my reception at the Hall, I soon discovered that *there* was a place of order, and instead of commanding, it was necessary that I should become the subject. This, to me, was a severe trial, and oft-times, when I had been reprimanded for some misdemeanor, would I retire to my room, and weep for hours. On these occasions my thoughts would vividly portray to me those scenes connected with my home: the swing in the old garret, the yard filled with flowers, my former playmates, and particularly the image of "Little Mortimer," would come up in life-like reality before me.

The change in my condition, however, was somewhat alleviated by the privilege allowed us by our superintendent, of walking out each afternoon for the purpose of recreation, and of viewing the beauties of the village in which my parents had placed me. Flushing is, undoubtedly, one of the most romantic and delightful villages on Long Island. The flower gardens of the Messrs. Prince, the nurseries of the Parsons, of Bloodgood, of King, and the grounds of St. Thomas's Hall, are all objects calculated to excite our interest and admiration. And then the beautiful country sites, and farms in the vicinity,—and more particularly on the roads leading to Clintonville, to Manhasset, and to Jamaica. In fact, one cannot walk or ride in or near the village of Flushing, without witnessing something calculated to dispel the most gloomy feelings.[3]

The enchanting objects which I have mentioned, compensated measurably for the restrictions under which I was placed at the Hall,—still, my memory would steal back to former times, and I would often long to hold an intercourse with my former comrades. But how should I hold a communication unknown to the superintendent? This thought puzzled me, as no letter was allowed to pass from the Institution without first being scrutinized by him. I ardently desired to hear from Mortimer, and I at length set my wits to work, to devise some plan of holding a private correspondence with him. I conversed with my school-mates on the subject of letter writing, and did not hesitate to express a wish that our letters might not be read by him.

On expressing this wish, several of the older pupils eyed me with particular attention, and it was not long before I received a particular invitation from one of them to visit her in her apartment at an hour specified.

At the hour appointed I repaired to her room, in which I found some half a dozen or so of the girls congregated. On my entrance, there were sundry knowing looks passed between them, and they immediately began to quiz me as to the reason why I wished to hold a private correspondence. My answers, of course, were all evasive. Enough, however, was elicited by them to know that I was fixed and determined on the point. The conference wound up by their telling me, that if I could keep a secret, I was at liberty to meet them again at another specified time. The truth now flashed upon me, that they had some plan to communicate, and I promised faithfully that I would meet them again, and that the secret, whatever it might be, should be faithfully kept.

On the third succeeding night, which was the time appointed for our second meeting, we again congregated in the same chamber. I was now put under a solemn pledge, that whatever they might communicate, should not be divulged by me.

They then went on to state, that they kept one of the servants in their interest by giving him certain bribes, and that if I felt disposed to contribute to the necessary fund, I might become one of their number, and share in the benefits of their association.

I did not hesitate to accede to the proposal. It was therefore agreed that I should contribute a certain sum out of the pocket money allowed me by my parents, as was done by the rest of them,—the amount of the contributions being punctually paid over at stated times, to the servant who transacted the private business, in the way of passing letters, &c.

After becoming initiated into this private association, I found no difficulty in getting up a correspondence in any quarter. I immediately wrote to Mortimer, requesting information relating to certain things in town, but did not intimate that I had any particular affection for *him*, giving him, at the same time, my fictitious address, which address was necessary, in order to screen the matter from our superintendent, and known only to myself, my correspondents, the members of our association, and the servant whom we had enlisted in our behalf.

The first reply which I received from Mortimer, I beg leave to insert here, as showing the true state of his feeling toward me. It reads thus:

"Dear Sophia,—

I have written to you on several occasions, but from some cause you have not received my letters, or else you have not condescended to answer them. You cannot imagine how I was transported on the receipt of the one to which I am about to reply. When I broke the seal, and discovered your signature, I kissed it again and again. I only wish I could see the writer, and impress as many kisses upon her lips as I imprinted upon the letter.

Sophia, although I am but a boy, scarcely turned the age of sixteen, I love you. I love you with a pure, a fervent, and a holy love. You are everything to me, and without you I am nothing. If you ever return to the city, you shall see how faithfully, how devotedly I will serve you.

Forgive me, Sophia, for thus early avowing my sentiments; but, I am aware that beauty like yours must win many suitors. It is, therefore, not safe for me that you should remain ignorant of my sentiments toward you. Those raven locks, those sparkling eyes, that sylph-like form, combining grace and dignity in the girl, are the only prelude, or evidence of superior beauty in the woman.

Sophia, accept of me as one of your suitors, and if I am the fortunate one, O the happiness that is in store for me!

In the exuberance of my feelings, I had almost forgotten to reply to the various questions which you have asked in your kind letter. Martha Steward has gone to West Chester to live with her uncle; Mary Bingham has gone to Jersey City; and Sarah Alstead has gone to the Female Seminary of Miss Adrain, at Jamaica, Long Island; John Stillman has entered the junior class at Columbia College in this city. The rest of our old playmates are in town, engaged in various avocations.

Write to me, Sophia, whenever you can get the opportunity, and believe me,
Yours, now and for ever,
Mortimer Bowers"

On receipt of the above letter from Bowers, I made no further effort to conceal my preference for him; consequently, it was not long before we fully understood each other.

Subsequent to the time of which I have been writing, I remained at the Seminary of Dr. Schroeder, for the space of two years, at the expiration of which time my parents considered my education sufficiently complete, and I was called to town to make my *debut* in the *beau mondes*.[4]

On the evening of my return to New York, my parents proposed to give a grand *fete* at the Broadway Mansion. The evening fixed upon was the 31ˢᵗ December, 1847. My parents in this case took the responsibility of inviting such guests as they intended for my future associates. Whether they acted prudently or not, shall be left for the reader to judge.

On my arrival at the Mansion, I found it brilliantly lighted, and every thing prepared in accordance with the circumstances of my father. I retired immediately to my dressing room, and having arranged my toilet to my satisfaction, descended to the parlor. Here I found myself surrounded by all the aristocracy of the city, and those who were not already acquainted eagerly sought the honor of an introduction. I was courted and flattered by every one, still I was ill at ease. My eyes wandered over the assembly in vain, in search of one who was dearer to me than all,—but he was not there. The only way in which I could account for his absence, was that he had not received an invitation. I ventured to ask my father if such were the case. He replied, coldly, that he did not wish his daughter to countenance young men of the standing of the one to whom I alluded.

This piece of information went like an arrow to my heart. The idea that for the future Bowers and myself were not to associate with each other, when hitherto we had thought ourselves living for each other alone!

The remainder of the evening had no charms for me. I could not enter with spirit into any of the amusements, but merely talked and moved mechanically.

When the company had dispersed, I retired to my chamber depressed in spirits, with gloomy apprehensions for the future, and almost for the first time in my life I fell upon my knees, and prayed in the fervency of the spirit. I then threw myself upon my pillow and wept. Sleep only came to my relief, but even that relief was partial. Representation of deeds of horror haunted me in my dreams. Subsequent, or recent events, have but too fully proved those dreams to have been ominous of the future.

In my dreams I saw Bowers and myself in almost every kind of imaginary danger. At one time we were on the brink of a precipice, at another we were suffering shipwreck; and again, we were in the midst of the flames.

I rose in the morning with swollen eyes, and with an uncommon pain in the head. I made my toilet, descended to the breakfast table, and after partaking of a cup of tea, felt somewhat revived.

After breakfast, the first thing which I did was to address a note to Bowers, stating my arrival in town, giving an account of the entertainment of the previous night, and expressing my disappointment at not finding him there.

I also informed him of the remark made by my father, when I inquired the cause of his absence, and of the consequent necessity of holding our interviews in private, knowing my father's disposition too well to suppose for a moment that he could be made to relent, when he had a fixed purpose in view. Although he had formerly been indulgent to me in the extreme, I understood him sufficiently well to know that when his determination was fixed there was no alternative.

A series of private interviews were therefore my only hope. I was under the necessity of watching the movements of my father, in order to screen these interviews from his observation, and to lull him into security in *any* case of suspicion. At the same time, I took every favorable opportunity of speaking of the good qualities of Bowers, and of watching the expression of the old man's countenance whenever those qualities were the subject of comment.

I noticed that on all such occasions the countenance of the old man assumed one of its darkest hues. "Eagles must sleep in an eagle's nest," he would say. "Let Bowers seek a wife in his own sphere."

Finding that my father absolutely refused to countenance any thing that might be said in favor of Bowers, I at length ceased to make his name the subject of conversation, in the presence of the old gentleman.

Our private meetings were still continued, and they mostly took place in the evening, after the old man had retired to rest. It was his invariable custom to retire at nine o'clock. During the remainder of the evening I was left at liberty to act according to my pleasure, without fear of restraint, so long as suspicion was not excited.

Bowers and myself generally contrived to spend an hour or two in the way of conversation and promenading, during several evenings of each week. Sometimes we would take a stroll on the Battery, and occasionally we would venture at the Museum. Policy required that we should not frequent public places in each other's society, as our association in such cases would soon become the subject of remark, and consequently reach the ears of my parents.

As already stated, I had the evenings mostly to myself after the hour of nine: my mother generally retiring at or before the time observed by my father, the delicate state of her health making it necessary for her to do so.

In the mean time I had many other suitors, whom, to please my parents, I always treated with courtesy and politeness, taking care, at the same time, that they should never trespass upon my appointment with Bowers.

The servants at home I managed to keep in my interest, so that I did not hesitate, on various occasions, to entertain Bowers in the parlor of the Mansion, after the old people retired to rest.

On one occasion, my father, either by accident or design, rose about an hour after he had retired, and made his way softly and silently to the parlor. There was no intimation of his approach. He opened the parlor door, and caught Bowers and myself in one of our most agreeable *tête à têtes*. He threw the door wide open, gazed upon us for a moment with an eye of scorn, and then turned away.

I trembled as I watched his departing footsteps, well knowing that the storm was now about to burst.

The next morning the old man did not make his appearance at the breakfast table, and my mother, when she presented herself, was in tears.

My father had ordered a cup of coffee to be brought to his chambers, and after *our* meal was over, I was summoned into his presence.

I obeyed the summons, and on entering the chamber, he calmly and silently pointed to a chair. His look was so cold and destitute of feeling, that I sank down with a shudder. After sipping his coffee a while, he commenced—

"Sophia," said he, "you are my only child. I have educated and brought you up in a way befitting my circumstances, and I have a right to expect in return, that you will show your gratitude, by associating with such persons only as are calculated to sustain the dignity of our family. With this object in view, on your return to town, I introduced you to the society of all the *elite* of the city. I also told you, on the night of your return, that I did not wish you to associate with any, except those of a certain class. In what manner have you complied with my request?

"If I am correctly informed, since your return to this place, and introduction to the world, you have sought the society, and cultivated the acquaintance, almost exclusively, of this Mortimer Bowers. And who is Mortimer Bowers? A young man without a fortune, without friends, and whose parents are in so straitened circumstances, that they with difficulty sustain themselves.

"Sophia, think not for a moment that I will consent to a union with *such* a family. On this point I must be obeyed. Deceive not yourself.

"I have now to request of you, that you discard this Bowers for ever, and I have also to inform you, that unless you comply with my request, you are to leave my roof immediately.

"Sophia, we live it is true, under what we call a republican form of government; but, our democracy exists only in imagination. It is merely a name, to tickle the fancy of the mob.

"We have our patricians and our plebians. Bowers belongs to the class of plebians, and his proper place is obscurity. You, Sophia, belong to the order of patricians, and with correct deportment on your part, your beauty and your talents, will obtain for you a place in the center of the circle of attraction.

"Sophia, I will give you three days to decide on your future course, at the expiration of which time I expect your answer. You may now retire."

I listened to this address of the old gentleman with downcast eyes, and in the most perfect silence. At the conclusion, I saw that the crisis had come. Despair gave me energy. I threw myself at my father's feet, and with a flood of tears, besought him that he would listen to *me*. He answered not a word. I then went into a vindication of my course of conduct, commented on the virtues of Mortimer Bowers, spoke of his superior education, as an off-set to his lack of fortune, and concluded by intimating, that although Bowers himself were poor, yet, if my father would sanction our union, the wealth of our family was sufficient for both—and, in the most suppliant manner, I besought him to change his purpose.

When I had concluded, the old man looked at me for a moment, then thrusting me from him with a repulsive hand, said he expected my answer at the expiration of three days.

With a heavy heart, I left *that* chamber, and retired to my own.

I again bent the knee in prayer, and earnestly did pray that the evils which threatened me might be averted. Still, I could not prevail upon myself to submit to the dictates of my parent.

After having to some extent composed myself, I threw on my bonnet, drew my wrapper about me, and went in search of Mortimer. I learned that he had gone to Wall Street on some business, and that he did not expect to return until afternoon.

I returned again to the Mansion, and after some further preparations, strolled down Broadway, in the hopes of meeting Bowers on his return. I met him as I had anticipated, and on taking his arm, and turning in the direction in which he was going, I related to him the occurrences of the morning.

When I had finished, Bowers, extending his arm about my waist, and taking my hand in his, bent upon me one of his tenderest looks, and replied to the following effect—

"Sophy, dear, you know that you are all and everything to me,—and it is a matter, in my mind, of the most sincere regret, that I am poor. I would not seek, dearest, to influence you in your decision, and the answer to the old gentleman. If you come to the conclusion that you will discard me, affluence for the future will undoubtedly be yours. If you resign all the attendant pleasures and comforts of wealth for my sake, I can only promise you, Sophy, that I will do all in my power to make you happy. If, however, you refuse to unite yourself with me, either at the present, or at some future time, all happiness for me is fled. I shall hope no more. What will life be to me, if the sole object for which I have lived is about to be torn away, or irrevocably lost?"

At this point of the conversation we had arrived opposite the Mansion, and we separated with the understanding that we should see each other again in the evening.

When I entered the house, I went immediately to my chamber, and packed up such portions of my wardrobe as were the most indispensable, in order to be prepared for any emergency—as I had already resolved in my own mind, that I would share the fortunes of Bowers, let the result be what it might.

As the evening approached I prepared myself for a walk, and kept a look out for the appearance of Mortimer. He did not appear so soon as I expected. The shades of night had fallen, and the moon had thrown her "silver mantle o'er the dark," and yet Bowers did not appear.[5]

Solitary and alone I sat in the front parlor, with the window half closed, anxiously scrutinizing the passers by, in the hopes that the next one might be Bowers himself. The moments dragged heavily away, and I had almost come to the conclusion that he intended to forsake me.

A light tap at the window at length told me that he was at hand.

In a moment I was at his side.

"Forgive me, dearest," he whispered, "for keeping you so long in waiting,— but I have been detained in some very serious case. As I was preparing to meet my appointment with you, my mother was seized with a sudden attack of cholera, and I was under the necessity of remaining to attend upon *her*. I stole myself away as soon as I could leave her with safety."

This explanation of Mortimer relating to his tardiness, was satisfactory, and I hesitated not to give him my entire confidence.

We directed our steps to the Battery, as being the most suitable place for our promenade, as we arranged matters for the future.

Bowers commenced the subject by asking me whether I had come to any conclusion. I told him, candidly and decidedly, that I had resolved never to wed with any, except with himself,—that I would share his fortunes, what- ever they might be, and that if my father persisted in his resolution, we could but live or die together.

When I had stated my determination, Bowers was so transported that he seemed for the moment to have lost his senses; and it was with difficulty that I prevented him from kneeling to me, even in the street. I suggested the idea of observing a little propriety, and he was obliged to content himself by im- printing a kiss upon my hand.

"Dearest Sophy," he replied, "this is more than I had a right to expect, but, since you are willing to resign all for me, I pledge myself, as a man of honor, that no effort shall be wanting on my part to make you as happy as my cir- cumstances will admit."

I told him, that poverty with him was preferable to wealth and luxury with- out him.

We then took into consideration the prospect of the future, and the ques- tion was asked whether it were not possible to appease my father to such an extent, that he would not put his threat into execution, of turning me out of doors.

At one time it was proposed that I should apparently accede to his wishes, by seeming to discard Mortimer, and that we should manage to continue our clandestine meetings upon a different plan from that which we had formerly pursued. It was then again proposed that we should elope immediately, before the old man had put his threat into execution, and trust to time to bring about a reconciliation,—and again, it was suggested that we should bide the expi- ration of the three days, and that I should then acquaint my parent with my determination, and throw myself upon his mercy.

The first of these propositions was rejected, on account of the supposition that, for the future, I would be watched with the utmost vigilance, and, therefore, we should have but few opportunities of seeing each other.

The second was thought to possess no particular advantage, and, consequently, we concluded to adopt the third.

Accordingly, at the expiration of the allotted time, I was summoned again into my father's presence. I entered his room with a firm and determined step, though not with a disrespectful air.

He drew a chair, and requested me to be seated. Before asking my decision, he addressed me to this effect—

"Sophia, you cannot suppose for a moment, that I, as a father, can entertain any but the kindest feelings toward you, or that I would not do any thing calculated to advance your happiness, consistent with the dignity of my family. I know it is sometimes the case that young ladies set their affections on a particular suitor, and exclude the more worthy, whether such conduct meet the approbation of their parents or not.

"I am confident, dear Sophy, that upon reflection you have decided in accordance with the dignity of your family, and that you have determined to select a husband from among the many wealthy suitors who are candidates for your favor."

When the old man had finished, I again knelt before him. I told him that I ought not to suppose him capable of doing any thing to make me miserable, more particularly as I was his only child, and that I was fully sensible I ought to subject myself to his guidance to any reasonable extent,—but, that the subject of matrimony was one in which every lady should have some choice of her own, as marriage was an event calculated to determine the happiness or misery of a whole life.

I told him that I had had a preference for Mortimer from his boyhood,—that I had never seen any who could compete with him in point of physical or mental endowments,—that his reputation was without a stain, and that his only misfortune was in being poor,—a circumstance entirely beyond his control, being nothing more nor less than a dispensation of Providence, or the result of the laws of the country.

In fine, I told the old man I could wed with none, except with Mortimer Bowers,—and I besought him, as he valued the happiness of his daughter, not to drive matters to the extreme which he had meditated. I promised obedience to him in every *other* thing, but, in the subject of matrimony I could not be controlled.

When I had finished my reply, my father's face was livid with rage. He rose from his seat, paced the room a few times, then turned to me and said—

"Sophia, the die is cast. Here is my purse, as I would not turn you penniless upon the world. This purse contains sufficient to provide for your present wants. The future will depend upon yourself. You are no longer the heir of Samuel Delaplain. You will leave this mansion before the hour of twelve tomorrow. If, after that time, you are found within its walls, I shall take the responsibility of handing you into the street. Farewell."

Thus the *finale* had presented itself, and it was now only left for me to obey the injunctions, and leave the house as soon as possible.

I had arranged with Bowers, that after the interview with my parent I should repair immediately to the Battery, where I should meet with him, that being the most convenient place of meeting, it lying in the direction of his business.

On arriving at that place I found Bowers already in attendance. I communicated to him the result of my interview, and the necessity I was under of seeking a new home immediately.

Bowers then informed me that the Ship Henry Clay was lying at the foot of Wall Street, and up for California,—that she was a staunch vessel, possessing every accommodation, and insured at the lowest rates,—that, as my father had driven me from his presence, he thought it advisable that we should seek our fortunes in the El Dorado of the West.

The California fever was then raging at its height, and it is not to be wondered at that I should lend a willing ear to the proposition of Mortimer.

The novelty of the thing was also exciting in the highest degree, and I was soon enlisted in it, with all the ardor of my feelings. The voyage around the "Horn" was entirely uppermost in my imagination,—indeed, so absorbed was I in the matter, that whatever regrets I might otherwise have felt, on being separated and driven from my home, under present circumstances, I was entirely free from any melancholy feeling.[6]

In order to add to the interest of the adventure, I had a fancy of appearing on ship-board, in the habiliments of the masculine gender. I suggested the idea to Bowers, and he, willing to assent to every thing to please me, made no objection.

The ship was to sail on the succeeding day, and I, having the privilege of spending one more night at the Mansion, did not find it necessary to seek any other abode in town. Mortimer repaired immediately to the vessel, engaged our berths, and paid the passage money. I was entered under the name of Harry Blain.

Mortimer Bowers and Harry Blain were thus duly entered as passengers on board the Ship Henry Clay, destined for California, and intending to sail on the first of May, 1850.

It is remarkable that neither Mortimer nor myself suggested the propriety of having the marriage ceremony performed before we left the shores of our native country. My attention was so much engaged in making preparations for the voyage, that the idea of the ceremony never occurred to me. May Heaven forgive me, for it was not designedly omitted.

With the contents of the purse which my father had given me, I found no difficulty in procuring the necessary male attire, and all other things required for the outfit,—and ere the sun had lighted up the horizon on the morning of the day on which my father had enjoined me to leave the Mansion, I was dressed in the accoutrements of one of the B'hoys, and on my way to the wharf at which the ship was lying.[7] I was accompanied thither by Mortimer of course.

Our baggage was immediately taken on board, and we found ourselves in comfortable quarters.

At the hour of 10, a.m., we hauled out from the dock, and the Steamer Osceola was ready to give us a tow beyond the Hook.[8]

As we were passing down the Bay, and I had a little time for reflection, I was for the first time led to realize the awkwardness of my position. I was on ship-board, in the company of Mortimer, and yet I was not legally his wife. I mentioned the oversight to him, and he, as well as myself, appeared exceedingly distressed. To make matters worse, I was dressed in male attire. No request could, therefore, be made of the captain on the subject, without subjecting ourselves to censure and disgrace,—even if an official could then be obtained to perform the ceremony, which was hardly probable. We therefore concluded to let matters remain as they were, feeling as though we belonged to each other, and that the ceremony was, at most, only a matter of form.

We were now fully embarked.

As no further occurrences of note transpired during our passage down the Bay, I shall make no other comment on this portion of our voyage.

The Steamer Osceola left us outside the Hook, at about 6 o'clock, p.m., of the same day on which we had embarked.

We now flung our canvass to the breeze, and stood forth into the broad expanse of the Atlantic. The wind was light, and so much to the south of east, that we were under the necessity of keeping our vessel closely trimmed, in order to bear away sufficiently from the land. Our progress during the night was but small.

On the morning of the second of May the weather was fair, the wind still continued light, and in the same direction. At about nine o'clock, a.m., we discovered a vessel at the south of us, and she immediately displayed a signal, which signal was promptly answered by the Henry Clay. A succession of signals were now displayed. The import of these, a portion of the crew, at any rate, did not understand.

At the close of the signals, the captain ordered the ship to be put about, and kept in a direction north of east.

This maneuver excited some surprise in Mortimer, as he expressed himself to me, saying that we were bearing sufficiently away from the land of our former course, and that now we were approaching the coast of Long Island.

We stood on in this direction, until the coast of Long Island, with its breakers, in reality, appeared distinctly in our view. The ship was again tacked, and run in a westerly direction, parallel with the coast. It was now on the afternoon of the 3rd. The coast of Long Island is known to be a dangerous coast for vessels,—and as we sailed along, and viewed the breakers in the distance, the occurrence of the wrecks of the Bristol and the Mexico, were strongly pictured to the imagination.[9]

The movements of the captain were not understood, and he refused to give any explanation.

At about three o'clock, p.m., the wind began to grow squally, and to blow directly from the south. Those who have resided on, or in the vicinity of Long Island, are perfectly familiar with the tremendous southerly winds which sometimes affect that coast. The captain began to evince considerable anxiety, and the wind rose by degrees to a perfect hurricane.

Every thing was now in a scene of confusion. The breakers were on the lee-ward, and the tide and wind setting us directly inward. Some prayed, and others loaded the captain with imprecations and curses, for bringing his ship in that position. As for myself, I clung to the arm of Mortimer, according to his directions,—and the tears which I shed on that occasion did but little honor to the male attire.

The wind continued to blow, and the breakers were now within a hundred yards of us. We every moment expected the ship to strike, when suddenly she seemed to be caught as if by an eddy, and she moved perceptibly to the wind-ward. To increase our hopes, the gale somewhat abated, and the vessel bore up gallantly to the breeze.

The change from despair to hope was so sudden that there was now as much confusion from excess of joy, as there had recently been from excess of terror,—and three cheers for the good old ship were soon found to be in order.

The vessel continued to bite her way into the wind until we were secure from the phantoms of Death which beckoned us to the lee-ward.

The captain now condescended to assign a reason why he had not continued directly on his course. He said he had yet to receive a portion of his cargo, for which purpose he intended to put in at the Breakwater, at the mouth of the Delaware,—that he did not wish to arrive there until all things were ready to come on board,—and that the signals which he had received from the vessel at the southward, were intended to apprise him of the progress of matters in that quarter; and that the said vessel would again telegraph to him, when the cargo which he expected to receive at that point, should be prepared; and, also, that he intended to stand off and on the coast, until he should receive the proper information.

This explanation was apparently satisfactory to the greater portion of the crew; but Bowers suspected that all was not right. Prudence, however, forbade him to express himself to that effect. The captain was solicited by all hands to keep a little further from the shore, and thus the matter ended.

After standing in a westerly direction for a while, we found ourselves nearly in the same position in which we were left by the steamer; and, on tacking ship, we bore away nearly in the same direction as we had taken on our first course.

The wind was now bearing south-west, and the gale having decreased to a good sailing breeze, the Henry Clay flew like a bird over the waters. On arriving at or near our first telegraph position, signals were again displayed, but, it appeared, with no better satisfaction to the captain, as he continued on his course.

We were now sailing directly on the route to California. The wind was fair, and I regretted that we had again to turn back for the purpose of stopping at the capes.

At about twelve o'clock on the night of the 4th, the captain changed his course, and stood in toward Cape Henlopen. At daylight he shot up a signal. This was immediately answered, and it appeared that all was right, as the ship was put into the Bay, and shortly after moored inside the Breakwater.

Now came the remainder of the cargo, which was closely packed in boxes, and marked "Sheetings," some with the stamp of the Powhattan Mills, and other marked "Lowell, Mass.," &c.

Next followed a quantity of passengers, so many that our ship was literally crammed. The suspicion of Bowers was again awakened, but he communicated nothing except to myself.

When all was on board, we tripped our anchor, and again bore away to the Atlantic. The circle described by our vessel as we sailed out the bay, was such as to give us a full view of the buildings and bathing grounds at Cape May, the beautiful appearance of which is peculiarly striking when viewed from the ocean. I shall omit their descriptions as not particularly connected with my story.

I now anticipated that we were entirely cleared for the gold mines, and gave myself no apprehension for the future,—and, although we were closely stowed on board, we had made up our minds to be as cheerful as possible.

On the night of the 4th we took the first comfortable sleep we had enjoyed since having been on board. The most of us had now no apprehensions. We little thought how soon apprehension was to be awakened.

On the morning of the 5th, we noticed that arms were distributed to certain portions of the crew, and that the military drill was the order of the day. We noticed, also, that the arms were taken from the boxes received on board at the Breakwater. There was now no longer any doubt. Something was wrong. A perfect silence was observed with regard to all questions which were asked. We noticed that about two-thirds of the ship's company were armed, and consequently were into the secret, whatever its nature might be. No information could be elicited on the day of the 5th.

On the morning of the 6th, the drum beat to arms,—and all those who *were* armed assembled in the proper order upon the deck. The captain then politely requested the remainder of the passengers to assemble on the quarter.

We complied with his request, and on being assembled he delivered to us the following short address:—

"Gentlemen, we suffered you to embark with us under the impression that you were going to California. This little deception was necessary on our part, otherwise we should not have been able to have escaped from the port. Our destination is Cuba. Since you have embarked on board our vessel, it is necessary that you should go along with us. If you will join in our expedition, we have arms sufficient for you. We would gladly have you to unite with us for the purpose of augmenting our numbers, and we have no doubt that our proposition will be acceptable to you, seeing that we are engaged in an enterprise intended to strike off the chains of slavery from the inhabitants of the island for which we are destined."[10]

At the conclusion of this address the passengers viewed each other, as if waiting for some one to reply.

Bowers at length stepped forth.

Addressing the captain, he spoke as follows:

"If Captain Bainbridge will allow us the privilege of holding a private consultation for a few moments, we shall then be able to give him a definite answer."

The captain assented to the proposition, and immediately withdrew to the forward deck.

Upon consulting, it was found that the passengers were, *en masse*, opposed to the expedition to Cuba, and that they were determined, if possible, not to be drawn into it. The question then was, whether they would accept the arms. This was decided in the affirmative,—considering that we should be better able to take care of ourselves, with arms in our hands, than without them. It was agreed that we should apparently accede to the captain's proposition, and subsequently project measures for the future.

The conclusion having been formed, Bowers walked forward, and told the captain that we acceded to his proposition.

Arms were then put into our hands, and we soon found ourselves drilling in martial order, upon the deck of the Henry Clay.

Every man of the ship's company was now considered as fully enlisted in the enterprise, and every information related to it was communicated without reserve.

We were informed that the plan of General Lopez was, to make a descent upon the island at three different points—that one of these points was at Cardenas, another at Trinidad, and the other (the one for which we were destined) was at St. Jago de Cuba.[11]

It was his design to land and establish himself at these points, anticipating that the presence of his troops at these different quarters, would encourage the people generally throughout the island to revolt and flock to his standard. He supposed, also, that the Spanish troops garrisoned upon the island would be easily subdued after having enlisted the people of his favor. His plan appears ultimately to have failed, except so far as the landing of the troops at Cardenas was concerned. So easily are frustrated the designs of man.

The destination of our company, then, was St. Jago de Cuba, situated on the southern extremity of the island.

All was now quiet on the ship-board, and, to a superficial observer, everything appeared to be going on well. The officers devoted their whole attention to perfecting the skill of the men in the use of their arms,—and Bowers, on account of his noble bearing, and the precision with which he went through the various drills, was promoted to the rank of captain,—a circumstance which excited no little pride in me, although it would have been impossible to raise him higher in my estimation than he already stood.

Although every one was outwardly submissive to the officers commanding the expedition, yet, there might be seen, whenever opportunity presented itself, small congregations of that portion of the crew who had embarked with the view of going to California. Various projects were proposed by them for thwarting the design of the expedition. No sure and decisive measure, however, presented itself, except that of open opposition,—and then the question was, whether we were sufficiently strong in point of numbers.

This question required a little consideration. After revolving the matter in our mind a day or so, it was finally resolved to make the attempt. It was determined that our party should wear their side-arms continually, in order that no suspicion might be excited when the opposition was about to be made.

Our party drilled themselves constantly in the broad-sword exercise,—the broad-sword being the weapon on which they mostly depended for the execution of their designs,—the muskets being deposited in one of the state-rooms immediately on the termination of each drill. Our plan was, to secure the state-room containing these weapons, and likewise to secure as many of the side-arms of the opposite party as could conveniently be done.

When the drills were past, some of this party ordinarily retained their side-arms, and others laid them away in such places as best suited their convenience. A great majority of them, therefore, were entirely unarmed except at the time of the drill.

It was thought by our party, that by securing the state-room containing the muskets, and each man seizing as many of the arms of the opposite party as came within his reach, when we were about to make the attempt, there would be little resistance, and consequently but little loss of life.

Such was our scheme. The time for putting into execution was fixed for the eighteenth of May, when it was expected that the ship would be off the coast of St. Jago de Cuba, and near the end of the voyage—or, rather, near the place of her destination. The attempt was to be made, also, at the hour of dinner. At that hour, we concluded, the energies of our opponents would be most universally relaxed.

El Dorado was to be the watch-word. It was first to be sounded by the man who secured the state-room,—at the sound of which every man was to look at his arms.

The eighteenth of May at length arrived,—and already the crew were gazing on the town of St. Jago de Cuba in the distance! Bowers had been appointed to command our party, a man had been selected to secure the

state-room, and each one had a position assigned to him. Every thing promised the most complete success.

Bowers had enjoined upon me, that I should keep by his side until the affair was over.

At the hour of dinner, each one of our party took the place assigned him,
and we did not wait long before the sound of El Dorado sounded from the
state-room,—the keys securing which were promptly thrown overboard.
Simultaneously, each of our men seized such of the weapons of our opponents as came near to hand, and the sound of "El Dorado" was heard from all
parts of the ship.

The arms of our opponents which had been secured were also immediately thrown into the sea,—our party being sufficiently well armed without
them.

Our men then immediately ranged in order on the starboard side of the vessel, and the shouting of "El Dorado" startled our opponents, and brought them
also to the deck. On arriving there, and beholding us arranged in martial order,
they looked at us with astonishment. Captain Bainbridge comprehended the
matter at once. But the most of his own men were unarmed. He tried the state-
room, but found it bolted and barred. He then waved his hand for his men to
come aft. The order was immediately obeyed, and seizing a hatchet, he ripped
open a box which had been deposited on the quarter deck, and covered with
canvass, and which, unknown to us, was filled with side-arms.

Each man seized a weapon, and thus in an instant, as it were, our opponents
were mostly armed, and stood arrayed against us. It was now too late for us
to retract, as the consequences would have been fatal.

The eyes of our party were now directed to Bowers, as if asking whether
they should strike. The countenance of Mortimer, at this juncture, was
thrilling in the extreme. I could only compare it to the Jupiter of Homer, when

> "He shakes his ambroissal curls in giving nod,
> The stamp of fate and sanction of a God."[12]

Bowers motioned his men forward, and it was now "Hand to hand, and
steel to steel."

Mortimer opposed himself to Captain Bainbridge, and after a few passes
between them, Bainbridge had taken passage for Eternity. The battle now
raged with the greatest fury. I kept by the side of Mortimer, as he had enjoined
upon me, and I was more than once indebted to him for warding a blow,
which would have been fatal to me.

A comrade who fought next to me met with a fate which was so horrible
in its nature, that the occurrence nearly unnerved me. He was attacked by two
of our assailants, and becoming bewildered by their impetuosity, he lost his
guard, and their weapons both took effect on him at the same time,—one
passing through his body, and the other severing the head therefrom.

The fight continued for about half an hour, when more than half the crew lay dead or dying upon the deck. The combatants began to grow weary, and their exhaustion, in connection with the horrid scene about them, caused them to suspend their fury as if by mutual consent.

Our number was so extensively diminished by the conflict, that it would now have been considered the height of folly to meditate a descent upon the island. It seemed to be the general wish, as expressed by the actions of the survivors, that the affray should be stopped. The weapons were therefore returned to the scabboard.

Our attention was now directed to the wounded and the dying. The day was exceedingly hot, and the cries for water were incessant. Our stock on board was nearly exhausted, and we were under the necessity of procuring more from *some* source. To obtain it, it was necessary that some one should go on shore, it was also necessary that whoever ventured to go, should go entirely unarmed,—thereby assuming a pacific character.

A call was made for some one to volunteer his services. No one was found to offer, and it is a fact, that among the survivors of those who intended to take Cuba by force of arms, not one remained, who had sufficient courage to venture alone upon the land to obtain a supply of water.

Bowers at length said he would go himself. It was therefore agreed that the vessel should be run in as near the land as could be done with safety, drop the anchor, and remain until the water could be brought on board.

This arrangement being agreed upon, and the ship being brought to the proper station, one of the boats was launched, with the water casks, and Bowers and myself stepped into her. The wind being light and fair, we put up a sail, and run into the land. After some search, we discovered a spring, and were in the act of filling our casks when we espied that the ship had tripped her anchor and was in the act of moving off.

We felt alarmed, but on casting our eyes to the westward, we discovered the cause of this movement. A Spanish brigantine was bearing down upon the Henry Clay, and those on board having no ordnance mounted to defend themselves, were unwilling, under their present circumstances to come in too close contact with the Spaniard, not knowing what he might be pleased to do. They had, therefore, concluded to take to their heels.

Thus Mortimer and myself were deserted, and left to the mercy of those into whose hands we might chance to fall. The ship crowded all sail, and what with her speed, and the coming on of night, she was soon lost to our sense of vision.

We were now upon the island without provisions of any kind, and neither of us understood the Spanish language. What was to be done? The best policy appeared to be, to make our way in the direction of the town, and trust to fortune on our arrival at that place.

On arriving at the town we sought a lodging for the night. The difficulty of making ourselves understood was some little hindrance, although we should have fared sufficiently well had not the brigantine sent word on shore that a vessel had been driving from the coast, and that the people of the town should be on the look-out. It was immediately inferred that we belonged to the strange vessel, and we were summoned into the presence of the chief magistrate. The name of this magistrate we afterwards learned to be Don Martin Mandrillo.[13]

On being requested to give an account of ourselves, Bowers frankly stated every thing connected with our history, from the time of our embarkation at the port of New York. Our persons were then subjected to an examination, and, unluckily for us both, my sex was discovered. This circumstance bore hard against us. They would listen to nothing which would tend to palliate what they considered to be a very grave offense,—and they considered, or pretended to consider, that those who were capable of falling into such things, were capable of others also,—and they immediately set us down as belonging to the expedition against the island, and consequently committed us to prison.

The prison in which we were confined was in the basement of St. Andrew's church. Whether this place was originally intended as a jail or not, I am unable to say: certain it is, however, that it answered the purpose well, and is well supplied with the instruments of torture.

We had obtained lodgings, but under circumstances, and in a place which was not calculated to excite in us any very agreeable feelings. We had no bed to repose on, except what the stone flagging of our cells afforded us. Our apartments were adjoining each other, and it was some consolation to hear the sound of each other's feet, as we paced to and fro for the want of a comfortable place to sit or lie.

Wearied with the exercise, we at length sank down upon the pavement, and denuding ourselves of a portion of our garments for the purpose of forming a pillow, sought to forget the realities of our situation by taking as comfortable a nap as our situation would allow.

Although we lay upon the stone pavement, we slept until awakened in the morning, by our jailer throwing open the doors of our cells and calling us to rise.

He told us that we were at liberty to walk in the room into which our cells opened,—and that he would soon furnish us with some breakfast. He retired, and we were left at liberty to examine the room in which he allowed us to walk. We examined that, and also examined the cells in which we had passed the night. We were firmly persuaded, from appearances, that all attempts to escape without some assistance from without, must be futile. The windows were small, and firmly secured with bars of iron. The walls of the prison also had iron bars extended across them, at the distance of about six inches apart. The floor was also in the same way. We were thus emphatically ironbound.

In about an hour the jailer reappeared, bringing with him a mug of water, and a small loaf of brown bread. These he deposited on a small table standing on one side of the room, and then retired.

At about three o'clock, p.m., we received another lunch of the same sort, and that was all the food we received through the day. At night we were again committed to the cells.

This was the manner of our living, with little variation, until the *finale* of the descent at Cardenas had presented itself. After the invaders had been driven back from that point, and the prisoners taken at Woman's Island, in connection with the seizure of the Georgiana and the Susan Loud, we were destined to experience a change, the circumstances connected with which I am about to relate.[14]

Early one morning, before our jailer had waited on us as was customary, we heard a bustle in the ante-chamber, seemingly caused by a number of persons passing about the room, and conversing with each other.

Our breakfast was also introduced into our cells,—a departure from the custom which had previously been observed.

At about the hour of ten, the doors of the apartments opened, and we were ordered to come forth. On approaching the ante-chamber, we found it fitted up in the shape of an auditory. A number of persons were in attendance; these, from their appearance and dress, we thought must constitute a portion of the principal citizens of the place,—and among them was Don Martin Mandrillo, the magistrate into whose presence we had previously been introduced.

A place had been fitted up in the form of a dock, in which, after the assembly had scrutinized us a few moments, Bowers was ordered to stand. I was remanded back to my cell.

Don Martin, with the assistance of those present, then proceeded to examine Bowers relating to the expedition, but was not able to elicit any thing more than he already knew. After the examination, Bowers was manacled and conducted back to the apartment.

I was then ordered to come forth and stand in the dock, and I passed an examination similar to that to which Bowers had been subjected. Nothing new was elicited from me. Irons were placed upon me, and I, also, was again incarcerated in the gloomy dungeon. We knew not our future destiny.

On the next succeeding morning we were again summoned into the ante-chamber, and were told that we must confess all we knew concerning the matter of the invasion, or submit ourselves to the torture. We both declared that we could communicate nothing more than had already been done.

A small rope, drawn over a pulley, was suspended from the ceiling, in the end of which rope was fastened a small hook, somewhat resembling a fish-hook, except that the beard was wanting.

We were now partially strangled, in order that the organ linguae might protrude from the mouth. The tongue was then perforated with an awl, and the hooks attached to the ropes were inserted therein. The ropes were then drawn over the pulleys, until they became so tight that we were under the necessity of standing on tip-toe to prevent our weight from being wholly borne by the tongue.

They kept us in this position for about fifteen minutes, when they released us, and remanded us to the dungeon.

A torture, on a par with the above, was inflicted every day during the space of one whole week,—we being requested on each occasion to divulge whatever we knew, and on declaring that we knew nothing more than had already been communicated, the torture was immediately applied.

In order that my reader may know, or form an idea of the nature of the Cuban Spaniard, I shall describe each torture separately.

On the second day, instead of one, there were four hooks attached to the rope, and one hook was inserted in each shoulder, and one in each hip, and thus we were suspended by these hooks, with our faces downward, until our persecutors were pleased to relieve us from the torment,—and this because we refused to communicate concerning a matter on which we were entirely ignorant.

On the third day we were suspended by the hair, and left to dangle until our persecutors were satisfied.

On the fourth day we were hung up with the head downwards, and suffered to remain a while in that position.

On the fifth we were scourged with a bundle of red hot wires.

And on the sixth, and last day, we were brought forth with great solemnity,—a Catholic priest being in attendance. The commands were now more particularly directed to Bowers, and he was ordered to confess what he knew, or this was to be the last day of his life. Bowers solemnly protested that he knew nothing more to communicate that had already been told.

He was then ordered to stand on a small platform, immediately in front of what appeared to be the image of a beautiful virgin. He was then told, that as he had a particular fancy for the ladies, as was evident from the fact that he had induced me to elope with him from my native country, he should have the privilege of embracing the beautiful image before him: and he was commanded to do so. Bowers leaned forward to obey the command, when lo! I was horror-struck at beholding the image raise its arms for the purpose of returning the embrace, and in the place of what should have been its arms, two sharp instruments, in the shape of sickles, presented themselves, and clasped the body of Mortimer in their embrace. Bowers writhed in agony, but all to no purpose. I was struck dumb.

The image continued to tighten its embrace, until the body of Mortimer fell, in four separate pieces, upon the floor.

I had no further recollection until I awoke, as if from a dream and found myself in the dungeon. It was some time before I could collect my thoughts,—but when I had been able to do so, the scene which I had witnessed was depicted to me in all its horrors. I now had no wish to live; in reality, I sincerely desired that my tormentors would put me also to death.

I was now suffered to remain both day and night incarcerated in the cell, and no further notice seemed to be taken of me, other than to furnish me with my daily allowance of bread and water.

After remaining in this condition for some days, I was surprised one after-noon to see the door of my cell open, and a lady, in company with the man who had acted as interpreter on former occasions, enter.

The lady introduced herself to me as Senora Mandrillo, the wife of Don Martin. She had heard of my case through the medium of her husband, and, it appears, her sympathies had been somewhat excited. She therefore wished to see and converse with me. I related to her my whole history without re-serve, and concluded by beseeching her to interpose in my behalf.

After hearing my story, she seemed for a while to be absorbed in thought, but finally promised that she would endeavor to ameliorate my condition. She then left me.

On the third day after the above interview, at about the time of night-fall, the same lady again entered my apartment, with a female attendant.

She immediately ordered the attendant female to take off her outer gar-ment, and requesting me also to undress, desired me to dress in the garment of which the other female had disrobed herself. She then threw over my head the scarf which her attendant had worn, and ordered me to follow *her*,—the attendant remaining behind in the cell.

We passed through the ante-chamber without exciting the suspicion of the jailer. On arriving outside, we found the senora's carriage in waiting.

We set off in the direction of San Salvador, at which place we arrived in the course of a couple of hours. At this place the lady had engaged a small boat to convey me down the river to an English vessel which was then lying in the bay, and bound for Baltimore.

By accelerating our movements, I found myself before the break of day safely shipped on board the brig Falmouth, and secure from the apprehension of any further insult or torture from the Spaniards.

Early in the morning our vessel weighed anchor, and after clearing Cape Cruz, stood to the eastward. As we run along the southern coast, we ran so near the land that I had an opportunity of taking a farewell view of the town of St. Jago de Cuba, a town not likely soon to be forgotten by me.

Our vessel now stood out through the windward passage, between the Islands of Cuba and St. Domingo, and I soon found myself again upon the wa-ters of the Atlantic. Nothing of note transpired during our voyage. We entered the port of Baltimore on the 15th July, 1850.

As already stated, the relation at Baltimore of my adventures excited so great a degree of interest, that I was induced to make the matter public, by presenting it in the form of a book. I know not that it is my duty to moralize on the subject, and, therefore, I shall leave my readers mostly to their own re-flections.

I would merely say, in conclusion, that, perhaps, had there been a little more discretion exercised, both by my parents and myself, I might have been spared my sufferings, and matters, at the present time, would be more agreeable for us both, and I would remind both the old and the young, that it is as necessary now as formerly, to observe the old adage—

"Look before You Leap."

I now only seek to retire from the world, and to spend my days in seclusion. Since the death of Bowers, I shall wait with patience for that coming eternity in which I hope to meet with him in that happy state in which sorrow is never known.

The Prisoner of La Vintresse

Mary Andrews Denison's (1826–1911) *The Prisoner of La Vintresse; or, the Fortunes of a Cuban Heiress* was published in 1860 and was one of the first of Beadle's dime novels. Denison was born in Cambridge, Massachusetts, a center of antislavery sentiments, and she married the Reverend Charles Wheeler Denison, who edited a New York antislavery journal called the *Emancipator*. She traveled to British Guiana with her husband in 1853 after he was named consul general and this may have contributed to her decision to write a novel about Cuba. Early in her career, Denison contributed to Boston-based story papers such as the *Olive Branch* and *Gleason's Literary Companion*, and she edited another periodical called the *Lady's Enterprise*. During the 1850s, she also published a seduction novel called *Gracie Amber* and an antislavery novel entitled *Old Hepsy*. She wrote several dime novels for Beadle and Company, including *Chip: The Cave Child* (1860), *The Mad Hunter; or the Downfall of the LeForests* (1863), and *Ruth Margerie: A Romance of the Revolt of 1689* (1862).

By making her plot turn on the key question of whether the heroine's fiancé is a spy for the filibusters who hope to "liberate" Cuba, Denison connects *The Prisoner of La Vintresse* to the news about filibustering expeditions and debates about U.S. plans to annex Cuba that pervaded the public sphere throughout the 1850s. But by 1860, many Northerners worried that annexing Cuba would mean extending slavery's sway, and Denison's representations of black slaves as degraded, abject beings and of wealthy Spanish slaveholders as decadent and licentious are probably meant to warn U.S. readers about the dangers of empire and the addition of Cuba as a slave state. Denison uses the genre of the international romance, made popular during the U.S.-Mexico War, to address questions about the relationship between the United States and Cuba, but since her heroine, Minerva, is of English "blood," the union between the Cuban heiress and "El Americano" does not signify optimism about the incorporation of Spanish Creoles and black slaves into the nation. Instead, the novel seems to advocate an intimate relationship between the United States and Cuba that does not involve annexation and the incorporation of new political subjects, but rather closer commercial relations and access to trade routes and markets. In other words, Denison's novel is aligned with an emergent form of imperialism that would become the dominant one in the "new empire" of the 1898 era.

THE PRISONER OF LA VINTRESSE;
OR, THE FORTUNES OF A CUBAN HEIRESS.

BY MRS. MARY A. DENISON

CHAPTER I

Escape and Disappointment

*T*he moonlight streamed broadly down upon the "Paseo De Ysabel Segunda"—the grand avenue of the city of Havana. Its two carriage drives—its two walls for foot passengers, glittered like silver in the splendors of the night; and the tree-branches that lined its sides were white with the glory of the full-orbed moon. The soft air was loaded with the scents of flowers that came from near and distant gardens. The blue field of stars glittered above, and the soft harmony of a full band of music, playing perhaps before the governor's house, their farewell march, came gently on the night-wind.

Two figures lightly but hurriedly crossed the lower end of the beautiful avenue.

"We did well with the guards, Minerva, now we have passed all danger, and I shall soon put you on board—good heavens!"

The lady looked up hastily at this exclamation.

"Do you see, Minerva, in the hurry and excitement, I have quite forgotten my portmanteau, containing all my papers—my drafts. In fact, I could not go without it. How unfortunate!"

"What *will* you do, dear Herman?" It was the musical voice of the young girl.

"There is but one thing I can do: put you on board and come back for it, then hasten to the ship. I don't think the tide is up. The boat that carries you will return with me, and it will not take thirty minutes. I *must* feel that you are safe."

"O Herman! it seems as if I dare not stay alone, and I am so fearful there may be trouble about your returning;" she said, half tearfully.

"Don't be afraid, dearest—the captain of the Eagle is a thorough gentleman, and I am well known here by most of the public authorities. Come, yonder is the boat, they are punctual—don't tremble so, my love."

"I fear—I hardly know what;" was the low reply.

"It is but natural;" returned the manly voice, "but you will soon feel safer when I am your protector. Here they are."

A boat approached the landing, propelled by two swarthy seamen.

"If I could only remain here till you return;" she murmured again.

"That would never do, Minerva. I'll see you at the vessel's side, however. What time do you set sail, men?"

"At twelve, to a second;" said one of the men.

"All right—I have an hour, then." Herman had pulled out his gold repeater—now he hastily put it back, secured Minerva in a comfortable seat, protecting her with lover-like energy against the upcoming of the restless waters as the sailors pulled oars lustily.

They reached the side of the black bulk. The captain's cheerful voice was heard.

"You are in good time, Mr. Goreham."

"Yes, sir; but I must ask the favor to be pulled back and waited for just ten minutes. By an unfortunate oversight I've left all my valuables, and this young lady, my cousin, of whom I spoke to you, will remain in your safe keeping."

"Ay, ay," responded the captain, "but I must limit you. Thirty minutes is the very longest I can spare the men, as I wish to set sail at twelve. Think you can do it?"

"I shan't be so long as that, captain, thank you. Now, be patient, darling," he whispered to the young girl as he helped her up the side.

Another moment and the sailors were off, Mr. Herman Goreham keeping them company, while Minerva was conducted to the handsome cabin, and shown her own pretty state-room, by the stewardess.

Here she dismissed the woman and sat down, listening intently that she might catch the faintest flash of the oars on their quick return. Strangely enough, a drowsiness crept over her, and, giving way to the sudden languor, she fell asleep. When she awoke, a midnight darkness was around her, and for a moment she knew not where she was. A sullen sound and uneasy motion convinced her all at once that the vessel was under way, and had been perhaps for hours. A blank horror seized her—could she be alone? The clattering of the doors, the trembling of the ship, convinced her that she must be at sea, and in a high wind. She tried the door of her state-room, standing up as best she could. A sudden lurch sent her out into the cabin where she caught at the long table and strove to steady herself, that she might look about her. There was no sign of life there. The lantern swung dismally, and the bolts and casings creaked and groaned. Overhead were sounds of tramping feet and shouting voices. Totally unacquainted with a ship as she was, she gazed from end to end of the long cabin in utter dismay. Of course Herman was on board. He had come at the appointed time, supposed her asleep and would not disturb her. Which of the state-rooms, whose gilding looked so ghastly in the dim light, could be his? And yet he might just have knocked at her door. Perhaps he did; she must have slept very soundly not to hear. A feeling of desolation came over her in spite of her hope, that sent the tears gushing to her eyes. If she could only see one human face—if the captain could come in, or the stewardess. But this horrible rolling—this deathly faintness that now crept over her, shrouding as it were, soul and body in its hideous mantle. At any rate, she must get back to her state-room, and there listen for the captain. It could not be very long till morning if the vessel started at twelve, and she had probably slept some hours. The damp sea-wind chilled her, and an undefinable fear weighed down her spirits. She returned to her state-room and sunk uneasily on her narrow bed. Ill as she felt herself growing, she did not call for

assistance, but waited patiently. It was evident that the calm wind of the previous night had freshened into a gale. The ship leaped and plunged, and the
ominous clattering as of ten thousand dishes, became every moment louder,
while the shouts above, grew more hoarse and continuous.

Sad was that weary watching till the dawn, and welcome the first gray streak
that slanted across the little state-room. Minerva attempted in vain to rise.
The fearful giddiness of sea-sickness was upon her—the ominous sinking and
depression that makes the malady seem tenfold more terrible. The gale had
somewhat abated its violence—but the ship yet plunged from one large wave-
top to the other.

Perplexing herself with wearying thought, she yet looked for some token
from Herman. He might be as ill in his state-room as she was in hers, but
surely he could send a message by the stewardess, or if there were other passengers, of which she was doubtful, by them or the captain.

The savory smell of coffee saluted her senses. Breakfast was being prepared,
then; some one might think of her. She was not mistaken. In a few moments
the door of her state-room opened, and the pleasant face of the stewardess
appeared, shining through the steam of the beverage she held in her hand.

Minerva greeted her with a smile.

It was good to see a human countenance, even that of a stranger.

"How are you, miss?" the girl asked simply.

Minerva shook her head; her look was expressive.

"Ah, you are not used to the sea," said the girl—"get all right in good time.
Take some strong coffee, that will make you better. Very pretty;" she added,
nodding her head approvingly, as Minerva shook the long curling hair that
had fallen from its fastenings, and hung in glittering curls all over the pillow.

The young girl smiled languidly and tasted the coffee. It gave her strength,
for she lifted herself in the narrow bed, and her eyes grew brighter.

"The gentleman who came with me," she said, turning to the stewardess,
who, with an admirable sea-gait, was placing the little state-room in order—
"is he ill, do you think, this morning? He said he was never sick at sea, but
then we have had a terrible storm, have we not?"

"Very bad," replied the girl, who, though she was Spanish by birth, spoke excellent English; "but who do you mean, by the gentleman? You came alone; I
saw no gentleman."

"Yes, I came over the vessel's side alone," said Minerva, "but my cousin was
in the boat. He had to go back to the shore after some luggage he had forgotten, but he returned directly. If I had my pencil, I would write a message to
him, and the steward could take it. It is strange that I have not heard from
him before now."

The stewardess stood regarding the young girl with a glance of perplexity.

"Are you sure he came aboard?" she asked after a moment of silence.

Minerva trembled at her look—her heart gave a great bound as she spoke.

"Sure, of course; he was to sail this voyage with me; his trunks are on board.

Why do you ask such a question?" she cried almost wildly. "Were you by when the boat came back?"

"No, not exactly;" said the stewardess; "but I was up in the cabin till long after the ship sailed, and I did see no one; but don't you be so pale and frightened, miss; I can very soon find out for you—the captain can tell. He might have possibly stayed out, you see, to watch the ship getting under way; sometimes our passengers do, in particular the first night. Do not be afraid—I will go see directly. What number is his state-room?"

"Seventeen;" said Minerva, faintly, sinking back on her pillow, for the bare thought of such a trouble sent all the blood to her heart and made her sick with apprehension.

Meanwhile, Bandola, the stewardess, made her way to the state-room designated by Minerva. It was locked—plainly the captain or the person who had secured it, was in possession of the key. She tried it, called through the key-hole, and managed to peek in under the blinds that made the upper half of the door. There was nobody there, that was very evident.

The captain came in, wet with salt-spray, pale and engrossed. He had been hard at work since the gale sprang up. Bandola went toward him; she was a great favorite with him.

"Well, Banda, we're about through," he said. "Did the storm frighten you? We had a fine taste of a tropical hurricane—one of the worst I ever saw. What?" he queried sharply, not hearing what reply the stewardess made.

"That young man, sir, who came with the young lady; is he any where on board?"

"Young man—on board—why of course he is," replied the captain. "You mean Goreham—in his state-room, likely."

"Oh! no, captain, I have looked."

"And what business have you to be looking after young men?" he asked, jocosely.

"Why, she, the young lady, sir, feels very bad about it. She wanted me to, and I saw him not in the cabin, at all, last night."

"The dickens!" said the captain, with energy. "Caulkings," he continued, turning to the first mate, who had come in to his breakfast, "is Goreham on board?"

"No, sir;" said the man.

"What! not on board? What do you mean, sir?"

"The men stayed nearly fifteen minutes after their time, against orders, sir," replied the mate, "and came back without him. You had turned in, and, you remember, given charge on no account to be disturbed. I felt a little uneasy when they came back and nobody with them, but expected every moment to see him alongside in some other boat, as he might very easily have done. Afterwards, in the hurry and confusion of getting off, it did not occur to my mind, sir."

"Well, well," muttered the captain, his brow clouding; "this is an unfortunate thing; a mighty unfortunate thing. Here we have this young lady on our hands, and the poor thing will be in a pretty mess. She'll fret herself to death, and who can wonder? There's certainly a mystery about it. Did he mean to stay?" he asked abruptly, as if questioning himself. "No—Goreham's the soul of honor—at least I have always found him so. Well, well, this is a pretty pickle, to be sure. Bandola, go to the lady and do what you can to comfort her. Say that he was probably detained for some trifling thing by some of those confounded custom-house people. It's very unfortunate, I'm sure, but it can't be helped, so I'll take breakfast."

But the worthy captain's spirits were low, that was easily to be seen. He ate and drank in silence, scarcely speaking to his companion.

CHAPTER II

Sad News

*B*andola went back to the state-room, with a slow step. Minerva had managed to rise, and had nearly completed her toilet. She looked very pale, and her large, dark eyes were supernaturally bright with excitement and expectation. She fully expected to see Herman, as the little door opened. A slight flush mantled her cheek—a smile broke over her face. It was changed to a sudden look of disappointment—and that again to an expression of vague terror, for there was that in the kind face of the stewardess that made her heart sink.

"What! has he not come!" she asked.

"Lady—"the girl stopped there—not knowing how to communicate the rest.

"It can not be that he is not on board!" cried Minerva, growing every moment paler.

"He will come in another ship;" said Bandola, catching at the *vinaigrette*[1] that laid on the pillow; "don't faint, lady; I'm sure he will come; he will take a vessel this very day; it will sail maybe quicker than this; you will meet him there, perhaps in New York."

"No—no—you can never know what reasons I have for fear—what terrible reasons;" the poor young girl almost gasped.

"But you will see him; you will certainly see him;" said the stewardess, the tears coming to her eyes. "Don't take on so, or you will be sick, and that will spoil your beauty;" she added, in the hope that an appeal to her woman's impulse might be successful.

"Oh! I am unfortunate;" wailed the poor girl—"*they* know that I have gone; they will waylay him; they will kill him; I shall never, never see him again. Is there no way for me to get back?—no way?—no returning ship? Oh, in mercy ask the captain; tell him I will pay him any price—and yet—it would be madness to return. Oh! why was I born to be the sport of fortune?"

All this time the stewardess was looking on pityingly, but wondering.

"Dear young lady," she said again, in her soft, soothing voice, "it can't be helped; don't weep so—you will be very ill."

"I think the captain is to blame; it was cruel, cruel in him not to send the men back; I will never forgive him, never!" she cried, the Spanish blood mantling her cheeks—her large eyes flashing anger. "Was it conspiracy? Is your captain a gentleman? an honest man?"

"What! Captain Wyllies? I will hear no word against him," cried the stewardess, almost angrily; "you have no right to blame him. He was worn out, and had to sleep, everybody was busy—they thought *he* would come in another boat, and it was all unfortunate and unhappy, but not on purpose. No one thought of such a thing. I am sorry for you, but you must say nothing against Captain Wyllies, because he is a good man. He would not do wrong for the whole world."

At that moment, the captain himself appeared. He looked quite pale and troubled.

"My dear young lady," he said, "this is very unfortunate; I assure you. I would give a great deal, if I were back in the harbor of Havana, this minute."

His frank, honest face, and real concern of manner, banished any lurking suspicion that had troubled her mind before.

"O captain! I can hardly think how to do or act," she said, her hands working over each other uneasily, her lips quivering.

"I think, under the circumstances, you had better let things take their course," he replied. "There is no way for you to return, unless I chance to speak a vessel bound to Cuba, and that is extremely improbable. If I do, however, and you should desire it I will place you on board. Very likely, Mr. Goreham was detained by some of the custom-house officers, who had, or thought they had, some other formalities to go through with, and he will take the first vessel bound for home, so it will only make the difference of a few days, perhaps even hours. I advise you to look upon the bright side, and be as cheerful as you can about it, every thing will come out right. There were several vessels ready to sail today, and be assured, he will take one of them. His anxiety will be almost equal to your own."

"Oh, but he knows where I am," said Minerva, piteously.

"And for that reason, his mind will be so much the easier."

"While I am deplorably in the dark, with reference to his fate," she added, the tears falling.

"I'll trust Goreham," said the captain, cheerily; "he's a wonderfully keen young fellow, and not one of the sort to get into scrapes. Don't you worry, we shall have a splendid run, always, do, with a storm at the outset; and in a week, trust me, you will meet in the good city of Manhattan."

"But—but—he has enemies," sobbed the young girl brokenly.

A dim suspicion of the truth, forced its way into the mind of Captain Wyllies.

This girl, though attired in thorough American costume, needed only the veil, the coquettish fan, the rich full silks and mantle of the Cubans, to transform her into a Spanish woman. Hers were the wonderful eyes of that race, the rich, black, luxuriant hair, the clear olive complexion, a shade lighter, perhaps, than the general line. The cousinship was, after all, a ruse, the two were flying perhaps from jealous rivals, this was the mystery. If so, there was certainly good cause for the girl's alarm. Those Spanish haters strike quick and deep, and fly justice. His pity grew, as the sad consequences of the whole affair flashed across him. Perhaps, the poor child was married, if so, and if harm had befallen him, a sad prospect stretched before her. Helpless and delicate, she seemed entirely unfitted for sorrow, or for labor. These thoughts, of course were his own, and rapid as lightning. They did not show on the surface, in troubled glances. On the contrary, the captain consoled her so much the more, as his own hopes fell. He assured her that he could look out for her comfort, and interest himself in her future fortunes. Bandola, he would relinquish to her. "She is a good girl," he said, "a *protege* of mine, and I'm going to educate her. She is not ignorant, now," he added, laying his hand lightly on her head, "so she may be some company for you. Cheer up, young lady, I prophesy a renewal of your happiness, on your return. I feel almost certain that young Goreham will meet you there."

Unconsciously, the happy, earnest manner of the captain, infused new hope into the sorrowful heart of Minerva, and, though she could not quite divest herself of her melancholy forebodings, yet she did not allow herself to give way to them.

CHAPTER III

The General and His Household

General Leindres de Monserate was one of the grandees of Cuba. A little man, shrewd, and sharp of feature, with nothing noticeable about his face, save a pair of magnificent black eyes, that, when he was pleased, wore a soft beauty, rare in the eyes of man, but when deepened by passion, their very repose was fearful. The general prided himself upon belonging to the *ancien regime*, and the scrupulous nicety of his white cravat and spotless dress coat accorded well with his polished manners. His dwelling, though one of the handsomest and most spacious on the island, did not look pretentious on the outside. It was within, that his ideas of magnificence all centered. The sun and the stars, could he have brought them down, could hardly have contented him with their brilliancy. The softest and most glittering fabrics, composed the hangings of his rooms, every thing was elaborately gilt, and yet good taste was predominant.

His conservatories were miracles of beauty and profusion, in which birds from every clime sported among rare, strange flowers, and fountains leaped in silvered spray to the crystal roof, keeping along the margin of the water, a continuous musical vibration, that made one hold the very breath to hear. The trees along the margins of his avenues glittered with golden fruit, and in front of the house bloomed the Tahiti almond, the mango, and the cedar.

General de Monserate, was literally the reigning head of his little household. Even his sister, Mancha, an angular, little, black-eyed woman, who would domineer over a kitten if she could find nothing else, was a mere cipher in her brother's presence. The rest of his family consisted of a niece, partly of Spanish, partly of English blood, a girl of seventeen, and a young man, whose guardian the general was, a fiery, passionate, and extremely elegant personage, and possessing an immense fortune in sugar estates and slaves. The general, in his own right, was poor; but through the favors of a will in his possession, obtained money enough to gratify all his nefarious and extravagant tastes. An old housekeep, with drooping eyebrows, served doggedly under Senora Mancha; a bright eyed octoroon was the dressing-maid of Senora Minerva. Don Carlos had his valet, and four or five black attendants, and the old general was seldom without his full complement of servants. The house was generally very gay, as the young senorita had not been long from one of the best American schools, and played and sang charmingly, besides possessing a variety of other accomplishments.

Preparations were evidently going on for a great party at the general's homestead. The servants were continually bearing hampers to and fro from the kitchen (which was a separate building) to the main residence. A happy set they seemed, showing huge ivories as they cracked their jokes, although they sweated under the apparent weight. The general's beautiful volante was oftener brought round than usual, sometimes occupied by the old gentleman himself, sometimes by the dashing Cuban, Don Carlos. Handsome as was this latter personage, an evil look permeated his countenance. His eyes, black and lustrous, pierced like stilettos, and had all their murderous keenness. A thick, black mustache covered his lips, save one dark crimson line; his forehead was low but massively shaped, and in bright black clusters, the curls grouped themselves about it. Every one has seen such men, men whose faces they at the same time admired and detested, and from whose attentions, if of pure mind and correct principles, they instinctively shrank. Once, as Don Carlos drove out of the courtyard, he turned and lifted his hat, at the same time smiling and bending. The young senora sat in the window, from which she had been throwing crumbs to a pair of Barbadian doves. She returned the bow, but at

the same moment turned back with a pained look. Her maid, who was intelligent enough to make somewhat of a companion, noticed the motion.

"I wonder what wedding Signor Carlos is going to attend?" she said smil-
ingly.

"Wedding!" the young girl spoke with pained surprise.

"I heard them talking about it, the general and Don Carlos, when they knew
nothing of my being near. It is to take place tonight, at twelve."

"Tonight at twelve," murmured the senora, looking blankly at the octoroon;
"tonight, at twelve, did you say? and my uncle?"

"Both of them," replied the girl, with a strange glance, "are to take part."

"They will never be so uncourteous as to leave their guests!" exclaimed
Minerva, her color heightening.

"No, they will not need do that," was the response.

"What do you mean, Althea!" asked the young girl, now thoroughly roused,
and not a little frightened. "There is something you wish to tell me, but dare
not. Don't leave me in suspense. My uncle and that man have been plotting,
I am sure of it; and oh, Althea, you would not see me suffer, if by a word you
could prevent it."

"No, indeed, my dear mistress," said the girl, "you shall be saved, if any word
of mine can do it. Tonight, Padre Rouez is to be here, and Heaven only knows
how it could be done, but you would be married."

Trembling from head to foot, the girl sprang from her seat, and began pacing the room.

"It would be monstrous," she muttered, "but they would not scruple, as
Althea says, it would be done,—I believe it. Now there is only one way to act,
I must appear to acquiesce, or my doom is sealed. Little they think that by
twelve o'clock, I shall be passing away from their hated influence. Althea, bring
me pen and ink."

The girl placed both before her. Steadying her hand, and controlling the
indignant impulse that almost shook her, so wronged did she feel herself, she
wrote, as follows:

> "Honored Uncle:
>
>   I have overheard that I am to be married tonight, at twelve. This anticipation
> of an event, which for some time I have known you to consider quite near,
> should not be approached without due reflection. I ask, therefore, that you will
> allow me to remain in the solitude of my own room, until the hour of mid-
> night, that I may more fitly prepare for the solemn duties about to be put upon
> me. Be so kind as to let me know by written word, whether or not, you comply
> with my request.
>
> Your niece,
Minerva Monserate"

In a few moments the octoroon returned, and handed a note to her mistress. The seal was hastily broken, and the senora read:

"Best of Nieces:
  You have my full consent to spend the evening as you choose. I will excuse you to our guests. I will send you a case of jewels that belonged to your mother. Accept my kindest wishes for your happiness.
                                        Your ever obliged, Uncle."

The senora tossed the letter from her, with a contemptuous gesture.

"Nothing else could be done," she murmured, below her breath. Then she turned to her dressing-maid.

"I have obtained permission from my uncle to remain at home, till the expiration of the time set for my wedding. You need not look so strangely, you see I am quite calm about it. Don Carlos will make a noble bridegroom;" the sneer was but half concealed.

"He is not noble; there is nothing noble about him," said the girl impulsively.

"Well, well, noble or not, you see how the case stands. I am not going down to this party—"

Althea started. "Not going!" she repeated.

"No, I shall stay in the solitude of my chamber, the greater part of the time," returned the mistress.

"And your beautiful ball-dress! Oh, not to wear it at all!"

"You forget I am to be married," said Minerva.

"Yes, but it will not be happy. You look anxious and pale, while you talk about it. Besides, it is mean in them to cajole you into it."

"Hush! Althea, remember you talk about my uncle. By the way, is that sister of yours still alone?"

"All alone," was the answer.

"And would you like to stop with her tonight?"

"What! of all things! tonight! When you need me so much? No, no, no, I can go just as well tomorrow. I shall want something then to take off the heartache, because, if you are married, you will go away."

"In any case, I shall," replied the young girl. The octoroon watched her mistress narrowly, as she said, "I wish you may carry a happy heart, wherever you go."

"Thank you, Althea. You shall hear from me," murmured the senorita; "good-by, and God be with you."

CHAPTER IV

The Search and the Attack

A beautiful little supper-room, whose table of Indian letter-wood, is spread for three. Enter Senora Mancha, brilliant in a head-dress, composed of red roses, gold foil, and rich lace. Though her face is sallow, her hair is ebon as midnight, and her manners still those of the Spanish nobility. The senora moved to the little stand of marble on which stood an apparatus for boiling tea. In a few moments the steam ascended in graceful curves, white as snow-wreaths. Presently, in came the general and Don Carlos. Punctiliously placing himself at the table, the old gentleman motioned for the rest to be seated.

"Yes, yes, I was never more surprised in my life," he said, as if upon some continued subject. "How could she have learned? I am at a loss to know. I think I can trust my sister."

"I *think* you may;" said the lady with no little emphasis.

"I don't care how it was found out, as long as it is known, and she don't object," said Don Carlos, displaying a magnificent diamond ring, as he helped himself to the delicate wafers near; "but the deuce is in it, too. How comes it that she makes no appeal, confesses no disinclination. My dear friend, I fear there's treachery at the bottom. Still, I am vain enough to believe that her playing off was only a girlish whim, for she well knows that I chose her from a legion who fain would be the mistress of my heart, to say nothing of other attractions;" he added with a sly smile.

"I am very glad the thing is settled at last," said the general, with a sigh of relief. "From tonight, I cease to hate America."

"Not so fast, my dear friend," spoke up Don Carlos, compressing his lips. "I saw Goreham today, radiant in whiskers and white in linen. The presumptuous fool! He was actually in conference with the governor. We are not quite out of the woods yet, general. There are vessels going out of the harbor every night—ay! and tonight."

The old Spaniard glanced up, alarmed. He met the wickedly smiling eye of his ward.

"I am not in the least concerned," said the latter. "It takes a great deal to disturb me. The senora's reproaches, here, even, fall upon me with the soothing influence of balmy showers. If my wife ever has hysterics, I shall study them."

The general nodded his head approvingly.

"As for El Americano, let him look out for himself, if he stands in my way, that's all. But I am forgetting my pretty bird. Senora, oblige me by filling a cup with this charming tea; and now, thank you—ah! with what grace it was done!

Now may I ask a very tremendous favor—that you yourself, with your own fair hands, will take it up to my pretty bird, with my compliments. Do not be frightened, my guardian," he added, as the old senora left the room smiling (for she was not averse to compliments, even insincere ones,) "I have only put in a little soothing powder; it will affect her volition, and perhaps her memory. Under ordinary circumstances, it would but make one sleepy, or more vulgarly speaking, stupid. She will not appear any the less interesting that she obeys implicitly. We shall astonish our guests who do not dream they are coming to a wedding."

The general's sister returned with the empty cup.

"How did you find her?" asked Don Carlos, wiping his mustached mouth, leisurely, with a napkin of exquisite texture.

"Apparently meditating," replied the senora. "She sat with her prayer-book before her, and seemed much pleased with the proof of your thoughtfulness."

"Ah! come round at last, like a good child," muttered the young man; and he opened his cigar case, offered it to the general, and both strolled out on the open balcony for a lounge.

Senora Mancha, however, after ringing in the servants to carry out the table, hurried from room to room to see that all the arrangements were perfect. Flowers bloomed everywhere, and fresher was their brilliant beauty, than the cold splendors of marble statuary grouped here and there. It needed but the flashing of the lighted candelebra to give a bewildering effect to the scene. An hour later and the rooms were revealed in their full magnificence. Soon there was heard the rattle of volantes—by couples came the gay beauties; diamonds, lustrous drapings, bright eyes, nodding plumes, and airy scarfs, with the fluttering of innumerable, gorgeous fans, gave a fairy-like brightness to this vision of Cuban loveliness. Among these throngs, celebrated for their various attractions, moved the elegant Don Carlos, and the stately little general. On this hand and on that, beautiful eager eyes awaited them, for each was, in a Yankee phrase, esteemed a great catch. Many inquiries were made for the Senora Minerva, all of which were skillfully parried or answered. The lady had begged to be excused till a late hour—she would soon make her appearance, etc, etc. Music abounded—the dance went on—the whist-tables were full—singing sounded bird-like, from one of the distant rooms—groups were partaking of ices in another. Suddenly appeared upon the gay, human parterre, Senora Mancha, her yellow face, puckered with wrinkles—her black eyes gleaming a desperate dissatisfaction. Here and there her gay head dress went bobbing, and more than one remarked that there was trouble somewhere.

"Where was the general? Oh! where was Don Carlos? Had any one seen either of them?"

Yes, the general had been last seen going into the conservatory with a countess, rich and distinguished. Possibly he might be found there. Distractedly Senora Mancha hurried to the conservatory; distractingly she looked about. No general. Then she plunged into the crowd again—caught a glimpse of Don Carlos, and made straight up to him.

He felt a pull at his coat-sleeve, and looked round frowningly. Dismay fell upon him when he caught sight of the yellow Mancha, working her toothless mouth.

"In the name of all the saints, what is the matter?" he asked.

"Gone, gone," was the muttered response.

"What! who?" exclaimed Don Carlos, who had not the most distant suspicion of the truth.

"Minerva, your bride."

The Cuban started; turned as pale as death.

"Do you mean that she has escaped! Was there not a watch near the chamber?"

"Yes, in the very next room, but she went from the window. The lace curtain is dreadfully torn, one of the best sets, and how I am ever to repair it—"

Don Carlos broke away, white with suppressed feeling. He soon found the general, and electrified him by saying: "Our plans are thwarted, your niece has escaped us. Do you still remain; I will find her—or—" A gleam of fire shot from his wild eyes. The general seemed struck with stupidity.

Instantly a light traveling volante stood at the door. Don Carlos drove rapidly to the custom-house pier. Springing out when arrived there, he sought out the superior officers. They had seen Herman Goreham only two hours before. He had taken passage in the Eagle, an American packet ship. Yes, there was a lady; his cousin. The Cuban showed his teeth at this.

"Then he has missed justice," he hissed. "He was a spy, the tool of the Yankee filibusters. It had come to his knowledge through papers recently found, a dangerous enemy had been suffered to leave the country. Peace and order were threatened. He had been, this American, the guest of the governor. He had insinuated himself into private confidence; in short, he was a scheming, double dyed villain." Don Carlos was furious. He frightened the officers thoroughly, and in less than ten minutes a private and concealed guard was posted from the custom-house up along the Paseo, and along the walls to the sea. It happened that Herman had landed but a few moments before, and hurried unsuspectingly along for his carpet-bag. The boat lay concealed in the shadow, and the sailors, idly waiting—two of them Spaniards—heard the conversation of the guards posted on the pier, and drew off silently where they could not be seen. Meanwhile, where was the Eagle? There was no time to be lost. A world of shipping lay in the harbor. The vessels all head into the streets. A belt of thick forest—mast after mast stretching away, and bayward, how close the vessels were! Screw frigates, ships-of-the-line, and no telling which is the Eagle. Don Carlos did not despair, however. A boat was in readiness, and slowly and laboriously it was maneuvered between the unwieldy hulks. He could find no boatman at hand, and dared not waste time in hunting one up, therefore he seized a pair of oars himself. Just as he passed under the side of a heavy Spanish sloop, a sudden flush, and a heavy weight made his boat rock again. It was the body of some unfortunate sailor, dead, of the fever, and in the moonlight he watched it sliding off with the current. Superstitious, as all Spaniards are, he regarded this event as a poor omen, and bent his energies toward finding the Eagle, with less hope for success than before. Baffled rage tugged at his heart harder than his hands at the oars, and as he glided from stern to stern, and at each attempt met with failure, he cursed his own fate, and particularly cursed Los Americanos.

Meanwhile, the Eagle had been got under way, and was now majestically making for the sea. Don Carlos had missed the sailors in their return to the vessel—had missed his bride and happiness, but it allayed somewhat the irritation of his mind to learn on his arrival on the pier, that Herman Goreham was a prisoner, and in the custom house ready to be carried to the guardhouse. It occurred to Don Carlos that he would, if possible, make the young man a means of conveying the Senora Minerva into his possession again.

Accordingly, he sought him. The young man stood under guard, looking sternly from face to face, as if still mutely questioning his captors.

"So, I see it all," he said, as Don Carlos came into his presence. "Villain, why have you deprived me of my liberty?"

"That shall be shown," said the Cuban, scowling back at him.

"It is no crime, I suppose, to steal a young lady from her home—from the arms of her affianced husband, on the very night of her expected wedding."

"Thank God! I have saved her;" said the young man, drawing a long breath.

Don Carlos sprang toward him, his hand under his vest, but in a minute he bethought himself and forced his heated face into calmness.

"Young man," he said, falling back, and commanding his temper under the scornful glance of his rival, "I have the power to place you in a dungeon where the light of day can never penetrate—where the walls ooze dampness—where you will have but the solitary crust and the jug of water—where your companions will be the worms and the rats, instead of the birds and the flowers of this beautiful land."

"Very poetical," said Herman, as the Cuban paused a second for breath. The white lips of the latter trembled with rage, but still he did not let his passion master him.

"Or I can give you liberty," he added.

"That is my right. Tomorrow I shall see if a citizen of America is to be captured for no crime; detained against his will by a jealous Spaniard."

The Cuban drew a long, deep breath; his eyes glittered—his fingers worked nervously against his vest.

"You are free if you deliver Senora Minerva into her uncle's custody."

"Impossible. The young lady is by this time on her way to America. The Eagle sailed at twelve. By consulting your watch you will find it is somewhat more than a half hour past that period."

"Perdition!" muttered the Cuban, now growing furious. "You shall answer for this, fellow—you shall rot in prison, or be hung as a spy, while I shall leave no means untried to recover the young lady. For your comfort, know that I shall take the fastest sailer in port, and it will go hard if, with my resources, I do not find the niece of General Monserate. Then, if she be not too much disgraced by your favor, I shall marry her."

It was Herman's turn to repel now. He sprang like a tiger upon Don Carlos, collared him, and before he could be reached, shook him till he was black in the face, and flung him at arms length almost senseless, and panting on the floor. At that moment, General Monserate entered. Herman was struggling in the hold of a powerful soldier. Don Carlos, his dress in disorder—his hair thrown wildly from side to side, his face purple and haggard, for the young American had held a choking grasp, was just rising with the aid of two custom-house officers, from the floor, covered with dirt, and sheet-white with passion. Blood had been shed, and Herman was marched off by the authorities, and thus ended a day that promised so much happiness at its dawning.

CHAPTER V

Minerva on Shore

Minerva Monserate, the young lady left so unexpectedly on board the American vessel, was, as our readers have already seen, the niece of an old Spanish grandee, and consequently of noble descent. We have hinted before, that English and Spanish blood mingled in her veins. Her father had married a young creature, Maria Wells, the daughter of a poor minister of the church of England. Much surprise was manifested at this unequal match, as it was called, but Senor De Monserate, the younger, was by the mere force of his character, as much feared as admired, and when he boldly returned for his travels, bringing his pretty British flower, nobody demurred in his presence, not even the domineering sister, Senora Mancha. The young man seemed very much changed after his marriage—put on the harness of labor, and went to work amassing a fortune. His whole heart and soul seemed absolutely given up to money-making. A child was born—it made little difference; his wife died—there was brief mourning; still he bought and sold, and people began to think there would soon be no end to his wealth. He spent as freely as he made. Though he never indulged in parties, hardly amusements of any kind, he allowed his sister sufficient to cover all such expenses, for in her young days, Senora Mancha was very gay. At last, in the midst of his processes for turning every thing he touched into wealth, he died, but his property possessed such accumulative force, that year by year houses, lands, and ships were added, so that his child was the wealthiest heiress in all Cuba. But of that fact, she was brought up in entire ignorance, as only her uncle, the lawyer who drew up the will, and a very few witnesses knew its conditions. Of this, however, more hereafter.

Minerva had become accustomed to the motion of the vessel which she called her sea-cradle. Though often troubled with spells of long and deep despondency, yet she endeavored to keep before her mind the evident certainty of meeting Herman as soon as they landed, or, at all events, shortly after. Whether she thought the winds would be more favorable to his voyaging, or that love might guide the helm so that both vessels should strike shore at the same moment, I know not; but the fact of the sudden storm having delayed the Eagle, and indeed put her out of her course, gave her expectations a more sanguine coloring. On the day before the vessel came in sight of port, she sat on the deck, her mantle thrown gracefully over her head so that its folds fell in artistic lines over her form. She was knitting, while very near her sat the stewardess, Bandola, reading aloud.

Suddenly the girl paused—the flush of her red blood was faintly visible under her dark skin.

"How I wish I was white, senorita, and had a lover like him. Ah! it must be very pleasant."

"Be contented with your lot, Bandola," said Minerva; "the sweetest rose has thorns, and you might find more sorrow than joy in the fate you covet. The captain says we shall sight New York in a day or two," she added, after some moments had elapsed.

"Yes, you have been there before, haven't you?"

"Oh, yes—twice, and each time stayed three years. I love New York dearly, it is a great, glorious place."

"Tell me what you came here for?" pressed the stewardess.

"For my fate," said Minerva, smiling and blushing.

"Your fate," queried the girl, wonderingly.

"No, no; to go to school. Didn't we have splendid times though, at Madame N—s school? There's where I first saw *him*," she added dreamily—then started, remembering who listened.

"Ah! I hope he will be there. What pleasure to see him standing on shore as the vessel goes in! Oh, I know he'll be there."

"I hope he will," said Minerva, her bright face clouding, as a gloomy doubt shadowed her mind.

"But were there no Spanish gentlemen who wanted you to marry them?"

"Oh, yes," said Minerva, smiling, "one in particular; the richest man in all Cuba."

"And why didn't you?"

"Because I didn't like him—because I detested him," she added passionately.

The shadow grew deeper on her brow; her work fell from her hands. The malignant face of Don Carlos, with its dark, vengeful eyes came before her. What if they had met, Carlos and Herman?—both quick, resolute men. Oh, the sickening apprehension that crept into her heart as the possible result suggested itself. And she alone in the world, poor and dependent, with but the temporary resort to her jewels to keep from famine. Well, better even that than the wife of that horrible man; better to earn her bread, though how those helpless hands were to accomplish such wonders could not even be imagined.

"There, now you are sad again," said Bandola.

"Yes, I was thinking."

"Why do you think? I never think long enough to make me unhappy. The way to enjoy life, I believe, is to think as seldom as you can."

Minerva made no reply to this sally. A dreadful foreboding had taken complete possession of her mind. She could not sit there in the clear breeze, the pure sunshine—but gathering up her work she went down into her stateroom. There, fumbling about the pocket of her traveling dress, she found a little purse, through whose meshes glittered gold.

"Poor, old uncle—he gave me this," she murmured; "he was good, kind, and liberal in all but one thing. Why would he force me, till I had nearly been sacrificed, to marry that dreadful man? What was the fascination Don Carlos exerted over him? I cannot think. Well, at least, I shall have sufficient to pay my passage, and to keep me in some hotel until"—here she paused. She would have added, "until I meet Herman," but her heart felt as heavy as lead when she thought of it. Even the captain's cheerful face and jovial language lacked their pleasant influence for her. She dreaded the sight of the shore, for she had never been so far alone, and now she had none but the captain and poor Bandola to depend upon.

Hearing the step of the former in the cabin, she lifted herself from her painful reverie and went out.

"We shall soon near land," said the captain, cheerily—"but see here, you are looking pale and ill again—I must not have this," and he shook his head.

With great effort Minerva kept back the tears.

"I suppose I must learn to transact my own business," she said, trying to smile, "so I am going to pay you my passage-money." She emptied the contents of her purse upon the table. "There, will you please see if that is enough to cover the expense of my voyage?"

"Tut, tut. Just put that money right back, my dear young lady. I'm the owner of my ship and have no one to consult besides myself—so you'll please oblige me by keeping what little money you have; you will need it all, yourself."

"Oh, I cannot, indeed I cannot be under such an obligation," said Minerva, the quick coloring coming. "I have other means." She faltered. "You will oblige me infinitely by accepting the passage-money."

"But I tell you my young friend, I fully expect to see Herman Goreham in the city of New York, and he agreed with me for the passage, so I shall settle with him, and you must let me have my way, for I generally do when I set out for it. I'm a very resolute man, you see."

Minerva sat quite perplexed and undecided. The captain lifted the purse and sweeping the gold into it, placed it in her hand.

"And now we must talk a little about the future," he said. "It is possible when you land, our young friend may not be visible. In that case where would you like to go? Have you friends or relatives in New York?"

"Some acquaintances, but no relations. I have made up my mind to go to an hotel."

"I know of an excellent private boarding-house," said the captain; but she exclaimed eagerly—

"Oh, not there—among the many I shall be unnoticed. I prefer an hotel; there I can be alone until I know my fate," she added in a lower tone, and with a quivering lip.

"Just as you please, though it is my opinion that you would be better suited in a pleasant family, but I will not attempt to dictate, you of course know best. Consult your own inclination, only remember to come to me as a friend in whatever circumstances of trial you may find yourself."

Two days after that Minerva was driven from the pier to the hotel she had chosen. Almost a stranger in a great city, her heart sank at times, though she strove to think that Herman would surely come—she should not have to wait but a little while. But how should she pass the time during that dreary waiting? Her little room, up many flights of stairs, had a cheerful look-out, but it grew monotonous to watch the ever-passing multitude, the same unvarying round of faces. Her dresses were taken out again and again, but there every thing was finished, and she dared not array herself in other than the plainest habiliments for fear of attracting attention. She little knew how often the question went the rounds, "Who is that beautiful girl dressed in gray, with the dark, Spanish eyes?"

One day she had been unusually sad. Captain Wyllies had been to inform her that as yet he had heard or seen nothing of Herman Goreham. He seemed, himself, perplexed and unhappy about it, and could no longer make excuses. He had come to consult with Miss Minerva—would she return to Cuba? He was nearly ready for the next trip, and he would see her safely back in the midst of her family.

"Never," was her reply, with a paling cheek. "I shall never return to Cuba. Captain Wyllies, you will inquire into this mystery—you will write me whether Herman be alive or—" she could not speak the word.

"Be assured I will use every means in my power to learn of his whereabouts. If there has been foul play—mind, I say *if*—the matter shall be brought to light as far as I have means and influence. I will not leave a stone unturned. Meanwhile if you find spies upon your path, you had better avail yourself of the kindness of a friend of mine, a very estimable lady, who, if you give her this card, will, for my sake be like a mother to you. Do not scruple to use my name, or to call upon me if you are in need."

When he had gone the young girl was more wretched than ever. She passed the time in writing. Seldom went out, and for the lack of exercise, began to grow thin and pale.

One day she was inspired with a sudden impulse to walk to the Battery. So arranging herself in her most unostentatious dress, she walked slowly along, her eyes looking straight forward as if she never again expected to see any thing of sufficient interest to attract their glances. The fresh air, blowing cooler as she neared the water, revived her, however, and brought a faint color to her cheek. A German band discoursed sweet music, and children in bright dresses running eagerly past her, made her heart beat faster with their happy smiles and cheerful voices. But as she hurried by all these and stood looking at the water, the old desolate, homesick feeling came over her. Only to hear a voice that had once been familiar, how sweet it would be! She sat down upon one of the benches, her pale face bayward, and the past with its happiness and its sorrows came over her in a tumultuous tide. She thought of her school-days—of the pleasant little parties of Saturday night when some of the young students who were well known by the principal, were allowed to mingle socially with the pupils. The bright face of Herman with its blue eyes and gold brown hair, seemed even now beside her as then. How little in those happy days she thought of any coming darkness? The merry girls in their bright dresses, all so eager to receive one smile from Herman, the prince of the college, as he was playfully dubbed, came thronging by. Southern eyes and night black tresses—Northern brows and fair golden hair, but he had turned from all to her. She lived over again the happiness of hearing him call her "beloved"—of listening to his voice that seemed to her of all music the sweetest. Noblest, bravest, most beautiful of all the sons of men he was to her! Then he had followed her to the sunny land of her birth. For two burning summers he had braved the pestilence to be near her. Shudderingly she recalled the first time, that Don Carlos thrust his dark presence between her and happiness—the evil hour when he grew jealous of *El Americano*, and became more impetuous in his suit. His dark hints and wicked insinuations sounded even now in her ears. His black, lurid eyes scorched her soul, and recalled the dreadful repugnance that had been sleeping in her heart since childhood when he was her constant tormentor. And now what had he done with Herman? Had he fulfilled his frightful threats? Did the golden hair lay matted in some foul corner, while the eye, bluer than heaven, sent stony glances after that they could never see? Before she knew it, the round tears were rolling from her eyes, and hearing voices coming that way, she hastily threw down her thick veil, and turned her face from the sea. Two young men passed her. She could not forbear one glance, and that sent a thrill of fear through brain and heart. The personage nearest her—tall, straight, and swarthy—was a foreigner. It needed but one glance at his thick, curling mustache and piercing eyes to recognize him. It was Senor Abrates, a Cuban, and boon companion of Don Carlos. Why was he here, following so quickly upon her absence, but as a spy sent by her uncle's ward? The horrible apprehension seized her that she was discovered—that Don Carlos had probably taken the next vessel that sailed after the Eagle, and they were on her track; they would hunt her down as the hound hunts the timid hare. She grew sick and cold at the thought, and gathered her veil in thicker folds. She fancied that the young man half paused as he neared her as if about to speak, and, as she hurried away with trembling limbs it seemed to her that she was followed. After a long, quick walk, however, she ventured to look round. There was no one in sight and she breathed more freely. . .

[In Chapter VI, Minerva gets lost in the city and is rescued by Senor Abrates, who returns Minerva to her hotel and asks her if he may call on her. Later, Senor Abrates tells his sister about his plans to "make the most of this affair." In Chapter VII, Senor Abrates calls on Minerva and tells her that he has come on behalf of Don Carlos but that he is willing to protect her by bringing her to stay with his sister, Dora, at the Abrates home, where she can live in seclusion. Minerva readily agrees, moves to her "new residence" and enjoys an evening with Dora and Manuel that is not even spoiled when Senor Velasquez, Don Carlos's spy, drops by. While Minerva's fears are for the moment put to rest, in the next chapter Denison shifts the scene back to Cuba.]

CHAPTER VIII

Herman Released

*D*on Carlos stood before a looking-glass. Many were his muttered imprecations as he met the gaze of a disfigured face. His right eye rejoiced in numerous colors beside its original black. A wound upon his cheek had not improved the appearance of his countenance. The don was dressed in a gay gown, and from his embroidered cap depended a heavy tassel of gold. His dressing-case was a model of luxurious beauty. Bottles chased with silver and gold—little cushions of satiny softness—brushes with handles of ivory—every thing rich, expensive, and rare.

"The scoundrel! he will pay dear for this," muttered Don Carlos as he lifted a cane from its corner and limped out of the room.

"Ah! welcome down-stairs, my dear Carlos," said the old general, rising with alacrity, while at a look from him, withered Mancha, who was embroidering on a bit of yellow satin, brought a light footstool for the invalid. "And how are you this morning?"

"A little stiff in the joints," said Don Carlos with a disagreeable laugh. "My good aunt, if you would be so kind as to leave guardy and me alone a few moments."

The senora humbly picked up her work and left the room.

"Now, my good friend, what have you heard and what have you been doing?" asked Don Carlos, turning to the general.

"Wonders! wonders!" exclaimed the general, rubbing his hands with intense satisfaction. "The consul has stirred himself in the business, and finds our prisoner guiltless of all conspiracy. My dear fellow, El Americano is to be pardoned instantly on condition of his leaving the country."

"Well?" queried Don Carlos impatiently, in a voice that betrayed that he expected more news of importance.

"Listen; this is my plan. I have bribed Salvetto, the keeper, and he is to have a private carriage at the door of the jail. There will be two strong men inside with ropes—you understand."

"And they will strangle him,"—cried Don Carlos with fiendish joy.

"Oh, no; not so bad as that. We would not commit murder, my boy, because I am old, and the sin would weigh heavily on my conscience. You have heard me tell of La Vintresse."

Don Carlos nodded his head.

"It was once the most magnificent estate in the environs of Havana. Ah! many a splendid party have I given there, but fire and the cholera and the hurricane have lent their united rigor to destroy it. You have no idea of the complete desolateness of the place. The walls are demolished—the fields have no boundaries—the water has overflowed, and only a part of the house stands, a melancholy ruin, and a part of the negro quarters. In this last, there is a strong room which on the plantation I used as a jail. Ah! you begin to understand. The prospect looks out upon a few stunted palm-trees, the distant hills, and an arid plain. There is not a creature living within a mile, and nobody passes there, for the place has the reputation of being haunted. It is haunted by the spirit of desolation. There is where, at night, I shall have this insulting American conveyed, and he shall learn that he cannot annoy a gentleman with impunity here, as in his own land. Old Jose who is cruel enough for any duty, shall live there and take care of him. Jose has a love for the old place, and is just lazy enough to covet such a life. He was born at La Vintresse, and I have had a room prepared for him. A dreary time it will be for El Americano. He will have no books, no papers, no amusement, little exercise; in fine, he will probably go mad, for I shall take an opportunity to supply him with news, and of no very cheerful kind."

"Guardian, that is a magnificent plan and worthy of your genius," cried Don Carlos, his green and black eyes kindling. "But," his face grew grave again—"we are no nearer to finding Senora Minerva. She has escaped us. Signor Abrates writes me nothing encouraging."

"Have no fear on that score—we shall find her. But I tell you it will not do to trust to others; we must go for ourselves."

"Do not I know that?" cried the Cuban vehemently. "Should I not have been there ere this, but for the vile clutches of that Yankee?"

"Patience, patience," said the general, "you will go there yet. You are nearly well. A sea-voyage will refresh you, and fully repair all damages. I have engaged our passage."

"What!" Don Carlos started from his chair—"and I this figure?"

"I tell you, you will be well enough by the time we land in New York. We will set out immediately to Saratoga, and it will go hard with me but we will find her."

"To Saratoga!—Zounds! no, not there, above all places."

"I tell you, yes; here is a letter found in the pocket of that intriguing Yankee; it is directed to his parents who, I should presume, are vulgar farming people in that same village of Saratoga. What more likely than that she should be found there? Once let me get her in my possession—the renegade child. I'll teach her that she can not lose old friends so readily."

Don Carlos mused. There is something in that he said. "She may have known of the fact that his people lived there."

"To be sure, and there's where she is, snug and cozy, setting them wild about him. We will make their ears burn, my don! We will make her glad to gain once more the protection of a home. As soon as the sun sets, Jose will be here with the carriage. Our volante will also be ready and we can drive immediately after to the Grand Carcel."

The evening was dark and the streets of Havana illy lighted or not at all. It was late into the night when the general and his ward took their seats in the volante, and were driven rapidly after the clumsy carriage that was to convey the prisoner from his dreary confinement to one as much more cruel as it was monotonous. The great building loomed up darkly, standing near the foot of the Punta. Palace-like it reared its regal front, and the dim starlight made it an imposing object. At that moment, Herman Goreham stood at the grated window of his cell looking forth and longing for liberty. In the two months and more of his confinement, he had changed from the self-reliant, dignified man, to the pale, bowed down captive. His cheek was thin, his beard and hair were grown, and in his eye glittered the restlessness of his soul. Captivity was not his only nor his greatest trouble—he mourned over the unknown fate of Minerva. His efforts to see the captain of the Eagle had all been fruitless. Some unseen influence outside his prison-walls, with more money and more power than he, was working him injury. He had attempted to obtain justice by sending a statement of his case to the American consul, but whether it had reached him he did not know. He had been able in this loathsome place, where punishment was regulated by the ability of the prisoners, to obtain a better apartment than the common cells where the sights he saw and the sounds he heard, offended his moral nature. But he was by no means placed in congenial society. His room-mates were, a military man who spent his hours in cursing and gaming, and a planter incarcerated for some political offense, who joined his comrade heart and soul in these elevating amusements. The room was large but not over cleanly. Great webs, black with age and dust, dangled from the cornices. The walls were disfigured with rude drawings and ruder scrawls in Spanish poetry. The floor was dirty and the ceiling obscure. The two prisoners were men of forbidding exterior, who when they found Herman averse to joining in their immoral practices, assailed him with vituperation albeit it was guarded by eloquent and elegant Spanish. He understood it all, for though unable to converse with fluency in the language, he could read it and translate with ease.

Tonight the image of Minerva had been more than usually present and distinct. He had fretted himself nearly into a fever in his vain attempts to imagine what she possibly might do, or where go. In the captain of the Eagle he had unbounded confidence—he knew that she would be placed in a good home. But what if, feeling her lonely and unprotected state, she should return? The thought gave him anguish. Suppose she was already the wife of that intriguing Cuban? It was horror to think. He tried to shut all such images from his mind, but they would return with redoubled vividness. He walked back and forth rapidly, and envied the two sleepers who had thrown themselves upon their cloaks and snored soundly.

Suddenly he heard the key turn in the lock of his cell door. A jailer entered with a *capitan de partido*, or local magistrate. The former held a small paper lantern in his hand and moved with a slow step, as if in the capacity he was, he desired not to be the bearer of good news.

The man came forward with his usual greeting, "Do you confess your fault?"

"I have nothing to confess," was the answer.

"It makes no difference," replied the jailer, calmly—"you are at liberty. A carriage awaits you at the door."

"At liberty!" Charmed words—the young man's face brightened—he straightened himself. "At liberty!" he repeated incredulously.

"You will walk this way if you please, senor," said the man.

Herman followed incredulously. He took down his hat, his linen oversack, and put them on as one in a dream. He moved out into the great black passage-way and felt the wind from the sea strike damp against his forehead. The jailer held up his lamp in the wide entrance. It flashed full in the faces of the general and Don Carlos;—evil omen! For a moment Herman drew back—he feared conspiracy, else why those two of all men, and here at such an hour, close upon midnight? The carriage stood just beyond.

"You are to go immediately from the country, senor," said the jailer.

"Am I to be driven to the pier?" asked Herman.

"I know nothing about it, senor, except that by order of the consul you are at liberty," was the reply, somewhat impatiently.

Herman drew a long breath and stepped out. The carriage door was flung open. He hesitated—placed his foot upon the step—there was a scuffling noise. His worst fears were verified—he was a prisoner gagged and bound.

Don Carlos and the general laughed out loud and long, then drove home to confer together. . .

[In Chapter IX, Minerva feels that she must either leave the Abrates house or accept Senor Abrates's offer to marry her, so she steals away to a boarding house

where she lives under an assumed name. But Senor Velasquez finds her there and declares his love even though he is Don Carlos's agent. She sends him away after pretending to accept his friendship, and then appeals to her landlady for help, vowing to "discolor" herself or stain her face if necessary in order to escape her persecutors. In Chapter X, she disguises herself as an old woman and returns to the Eagle to makes inquiries about Bandola, only to discover that her faithful friend has apparently disappeared. She manages to fool Senor Abrates when he suddenly appears at the ship, but on the way back to her boarding house she spots Senor Velasquez following her and realizes that he has penetrated her disguise. At the end of the chapter, she finds that a thief has stolen her remaining money and worries about whether and how she will be able to eat and pay her living expenses in such dire circumstances.]

CHAPTER XI

The Home of Father Goreham

A plain, white farm-house, nestling down amid trees of a century's growth, surrounded by noble orchards and fields, whose grassy billows were always in gentle unrest, overlooking a sparkling trout stream; in the rear the solid granite hills, with here and there silver tubes of water laid along their rough sides. Such was the home of old Farmer Goreham, or, as he was better known, honest old Ben.

Nothing was wanting to complete the picturesque effect of this woodland home scene. The well, with its grassy mosses mingling with brown, and its high-curved sweep was there; the garden, with its borders of lilacs and roses; its full-seeded sunflowers, browning in the summer heat; its crowing hens and brooding chickens; its bright array of milk pans and cans; its great white and black dog, in leather collar, stretched along, his bushy head on his right forepaw, and the eyes looking up now and then, with almost human intelligence; the long entry, dark and yellow, spotted with straw mats of snowy whiteness; everything bespoke comfort, neatness, and a farmer's rude wealth. The rooms were nearly all of the quaint pattern, large, high-ceiled, and heavily-corniced, with oaken framing, and but one was fitted up in modern style. This was the front room on the east side of the dwelling, and rejoiced in a carpet of rich pattern and coloring; a pianoforte, two or three couches, a beautiful desk of some West India wood, and chairs massive and polished. Here might often be seen little Jessie Goreham, the fair lily of the family, her soft, light hair braided above a brow of surpassing whiteness; her blue eyes wandering dreamily from object to object; her little fingers busily plying knitting-needles, or touching the notes of the piano, her father's birth day present. When she played after the day's work was done, Farmer Goreham might always be found outside of the parlor-door on the broad straw settee, handkerchief over his face, listening to every music-dropping note. Honest Ben stood six feet and four inches. He was a powerful, swarthy-browed, and handsome man; had been a hard, earnest worker, and as laborious a thinker. Authors of wondrous research stood upon the shelves in his library; books that were born of and for capacious and far-reaching intellect were his daily study. His wife was what would be called a gentle, ladylike woman, famous for her house-keeping qualities, and noticeable for her great reverence for her tall husband. They had but two children, Jesse and Herman, their pride, and their greatest earthly blessing.

It was a pleasant, red twilight, just after a refreshing shower. Mrs. Goreham was walking reflectively through rows of early pears, all put up in baskets as white as drifted snow.

"Sarah," she said, to a red-cheeked girl, "I know Mrs. Wise at the hotel would like some of these pears; suppose you pick out a hand basket full, and carry them up in the morning."

"I'll do so," said the girl.

"And don't let anything happen to the eggs again—you broke three this morning. Not that I care for the eggs, but your habits are somewhat careless, and I wish you to correct them."

"Yes'm," said Sarah, demurely.

In the door-way, watching the great piles of drifted clouds, stood Jessie and her father. Both of them wore a touching sadness in cheek and eye. The mother, as she looked at them, grew sad also, even to tears, for she took out her handkerchief, and silently wiped her eyes.

"There he is," said Jessie, in a low, almost broken voice.

"And no letter, I fear, from our poor boy," said honest Ben, as he watched the motions of the coming lad with eagle eyes.

The boy came nearer—handed a letter; the father took it, and shook his head as he sighed, "Not from Herman."

"And nearly five months," murmured the farmer's wife, gently.

"Yes, nearly five months since we began to wonder whether the poor boy were dead or alive. Well, Heaven give us strength."

"We thought so much of him," mused the fond mother.

"If we could hear aught—but this dreadful uncertainty," groaned the farmer.

"Terrible! and in that place where they strangle men with the garotte, for no offense but that of loving liberty," sighed the wife, in response.[2]

Jessie had crept into the parlor, and opened the lately-unused instrument. As she touched the familiar chords, her hands trembled, and the tears rolled down her pale cheeks.

"I can't bear to hear it," said the old farmer.

"Nay, father, let the child alone; it soothes her. She feels the loss as keenly as either of us," pleaded his wife. "Ask her to play for us; it will cheer her up, poor little thing; and he loved music—why should not we? Play, Jessie, play, dear," she called, through the open door; "one of thy father's favorites, my child." So Jessie sat there, and, by the moonlight, played softly all her father's favorite harmonies.

The great corner-clock in the entry struck nine, when there was a hurried knock at the door. It was the post boy again.

"I knew you were looking all the time for letters from away," he said; "and so, as this came in late, I made bold to bring it."

The farmer thanked him. His great, brown hands trembled as he took from the case his silver-rimmed spectacles, and fumbled over the letter long before his eyes rested upon it. He dreaded to read the superscription. Alas! he was doomed again to disappointment. The hand was femininely delicate; it was post-marked New York. He threw it on the table, and turned away impatiently.

"Oh, father, won't you read it? What beautiful writing!" cried Jessie.

"No, I don't want to read it. It's an order, likely, for fruit or butter—it's nothing that I want to see."

"Benjamin, Benjamin, thee must be more reconciled," said Mrs. Goreham, who, having been brought up a Friend,[3] used the language of that sect whenever she felt strongly excited.

"May I read it, father?" asked Jessie.

"Yes, read it, child, read it."

Jessie opened the letter, but she had scarcely read the first dozen lines, when she uttered a great cry of joy.

"O mother! O father! it is of Herman, after all. So wonderful! still he's not found; but she—oh! stop, I'll read it, you'll be so astonished—perhaps so delighted—I don't know; it's very sad;" and thus, alternating from joy to pathos, she commenced as follows:

"Mrs. Goreham—Dear Madam:
I felt toward you the emotions of a daughter when I first heard my Herman (pardon me, but in life or death he is still mine,) speak of the virtues of his sweet mother. I should not take the liberty of addressing you thus, though probably my name is not new to you, were I not driven to the direst necessity. Your son took passage for himself and me in the bark Eagle, from Cuba; put me on board, then returned for some important matters left behind, and I have not seen him, neither heard from him from that day to this. Where he is, how dealt with, God only knows! to that Great Being I have confided him, and await patiently the result. I am an orphan, far away from my family, who have conspired cruelly to unite me with a man for whom I have neither affection or even esteem, and I dare not return, for I am certain the wicked purpose that has been the aim of their lives would be put in execution. There are spies surrounding me, so that I am under the necessity of wearing a constant and disagreeable dis-

guise, and even under that I fear I am recognized. I must tell you the whole of
my miserable story I have begun. I have thrown myself upon your kindness; I
must not shrink, however pride may counsel me. I am compelled to add, that
I have not now, and have not had, sufficient food to sustain life comfortably. I,
who have all my life had delicacies at my command, am starving; my only food
and drink has been a little dry bread and water. There, it is told; my trembling
fingers have performed an unwilling task, but what could I do? If it were not for
the hope I have of seeing him once more, I would give way to fainting nature,
and die; but my faith forbids, and counsels me to take every needful precaution
to sustain life. May I come to you, if only for a while? I should have been the
happy wife of your son, if ill fate had not intervened. I can scarcely guide my pen
for weakness and dizziness, and can only add, that, if on Thursday you will
come, or send for me—for I have no means—you will find me at a grocer's on
the corner of A——— and L——— streets.

Very truly yours,
Minerva de Monserate"

"The poor child!" cried the farmer's wife, tears in her eyes.

"Isn't it terrible, mamma?" murmured Jessie, her fair face troubled, and her
large eyes distended; "it makes me shiver from head to foot to think of any one
suffering, actually *suffering* for want of food, and only think of our abun-
dance."

"Well, what would you do, mother?" asked the farmer, hastily.

"Do? take her home here, the poor child; take her right home. Do you go
after her, father? she shall find rest here; think! she would have been the wife
of our dear boy." Here the motherly heart gave way, her voice faltered and fell;
she arose, and hastily left the room.

"And Herman used to write such beautiful letters about her," said Jessie;
"how I long to see her. He told me I should love her, and I know I shall. Father,
is it not strange? What can we do to find Herman? We must go to Cuba, father; we must search from one end of the island to the other." Her beautiful
eyes were bright and humid with tears.

"Yes, yes, child; but if they have put him out of the way—these Spaniards
are devils when their blood is hot," he said huskily; "I wish he had stayed at
home, the poor boy."

While they were thus talking, Minerva sat in the dimness and solitude of
her own room. Candle she had none, but the moon shone now and then with
a brightness that penetrated even into the somber corner, and played about
her poor, pale face, with its white lips, and burning eyes. Every day for nearly
a month she had known that the prowling Spaniard walked to and fro before
her door, as if fiendishly to intimate that go where she would, he would keep
guard, and be in readiness to deliver her, if possible, into the hands of her
uncle. This unmanly surveillance on the part of her persecutor had worn

down the poor girl, till she had become almost emaciated, and the want of proper food, added to her constant mental anguish, threatened to prostrate her with a long and dangerous illness.

Once the man had written to her—she had flung his letter in the fire. Scores of times he had attempted to see her, but she was resolute, and had never allowed him to enter her door. Weak and despairing, she had give up hope, and looked forward to death with longing. She had even, when the delirium of hunger was upon her, revolved in her mind the different modes of suicide, and once she had actually obtained some charcoal, and closed her doors and windows, in the expectation of putting an end to her unhappy existence. It is strange how often, by the merest chance, the contemplation of a crime becomes suddenly as horrible as it had before seemed plausible. The simple fact of an humble neighbor, sent at the night-time by an overruling Providence, with a basin of soap, with the modest assurance that she had thought the lady looked ill, and would relish it, changed the current of her destiny. The air of the room seemed fierce and hot; its darkness tomb-like, and Minerva, like one waking from a trance, rushed to the windows, and, throwing them open, breathed once more (her tears gushing the while,) the delightful air, murmuring, "I was insane, Father, forgive me! help me to bear the burden till thou shalt see fit to remove it." This little prayer gave her relish for more. Strengthened and comforted by the nourishment, she still farther supplicated that the Almighty would deliver her from the power of her oppressors, and arose, feeling a certainty that in some way help was soon to come. That afternoon she overlooked her slender wardrobe. Noticing that there was some rattling substance in the pocket of an apron, she drew out an old letter, one she recognized immediately as having been written by Herman while he was at his home. "Saratoga"— the name she had tried so often and vainly to remember. An impulse seized her, of which she determined to take instant advantage. She would write a letter to his home—to his mother, and throw herself upon their protection. The idea was as suddenly acted upon, the letter written, and sent as cautiously as she could manage it, and now she gave herself time to think. What the result would be, she did not dare imagine. Sometimes she was bewildered with hope; again, fearing that she might be deemed an imposter, her heart sank; but be as it might, she believed that in some way deliverance would come.

The third day, early in the morning, she dressed herself in her wonted habit, and, taking a few articles with her, set out on her promised errand. The man at whose shop she rested offered her a chair, remarking that she looked weary. He had seen her before, and doubtless thought her appearance as remarkable as it was unique, so singular was the blending of youth and age in her countenance—the gray hair, the large spectacles, the mimic furrows, and the bright young eyes and lips, full, though not blooming. Trembling, even shivering as one in an ague, she sat near the warm sunlight of an August day, waiting, dreading, hoping—above all, hoping! At the sound of wheels, how wistfully she looked forth! Now it was the baker's cart, now a market wagon—oh! after all her longing desires, was she to be doomed to disappointment? Presently a light Jersey wagon, covered, drawn by a handsome gray horse, came by—drove more slowly—backed a little, and stopped. Poor Minerva! her eyes grew dim—she clutched at the counter convulsively. That face—the handsome, brown, kindly face, so like the son's. Oh! she could have shrieked for very joy. It must be for her.

"Is there a lady waiting here to go out of town?"

"Yes, yes," cried Minerva, eagerly; he turned, astonished, glancing at her narrowly, looked at the small, white hand, now ungloved, smiled as he gave another scrutinizing gaze at the oldish bonnet and the odd face, and clasped the little fingers in his, locking his lips together. His eyes shone suspiciously, his lips trembled as he said, "Are you all ready?"

"All ready," she replied, low and brokenly.

"Then come," he drew her arm in his, as tenderly as if he had been twenty-one, and she a bride, assisted her into the wagon, and drove off at a brisk pace. The hunted fawn was free, at least for the present.

CHAPTER XII

Two Arrivals

*T*en minutes had not elapsed, when a lumbering carryall, drawn by an impatient, high, black horse, drove also up to the grocer's store. A man dressed in a farmer's suit of gray, with long hair, that dangled beneath his hat in glittering skeins, keen, dark, eyes, encased by horn spectacles, and a hand singularly small and well gloved, sprang out and entered the store.

"Is there a lady waiting here to go in the country?" he inquired, hastily, after a quick scrutiny.

"You're too late, old gentleman," said the grocer, speaking very slowly, as he always did when he was busy; "she's gone with the t'other old man, maybe he was your brother."

"How long has she been gone?" queried the man, with short, imperative words. His manner offended the grocer.

"Well, it may be half-an-hour, it might be five minutes; I don't keep the run of all the people who go out of my shop, the run of their custom is all I care about," he replied, slower than before.

"So much for the cursed breakage," muttered the man, as he walked to the door, and scanned first up and down the street. "If the rotten shaft had held good, just twenty minutes longer, she would have been in my possession, now it remains to head her off in that direction, and that will be difficult."

As he said this to himself, he had sprang into the vehicle, showing a row of teeth, glittering and white as milk, while his upper lip, shorn of a recent mustache, proved by his quivering jerks, the agitation of his mind, and the fierceness of his temper.

Meanwhile, the gray had cleared the lower part of the city, before the old farmer turned his attention from the prospect before him. Then, when they were past all danger, for the horse was spirited, and pricked up his ears at the sight of a bridge or railroad track, he said, pointing to the bottom of the carriage, "There's a little basket there, mother put me up a few sandwiches and cakes, for, to tell you the truth, I started without my breakfast. Perhaps you will help me eat them, it's not so pleasant to eat alone."

Minerva thanked him, blessing him in her heart for his thoughtfulness and delicacy, blessing him for the food, for she was hungry.

"I must look strange to you, in this disfiguring dress," she said, and as she spoke she lifted the bonnet, cap, and false front from her head. Her own curls fell on the instant in thick masses about her face, that now, divested of spectacles, though white and thin, was still youthful and very beautiful.

"Poor child!" said the old man, and there he paused. The past crowded on his soul, Herman, his face exultant with love and triumph seemed at the moment shadow-like, to sit beside his betrothed.

"You are ill," he added, a moment after, controlling his feelings; "how much you must have suffered! But we'll soon get you up again in our good country-air, clear and bracing, and my little Jessie longs to welcome you as a sister."

"O, yes, little Jessie," murmured Minerva; "he used to speak of her. How I shall love her!"

"I want to talk with you about my boy, when we get home," said the farmer; "I can't do it in the noise of these rattling wheels. But perhaps, if you have found it necessary to wear your disguise, it is not prudent to take it off now, even though we are on the road to the country."

"It seems so pleasant to be free from the odious thing," said Minerva childishly, "but I will replace it, and content myself with the beautiful fields, the clear sweet breeze, oh! how sweet!" She sank back in the carriage, and let her eyes rove delightfully round. Here, for the time, was peace and content. Herman's father had believed her, she was beside him, how strong and beautiful he seemed! And, oh! to be folded to his heart and called daughter; was that blissful time ever to be? should she who had been denied so long know the blessings of a parental love? Quietly she sat there, too happy even to think, wanting to cry out with all her heart at the fresh beauty of the scarlet thorn-berry, and the clusters of ripening barberries, that made the road like a picture, at the yellow hay-stacks in the fields, flinging invisible censers of perfume, at the cottages and farmyards, laughing to herself with an almost infantile glee, as she thought of Senor Velasquez, pacing back and forth, the self-constituted sentry over an empty room. Little she dreamed how near she had been to falling in his hateful power, but the space of fifteen minutes ago.

That morning was one of excitement and anxiety, at the pleasant farm-house. It had been impossible for honest Ben to eat the nice breakfast, so neatly prepared by his wife, and Jessie was fluttering from mother to father, restless almost to tears. She did cry a little, when her father set out, and said, with her last kiss, "Be *sure* and bring her, father."

Her mother seeing that she grew more nervous as the time wore on, planned that she should carry some little delicacy to the sick lady at the hotel, and put up for her some of her choicest fruit. Mrs. Wise had been an early friend of Mrs. Goreham, and in her sad illness had wished to be near her. Jessie was an especial favorite with the sick woman, and she loved to see the bright, young face in her darkened chamber. Jessie was there perhaps an hour. She came home brimful of news.

"Mother, what do you think?" she exclaimed, her voice eager, her eyes shining; "who do you think has come to the hotel?"

"Some great personage, I should judge, by your manner, my daughter," was the quiet reply.

"Yes, a general with a long name, a Spanish general from Cuba, and there's no telling how rich he is. They say such quantities of baggage as he has brought, and so many servants! I saw a chariot myself, or rather, Mrs. Wise called it a volante, open; and the harness glittered with silver and gold, and there was a negro sitting on one of the horses, I declare I never saw such a splendid uniform—and—"

"Livery, my child," said Mrs. Goreham.

"Oh, yes! well, it was as brilliant as it could be, and such horses! I thought father's gray was the handsomest horse I ever saw, but these are both milk-white, two beauties. Then there's a sister, I haven't found out yet whether young or old, and a very handsome Spanish gentleman, Mrs. Wise says, though she don't like his eyes."

"Well, and what does it all amount to?" asked the mother, not at all dazzled by this enumeration.

"Why, nothing—that is," said Jessie, slowly, hesitating as she wound the blue strings of her hat round and round her finger; "of course they are people of distinction and wealth, *enormous* wealth, Mrs. Wise says."

"But there are a great many people of wealth and distinction, here," said Mrs. Goreham.

"Yes, but nobody has made such a sensation, so Mrs. Wise says; everybody is talking about it, and he has engaged almost a whole floor, two parlors, three or four bedrooms, and two or three rooms besides. They have their breakfast carried up to then, for I suppose they feel themselves too good to eat with the rest of the boarders. Mrs. Wise says she heard they carried their priest with them, for they are all very pious. Oh, dear! How I should like to see them!"

"Some one is coming, I shall like to see far better," said Mrs. Goreham, rising and shaking out the folds of her dress; her quick ear had detected the sound of coming wheels.

"Oh, patience, me! yes, I'd almost forgotten," said Jessie, with flushed face; "I wonder who she will look like? I wonder if I shall like her? Oh, dear!" and her little face fell again; "these great people came from Cuba. I almost hate the name, but, perhaps, why, who knows, they may help us find Herman?"

Mrs. Goreham smiled sadly at the ludicrous idea. That these grandees were in any way connected with the fate of her boy, a plain farmer's son, never remotely occurred to her mind.

The wheels were nearer; even father's voice could be heard speaking to the boy who tended the gate. The mother fell back a little; Jessie grew very solemn as the carriage came in sight. At first only the portly form of the farmer was visible, and Jessie was ready to cry out with disappointment, but in another moment it was plainly to be seen that a woman occupied the seat behind.

Minerva had disengaged her uncomely disguise before she was handed out. The flush of expectation crimsoned her cheeks—her eyes were eager, large, and bright as diamonds.

"See what I've brought you home," said the old farmer. His wife received the stranger with open arms, kissed her fondly, pressed her hand with earnest love. Jessie put her arm around her, thinking to herself, "Oh! how beautiful! I am sure I shall love her dearly!"

"Take her right up stairs, Jessie, daughter," said her mother, gazing with yearning fondness on the gentle girl for her son's sake, "and when she has rested, both of you come down to breakfast."

It seemed like heaven to Minerva, after her prison-like life, thus to be brought into genial sunshine, among simple, kindly hearts. She looked around the large chamber so scrupulously clean—everywhere only white, from bed-hangings to the lilies resting in clear crystal on the mantel-piece. She looked out—there were no lawns, no fountains, no ornamental grounds, but the handiwork of the great God, grander than all the arts of men, was stamped upon crowned hills, and the blue and amber skies.

"This is rest," she said to Jessie, who was as fully occupied as she could be in gazing her fill at the lovely stranger, and wondering so heartily where Herman could be. And when they went down stairs to the simple luxuries spread out before them—the fresh honey, the stamped butter, the white breakfast-cakes, Minerva thought she had never seen so much elegance. Meantime the farmer and his wife, after consulting together about her, had determined that she must still be kept as secluded as possible, and that every means must be taken to restore the faded bloom to her cheek. That evening, the farmer held a long consultation with her. He did not dare to tell either her or his wife that he had just heard how a vessel had been wrecked off the coast of Cuba, at or near the time that Herman had intended to sail. . .

[In Chapter XIII, Manuel Abrates and his sister Dora decide to go to Saratoga, where Manuel secretly hopes to meet Minerva. In the chapter that follows, Denison moves the action to Saratoga.]

CHAPTER XIV

The Cuban Lion at Saratoga

A picture of indolence and high life almost unequaled. A long, private parlor, gorgeous with upholstery, some of which is imported expressly for the use of the occupant. The high windows, rich with hangings of gold-embroidered lace. A lounge of crimson velvet, drawn up to the central casement, and reclining thereon in voluptuous elegance, Don Carlos. Nothing could be more splendid than the oriental magnificence of his costume; it is an emulation of princely expenditure. It flushes if he lifts an arm as if embroidered with gems. The light trembles from shoulder to hem if he but moves. An amber pipe, gold-mouthed, and falling in many serpentine folds, is gracefully suspended from his lips. His smoking cap is of massive gold braid, with perhaps here and there a jewel touching its points. He is the king of loungers, this Don Carlos, with unbounded wealth—this heir to luxury.

He has been out today, but no languid and well-dressed belle was honored by a seat at his side in the beautiful volante. It has not yet come to that. The don uses his gold, brilliant-mounted eyeglass, now and then, drawls "rather pretty," and that is all. His selfish heart is steeled against bright eyes—the charmers charm in vain. He is watched through closed shutters—watching stealthily through half-open doors. The young fledglings go into ecstasies over him—his walk, his air, his bow, his smile, all are perfection. Decidedly he is the lion of Saratoga. And then there is such a romantic story going the rounds, how he is breaking his heart for some fair lady who ran away on the night she was to be a bride—poor man! no wonder he shuns the sex and keeps so much in solitude. And that dear little elderly lady! did you notice her laces? Every day something new, and the plainest far more costly than the richest specimens that adorn the arms and bosoms of the fair Americans. What yellow glances some of those women bestow upon them—deeper than even the chronic jaundice-tinge of the wonderful webs. As for dresses, the ladies might search their wardrobes in vain to find any thing that will approach their marvellousness. She is an object of envy in spite of her diminutive face, and prospective wrinkles. Even the gold-mounted fan is a talisman in her hand. Who could hope to approach that subtle maneuvering that makes every motion a word? And so that is the aunt of the magnificent don, they say, and her diamonds fairly blind one.

Don Carlos still smokes and lounges. On an inlaid table near are the evening papers, which by their rumpled appearance, he has probably consulted. By-and-by he needs something and calls his valet, who is in an outer room, to pull the bell-rope. Marques is a small, yellow man, very handsomely dressed. He walks with dignity up to the cord, gives it a delicate touch, and retires gracefully. One of the servants of the house appears.

"Call my waiter," says the don, with an air.

Presently the waiter, a thoroughly black negro, dressed in white, enters, bowing obsequiously. Don Carlos points to the little gilt basin in which his pipe rests; it needs replenishing. The waiter, with another servile inclination, performs his master's bidding. This only to give an insight into the private habits of the Cuban lion.

A little later General Monserate entered, precisely dressed and perfumed.

"Well, guardy," said the young man, turning upon himself a little as the general threw his delicate frame upon another lounge; "what have you been doing today?"

"Scarcely any thing of importance," was the reply. "I am waiting to gather up my force-we are making an impression now."

"Are we?" queried the don, languidly, casting his eye along his dressing-gown; "well, that is what we came for, you know."

"I don't see as we get any nearer to the matter in hand. This story Velasquez repeats in his last letter, leaves us where we were before."

"You mean that Abrates has concealed her?"

"Yes."

"Married her, perhaps," said the don, in an undertone, his face growing gray.

"Perhaps."

"If he has!" murmured the young man, between his teeth.

"What can you do?"

"At least kill him," shouted the don, with ferocity.

A servant came in and handed the general a note, then disappeared.

"Aha!" cried the general, as he read; "this brings news. Senor Velasquez is below-stairs."

Don Carlos started bolt upright.

"Let him come up immediately," he said, taking an easier attitude.

It was not long before the door opened, and a tall man in the dress of a clergyman entered. He was smoothly shaven, wore his hair low upon the forehead, and spectacles of a greenish color disguised his eyes. Both the general and the don expressed by their glances the utmost astonishment.

"We had looked for a friend," said the general, frowning at this intrusion as he considered it.

"And not for an interloper," added the don, haughtily.

The incomer was silent, but with one movement his shining black hair was thrown back, and the spectacles displaced.

"Senor Velasquez!" cried the general.

"Hollo! Old friend," ejaculated the don, laughing heartily. "Where in the world did you study theology?"

"My theology all came out of your books," said the senor, smiling, as he seated himself, "So you did not know me; I was certain you would not. I flatter myself that few can carry out a disguise better than myself. Well, I'm glad to see you. So you thought best to follow my advice, and come here in person?"

"We followed the dictates of our own judgment," said the don, more coolly. "I intended to come from the first; a slight indisposition prevented me, however."

A lurking smile grew deeper on the thin lips of Senor Velasquez.

"Well, what's the business?" asked the don, laying his costly pipe aside. "What have you found out—what do you know?"

"I have by letter given you a precise account of my doings up to the present time," said the senor. "I have now only to exonerate Senor Abrates; she escaped him, as well as myself."

"How do you know?" inquired the don.

"I have seen her," was the reply.

"Where? when?" cried Don Carlos, excitedly.

"Patience, my dear friend," said the senor, softly; "I will tell you the whole story. For some reasons, probably of importance, Senorita Monserate left the house of Senor Abrates. I tracked her to a common boarding-house, where she had taken rooms under the name of Smith. For some time I watched her, waiting for an opportunity to surprise her; but before that could happen, she had changed her name again, and her lodgings. For weeks I tried in vain to obtain an interview with her. I have waited patiently before the house in which she was, for hours at a time. I have tracked her to stores and the post-office, but she was too cunning for me. I have every reason to suspect that she knew me. One day I saw a boy go from the house with a letter. I knew then that she would not venture out. I followed the boy and overtook him. I wished to see the letter—he was not to be threatened, I bribed him; he carefully unsealed it, for the seal was not yet wet, and, for a half-sovereign, allowed me to read it. It was a plan for flight. On a certain day she was to meet the man to whom she had written, and place herself under his protection. Thus forewarned, I thought I might outwit her. I obtained country suit and wagon, and should have assuredly been successful but for the breaking of my shafts in going down hill. The accident delayed me nearly half an hour, and I was in the vicinity of no other carriage. When I arrived there, she had gone. If I had found her"— he paused here, but "*you* would never have seen her," gleamed in his crafty eye.

"Too bad!" muttered the don, making as if he would walk, then changing his mind, throwing himself down again, where he crouched with folded arms, deep in thought.

"Had you no clue in the letter by which you might trace her?" asked the don, excitedly.

"I certainly had," was the reply.

"Well, well; where was it?"

"I have gone beyond the bonds of my contract already," replied Senor Velasquez, evasively.

"Five hundred dollars for the information," said Don Carlos; adding, with a sneer, "you make money on me."

"That's the way I live," was the reply.

"I'll give you a check, now, for the information."

"Well, then, she is at this moment not a hundred miles from this hotel," was the crafty reply.

"I thought so!" exclaimed Don Carlos, springing up. "But where—where?"

"That I must first find out myself," replied Senor Velasquez. "The greatest caution is necessary, now, for she is with powerful friends. In this disguise, however, I hope to succeed. You have, of course, taken the precaution of entering another name on the books?"

"Yes," replied Don Carlos; "the general assumes the name Ameyda, and I that of Don Johan—ha! ha! My venerable aunt, who had the liberty of choosing her own sobriquet, is Dona Marguerita—quite fanciful. Our servants are drilled, so there's no fear, unless the lady sees our precious faces."

"That is all well; in my ministerial character, I flatter myself I can succeed in reaching her presence. This much I have learned, that she is in a large farm that is very favorably situated for the purpose of abduction; for it must, I fear, come to force at last. Leave me alone to manage by what artifice I can best serve your purpose. In the mean time, we are to have two more of our friends here, Senor and Senorita Abrates."

"How do you know that?" inquired the don.

"Their names are booked. I don't doubt but that they will be here today."

"I remember the little senorita," mused Don Carlos; "she was a pretty little thing, and quite took my fancy. Of different stuff from Senorita Minerva, she would allow caresses; while my little playmate (a shadow crossed his forehead), what a life she led me! But I will show her yet whose turn it is to be master. . . ."

[In Chapter XV, Ben and Jessie Goreham go to Washington to visit family and make inquiries about Herman. After they leave, Senor Velasquez, who is masquerading as a minister who once knew Herman, visits Mrs. Goreham and obtains a private key to the Goreham grounds. In Chapter XVI, Dora becomes the "belle of Saratoga" and flirts with Don Carlos, who seems to be infatuated with her but who reassures the general that he will not be satisfied with such "small game" and still plans to force Minerva to marry him. Then, in Chapter XVII, Senor Velasquez plots to abduct Minerva and take her back to Cuba on a ship whose captain has been told that Minerva is a madwoman.]

CHAPTER XVIII

An Abduction

*M*ore than a week had elapsed, and Minerva sat at the window of her large cool room, reading one of Jessie's innocent letters. She was having such capital times. "O! Minerva could not begin to imagine how happy she was. She found that her uncle, though very rich, was not at all proud," she said, "and his daughters though they were educated at the convent (didn't it seem funny though?) were as good Protestants as she was. And oh! she had actually seen and shaken hands with the president; and had been to the White House with her cousins, and such an array of splendid dresses, fair faces, and noble-looking men, she never saw before. She had visited every place of interest, had been to two or three parties, and oh! she was perfectly wild with pleasure. But the best of the news, and what she was sure would seem to Minerva more glorious than all, was, that the men with whom her father held audience, were to see what they could do in the case of dear Herman. There had been so much fuss of late with filibusters, and all that sort of thing, that they supposed he might be imprisoned by the officials of Havana, or be the victim of private malice; in either case, they would do what they could." Then followed words of love and caution, so that Minerva sat with tear-filled eyes, quite happy, looking out upon the beautiful prospect. Her faith in seeing Herman again had strongly revived—perhaps I should say *strangely* revived, by as simple a thing as a dream. She had heard his voice—the tone was that of gladness. She seemed to be brought to his side as by a miracle. To her he looked for hope, for help, almost for life. Never had her heart beat with such mingled emotions as when she awoke from that vision. She was so happy! She felt almost as if wings had replaced her slower powers of locomotion, and she could hear still the whisper of his voice through the quiet air.

The time was after dinner, nearing three o'clock of the afternoon. When she had read Jessie's letter, she hurried into the room of Mrs. Goreham, who was partially an invalid.

"Are you well enough to walk, this afternoon?" she asked.

"Not quite," was the reply. "But don't stay for me, your exercise is so limited, that I dare not have you give up your walk. Take Bruno, and I am sure the gardener's wife will go with you."

It was a lovely afternoon, and Minerva longed for the solitude of the great oaks, where she was wont to rove. Truth to tell, it suited her best to be alone, though the company of the good farmer's wife was no intrusion, for her tastes were refined, and her conversation was instructive. She left the room silently to prepare herself, and on the way met the gardener's wife, who to her response "*Be* you going out?" received no reply, save the quiet, "yes"; for Minerva

could not run the risk of spoiling a lovely walk by the common-place society
of the fat gardener's wife. So, after throwing on bonnet and mantle, she saun-
tered through the long, shaded entry, out upon the shadowed grass plat, covered with snowiest laces, and called Bruno. At the sound of her sweet voice, the
dog, who was lying near his house, at the farther end of the garden, sprang up
with a joyful cry, and ran toward her. She patted him on the head as she stood
there, a pretty picture, her dark curls blown about her cheek by the breeze,
and the dog with half-human eyes, fixed upon her beautiful face.

"Bruno, will you go with me for a walk?" she asked, showing the little book
that she usually carried upon such excursions.

The dog gave a sharp bark, that might have been interpreted "yes."

"Well, come along then, but you must not run; here, here, stay close beside
me, for I have no other protector but you, today."

The faithful creature surely understood, for he fell back on the instant, and
moved with her step for step, looking momently up as if he said, "you see I am
trying to take the best of care of you." Quietly they walked along the grassy
path that led to the broad fields. These they passed, under the shade of the
apple-trees that lined either side. The low hum of insects in the under-brush
and along the hedges, the quick, soft twitter of birds in the branches overhead,
the ripple of a brook not far off, all these combined to add the delightful re-
flections with which Jessie's letter, so sweet, so guileless, had filled her mind.
They passed here an orchard, with its wealth of ripening fruit, there a patch of
some choice vegetable, and again, a field of waving corn. Presently, the paths
became more like roads. A thick and pleasant foliage came soon in sight, and
the cool smell of the groves greeted the senses deliciously. A light stile taken
down—Bruno had leaped it previously—and Minerva was in her favorite
haunt. How silvery green the trees were, with the sun sending, between their
branches, soft pencil-rays of light! Far as the eye could reach, there was a roof-
ing of green, for here the beautiful elms had been trained in arching sprays,
that met, forming lines of beauty. Away, on every hand, these cool, dark paths
extended, and seats were placed at intervals, for resting places. Minerva strayed
on, smiling to herself, and talking to Bruno for growling, as he went.

"Bruno, you're a bad, naughty boy; did you know it, Bruno? And Bruno, I
shall report you to your master, when he comes home, your *young* master, I
mean; fie, fie, stop growling, you ought to give a laugh-bark, when I speak of
him, did you know it, sir? I wonder if you'll remember him, you bad boy! of
course you will, though, a year's absence doesn't matter much to a dog, does it,
Bruno? What! growling still? What is it at, I wonder? at the beautiful pieces of
blue sky up there? or the scent of these sweet wild flowers? for shame! a great,
intelligent dog like you, to see nothing lovely in this charming place! Is it a
snake, Bruno? I wonder what can ail the creature? He has done so three or four
times, lately. Who's here, Bruno, good dog! you'll protect me, won't you? Yes,
yes, fine old Bruno, only I don't half-like that growling," she added musingly.
"Of course there's nobody here, but I'm nervous, I believe, nevertheless, ah!"

She uttered a short, shrill scream, and sank back, pale, almost helpless. The report of a gun had sounded near, and alas! Bruno, the good, noble dog, had rolled at her feet covered with life-blood.

"Oh, my God, protect me!" cried Minerva; "Oh, Heaven, which way shall I go?"

"Not that way, for your life," cried a deep voice, and in another moment, the man in green spectacles stood before her. "Pardon me, madam," he added, in a tone of deep respect, and pointing to the path he had come; "I think there are villains there. Some one is lurking round, this poor creature is a prey."

"Oh!" Minerva shuddered; "what shall I do? I have enemies, dreadful enemies, which way must I go to escape them?"

"Will you trust yourself to my guidance? your friend at the farm-house, Mrs. Goreham delivered this key in my keeping, that I might have an opportunity to inspect the place."

Minerva felt comparatively at ease. Surely Mrs. Goreham would never have lightly done a thing like that, unless she had perfect confidence in the man.

"If you will conduct me home," she said, trembling in every limb, as she accepted his arm, glancing with so innocent, supplicating a look in his face, that his heart must have been a stone, to resist its pleading.

"There is a road not far from here," he paused to listen, as if suspicious that some one was near, "that leads to the public highway; once there, you are safe"; all this time he was leading her rapidly.

"I seem to hear horses' feet," she said; "I am full of terror, oh, it was so cruel to kill poor Bruno! how could they have the heart? Why! here is a carriage in the private grounds, what does it mean? I—" a sponge applied to her lips and nostrils, cut short the sentence, the door was opened, the unconscious girl lifted in, Senor Velasquez entered after, the door slammed to, the vehicle was driven rapidly out, a boy posted at the stile, with a key, locked the gate and threw it into the carriage; in return, the senor tossed him a piece of silver.

When Minerva again came to consciousness, she lay on a bed in the captain's state-room, which had been given up and arranged for her. There was the eternal sound of the waters beneath, the plashing against the vessel's side, the swift, uneasy motion. After a moment of bewilderment, she closed her eyes with a smile, murmuring, "Thank God, it was then only a dream, and we have started, and Herman is on board—"

She glanced slowly around the cabin. It was certainly different in size and appointments from the one she had gone to sleep in. Bewildered and surprised she tried to gather her thoughts as she murmured, "If only Bandola would come in, then I should know; if my head would only stop aching, and Bandola would come."

The door opened, for a moment her heart beat violently, but sank again when she saw enter, not Bandola, but a stout negress, whose face was most unpleasant.

"It was no dream, then," she murmured; "it was no dream. Oh God, help me!"

"What's a matter, chile?" asked the woman, standing off, as if not quite decided, whether it was safe to approach nearer.

"They have brought me here against my will," she cried, bursting into tears, and striking her forehead with clasped hands.

"They always says so," muttered the woman. "Well! So long you's not violent, you'll fare well, chile, but ef you begins to git wrathy, the Lord help ye! ye'll have to have straight-jacket right on, no mistake."

"A straight-jacket—me? oh! what *can* you mean?" cried Minerva, white with new and sudden terror.

"Never mind, honey, on'y try to keep right dat's all. The man as brought you here, told me jest what to do, so you needn't talk none, honey, no use for you to tell ole story, you knows, might's well keep yer grief to yerself."

"God help me! I don't know what you mean," said Minerva, quite despairingly.

"No, no, you never does," said the negress, shortly; "I've seen 'em in irons and jackets and every thing, an they never knows what it's for."

A little light began to glimmer on the poor girl's brain.

"Where are they taking me?" she asked, faintly.

"To Cuby, chile, back to your old father and mother, breaking dere hearts for ye, honey."

"I haven't any father and mother, they both died years ago."

"Oh, no! I 'spects not," said the negress, pleasantly, laughing a little to herself. "If I'd said they's dead, 'poze you'd a thought 'em living, eh? But, don't make no difference, noways, you's going back to Cuby; 'spects you never was in Cuby, neither."

"Oh, yes! That was my home, I was born in Havana," said Minerva.

"Well, that's might reasonable, now, considering, thought as maybe you wouldn't recollect, p'raps."

"I recollect too much," murmured the young girl, grievingly. A moment after she said, "Can I not see the captain?"

"Well, I guesses not, captain doesn't like to go in ladies' state-rooms; if you wants de steward now, he'll bring you any thing you orders. Say, piece of grill chicken."

"Oh, no, no, no," exclaimed Minerva, in tones of intense disgust. To think of food in her misery, was too much.

"Well, I doesn't insist on nothin'," replied the negress; "'xcept ye must be very quiet and still, 'cause there'll be danger to ye, if ye be; but I've known some folks in your state, to be let right down in the water, when de paroxysms come too strong, so try to be still, honey."

"What is your name?" asked Minerva, after she had watched the woman with pitiful eyes for some moments.

"I's called Mrs. Roxy," was the reply. "Well, chile, stop looking at me, yer eyes kinder haunt me; what is it you wants?"

"Oh, Mrs. Roxy," murmured Minerva, plaintively; "won't you leave me for a little while? I should like to be alone for a short time."

"Orders is to watch ye close, chile, see't you don't do no mischief," was the short reply.

"But you needn't be in the least afraid, I'm persecuted by wicked people, who wish to injure me; I assure you, I have all my faculties, I know all about it, and I shall submit, because I must. I am in the power of bad people, and must wait till God delivers me out of their hands."

"All sounds wise and natural," said the negress, "but I ain't no fool, I tell ye, I's seen people jest your way; ye'd never know 'twasn't jest as they said, if want for 'sperience; you see, chile, I's got 'sperience."

For a moment, Minerva was hopeless, but after she had thought a while, she said:

"Will you let me write something with a pencil, and will you give it to the man who brought me?"

"Oh, yes, anythin' in reason, honey; I ain't 'clined to be onreasonable," was the reply.

Minerva lifted the little gold pencil attached to her chain, and wrote as follows:

"Senor Velasquez:

For it must be you, although your disguise deceived me thoroughly; you can perhaps contemplate the act you have performed with complacency. I leave you and your conscience with God, who is the Judge and the father of the orphan. I only beg you, as you hope for mercy hereafter, to let me be alone, whenever I wish. The face of the old servant who attends me is disagreeable, I do not want her in my state-room. Say what you will to them all, I shall put my case in the hands of God, and leave with Him, also, the retribution; but let me not be annoyed with any attendance.

Minerva de Monserate."

The negress carried the note. In a few moments she returned looking somewhat crest fallen. In her hand she carried a folded paper, on which was written:

"Your request shall be complied with, I have given orders."

The young girl smiled bitterly.

"I knew he would not dare to do otherwise," she said to herself.

[At the beginning of Chapter XIX, Mrs. Goreham learns that Minerva is missing and becomes "prostrated" with fear and grief, hastening Ben's and Jessie's return. Soon thereafter, Farmer Goreham goes to Saratoga to confront Don Carlos and the general.]

CHAPTER XIX

—

*A*fter some consultation, the old farmer, whose suspicions had been more than awakened in the direction of the great people at the hotel, decided to go, and, as he expressed it, have a little honest talk with them. He was, accordingly, ushered into the great parlor, during the don's morning lounge, and where the general made it a practice of reading the news. Don Carlos was, as usual, stretched in a silken laziness, puffing slowly at his meerschaum. The don had the civility to nod his visitor to a seat, and then, with a stare of cool impudence, awaited his communication. "I have come on the behalf of a young lady who is a countrywoman of yours," said the farmer, sitting entirely at his ease, and returning the don's cool stare with a glance every whit as cool.

"Ah!" ejaculated the Cuban, while the general's newspaper rattled as he turned it; "what does the young lady wish?" and he puffed again, this time regarding the ceiling abstractly. "I cannot tell what she wishes," said the farmer, whose warm feelings were rapidly getting the better of him; "but in plain terms, a young lady, by name Minerva de Monserate, has been abducted from my home, where she was placed for safe keeping; and, I have no doubt, you know enough of the affair, to inform me if she is in good hands, at least."

The paper rattled again with an exultant motion, while the don, very slowly removing the pipe from his mouth, turned contemptuous eyes upon the farmer, as he said:

"Old man, what do you suppose I know about young ladies who find an asylum at your house?"

"If I knew as much as you do about it, I think I could lodge you in an American institution, such as you have not yet visited," said the old farmer, the hot blood surging to his temples. "It is my firm belief that you are here under an assumed name, and that you have either abducted the young lady of whom I speak, and who was to have been married to my son, for whose disappearance I shall call you also to account at the proper time."

"Old fellow, you are insane," said the don, rising, and insolently stretching himself.

"Don't you call me old fellow, you rascally foreigner," cried the farmer advancing toward him. "We American citizens do not allow even Spanish dons to insult us with impunity."

"My good man," said the little general fiercely, "do you know who you are talking to?"

"Well, yes, I believe I do," replied the farmer with bitter emphasis, standing very straight, and looking terribly grand. "I am talking to men who call themselves *gentlemen*, but have never learned to treat gray hairs with respect. I'd whip my dog Bruno, who is but a brute, if he had so little manners."

"Shall I ring for my servant to show you the way out?" queried the Cuban don languidly.

"Ring for what, you puppy you!" thundered the old man, in tones that drove both the general and the don some paces backward; "ring for your niggers to show me out? If you dared do it, I'd pitch them and you out of the window;" and his great muscles and strong chest quivered for the action, as he threw his arms out. "You'd look well ringing for your servants to show me the way over my own land. The ground these premises stand on (he stamped with his foot) is mine every inch of it; and you and your niggers, all sold, together, wouldn't bring what it's worth to me. You had better take care how you insult a man who is king on his own soil. I came here peaceably, to ask you a civil question, which you haven't attempted—no, nor haven't *dared* to answer, yet."

"Come, we want none of your pretensions," exclaimed the don, sauntering a little as if elegantly indifferent. "We are accustomed to the privacy of our own apartment; and, in Cuba, between *gentlemen*, the sword would have settled any questions of this kind before now, if such words had been employed. You put me under the necessity of ringing my bell."

Like a lion with glaring eyes, the old farmer (who had probably never heard a disrespectful word uttered in his presence,) stood for one moment, his brow flaming, his lips looked like iron, his chest dilated—then, it seemed almost without moving—he gave one lunge, and sent the don off his slippered feet, nearly the whole length of the room; and, before a word could be said, or a motion made, was outside the door. None would have suspected the farmer, to see him nearing his own home, that he had stirred a muscle, or drawn a deeper breath than usual, since he left it an hour before. He felt as if he had done his duty; and, unconsciously, the blow was for his son, whose fate he now, with more certainty than ever, connected with the Cuban aristocrats. At the great stone step he was met by Jessie, who had been watching for him.

"O father!" she cried, "I am glad you have come home."

"Is mother worse?" asked the farmer, standing still.

"No; but there's a gentleman in the parlor waiting for you, and he has been talking with me this half-hour. He knew Minerva and all her family."

The farmer hastened in, followed by his daughter, whose attention had been powerfully attracted by the handsome face of the stranger.

It was Senor Abrates who introduced himself to the farmer. He had heard of the abduction, he said, and, being interested in the young lady, had come to see what he could learn about it. He had been, in earlier years, a playmate of Senorita de Monserate, and both his sister and himself regretted the unpleasant turn which the affair had taken. Understanding, to some extent at least, how matters stood, he believed that the senorita had been forcibly carried away; and the probability of her fate, if she were in the hands of Don Carlos' deceiving agent, filled him with dismay, for he did not believe the latter was at all scrupulous in the fulfillment of his engagements, nor could he believe him under oath.

This testimony placed matters in the most unfavorable light. Tender-hearted Jessie walked to the window to hide her tears, and the old farmer, resting his cheek on his brown hand, mused silently. At last he said fervently:

"Well, I believe I'm one of the Old Testament Christians, for I'm dreadful apt to take judgment in my own hands where I think the Lord allows it. And I've got the faith of those times, too, as well, for I believe the God of Moses will protect that poor child; ay, and bring my son back to me from a foreign land. It may not seem consistent to say that I shall pray for this, when you hear, maybe, that I knocked down that Spanish puppy at the hotel up yonder for his insolence; but my blood is quick, and the man deserved it. Think of his calling his *niggers* to order me—*me* out of his room. I'd do it again."

Senor Abrates laughed heartily, "That makes the second time," he said.

"Why, what do you mean?" queried the old farmer.

"Your son did the same service for him, so I have understood, when, through his contrivance, he was ordered to prison."

"Ah!" said the old man, thoughtfully, "Is that so? Herman was always a plucky boy, but I never knew him to fight. It must have been a great provocation, as in my case; and certainly it is the first time I have ever laid hands on any man."

It is needless to say, that after the interview with the young Spaniard, who promised to leave nothing undone in this matter he could do, the old farmer suffered some remorse for the deed of the morning. His conscience, quick and clear, took him to task, in spite of his self-gratulations on his old-fashioned religion—"an eye for an eye, a tooth for a tooth."

CHAPTER XX

The End of Senor Velasquez

The voyage to Cuba in the Aspinwall threatened to prove tedious. A succession of head-winds and baffling storms, that make the captain protest, not always in the most decorous language, that he believed there was a Jonah on board, detained them daily; and, to add to the general uneasiness, the captain had Senor Velasquez on his hands, sick with what threatened to be a dangerous fever. Day after day Minerva remained in her state-room, until the captain, thoroughly alarmed for his patient, and believing, from the incoherent self-accusations he had listened to, that Minerva's story was the true one, run the risk of her sanity, and sent for her. After some conversation, his brow cleared.

"If I had known this sooner," he said, "I should have let the villain die, for he is not fit to live. Here I have been nursing and doctoring him, giving him the time my duties absolutely required, and all for a lying imposter."

"What can I do?" asked Minerva, anxiously; "I am tired of inaction. Let me aid you in some way."

"You," exclaimed the captain, with some vehemence; "I'd see the wretch rot before you should help him. What! after he has tried to murder you by inches?"

"I am required to help my worst enemy in his need," said Minerva, gently. "That, at least, I have learned in all my troubles to cherish no malice, and to return good for evil."

"Well, I'll be blest, then, if you ain't a thorough-going Christian," said the sailor, in his rough way; "nothing else could do it—no," he added, sotto voce; "and, even then, nothing else but a woman!"

So, when she was able, Minerva took her post by the state-room in which Senor Velasquez lay. Frightfully changed he was in the short struggle he had had with the fearful typhoid. When the delirium was on him, he talked much of Minerva, and exposed his plans with diabolical minuteness. One night, Minerva, whose state-room was opposite, heard the name of Herman on the frenzied lips. The moon threw its silvery light in at the stern windows, so that every object was clearly visible, and Minerva, anxious to hear whatever concerned that beloved name, glided softly from her state-room and crept to the other side of the cabin. The negress, who was employed as nurse, sat on the floor just beyond the door, asleep, her bowed head resting on her folded arms. Senor Velasquez was talking very softly now, so that Minerva crept closer and closer to listen. Terrified at his face, she turned her eyes from the ghastly picture. The steward had shaven his head, and his eyes weirdly wild, large and ebon, rolled from side to side in their loose sockets.

"Yes, yes, Don Carlos," muttered the sick man, "I'll keep the secret of La Vintresse. Are you sure you have him safe there? Los Americanos are very cunning—very strong! Ah! old Jose is with him, the treacherous old dog! He knows how to torture—let the prisoner look to it—La Vintresse. I was there myself once—heaven preserve me from the recollection! The walls were half down—rotten posts stood tottering, sunk at their base in pools of mud and water. There was not a green spot—the man will die of desolation. He will choke himself with his own hands; he will beat his brains out against the horrid walls; yes, yes, he will go mad!"

Minerva listened shudderingly. Presently he broke out in a wild cry— "Bring the priest!" It was a strange fancy, but, nevertheless, it occurred to Minerva to repeat the word "confess."

"Ah!" cried the senor, eagerly, "are you here, holy father?"

"I am," said Minerva, in a low voice.

"No, no—but stop—I see the crown of your head—yes, yes, the shaven head, and the rosary, and the robe"; and here began a confession, now and then coherent—at times too shocking for human hearing, but still the shrinking girl listened in the strange silence that was not silence, for the waves, as they washed up, answered the sick man's moan. At last he came to his later life. "Father," he said, "listen. I wanted the girl, and I was promised a fabulous sum if I secured her to the old general, her uncle. But I was cunning," he added, in a tone of triumph; "I made them pledge the money to me, and, after all my planning and theirs, I meant to marry her myself, and secure the fortune. Half should have gone to the church, holy father, so I should be absolved. I put her on the vessel, I carried her to Cuba, and there the fiends got me. See!" he cried, for the confession had gone from his mind, and his raving grew so fearful that Minerva was obliged to waken both the steward and the captain. Their tardy steps were, however, too late; the state-room was empty, and the black nurse sat crouched up in a heap, her eyes glittering with terror while she cried, "O captain! the devil! the devil!" The man at the wheel averred that something, either man or ghost, came up the cabin stairs and flung itself over the ship's side. In an instant every measure was taken, every effort made to recover the ill-fated Cuban—the tool of worse men than himself—but all in vain; the miserable man had gone to the bottom in the midst of his iniquity, with all his sins on his head.

CHAPTER XXI

La Vintresse and the Rescue

Minerva had scarcely recovered from this shock, when the pleasant shores of her birthplace came in view. The scene, however, brightened her drooping eyes, and gave a little color to her pale cheek as she saw the tall Castle Moro; the flags and the signals; the houses so near the water; the innumerable masts of a heavy commerce. Her plans had been well matured. Secure in her very loneliness, she did not fear for their ultimate success. The captain was ready to stand by her, and, indeed, he would not allow her to leave the ship without close attendance. How strange, and yet familiar seemed the surroundings, as she drew near the place of her former residence. But for the bitter reminiscences connected with past scenes, she could have kissed the smooth trunks of the gorgeous palms. The city was unusually silent; it was the fever-season, and, in addition, they heard that the cholera had broken out with dreadful violence. The house, as they drove up the grand old avenue, had a deserted look. There were but few servants left, and the main building was closed. Minerva went round the wide veranda till she came to the kitchen enclosure. A woman, on her hands and knees, was fanning with her breath a few white coals, while beside her laid a bunch of herbs, and a pan of water. In another moment the flame darted up. The servant turned impatiently at the sound of a footstep echoing through the hollow dreariness of the great cook-room.

It was Bandola.

The girl gave a shriek of mingled joy and terror, sprang to her feet, looked on all sides with vague fear, ran toward Minerva, and fell, weeping, on her shoulder.

"Oh! it is you, then! I never, never expected to see you again. It is too much joy—I shall die of joy."

"No you won't, Bandola, you must live to help me in my plans. Do you want to go back to America?"

"Oh! God knows!" cried the girl. "Do you think I have never given your letter to the consul? It has almost killed me. Don Carlos came on board when the vessel was in port, and what he said I know not; but the captain told me to go with him, and here I have been kept as a prisoner all these months. I know they have been months, though they have seemed like years. I should never have been here, perhaps, only the servants have been sent to the hospital to tend the sick, and the old housekeeper was taken with the cramps, and let me out to give her medicine. But, oh! if *you* should be ill!"

"Don't fear for me," said Minerva; "God will take care of me. Who is in the house besides you?"

"Nobody but the housekeeper—and there! did you hear wheels? It is that horrible Jose. I have seen his face go past my window every day, till I am tired of it."

"Where does he come from every day, Bandola?" asked Minerva.

"That I don't know. I've asked the housekeeper many times, but I suppose she never knew either, for she never told me. He brings something in a basket, and carries something away; what it is, I know not. Oh! I can't get tired of looking at you," she added, in an ecstasy. "Are you sure I am awake? I have frightful dreams, sometimes; but if this is a dream, I want to sleep always."

"You are wide awake, Bandola; so am I. You shall not remain here, but go back to America with me, if all things come right," said Minerva.

Tears of gratitude stole down the dark cheeks of the grateful girl, as she uttered the low, fervent cry, "God be thanked!"

"I must see this Jose; where is he?" asked Minerva.

"Around at the stables, I suppose," was the reply.

"Lead the way to the housekeeper, Bandola."

The girl held up her head, and marched like a soldier.

Minerva stood before the housekeeper, who gave a shrill cry, and seemed inclined to faint.

"Do not be frightened, my good Monte," said Minerva, soothingly; "you see I have dropped from the clouds. I wish you to give me the keys of the main body of the house."

"Against the orders of Don Carlos," murmured the housekeeper.

"I am mistress, now," said Minerva, with dignity.

The woman unloosed the keys with trembling eagerness, and placed them in Minerva's hand. Bidding Bandola follow her, she entered at once into the long-closed-up passages, and unlocked the business room, where every thing remained just as the general's steward had left it, with a view, probably, to trimming it up before the family returned. Here she sent for the old negro, Jose. He came in very soon, a tall, bony, cruel-faced man, whose complexion, black though it was, seemed to change to a yellow pallor, when he saw what seemed to be an apparition, for he could scarcely persuade himself of the reality of her presence.

"Jose," she said, sternly, "have you come this morning from La Vintresse?"

The man was dumb for a moment. At last he managed to answer that he had.

"What horses are here?" she asked.

"Rose and Charlie," he replied.

"Put them into the carriage immediately," she exclaimed.

"Into the carriage, senorita?"

"Into the carriage, I said; then come back. Be quick!" she added, in a sharp, authoritative voice.

He was gone, absolutely lost in wonder and did nothing but roll up the whites of his eyes as he muttered to himself: "Wha' in Harry she gwine to do nex'?"

"Carriage in senora," he said, humbly.

"Very well, I'm going to La Vintresse; you may drive me."

If the negro's mien was astonishment and wonder before, it was now simply horror.

"You," was all he said, slinking back shufflingly.

"Yes, I, certainly; I am going to La Vintresse. You comprehend, perfectly, you are to drive."

"*You*,—to La Vintresse?" he muttered again, his lips scarcely moving.

"I am out of all patience with you; are you so stupid? Either you may carry me there, peacefully, or I shall appear to the consul to let the police go with me. I am your mistress, now, and Senor Herman is to be brought from La Vintresse, by my orders."

"But he is sick," muttered the negro, with ashen lips.

"Then see that pillows and a bed are placed in the carriage, go, Bandola, and bring them from wherever you may find them. Be quick, girl," she added, her heart sinking, as she thought little she might know *how* sick he was. Still the negro stood irresolute, staring at her.

"Have you taken leave of your senses, Jose?" she cried, threateningly, stamping her foot in feigned passion. The man muttered an incoherent word or two, and went slowly out. A bed was soon improvised, and bearing a few necessary articles, Minerva entered the carriage with Bandola.

"Stop a moment," she cried, as the man was mounting to his seat; "you will want another man to help, in case he will need to be lifted."

"I lift him," answered the man, surlily, and sprang on the box.

"Are you not afraid?" murmured Bandola.

"Afraid, oh, no, good Bandola, I have not once thought of fear," said Minerva, as the carriage rolled swiftly along. "Jose dares not disobey me, it is *he* who fears, I think; he is a hard, cruel man, but I believe now he fears me. He knows I have power to expose him to the authorities, and he will be the abject slave, till I have done with him. But, O Bandola! What are we going to see, I know not; there I fear every thing."

"It is not possible you believe Mr. Herman is there!" exclaimed the girl, shrinkingly.

"Yes, I believe they have buried him alive, but we shall know soon; we must be nearing the outskirts of Havana."

"And shall you take him back with you?"

"If it is possible, immediately to the ship," was the reply. "The captain was to have every thing in readiness, and perhaps a doctor on board. We shall not sail for a week, and he will be perfectly quiet there. We are coming to a dreary place," she added, looking out over the prospect where nature had been subjected to various tortures by fire and by flood! "Oh! what a miserable quiet there is here! so unearthly."

In truth, the very air seemed as stagnant as the ground. The gullies in the road were deep with green water, the stunted palms seemed each to be laboring under some deformity, the fields were arid, and presently the wretched ruins of La Vintresse came in view, a sickening mass of black and tottering walls.

"Very dirty here, senora," said Jose, as the carriage stopped at a large out building; "but if the senora will wait, Jose get planks and lay them."

In a few moments there was comparatively a dry path. Minerva with difficulty controlled her feelings, as she stepped into the narrow hall of the building, that had for so long been Herman's jail.

"The senora I hope will not punish Jose," said the negro, humbly; "he did but what his master ordered."

"You shall not be punished, Jose, only lead me to him."

Up the narrow, dirty stairs went the old negro, applied the key reluctantly to the lock, the door opened with a harsh creak. Bandola had placed one arm about Minerva, for what with vague terror and excitement, she could scarcely stand. The room was large, bare, with miserably defaced walls, and high-barred windows. Neither table, nor chair, nothing but a low pallet spread in one corner, and a camp stool near one window, as if the prisoner had lifted himself to see the dreary sight without.

Minerva gave a low, shivering cry. What was that extended on the pallet, ragged, scarcely human? "Oh! can that be?" she wailed pitifully.

Jose shrank away from her real sorrow. Slowly she went up to the prostrate figure, half-hoping it might not be him. The man seemed asleep, though his hollow eyes were not much more than half-closed. His skin clung tightly to the bones of his face, and was so painfully bright, that it suggested the thought of varnish. The beard had grown frightfully profuse, and fell on his throat and chest, in matted, tangled masses. Language cannot convey an idea of his extreme emaciation.

"Oh Bandola!" sobbed Minerva, the tears raining down; "can he be alive? can he be alive? oh! cruel, cruel fiends! How could my uncle and Don Carlos bring an innocent man to this? What shall I do? I fear to touch him, he looks so frail; O Herman! O Herman! if you could only speak to me?"

"He sleeps a good part of his time," said Jose. Minerva dared not trust herself to reply; she knew the man before her must have been as black in heart as in complexion, to see a fellow-being suffer as he must have suffered; there was inherent cruelty in a nature like that. Kneeling down on the wretched floor, she softly kissed his forehead. The motion, slight as it was, roused him. He opened his eyes, glassy and restless; they fell upon the loving glance of Minerva. A singular change came over his face, the whole countenance lighted as if a thin red flame had suddenly run from vein to vein, under that fearful whiteness. He sprang upright in the bed, cried out in a hollow voice: "At last! at last! O God!" and sank back lifeless.

"I have killed him," cried Minerva, as the negro went toward him.

"He's been so two or three times, senora," said the man. "If you will go down stairs, I will get him ready to go in the carriage. I doesn't think he's dead."

Sobbing like a child, giving way to utter abandonment of grief, Minerva went down the stairs, and walked to and fro in the narrow entry, Bandola trying in vain to console her.

"We must go in the carriage," said the faithful girl; "to hold him if he needs. Only think, he will be taken from this dreadful place, it ought to make you happy."

"Oh! but Bandola, I fear I have killed him," cried Minerva, piteously; "it might have all been managed so differently, and now he is dead, dead," she wailed, piteously. She was prevailed upon, however, to enter the carriage, where she adjusted the pillows, and sat dreading to see the lifeless form, that a child might almost carry.

Presently it came. Jose had replaced the miserable rags he wore, with the suit that had been taken from him, prison-fashion, when he was carried thither. Still seemingly dead, he lay white and nerveless upon the soft bed prepared for him. He was yet living. The fresh air, the motion of the carriage revived him. Slowly the luxury of his surroundings dawned upon him. He smiled feebly like a child; he had no longer the strength to speak.

Minerva had given directions to be driven immediately to the pier. The captain stood in readiness, the usual formalities were hurried through, and in a short time, the poor invalid lay on a bed of down, surrounded by careful friends and the best of nurses. A skillful doctor pronounced his case one of slow starvation and complete inanition, giving it as his opinion that a year's time would scarcely complete the process of restoration, so entirely had all his faculties succumbed. "And I think if you had delayed till tomorrow," he added, "he would not have been alive, the light was so far spent."

Minerva listened in silent gratitude; she had no words, but thankful tears.

CHAPTER XXII

All's Well That Ends Well

Jessie sat in the pleasant parlor of the old farm-house, playing a few pleasant chords. Her mother, pale and feeble, listened from her wheeled chair near the window. There were fitting thoughts in Jessie's mind that found expression now and then in a sweet smile, or else in a profound bending of the pretty head, while the eyes looked thoughtfully far away.

Presently in came the farmer, but a changed man was he. His cheek was flushed—his face serious yet beaming, while in his great brown eyes could be seen the shadow of tears.

"Jessie," he said softly—"Jessie, come here."

The girl arose, paused a moment, seeing that her mother had fallen asleep, then hurried out to meet her father.

He led her rapidly around the path that led to the grape-arbor.

"Jessie," he said, and the girl caught his hand, for the manly voice was smothered—"Jessie—O God—be thanked! your brother is coming home to us."

"What father—what father?" half-shrieked the girl—"Herman coming?"

"He will be here tomorrow—think—think Jessie—Minerva, the noble girl!" His voice choked again—his breast heaved—he could say nothing more, but sat down quite overcome, his face hidden in his hands.

"O father! father!" and Jessie hid her face on his shoulders, sobbing. It was a solemn joy—broken only by the sweet words "my brother," and "my son."

"Are you going after him, father?" asked Jessie, lifting her tear-stained face to his.

"No, darling—they will be here tomorrow in a closed carriage. Herman is, I believe"—his voice trembled again, "quite an invalid. We must be prepared to see a great change in him. Minerva says he has suffered terribly—my poor boy! Those proud Spaniards shall pay for it."

"They have gone home, father."

"Yes, but we can reach them. Now, how shall we tell your mother?"

"Father, *I'll* tell her," said Jessie.

"Very well, my darling—break it to her as gently as you can," and with a grateful heart he kissed the fair white forehead.

One can imagine the emotions of the little party gathered to welcome the wanderer home on that eventful morning. It proved a clear and beautiful day, and God was not forgotten for his glorious sunshine, for all his tender mercies. The pale lips of the invalid-mother moved often as if in prayer. At nine o'clock Senor Abrates came over from the hotel, as seldom a day had passed of late that he did not.

Oh! that sound of carriage-wheels! Jessie cannot endure the silence—she starts forward screaming that Herman is coming. But when she sees that pale being, lifted in the stalwart arms of his father—that white figure not at all like the brave, handsome brother who went away—she starts back, trembling and in tears. A joyful kiss was on the cheek—soft arms around her neck—it was the embrace of Minerva. For many minutes the silence was something solemn and heart-breaking, but Herman laid his poor head upon his mother's breast, and felt stealing over him the old content of his boyhood. When words came, the confusion was appalling. Jessie hovered round the couch, kissing and caressing, while her father walked the room with glad and rapid heart-pulsings, praying audibly in thankfulness for this unlooked-for blessing. Minerva knelt down by old Bruno, quite overcome at sight of him, for she had long thought him dead, and the faithful creature gave a low whine of delight.

The proud but crest-fallen Don Carlos had returned to Cuba, but before he went, to the extreme indignation of his guardian, he had made the pretty butterfly, Dora, his wife. The poor general never held up his head afterward—poor, for he was now impoverished since he learned through Senor Abrates that Minerva had been put in possession of knowledge sufficient to secure her fortune to her, and that the oath of allegiance taken by Senor Velasquez was not proof against the wild vaporings of a disordered brain. Neither did his uncle dare take any steps to recover the lost heiress, who, in time, made them sufficiently aware that she "knew her rights, and knowing, would maintain." Herman persuaded his father to take no steps toward restitution, feeling fully repaid for his sufferings in the constancy of his charming betrothed. But those days of sorrow had left and would leave for years, perhaps during life the traces of their terrible endurance. As for Senor Abrates, relieved of the responsibility of his sister's care, he had, through the influence at Farmer Goreham's, become a changed man, and saw life through a far different medium than that of his recent past. Imperceptibly, sweet Jessie Goreham was taking the place of his old love, and surely a purer, lovelier creature could not be found. He contemplated putting together the remnant of his fortune and buying out some good business in which Herman might be his helper.

In the great mansion of Don Carlos, Dora queens it. The don is quite fond of her, and though he is growing a desperate lover of pleasure, he allows himself to be influenced somewhat by his bright, willful little wife. But the truest happiness reigns in the household of the farmer where the pale son and his beautiful bride, make the home an Eden. Bandola has never left her mistress, and probably never will.

A miserable old man rises at eleven in his little old house leading from the Paseo in Havana. He is to be seen generally at dusk—peevish, thin, and repulsive-looking—arm in arm with a withered little old woman of some sixty years, walking slowly through some retired street. The house and a pension for both is the kind bounty of Minerva, but the old general is both ungrateful and unthankful, and to this day berates his niece bitterly, because she did not marry the man she detested that he might be enriched. Who would recognize in those two shriveled grumblers, the haughty general, famous at Saratoga, and the little senorita, whose rich apparel was the envy of feminine eyes?

In time Minerva learned what she had never known before. Her father when only nineteen, had loved a Cuban lady,—a Dona Marie St. Lunan. From all accounts, she was very good and lovely, and the young man had adored her. News came however, while he was sojourning in England for a time, that she was false to him, and following rapidly, the fact came out that she was married. In despair the young man first attempted his life, then thought better of it, and out of revenge married the first woman who would have him— the beautiful English girl, the mother of Minerva. When he arrived at home, he learned the truth of the matter—she had been sold, forced into marriage with a rich old don. She would never see him till, her life fading away, she sent for him when she was dying. Her only child, the babe of a few months, slept by her side.

It was an anguished meeting.

"We have been unhappily parted," she said, "but I have a son and you a daughter! Promise me that if it is in your power, they two shall be united. Thus, through our children we may once more know a true and worthy love."

"I promise," he said.

Thus it came to pass that both children were reared under the roof of General Limenes de Monserate. The old don was induced before he died (being also a friend of the general) to give the guardianship of his son into his hands, and the will of Minerva's father provided that if the two children, coming of age, married, half the property was to go to General Limenes as a reward for his endeavors, but that if she married any other man, he (the general) should forfeit all interest in the will. There need be no further explanation, of course the reader sees the result.

General Limenes de Monserate is living yet, and so are all the rest of my characters. Perhaps there are those who knew some of them in Saratoga.

THE END.

EXPLANATORY NOTES

Unless indicated otherwise, the Texas and U.S.-Mexico War references were culled from Mark Crawford, *Encyclopedia of the Mexican-American War* (Santa Barbara: ABC-CLIO, 1999); and Edward H. Moseley and Paul C. Clark, Jr., *Historical Dictionary of the United States-Mexican War* (Lanham, Md.: Scarecrow Press, 1997). General notes were gleaned from standard reference sources. When entries overlap, the second note will reference the first by the appropriate title and note number.

The Female Warrior

1. "'Tis strange,—but true; for truth is always strange— / Stranger than fiction" (Byron, *Don Juan*, XI, 101).

2. The 1837 Panic occurred mainly because President Andrew Jackson vetoed the charter of the Second Bank of the United States in 1832, putting it out of business by 1836. Centered in Philadelphia, the bank was the main financial institution for individuals, businesses, and the federal government until Jackson withdrew the government's holdings in 1835 and deposited them in state banks and required all government land purchases to be made with specie. With land speculation fueling the economy throughout 1835, state banks loaned money beyond their reserves and printed new currency, while foreign investors offered large loans to industrialists and businessmen. When inflation rose, creditors began to call in their loans to be paid in gold or silver. With specie in short supply, banks in debt beyond their reserves, and paper currency that lacked value, banks and businesses went bankrupt, economic growth dwindled, and people who had money in state banks lost it all by 1837. See Edward S. Kaplan, *The Bank of the United States and the American Economy* (Westport, Conn.: Greenwood Press, 1999).

3. Galveston, Texas, is a port city along the Gulf of Mexico that served briefly as the capital of the Texas republic.

4. Texas and Mexico were embattled during the years between Texas's 1835 rebellion to its 1845 annexation into the Union. Before Mexico gained its independence from Spain, the Spanish government agreed to allow Moses Austin to settle Mexico's far northern frontier, Texas. When the elder Austin died, his son Stephen arrived in San Antonio, Texas, in 1821 to claim lands promised to his father. The newly independent Mexico recognized the colonization plan because it required the settlers to acknowledge the authority of the Mexican government and the Catholic Church. The new arrivals did neither, so Mexico prohibited further colonization in 1830 but had little power to enforce the decree and less support from President Jackson to uphold the mandate. After taking the presidential office in 1833, Santa Anna's attempt to consolidate the central government's power incited rebellion across Mexico—Yucatán, Sonora, Texas, and other regions supporting federalism rebelled. Texas revolted in 1835, and in March 1836 it proclaimed its independence. Almost immediately, Santa Anna led an army to quell the rebellion. By the end of March, he led a successful siege of the Alamo and earned a victory at the battle of Goliad, where he

ordered the execution of 445 captives. The following month, he met General Sam Houston at the battle of San Jacinto, where the Texas army captured the Mexican general and president and forced him to concede Texas's independence through the Treaties of Velasco. While President Jackson recognized Texas in 1837, the Mexican government never ratified the treaty, so when Santa Anna briefly took power in 1841, he turned his attention again to Texas. By October 1842, Santa Anna retired from the presidential office, but the Mexican army had already invaded and captured San Antonio twice during the year. The skirmishes continued until 1845, when the United States annexed Texas and inherited its war with Mexico. For the 1842 San Antonio battles, see Joseph Milton Nance, *Attack and Counter-Attack: The Texas-Mexican Frontier, 1842* (Austin: University of Texas Press, 1964).

5. Sam Houston (1793–1863) was the first president of the Republic of Texas from 1836 to 1838, a position he secured because of his military and political prominence during the 1836 Texas Revolution. Under Houston's command, the Texan army defeated General Santa Anna at the 1836 battle of Jacinto and thereby secured Texas's independence from Mexico. Houston also served as a U.S. senator from 1846 to 1859 but lost his seat when he refused to support Texas's secession from the Union in 1861.

6. San Antonio de Béxar, or San Antonio as it is now known, is the home of the Alamo mission, where General Santa Anna defeated Texan rebels, including William Travis, Jim Bowie, and Davy Crockett, after a thirteen-day siege in 1836. The Mexican army returned to San Antonio and briefly captured it in March and September 1842.

7. Hernán Cortés founded Vera Cruz, a port city along the Gulf of Mexico, in 1519. It has served as the main dock for invasions, commerce, and trade throughout Mexico's history, mainly because the path to Mexico City is approximately 260 miles inland.

8. Antonio López de Santa Anna (1794–1876) dominated Mexico's political and military scenes from the 1820s to the 1850s. He was elected to the presidency in 1833, and three years later, he mobilized the Mexican army against the Texas rebellion. He gave no quarter at the battle of the Alamo in March 1836 and ordered the execution of several hundred Texan prisoners at the battle of Goliad a few days later. In April 1836, Santa Anna lost at the battle of Jacinto, leading to Texas's independence. His actions at the Alamo and Goliad fostered his reputation in the United States as a vain, ruthless, despotic, lecherous, and duplicitous leader. His standing in Mexico was equally vexed. After losing Texas, Santa Anna was exiled to Cuba, but on the eve of the U.S.-Mexico War (1846–1848), he brokered a deal with President James K. Polk to oust Mexico's president and agree to settle affairs with the United States amicably. He was smuggled through the U.S. blockade; he was successful in his presidential coup; and then, instead of completing the deal with Polk, he mobilized his troops against American forces. He was exiled from Mexico in 1855 and did not return until the year of his death.

Magdalena, The Beautiful Mexican Maid

1. Captain Charles May (1817–1864) served as the chief of cavalry in General Zachary Taylor's Army of Occupation. He performed several reconnaissance missions and saw action at the battle of Buena Vista.

2. The Army of Occupation served under General Taylor and dominated the warfront in Mexico's northeastern states, gaining victories at the battles of Resaca de la Palma, Palo Alto,

Monterrey, and Buena Vista. The narrative opens with an inaccurate but revealing date that we have left uncorrected: Taylor's army was in Corpus Christi, Texas, in March 1846; not "March 11, 1847." By March 1847, most of the historical action the narrative recounts was already over, but the 1847 date suggests that Buntline wrote *Magdalena* between 1846 (the publication date listed on the original copyright page) and 1847 as news of the war made it to the home front. Definitely, the novelette could not have been published before the May 20, 1847 publication of Whittier's poem included at the conclusion of the narrative.

3. General Zachary Taylor's (1784–1850) career as an Indian fighter throughout the 1820s and 1830s earned him the nickname "Old Rough and Ready" for his casual demeanor and strong leadership. In 1845, he deployed to Corpus Christi, Texas, and then in 1846 moved to the left bank of the Rio Grande into disputed territory. The Mexican army considered it an act of invasion, and the U.S.-Mexico War commenced. Taylor led successful campaigns during the first four battles of the war and was elected as the twelfth U.S. president in 1849. He died the following year.

4. William Wallace Smith Bliss (1815–1853) served as General Taylor's adjutant general and chief of staff. Captain Samuel Hamilton Walker participated in the Mier Expedition, and his company of Texas Rangers served as volunteers, scouts, and guerilla fighters in Taylor's army.

5. Francis Marion (c. 1732–1795) was a brigadier general in the South Carolina militia during the American Revolutionary War, where his guerilla tactics earned him the name "Swamp Fox." See Hugh F. Rankin, *Francis Marion: The Swamp Fox* (New York: Thomas Y. Crowell, 1973).

6. In response to the 1842 Mexican attacks on San Antonio, General Houston raised a volunteer army that invaded Mier, a town located near the Rio Grande in Nuevo León, Mexico. Generals Pedro de Ampudia and Antonio Canales captured the 262 Texans, and Ampudia led them on a forced march to Mexico City. En route, some of the Texans staged an escape near Saltillo at Hacienda Salado. The prisoners were recaptured in March 1843 and sentenced to decimation by lottery. One hundred and fifty-nine white beans and seventeen black beans were placed in a jar, and the Texans were forced to draw. The seventeen who had black beans were executed; the rest continued their march and were imprisoned at Perote Castle. Several Texans, including Samuel Walker, escaped from the prison, and Santa Anna released the remaining Texans in September 1844. See Joseph Milton Nance, *Dare-Devils All: The Texan Mier Expedition, 1842–1844* (Austin: Eakin Press, 1998).

7. General Taylor and Brackett are discussing the route Taylor took against orders from Secretary of War William Marcy and that led to the battle of Buena Vista. After Taylor captured Monterrey, Mexico, in August 1846, Marcy ordered Taylor to halt, but Taylor marched approximately eighty miles south to capture Saltillo, the capital of the state of Coahuila. Taylor then returned to Monterrey and left Saltillo under the command of General William Jenkins Worth, but General Winfield Scott ordered Worth toward Veracruz. Hearing of Taylor's weakened position at Saltillo, General Santa Anna moved his army north from San Luis Potosí, an important staging area northwest of Mexico City. In February 1847, the two armies met a few miles south of Saltillo at the battle of Buena Vista, where Taylor took the field after two days of battle.

8. Brackett is dressed as a ranchero, a Mexican guerilla fighter. Rancheros were mostly vaqueros armed with lassos, familiar with Mexico's northern terrain, and used to hard horseriding; their raids plagued Taylor's northern war theater.

9. As a Carlist, Don Ignatio supported Don Carlos's (1788–1855) claim to the Spanish throne as Charles V following the death of his brother, King Ferdinand VII. When Ferdinand died in September 1833, the First Carlist wars raged in Spain as the king's brother, Don Carlos, unsuccessfully attempted to take the throne from his niece, Isabella. The conflict pitted traditionalism (Don Carlos) against liberalism (Isabella) and lasted until 1839, when Don Carlos was defeated. Tomás de Zumalacárregui (1788–1835) was one of Don Carlos's most effective military tacticians, whose death crippled Don Carlos's campaign.

10. Antonio Canova (1757–1822) was a Venetian sculptor whose marble works often rendered nude subjects. Salvator Rosa (1615–1673) was an Italian painter and etcher known for landscapes. Diana Vernon is Frank Osbaldistone's love interest in Sir Walter Scott's 1817 novel *Rob Roy*.

11. Orizaba is a town in the state of Vera Cruz, Mexico. The highest mountain in Mexico, the Pico de Orizaba, overlooks the valley town.

12. Buntline's Spanish is imprecise, so following his English translation of Magdalena's song, the translation of Brackett's ditty can be rendered as:

> "It's true that in this house I am the master.
> My father I love, my mother I adore,
> But a dear little wife far better would be,
> Oh, a dear little wife a treasure to me."

13. On May 8, 1846, General Arista and General Taylor met at the battle of Palo Alto. General Arista had earlier sent General Pedro de Ampudia to attack Fort Texas, later to be named Fort Brown in honor of Major Jacob Brown, who held the fort but suffered a mortal wound. Arista recalled Ampudia, and the 4,000-man Mexican army was set to meet the 2,200-man Army of Occupation. Topographical engineer Lieutenant Jacob E. Blake reconnoitered the battle lines before hostilities began at 2:30 p.m. Dueling artillery fire characterized the battle, with the U.S. "flying" artillery forcing Arista's retreat and giving Taylor the field but not before the architect behind the light artillery, Major Samuel Ringgold, sustained a mortal injury. Captain John Page similarly suffered a cannonball injury and, alongside Ringgold, died at Point Isabel a few days after the battle. Ringgold's death evoked national sympathy and inspired commemorative poems, songs, and lithographs.

14. Colonel Trueman Cross was killed on April 10, 1846, while on a horseback ride north of the Rio Grande. Two weeks later, Captain Seth B. Thornton and a patrol of sixty-three dragoons fell into an ambush on the north side of the Rio Grande. Eleven Americans were killed, six were wounded, and Thornton and the rest of his dragoons were captured. The ambush gave President Polk the cause to take his war speech to Congress, which declared war against Mexico on May 13, 1846.

15. Joachim Murat (1767–1815) commanded Napoleon's cavalry and was one of Napoleon's ablest officers during his rise to power. Murat was named king of Naples from 1808 to 1815.

16. Willy-nilly.

17. On May 9, 1846, Generals Taylor and Arista met at the battle of Resaca de la Palma. The

day was disastrous for Arista, while Taylor's victory paved the way for him to capture Matamoras. Captain Charles A. May and his cavalry are often credited with turning the tide of the battle, but May's charge was in reality unsuccessful. May was also erroneously given credit for capturing General Rómulo Díaz de la Vega (1804–1877). Lieutenant Zebulon M. P. Inge of the 2nd Dragoons was killed at Resaca, while David Emanuel Twigs (1790–1862) earned the rank of brigadier general for his leadership at the battles of Palo Alto and Resaca de la Palma.

18. On May 6, 1846, Major Jacob Brown suffered a mortal wound during General Ampudia's siege of Fort Texas, located on the north bank of the Rio Grande. Captain Edgar S. Hawkins assumed command and withstood the assault until U.S. reinforcements arrived. General Taylor renamed Fort Texas Fort Brown in honor of Major Brown.

19. American forces defeated the British at the Revolutionary War battles of Saratoga (September–October 1771), Yorktown (August–October 1781), and Brandywine (September 1777).

20. Major General Mariano Arista (1802–1855) commanded Mexico's Army of the North at Matamoras in April 1846. He suffered defeats at the battles of Palo Alto and Resaca de la Palma before Santa Anna relieved him from duty and recommended him for court-martial. He was absolved of misconduct, served as the Mexican president (1851–1853), and then resigned the position and retired to Portugal, where he died.

21. Brackett is probably referring to one of the two 1842 skirmishes between Texas and Mexico that took place in San Antonio.

22. General Taylor did not take his army all the way to Mexico City, but the "prophecy" refers to Taylor's plans to cut a path south of Monterrey and Saltillo to Agua Nueva, via Buena Vista, which lies between Saltillo and Agua Nueva.

23. Located on the Rio Grande in the state of Tamaulipas, Matamoras is the first foreign city to be occupied by U.S. forces. The battle of Monterrey (September 21–23, 1846) was General Taylor's third victory against Mexico's Army of the North, but his forces tallied considerable causalities and Taylor suffered criticism from President Polk for agreeing to a generous armistice with General Ampudia. The U.S. Army occupied Matamoras for the duration of the war.

24. General William Jenkins Worth (1794–1849) distinguished himself at the battle of Monterrey and briefly served as the city's military governor. His longtime friend General Scott ordered him to join the siege of Vera Cruz, and their friendship ended in bitter rivalry about disputes over leadership and power struggles. After the war, he took command of the Department of Texas, where he died of cholera.

25. The first verse of "La Ausencia"—"The Absence"—can be rendered: "The magic is gone from my heart, and my joy is gone too"; followed by, "And in an instant, everything was lost. Where have you gone, my dear?"

26. Brackett's narrative places him at the 1836 battle of San Jacinto, which secured Texas's independence from Mexico, and the ill-fated 1843 Mier Expedition, which exacerbated anti-Mexican sentiment in Texas and the United States. (See above, *The Female Warrior*, note 4, and *Magdalena*, note 6.)

27. Defying orders from the secretary of war, General Taylor proceeded south to Saltillo after capturing Monterrey. In November 1846, the U.S. Army took Saltillo peacefully, and

General George Jenkins Worth was left in command of the city until January 1847, when he was called to join General Scott's siege of Vera Cruz.

28. General Ciriaco Vázquez (1794–1847) is possibly the general Brackett befriends. Vázquez led an infantry in the Army of the North and maintained a position around the state of Tamaulipas before he joined his army with the Army of the East. General Vázquez did not participate in the battle of Buena Vista.

29. "The native rum of the country." (Original footnote.)

30. Approximately seventeen miles south of Saltillo, Agua Nueva served as a staging ground for both armies in the days leading to the battle of Buena Vista, which was fought at the hacienda San Juan de la Buena Vista, about five miles south of Saltillo.

31. King of Sparta, Leonidas led his small Spartan band against a larger, invading Persian army at the 480 BC battle of Thermopylae.

32. On February 23, 1847, Santa Anna's Army of the North met Taylor's Army of Occupation at the battle of Buena Vista. After learning that much of Taylor's army was redeployed to Vera Cruz, Santa Anna marched his army north toward Agua Nueva. Taylor's forces retreated to a defensive locale, the hacienda San Juan de la Buena Vista, and fortified their position to meet Santa Anna's army. For most of the day, the U.S. light artillery and Mexican lancers exchanged the field, and cavalry charges from both sides often ended in hand-to-hand combat. By nightfall, the battle was over, and even though Santa Anna's army seemed to have carried the day, he retreated to Agua Nueva, his grand Army of the North having suffered considerable casualties, injuries, and desertions during the encounter. The defeat demoralized and depleted Mexico and its army. Taylor's surprise victory at Buena Vista was also his last one in Mexico: he and his Army of Occupation returned to Monterrey, where they remained for the duration of the war.

33. At the June 18, 1815 battle of Waterloo, British and Prussian forces defeated Napoleon's army and ended his reign on the French throne.

34. John Macrea Washington (1797–1853) commanded the 4th U.S. artillery. Brigadier General Thomas Marshall (1793–1853) was perhaps responsible for the battle of Buena Vista when the top-secret order addressed to General Taylor that he opened fell into the hands of Santa Anna; it was from this order that Santa Anna learned of General Scott's redeployment of Taylor's men. John Paul Jones O'Brien (1818–1850) earned the rank of major for his effective use of artillery at Buena Vista, while the 2nd Indiana under Colonel William A. Bowles retreated when they met Major General Francisco Pacheco's division. Captain George Lincoln served as the assistant adjutant general under General Wool. Colonel John J. Hardin led the 1st Regiment of Illinois Volunteers and died at Buena Vista, while Captain Albert Pike (1809–1891) commanded an Arkansas cavalry that held the rear line during the battle.

35. Former congressman and governor of Arkansas, Colonel Archibald Yell commanded the 1st Arkansas Volunteer Calvary, a motley crew known as the "Arkansas Ransackers." Yell died at the battle of Buena Vista, as did First Lieutenant and Adjutant Edward M. Vaughan of the Kentucky Calvary.

36. Captain Braxton Bragg (1817–1876) commanded a field artillery battery that proved crucial in stopping a Mexican advance during the battle of Buena Vista. Bragg turned the tide

of the battle when he gave the Mexican army "more grape," a bunch of balls held in place by two wooden blocks and then fired.

37. John Greenleaf Whittier's (1807–1892) "Angels of Buena Vista" appeared in the May 20, 1847 issue of *The National Era*, an abolitionist organ Whittier edited at the time. The poem appears here with some changes from the original publication as well as the 1857 version in *The Poetical Works of John Greenleaf Whittier*, vol. 1 (Boston and New York: Houghton, Mifflin, 1892). The most significant change is the use of quotation marks, so we have restored the use of quotation marks, following the 1857 text, to clarify the speakers in the poem but have otherwise left Buntline's alterations uncorrected.

'Bel of Prairie Eden

1. The manuscripts that provide the epigraphs throughout the text are fictions within a fiction.

2. The opening setting is one of the two attacks the Mexican army waged against San Antonio, Texas, in 1842. (See above, *The Female Warrior*, note 4.)

3. The Grywin family arrives in 1840, four years after Texas gained its independence.

4. See above, *The Female Warrior*, notes 4 and 8.

5. See above, *Magdalena*, note 8.

6. See above, *Magdalena*, note 6.

7. A hidalgo—"son of something"—is a low member of the Spanish nobility who enjoyed social prestige without necessarily being wealthy or owning property. The reference to 1716 is obscure but generally indicates an era of decline for hidalgos and also points to the year that the government of New Spain (Mexico) sent colonists to settle the region of Texas.

8. The Castle of San Juan de Ulúa guarded the port city of San Juan de Ulúa, near Vera Cruz. Its well-fortified position obstructed a direct amphibious invasion of the area. In March 1847, General Scott's navy bombarded the fort, along with Vera Cruz, until the Mexicans surrendered both on March 27, 1847. About three miles offshore and south of Vera Cruz, the Isla de Sacrificios provided the U.S. Navy cover to stage an amphibious landing at Collado Beach during the siege of Vera Cruz.

9. A disease carried by mosquito, yellow fever (*el vómito*) raged along Mexico's low-lying gulf coastline during the rainy season (April and May). The headaches, fever, vomiting, and constipation made it a dreaded disease. General Scott tried to time his siege and invasion of Vera Cruz before the rainy season, and while he did manage to take the city before the end of March, many of his men contracted *el vómito*.

10. The Castle of San Juan de Ulúa, Fort Concepcíon, and Fort Santiago defended Vera Cruz and prevented a direct invasion of the city from the water.

11. See above, *Magdalena*, note 11.

12. The USS *Princeton* warship received President John Tyler and his cabinet for a cruise down the Potomac River on February 28, 1844. One of the ship's guns exploded during a demonstration, killing the secretary of state, the secretary of the navy (who had requested the demonstration in the first place), and other members of the presidential cabinet. Twenty people, including the captain, were injured. See *Dictionary of American Naval Fighting Ships*, vol. V (Washington, D.C.: U.S. Government Printing Office, 1970).

13. In July 1814, General Winfield Scott successfully led American forces against the British

in the Niagara campaign to occupy Canada during the War of 1812. After Scott's forces took Vera Cruz during the U.S.-Mexico War, the army followed the same route Hernán Cortés cut on his way to conquer Tenochtitlan (Mexico City) between 1519 and 1521.

14. See above, *Magdalena*, note 24.

15. The narrative shifts to the Spanish conquest of Mexico from 1519 to 1521, over three hundred years before the U.S.-Mexico War.

16. Montezuma II (c. 1466–1520) was the reigning Mexica (Aztec) emperor when the Spanish arrived to conquer Mexico. History often portrays him either as a superstitious ruler too passive to lead his people against the Spanish or as the ill-fated emperor who happened to be in power during the European invasion.

17. Lippard juxtaposes the Mexica practice of sacrifice with the tortures of the Spanish inquisition, the idolatrous sacrifices to Moloch in the Old Testament (Leviticus 18:21; 20:2–5), and the tortures exerted during the sixteenth-century Protestant Reformation in Geneva led by John Calvin.

18. Quetzalcoatl, the Feathered Serpent, was not necessarily a god of peace but one of learning and creation. The Mexica believed that Quetzalcoatl, who had departed from the region, would keep his promise and return to the land of the Mexica, a belief that made Hernán Cortés's arrival seem mythic to the Mexica and fortunate for the conquistador. See Thomas, *Conquest: Montezuma, Cortés, and the Fall of Old Mexico* (New York: Simon and Schuster, 1993).

19. Along with a blue cross, "*In hoc signo vinces*," or "In this sign you shall conquer," is believed to be part of the script on Cortés's standard. See Thomas, *Conquest*, 156.

20. Father Bartolomé de Olmedo was a well-educated friar who advised Cortés during the conquest of Mexico. Pedro de Alvarado was one of Cortés's closest confidants during the conquest and also one of the more brutal conquistadors.

21. Ruth 1:16.

22. "Mariana" references Malintzin, the daughter of a Náhua leader who was sold into slavery and then offered to Cortés as a gift by the Maya Indians near Cozumel. Malintzin spoke Nahuatl, the language of the Mexica, and served as Cortés's translator and lover. She was baptized as "Marina" and is either remembered as "Doña Marina," Cortés's helpful concubine, or as "Malinche," the native woman who betrayed Mexico's indigenous people.

23. Harry Grywin's escape from the Mier execution is based on the story of James L. Shepherd, a seventeen-year-old Texan who faced the firing squad at Mier, was shot in the cheek and arm, feigned death, and then escaped to the mountains at night. A few days later, his injuries forced him back to Saltillo, where he was recognized, taken into custody, and executed a second time. See Nance, *Dare-Devils All*, 296.

24. A duenna is a female chaperon, and Argus is the one-hundred-eyed giant of Greek mythology.

25. Mexitli—rather than Mexitili, as Lippard writes it—is the war god that led the Mexica to power before they worshiped Huitzilopochtli as their war god.

26. The citizens of Syrabis, a Greek colony near Italy founded around 720 BC, were renowned for their wealth, luxury, and splendor. In 510 BC, Syrabis lost a war with nearby Crotona, and the Crotoniats diverted the Crathis River to flood the city of splendor and bury it beneath the river's sediment.

27. The reference is obscure.

28. In 1682, William Penn, a Quaker, founded the "city of brotherly love," Philadelphia. "The Quaker City" is also the title of Lippard's 1845 urban gothic novel *The Quaker City; or The Monks of Monk Hall* and served as the title of his own story paper.

29. On April 18, 1847, General Scott's forces met General Santa Anna's army at the battle of Cerro Gordo near Xalapa, Vera Cruz, Mexico. Santa Anna suffered a crushing defeat, with an estimated four thousand Mexican dead and five Mexican generals captured.

30. Edwin Forrest (1806–1872) was a Philadelphia-born actor whose rivalry with William Charles Macready, the British actor, fueled the 1849 Astor Place Riots. Forrest often played the lead role in Sir Edward G. D. Bulwer-Lytton's (1803–1873) *Richelieu*, a play about the French cardinal Armand Jean de Plessis de Richelieu (1585–1642), who served as King Louis XIII's chief minister and helped consolidate French royal power. See Dennis Berthold, "Class Acts: The Astor Place Riots and Melville's 'Two Temples,'" *American Literature* 71, no. 3 (1999): 448–449.

31. Funded by a bequest from Stephen Girard, Philadelphia's Girard College opened its doors in 1848 as a boarding school for fatherless boys. Girard (1750–1831) was a French-born American banker and philanthropist who financed the War of 1812 and backed the first and second Banks of the United States.

32. Characterized by its mausoleums and monuments, Laurel Hill Cemetery was founded in 1836 as a burial ground for Philadelphia's wealthy. Its location outside of the city promised a final escape from Philadelphia's industrialization and cramped, poor urban population.

33. "An epitaph something like this is recorded on a marble pile in the great cemetery near Paris." (Original footnote.)

34. John Randolph (1773–1833), commonly known as John Randolph of Roanoke, was a Virginian who served various terms as a U.S. representative and a senator between 1799 and 1827. He was a leading "Old Republican," a political group that advocated limited power of the federal government in relation to individual and state's rights. He opposed the purchase of Florida, the War of 1812, and the Missouri Compromise, and, later in his political career, he strongly supported sectionalism. He died in Philadelphia on May 24, 1833, and his will granted freedom to his slaves. John Greenleaf Whittier memorialized Randolph's act of emancipation in the antislavery poem, "Randolph of Roanoke," which appeared in the January 7, 1847 issue of *The National Era*. Lippard is echoing Whittier's poem, which imagines that "Remorse!" is Randolph's last written word, as one of his slaves attends to him bedside. See Norman K. Risjord, *The Old Republicans: Southern Conservatism in the Age of Jefferson* (New York: Columbia University Press, 1965) and John Greenleaf Whittier, *The Poetical Works of John Greenleaf Whittier: Anti-Slavery Poems, Songs of Labor and Reform*, vol. III (Boston and New York: Houghton, Mifflin, 1892).

35. Deuteronomy 32:35; Romans 12:19

A Thrilling and Exciting Account of the Sufferings and Horrible Tortures Inflicted on Mortimer Bowers and Miss Sophia Delaplain

1. Eighteenth-century German pseudo-science believed the Circassians, a tribe from Russia's Caucasian region, were the origin of humans and maintained the pure beauty of the white,

Caucasian race. By the 1850s, "Circassian beauty" appeared in the United States as a popular notion of white purity that was often linked to women, and by the 1860s, P. T. Barnum displayed female "Circassian beauties" at freak shows. See Robert Bogdan, *Freak Show: Presenting Human Oddities for Amusement and Profit* (Chicago: University of Chicago Press, 1988).

2. Reverend Doctor Frederick Schroeder headed St. Ann's Hall, an all-girls school established in Flushing in 1839. The school featured a gymnasium and emphasized exercise and horsemanship. See Henry D. Waller, *History of the Town of Flushing, Long Island, New York* (New York: Harbor Hill Books, 1975 [1899]), 187.

3. The gardening and tree nursery businesses of William Prince, the Bloodgood Nurseries, and Parsons & Co., helped to establish Flushing's early economy. St. Thomas's Hall was a school for boys established in 1839, and Clintonville, Manhasset, and Jamaica are neighboring villages to Flushing. See Waller, *History of the Town of Flushing*.

4. A formal event of the aristocratic class, a "debut" in the "beau monde" is an event announcing the coming of age of a young woman into high society.

5. "now glow'd the Firmament / With Living Sapphires: Hesperus that led / The starry Host, rode brightest, till the Moon / Rising in clouded Majesty, at length / Apparent Queen unveil'd her peerless light, / And o'er the dark her Silver Mantle threw" (Milton, *Paradise Lost*, IV.604–609).

6. Before the building of the Panama Canal, sea travel from the East Coast to gold-rush California required the circumnavigation of Cape Horn, one of the headlands of the Tierra del Fuego chain of islands south of Chile. Named after the Kentucky statesman and founder of the U.S. Whig Party, the *Henry Clay* was a 1,400-ton, triple-decker merchant ship launched in March 1845. Its service from New York to Liverpool made it primarily an immigrant ship. See Carl C. Cutler, *Queens of the Western Ocean: The Story of America's Mail and Passenger Sailing Lines* (Annapolis, Md.: U.S. Naval Institute, 1961).

7. Originally connected to the gangs of New York's fire crews, the B'hoys—short for "Bowery B'hoys"—embodied an urban, working-class white nativism that was democratic and jingoistic. Ned Buntline made the "B'hoy" a popular literary figure in *The B'hoys of New York: A Sequel to the Mysteries and Miseries of New York* (New York: Dick and Fitzgerald, 1850).

8. The steamer that pulls the *Henry Clay* is named after the leader of the Seminole Indians during the Second Seminole War (1835–1842). Osceola was not an appointed chief, but his small band of Seminole fighters kept nearly 40,000 U.S. troops on the defensive throughout the second of three Florida wars. He proved impossible to defeat by warfare but was captured after arriving for an ostensible peace negotiation. He died of malaria in 1838. See John K. Mahon, *History of the Second Seminole War, 1835–1842* (Gainesville: University of Florida Press, 1992). "The Hook" possibly references Sandy Hook, a barrier peninsula along the eastern coast of New Jersey.

9. In November 1836, the *Bristol* arrived along the Long Island coast from Liverpool. Violent weather drove it to the Rockaway Shoals, about half a mile from the shore. Eighty-four people perished in the wreck, including a majority of the immigrants the ship carried. In January 1837, the *Mexico*, another Liverpool immigrant packet, suffered a similar fate ten miles from the *Bristol* site. One hundred and sixteen people died in the *Mexico* wreck.

10. Because of the 1818 Neutrality Act, the U.S. government did not openly condone filibus-

tering missions to nations at peace with the United States and in fact halted Narciso López's July 1849 attempt to take Cuba. López was able to outfit his 1850 expedition and amass an army of American volunteers because his recruiters claimed to be setting out for California. It was an open secret to most of the volunteers that they were enlisting for Cuba, but when plans for the attack on Cuba were revealed, several volunteers deserted the mission. López's filibustering missions were not abolitionist in regards to black slavery; instead, Captain Bainbridge echoes a popular revolutionary, republican rhetoric of the time that viewed white Cuban elites as enslaved by Spanish monarchy. See Tom Chaffin, *Fatal Glory: Narciso López and the First Clandestine U.S. War against Cuba* (Charlottesville: University Press of Virginia, 1996).

11. This tripartite plan was not part of López's 1850 invasion of Cárdenas. Rather, the three enlisted ships—the *Georgiana*, the *Susan Loud*, and the *Creole*—rendezvoused at Las Mujeres Island, off the Yucatán coast, where the volunteers boarded the *Creole* and proceeded to Cárdenas in one ship. Santiago de Cuba (St. Jago) was not included in the invasion plan.

12. From Alexander Pope's translation of Homer's *Iliad*: "He spoke, and awful, bends his sable Brows; / Shakes his Ambrosial Curls, and gives the Nod; / The Stamp of Fate, and Sanction of God" (I.684).

13. A "mandrill" is an African baboon, while *mandrillo* in Italian means "ape."

14. "Woman's Island" is a translation of Las Mujeres Island, López's rendezvous point before the Cárdenas invasion. Over a dozen men deserted the expedition when they were sent to the island for fresh water (Robert E. May, *Manifest Destiny's Underworld: Filibustering in Antebellum America* [Chapel Hill: University of North Carolina Press, 2002], 128). As for the May 18–19, 1850 Cárdenas invasion, it was initially successful. During the night, the filibusters took the local garrison and captured the lieutenant governor but not before he could send word of the invasion to Matanzas. By the next afternoon, with Spanish reinforcements en route, López's army hastily boarded the *Creole* and, under fire, set out for Key West, leaving five volunteers behind at Cárdenas. They were executed by firing squad (Chaffin, *Fatal Glory*, 139).

The Prisoner of La Vintresse

1. A small, ornamental bottle for holding smelling salts.

2. Mrs. Goreham is probably referring to the execution of Narciso López, who was strangled to death with a garotte (usually an iron collar, although it could also be a chain, rope, or wire) in Havana on September 1, 1851, after the failure of his third attempt to take over Cuba.

3. A "Friend" is a Quaker, otherwise known as a member of "The Religious Society of Friends," a Christian denomination that emerged in England in the mid-1600s.

ABOUT THE EDITORS

Jesse Alemán is an associate professor of English at the University of New Mexico, where he teaches nineteenth-century American and Chicano/a literatures. He has published in a variety of journals and edited the reprint of Loreta Janeta Velazquez's *The Woman in Battle*.

Shelley Streeby is an associate professor of U.S. literature and cultural studies at the University of California, San Diego. Her first book, *American Sensations: Class, Empire, and the Production of Popular Culture*, was awarded the American Studies Association's Lora Romero First Book Prize.